American Arabists in the Cold War Middle East, 1946–75

ANTHEM MIDDLE EAST STUDIES

The Anthem Middle East Studies series is committed to offering to our global audience the finest scholarship on the Middle East across the spectrum of academic disciplines. The twin goals of our rigorous editorial and production standards will be to bring original scholarship to the shelves and digital collections of academic libraries worldwide, and to cultivate accessible studies for university students and other sophisticated readers.

Series Editor
Camron Michael Amin – University of Michigan – Dearborn (USA)

Editorial Board
Benjamin Fortna – School of Oriental and African Studies, University of London (UK)
John Meloy – American University of Beirut (Lebanon)
Lisa Pollard – University of North Carolina Wilmington (USA)
Mark L. Stein – Muhlenberg College (USA)
Renée Worringer – University of Guelph (Canada)

American Arabists in the Cold War Middle East, 1946–75

From Orientalism to Professionalism

Teresa Fava Thomas

ANTHEM PRESS

Anthem Press
An imprint of Wimbledon Publishing Company
www.anthempress.com

This edition first published in UK and USA 2019
by ANTHEM PRESS
75–76 Blackfriars Road, London SE1 8HA, UK
or PO Box 9779, London SW19 7ZG, UK
and
244 Madison Ave #116, New York, NY 10016, USA

First published in the UK and USA by Anthem Press 2016

Copyright © Teresa Fava Thomas 2019

The author asserts the moral right to be identified as the author of this work.

All rights reserved. Without limiting the rights under copyright reserved above,
no part of this publication may be reproduced, stored or introduced into
a retrieval system, or transmitted, in any form or by any means
(electronic, mechanical, photocopying, recording or otherwise),
without the prior written permission of both the copyright
owner and the above publisher of this book.

British Library Cataloguing-in-Publication Data
A catalogue record for this book is available from the British Library.

ISBN-13: 978-1-78527-180-9 (Pbk)
ISBN-10: 1-78527-180-6 (Pbk)

This title is also available as an e-book.

CONTENTS

Acknowledgments — vii

Introduction: America's Middle East Area Experts — 1

Chapter One   The Orientalists Fade Away — 19

Chapter Two   The Middle East Hands Emerge — 33

Chapter Three   Landfall: Language Training in Beirut, 1946 — 47

Chapter Four   Filling the Cold War Linguist Gap: The Middle East Area Program in Beirut — 65

Chapter Five   "The Departure of Kings, Old Men, and Christians": The Eisenhower Years — 85

Chapter Six   Quiet Diplomacy in Action: The Kennedy and Johnson Years — 109

Chapter Seven   Kissinger's Arabesque: The Nixon and Ford Years — 135

Epilogue: Beirut Axioms; Lessons Learned by the Middle East Hands — 169

Appendix: Brief Biographies — 191

Notes — 197

Bibliography — 231

Index — 241

ACKNOWLEDGMENTS

This book has taken a far longer path from its origin, as my dissertation at Clark University, than even I could have imagined. This work is rooted in oral history as well as the documentary record, and this has necessitated the assistance of many persons who were willing to talk about their experiences representing America abroad. I have incurred tremendous debts to many people but especially to many Middle East hands as well as their families.

At Clark University Professor Douglas Little offered a model of what a scholar should be and patiently gave a lot of valuable advice. Professor George M. Lane, as both teacher and diplomat, encouraged and guided this work. Their advice was always the most cogent and wise. I have tried to follow their guidance, and any errors are entirely mine.

Institutional support from Clark University and Fitchburg State University (FSU) has enabled me to attend conferences, travel to archives and conduct interviews. FSU's head librarian Robert Foley and his staff have patiently dealt with endless requests for interlibrary loans.

The National Endowment for the Humanities (NEH) enabled me to spend a summer in Washington, DC, attending the NEH seminar on the New International History of the Cold War led by Professor James Hershberg and an array of Cold War scholars, including Raymond Gartoff. It was a wonderful opportunity to explore the National Security Archive's document collections. This support opened new vistas for me on foreign policy. I also must express my deep appreciation for the hardworking and helpful staff of the National Archives facilities in Washington, as well as College Park and Suitland, Maryland. Over the years the Society for Historians of American Foreign Relations (SHAFR) conferences have been a very helpful venue for presenting my work. I have greatly benefited from the comments and suggestions of many SHAFR members.

The Middle East Institute library in Washington, especially with the aid of librarian Betsy Folkins, was a wonderful source of materials on the American interaction with the Levant and the careers of Raymond Hare and Malcolm Kerr. The archivists of the John F. Kennedy Presidential Library, especially Mary Kennefick, as well as the staff of the Lyndon Johnson Presidential Library, have been very helpful in locating key documents. This work has been enriched by materials from the oral history collections of Princeton University's Mugar Library, as well as the William Yale Papers at Boston University's Mugar Library. The staff of the Government Documents Depository at Harvard University's Widener Library has been very helpful as well.

Dr. James Snow of the Foreign Service Institute generously offered much time to discuss the ingenious scientific linguists as well as his tenure as head of the Arabic language training program at Beirut. The former president of the American University of Beirut (AUB) David Dodge patiently read early chapters and discussed his career. AUB President Robert Haddad and Dean Lufty Diab also provided materials on the course of studies for American diplomats from the AUB archives.

The oral history interview project of the Association for Diplomatic Studies and Training (ADST) has been instrumental in the completion of this work. Their transcripts, originally housed at Georgetown University and then at the Foreign Service Institute, are now online. The ADST oral history project, led by Charles Stuart Kennedy, has done an incredible job of interviewing an array of American Foreign Service officers and recording their perspectives on the formulation and implementation of foreign policy. No words can express the extent of my gratitude to Charles Stuart Kennedy, Dayton Mak, Stephen Low, Marilyn Bentley and many others who have carried forward the ADST's commitment to diplomatic history.

So many diplomats kindly gave their time, including (but not limited to) William R. Crawford, Hermann F. Eilts, Paul J. Hare, Raymond Hare, Andrew I. Killgore, George M. Lane, Dayton S. Mak, Richard W. Murphy, Richard B. Parker, Talcott Seelye and Michael E. Sterner—many thanks to them and to their families for allowing me to interview them about their experiences. Many others generously gave of their time to discuss their careers via telephone or by correspondence, including Donald Bergus, Hume Horan and William Lakeland.

Finally thanks to my parents, John and Bianca Fava, who always encouraged my academic endeavors, as did Paul Moretto. My greatest debt is owed to my husband, Arthur F. Thomas, and my daughter, Ann, whose support and encouragement are most deeply and sincerely appreciated.

INTRODUCTION: AMERICA'S MIDDLE EAST AREA EXPERTS

In the summer of 1946 Donald Bergus, William Sands and their instructor Dr. Charles Ferguson landed in Lebanon. Their destination was the American embassy in Beirut, where Ferguson established a new State Department program to train diplomats in the Arabic language and Middle East area studies.

Their goal was to create a small group of area specialists who could communicate with the people of the region in one of the hardest of the "hard languages" (Russian, Chinese, Japanese and Arabic). It takes approximately four years for an English language speaker to achieve skill in the fundamentals of Arabic, but Ferguson had been allotted only six months.

Lebanon was then the region's financial and commercial center and almost lived up to its billing as the Switzerland of the Middle East. The Lebanese had a well-deserved reputation as the area's most sophisticated businessmen, building their fortunes on the capitalistic ideals learned from decades of close contact with American missionaries, educators and diplomats. But beneath the surface lay the germs of conflict and war, dormant for the moment, as the first group of American diplomats began their exploration of the Middle East.

Within a decade the Eisenhower administration would make a major investment in the program and regard these area specialists or Middle East hands as the American frontline in the Cold War.

Between 1946 and 1975 the Middle East Area Program (MEAP) expanded into a highly selective, rigorous training program, which produced a small corps of professional diplomats known as Arabists or, as I would term them, Middle East hands. This book examines 53 of them, men and women, who staffed American embassies from Morocco to Afghanistan over the decades from the Eisenhower era through the Ford administration (see Brief Biographies in the Appendix), as America's Middle East foreign policy crystallized into three general objectives: to keep the Soviets out, secure access to oil at a stable price and maintain the special relationship with the state of Israel.

These diplomats were very different from those who had worked in the old Bureau of Near East Affairs (NEA) in the 1930s and 1940s: the modern Middle East hands were far more middle class, far less Ivy League and had for the most part no connection to the old missionary community or the East Coast elite. Most often they were veterans of the US armed forces, educated in public universities and possessed not only undergraduate but graduate degrees in foreign affairs. But they all had one clear characteristic that few other people possessed: they had the skill to learn hard languages and acquire them rapidly.

Those who became Middle East hands were involved in events that still reverberate for America. Over these decades Middle East policy was increasingly formulated at the highest levels, and Washington often ignored their area expertise. Even though Middle East hands grounded their policy recommendations in their knowledge of the region's history, politics and languages, their views often ran against the conventional Cold War wisdom. Although their views were not homogenous, such as on how to handle Gamal Abdel Nasser, they did reflect a depth of knowledge about the region and the political forces within it. American foreign policy is always presidential policy, but Middle East policy increasingly became a battleground at the highest levels, and area specialists, much like the China Hands under McCarthyism, suffered for it. Important factors that affected Middle East policy were the Cold War imperative to counter Soviet influence in the region, the developing special relationship with Israel, as well as the effective lobbying of the American Israel Public Affairs Committee (AIPAC) since it was established in 1951. Ironically, as the careers of the Middle East hands advanced, their role in the policy making process was reduced.

Their policy outlook was centered upon a belief that the only solution to the region's most prominent problem, the Arab–Israeli conflict, was via a negotiated comprehensive peace with defined borders and a resolution of the refugee problem. In addition, they cautioned that the United States should not ally itself too closely with any state or regime, whether Arab or Israeli. They did not view the Soviets as the primary threat in the region but instead feared Moscow might make substantial gains by fishing in troubled waters. Arms transfers and nuclear proliferation, always a State Department priority, were particular areas of concern in a region where civil wars and border conflicts were endemic. Finally, Middle East hands repeatedly argued that a dispassionate analysis of what was in the US national interest must guide American policy.

Middle East hands supported a number of diplomatic initiatives to diffuse the conflict, including the Eric Johnston Plan, the Joseph Johnson Peace Plan, the Rogers Peace Plan, and they persistently worked at what they called quiet diplomacy to avert conflict in a volatile region.

Ironically, when the people of the region sought to protest American policy they most often targeted American embassies and diplomats. Thirty years after the training program began at Beirut one lone graduate of the program, George Lane, stepped off a US Navy landing craft onto the beach wearing a flak jacket. His assignment in 1976 was to reestablish the American presence after the murders of the US ambassador to Lebanon, his aide and their driver. It was only the beginning of a tragic conflict that began as a civil war and ultimately drew into the fighting Syria, Israel, the Palestine Liberation Organization (PLO) and a myriad of Lebanese factions. More than 150,000 people died in more than a decade of warfare, both American embassy buildings were repeatedly bombed, and among the dead were many American diplomats and employees. The Marine Battalion Landing Team headquarters was attacked by a truck bomber and destroyed with the loss of 241 US Marine peacekeepers.

America became the target of terror; many of the Middle East hands were among its most victims. As Harry Truman said, foreign policy was made by the president and not the State Department, but those who carried out presidential policy had to live (and often die) with it. Within little more than a decade 5 of the 53 Middle East hands in this study were dead. In addition numerous support personnel and embassy staff were killed in attacks and bombings. Almost every Middle East hand suffered some disaster: embassy bombings, hostage takings or assassination attempts.

They were also often the targets of journalistic attacks. Ironically, as their policy influence was shrinking, political pundits often blamed America's problems in the Middle East on State Department Arabists who were cited as being a powerful force controlling American policy.

It is important to examine the policies they did recommend and to measure what influence, however limited, they did have on policy. In retrospect the primary thrust of their counsel was to advocate an active role in resolving the Arab–Israeli conflict. Their goal was to mitigate the escalating violence, avert warfare and secure American interests.

The Middle East hands have been the target of political pundits as well as terrorists but rarely the subject of scholarly study. They argued for what they saw as America's vital interests. Yet they, more than any other regional specialists since the China hands in the McCarthy era, have been attacked and had their advice ignored.

The primary charges against them have been that they were pro-Arab or even anti-Israel and that they controlled US policy. Assistant secretary for the NEA Richard Murphy pointed out that rather than steering policy to their own ends, the Middle East hands had offered advice and carried out their orders but had wielded little influence: "This is not an enemy force hidden in the State Department offices undermining presidential policy. That is a fantasy."[1]

American presidents were enmeshed in Middle East crises: Truman and the founding of Israel, Eisenhower and Suez, Johnson and the Six Day War, Nixon and October War and oil embargo and Ford's efforts on the Sinai withdrawal. Yet, there has been little examination of their advisers and the counsel they offered.

While their advice was based upon what State Department policy makers thought was best for American interests, a variety of accusations have been used to undercut them. Israelis and their US supporters, most notably the American Israel Public Affairs Committee, argued that the Middle East hands wanted Israel to take risks to achieve a peace settlement.

To the Middle East hands a negotiated peace agreement was inherently less dangerous than the risk presented by a prolonged and potentially escalating conflict. After the 1948 Arab–Israeli War, bitter disputes were fought over borders and the right of return for Palestinian refugees. After the 1967 Six Day War, the occupied territories immensely complicated the quest for a solution. When Middle East hands urged negotiation under the Rogers Peace Plan, they were accused of anti-Israeli bias, hostility and even anti-Semitism.

The most succinct description of how effectively such charges were used against them was offered by Undersecretary of State George Ball. In 1976 Ball argued it was in Israel's best interests to negotiate a peace agreement because "a continuance of the present stalemate is more dangerous than the concessions required for peace." But Ball gloomily noted the fate of anyone who might suggest such a course: "To suggest that America should take a stronger and more assertive line in the search for Middle East peace is to risk being attacked as a servant either of Arab interests or of the oil companies, or being denounced as anti-Israel, or, by a careless confusion of language, even condemned as anti-Semitic.[2]

The "careless confusion of language" has often led to false charges of anti-Semitism against the Middle East hands and has damaged, and even ended, a number of careers.[3] It has also severely limited their ability to openly address a number of issues (particularly the role of the PLO in peace negotiations) and marginalized their views. In effect they were silenced, much to the detriment of the US position.

One critic, Michael Lewis of AIPAC, characterized what he saw as the typical Middle East hand's point of view, circa 1988. He observed that the State Department's NEA Bureau "has been the bureau most recalcitrant in the face of change, persisting with many of its old views, for example, on the need to include the PLO in Arab–Israeli negotiations [...] They hold that close relations with Israel damage American relations with the Arabs, that the Arabs would be forthcoming to Israel if only Israel made concessions, that Palestinian terrorism can only be addressed by resolving the Arab–Israeli conflict and that the conflict cannot be resolved without inclusion of the PLO."[4]

In fact, that "recalcitrant" and "old views" became Israel's policy when it opened negotiations with the PLO in Oslo and then signed the Declaration of Principles in 1993. Where borders were defined, as in the Camp David Accords between Israel and Egypt, conflict ended. The Oslo approach was independently adopted by Israel under the leadership of Yitzhak Rabin, but Middle East hands had long urged that American policy be based on such negotiation for decades. The aim was to avert more of the tragic violence that had marked the Arab–Israeli conflict.

The critics have raised important questions: Was the Middle East hands' advice pro-Arab? Was it harmful to Israel? Journalist Robert Kaplan, in his book *The Arabists: The Romance of an American Elite*, has contended that they were "the secret drivers of America's Middle East policy since the end of World War II."[5]

To address these questions, this book is divided into two sections: the first half examines who the Middle East hands were and how their policy views developed. Chapter two characterizes the Orientalists who preceded them in the old NEA; the next chapters describe the typical Middle East hand, the development of Arabic language training and the MEAP, the methods of instruction and their experience in the field. The second half of this work explores the development of diplomatic careers of the Middle East hands and their experiences during the Eisenhower, Kennedy, Johnson, Nixon and Ford administrations. Their views on American foreign policy as lessons learned, are summarized in "The Beirut Axioms" and the appendix contains a series of brief biographies of typical Cold War–era American Arabists.

Nowhere but in the Middle East is there more disagreement over words and their meaning; therefore it is important to define the terms central to this discussion: Arabist, Orientalist and professionalism. For the purposes of this study an Arabist or Middle East hand is any US Foreign Service Officer (FSO) who completed the State Department's MEAP between 1946 and 1975 and then continued to work in the NEA. It excludes those who attempted the program but failed to meet its demanding requirements or those who later pursued careers outside of NEA or in the private sector.

The State Department, through its Foreign Service Institute (FSI), developed a program that was not merely an intensive course in Arabic but rather a language and area studies program that aimed to develop genuine area expertise in the entire region. That required skill, determination and a major investment of time: up to two years out of a career to learn a hard language, as well as the history, politics, culture and economic systems of the area—both Arab and Israeli.

Some critics have contended the Middle East hands did not understand Israel, but in fact their training was not limited to the Arab side. They studied and visited Israel, and many held posts there. At first senior State Department administrators refused to send any graduate of the Arabic program to Israel on the premise that no Arab states would later accept them. This was illogical since many of the program candidates had already served in Haifa, Tel Aviv or Jerusalem before applying to the program. During the 1960s one of the program's graduates, William R. Crawford, was in charge of NEA's personnel policy and reversed it: "I insisted that everybody who went through Arabic had to have an equal exposure to Israel" since Middle East specialization "must entail equal knowledge of both cultures." Thereafter all MEAP graduates were routinely posted to Israel.[6]

Years later, William Quandt, an advisor to President Carter and a Brookings Institution fellow, testified before Congress that "the results [of posting diplomats to both sides] are impressive." Quandt recalled that "Arabists are sufficiently suspect [of being anti-Israeli] that only one Assistant Secretary of the Bureau for Near East and South Asian Affairs in the past twenty years has been an Arabist. Incidentally, during his tenure, US–Israeli relations reached unprecedented high levels of cooperation."[7]

The term "Arabist" has taken on a negative, if not pejorative, air in the United States. While British dictionaries define an Arabist as an Arabic linguist, most American dictionaries add a second definition, which asserts pro-Arab favoritism and reflects the polarization of the Middle East debate.[8] Outside the United States and in the world of linguists, an Arabist is a specialist in the Arabic language and the use of that term is unavoidable when discussing language study.

Middle East scholar Bernard Lewis observed that for some, the term "means an advocate of Arab causes." In defending the original usage, Lewis observed: "The term Hispanist does not mean an apologist for Central American tyrants or terrorists, an admirer of bullfighters, an observer or practitioner of Spanish affairs, or a purveyor of bananas. It means a scholar with a good knowledge of Spanish, specializing in some field of Spanish or Latin American history or culture. The word Arabist ought to be used in the same way."[9]

A more broadly descriptive term is required since their work encompassed the entire region, not merely the Arab world. Israelis, of course, speak Hebrew, Yiddish as well as English and in recent years have also welcomed large numbers of Russian- and Ethiopian-speaking immigrants. Iran's culture is historically Persian and most Iranians speak Farsi or dialects of Arabic. Other states, in particular Lebanon and Egypt, include a broad mix of religious and ethnic identities, which include people who may be Islamic or Christian and may not necessarily speak Arabic or identify themselves as Muslim. The Kurds occupy a borderless region that spans five countries, speak their own unique language and the issue of their nationality is contentious. The MEAP was faced with the challenge of teaching about peoples and languages far beyond what is perceived as traditional Arabist studies. For these reasons I have adopted the term "Middle East hand" to describe the program's graduates.

The original term for the study of the region, Orientalism, is rooted in the nineteenth-century European (especially British and French) colonial domination of the Middle East and carries with it romantic, exotic and even bizarre overtones. It also serves as the generic term for a largely European school of writers, travelers and diplomats who translated "the Orient" for the West. These were people like Sir Richard Burton and Lawrence Arabia, Gertrude Bell, a British diplomatic adviser who drew the borders of Iraq, and adventurers like Freya Stark. There was a strong link between those amateur experts and the British Foreign Office, who called these advisers "Oriental Secretaries" and gave them a dominant role in foreign policy.

The modern usage of the term "Orientalist" was defined by Edward Said's 1978 work *Orientalism*, which described the imperialist condescension inherent in the term.[10] Said focused on the late nineteenth- and early twentieth-century colonial era and decried the power relationship implicit in one nation controlling and classifying an entire region as "other." Said observed that Orientalism connotes "a British and French cultural enterprise" peopled by "a long tradition of colonial administrators." It is based in what he terms "positional superiority" or the upper hand over another people.[11]

He also defined Orientalism as "a Western style for dominating, restructuring, and having authority over the Orient." But, he errs when he connects nineteenth-century European Orientalism to modern American diplomacy. Said veers into unsubstantiated polemic when he dismissed American Arabists in a single sentence: "The legendary Arabists in the State Department warn of Arab plans to take over the world." He did not explain where he got the idea nor present any evidence to support it.[12]

Furthermore, Said viewed the United States as having established a new postcolonial form of Orientalist dominance, having made the Arab world into "an intellectual, political and cultural satellite of the United States." He also pointed out that this extended into the classrooms where Arabic was studied since "[m]ost elementary courses in Oriental languages are taught by 'native informants,'" which in fact was the method used by FSI in Beirut where Arabic speakers coached students while the program was run by State Department instructors. But for Said those "native informants" did not hold "power in the system (in universities, foundations, and the like) [which] is held almost exclusively by non-Orientals." Although the Arab oil companies had wealth, the appeal of American exports had made them "totally absorbed by the United States economy."[13]

But the critical implication of his work, for this study, is his explanation of the shallow and amateurish aspects of what once passed for serious scholarship and diplomatic practice. Any shelf of interwar texts on the Middle East would be populated by European travel memoirs, works by Gertrude Bell, Freya Stark and Lawrence of Arabia. For decades few authors from inside the region reached a Western audience with books about contemporary politics. One of the few exceptions was George Antonius's *The Arab Awakening*, a 1938 political study of Arab nationalism. The Beirut FSI program used the Antonius book as a starting point and focused on the contemporary history and politics of the region.

Arabic language study in the United States hardly existed before World War II and serious study was limited to Classical Arabic in divinity schools where it was studied in long-dead forms, far different from modern usage. A handful of scholars, most notably Philip Hitti at Princeton, became the first generation of modern Middle East professors in the 1940s. Area studies, a combination of language study with regional history, politics and religion, would not develop fully until after World War II. A bold manifesto, written by scholar H. A .R. Gibb, demanded an intensive effort to develop modern Middle East studies at a very late date: in 1963.[14]

Edward Said's *Orientalism* also criticized the power that Gibb wielded in his position as a scholar once he moved to Harvard University, as well as the development of professional organizations like the Middle East Institute founded in 1946 and the Middle East Studies Association, which he saw as captives of the "powerful support" they received from the Defense Department and oil companies. For Said, those sources of support perpetuated "the traditional Orientalist outlook."[15]

The Department of State developed the first language program that was divorced from Orientalism, taught modern language forms of Arabic and took a serious, academic approach to the Middle East. The antecedents of this program began during World War II, when the US Armed Forces desperately needed experts in almost all of the hard languages (especially Arabic). The Army Specialized Training Program (ASTP) was hastily organized by a handful of young scholars who were experts in scientific language training. The ASTP staff was quickly mobilized for the duration of the war and produced language texts, records and organized intensive courses in all of the hard languages.

When it disbanded in 1946, the key members of the ASTP staff were recruited by the State Department to become the core of the newly established FSI and its Arabic program. The State Department also recruited veterans who had graduated from the ASTP. The model diplomat sought by the State Department in the postwar decades was an armed forces veteran with proven skill at learning hard languages. This attracted a new, very different group, as many middle-class armed services veterans used both their ASTP experience and the GI Bill to get on the fast track to a postwar diplomatic career.

Most of the postwar hard language programs at the State Department could build on prewar experience, but the MEAP had no predecessor. Therefore its development was unique. The story of how it evolved is also part of the story of how modern Middle East area studies developed in America. Many of the Arabic training methods of the FSI were adopted by universities as the small core of scientific linguists who shuttled between the FSI and academia. After one of its first directors Dr. Charles Ferguson left MEAP, he was hired by Harvard University's Center for Middle East Studies.[16]

The MEAP is also the key to understanding how these US diplomats learned about the region and how they were later marginalized. One of the most important instructors in the area studies program in Beirut was Dr. Malcolm Kerr. He was influential not only as an instructor but as the model of an incisive analyst on America's Middle East policy. After the death of Raymond Hare, one of the earliest Middle East hands, his papers were stored in the library of the Middle East Institute. Among them was a substantial collection of original draft speeches and articles written by Kerr. Those materials are used here to give insight into the views of those who trained and shaped the careers of Middle East hands in the State Department.

Few Americans, especially policy makers in Washington, knew anything about the history or politics of the Middle East. Lobbyists found it was far easier to undercut the Middle East hands if (and such was the case) policy makers had no fundamental understanding of the past and were reluctant to be disabused of the conventional wisdom. More importantly, the Cold War led to a simplistic division of the area into Soviet and American clients at a time when the region was swept by successive waves of nationalism and neutralism.

For purposes of this study the term "Orientalist" refers to the missionary sons, oilmen and others who learned their Arabic, if they learned it at all, while living or working in the region and joined NEA before 1946. Prior to that time there was no Arabic training for diplomats, but instead the old NEA was staffed by anyone who could be found with any link to the area. This policy drew upon an expatriate community of former missionaries and oilmen, who often viewed the Arabs as clients.

Orientalists often felt passionately about the importance of linking America to the Arab world and saw Zionism as a threat. Some sons of missionary families became State Department Orientalists who spoke of the fight in Washington over the establishment of Israel as "the Battle of Palestine." They often cultivated a romantic and adventurous air, and were single-mindedly determined to shape American policy between the 1920s and 1940s.[17]

Two notable exceptions who emerged at the end of World War II and the end of the Orientalist era were Raymond Hare and Parker Hart. Neither of these American diplomats were the sons of missionaries, nor oilmen, but they developed facility in Arabic and expertise in the area and rose to become ambassadors. In many ways they fostered the careers of many junior officers and could be considered the founding fathers of the Middle East hands.[18] Hare and Hart were both talented men who aspired to a career in diplomacy built upon linguistic skill and area knowledge rather than social connections. They remained the only genuine Arabic language specialists among the ambassadors who served President Eisenhower and mentored the next generation of Middle East hands who were just beginning their careers.

The term "professionalism" in this work refers to the changes following 1946 in the selection and training of America's Middle East hands. Arabic was the last of the hard language programs to be established and for that reason originated under different circumstances. The MEAP of the FSI attempted to train the post-1946 group as objective political reporting officers. The candidates they recruited and selected were a small group of young veterans who gambled that language training would be their key to career advancement and ultimately to an ambassadorship.

Completing the MEAP was a rite of passage and built a sense of professionalism, objectivity, as well as institutional loyalty. Moreover, spending two years in Beirut not only defined their expertise but shaped their outlook. Middle East hands viewed the demands of training and the hardship of living at remote posts, as the means to reach the top in a highly competitive milieu.

Since the FSI selected candidates on the basis of proven language learning ability, the program built up a core group with no common social background or regional links (as Orientalists had) to predetermine their views.

By the Kennedy era the State Department set aside a number of positions in embassies as "language-designated posts," limiting them to graduates of the program. In addition, the MEAP developed a rigorous testing program, which rated language skills and was made part of a diplomat's personnel record. Thereafter, graduation from MEAP put a diplomat on the career track and defined the group's professionalism.

In a study entitled "The Trashing of Professionalism" Louis Menand discussed how a wide range of professionals have been criticized and described how "superior expertise is now almost automatically equated with elitism." There are distinct parallels between Menand's study and the experience of the Middle East hands. Training was their credential, and rigorous testing eliminated many aspirants who could not reach a high skill level.

The graduates of the MEAP have been termed "an American elite" by Robert Kaplan, but in terms of social class they were much less elite and more middle class than the Orientalists. Although Menand's study deals with professionals in general, his observations also fit the Middle East hands. Menand argues that professionalism is developed within "credentialing systems" and produces a specialization, defined as the "knowledge and skills needed in a particular endeavor, [which] are not transferable" and are based upon a "standard of disinterestedness." In other words, beyond being credentialed in a system that excludes amateurs, the true professional must be objective. Menand finds professionals under attack by the uncredentialed, who are fired by "the deep sense of skepticism about the possibility of independence of mind."[19]

Who were their critics? Much as Menand describes, they were often deeply skeptical, lacked formal training and were partisans of one side or another. Indeed, most of the material written about American Arabists has been either critical, even antagonistic.[20] The Middle East hands were often attacked by journalists and even politicians who questioned their objectivity and termed them pro-Arab. Most Middle East hands, however, would see in Menand's definition that their training was aimed to create area expertise that was based upon a "standard of disinterestedness" neither tied to Arab nor Israeli interests but defined by American interests.

Why the antagonism? The policies that they recommended were predicated on independent thinking and a regional focus that clashed with the dominant Cold War consensus. Their primary goals, which I have termed "the Beirut Axioms," were to reach a comprehensive settlement of the Arab–Israeli conflict, define regional borders, resolve the refugee problem and seek a resolution to what seemed (and seems) an insoluble conflict. This was also the best defense against the expansion of Soviet influence. They aimed to protect US interests and tried to develop diplomatic initiatives to build a positive image for America in the region.

The Middle East hands recognized the enormous dimensions of the task. Donald Bergus addressed these difficulties in the spring of 1956, shortly before the Suez crisis, a time when a solution to the Arab–Israeli conflict would have been far less complicated. He said he wished that he could "outline some new gimmick, some easy way, some royal road to the permanent lessening of tensions" but there was no "royal road" to peace unless both Arabs and Israelis were willing to compromise: "There is no solution which can succeed without a common will for peace and a readiness to make the contributions necessary to achieve that peace." He warned that unless both sides moved forward the next generations of Arabs would be convinced that "[t]hey must seek by war a solution to problems which were created by war." He also cautioned against the view among some Israelis "that for the indefinite future they must stand on the ramparts of a garrison state."[21]

When Israel and the PLO signed the Declaration of Principles in 1993, Middle East hand James Akins argued that "a just peace in the Middle East" had always been the goal of the Middle East hands. He also observed, "We certainly talked about a just peace in the area longer than almost any Palestinian or Israeli."[22]

The Middle East hands' regional focus clashed with the dominant Cold War view of Washington policy makers. Middle East hand Michael E. Sterner pointed out that the American focus was on the Middle East as a Cold War chessboard where the rivalry with the Soviets played out. Yet, Sterner and his colleagues argued that communism held little appeal in the Arab world but that the Soviets were opportunists, eager to fish in troubled waters. The best way to reduce Soviet influence was to remove the Arab–Israeli conflict as an excuse for Arab reliance on the Soviets or "there would be a shift in the global balance of power."[23]

For American presidents, from Eisenhower to Nixon, the Cold War outlook dominated policy, and there was an inherent conflict between the regionalist viewpoint of Middle East hands and Washington's globalism. What might be termed the globalist or Cold Warriors' school of thought, according to historian (and former MEAP instructor) Malcolm Kerr, "is based on the idea of the balance of power" and "cultivating local clients." Its founding father is Hans Morgenthau, with his intellectual heirs being John Foster Dulles and Henry Kissinger. The regionalist school, according to Kerr "does not deny the importance of the American–Soviet global rivalry, but denies that local issues around the world should be primarily approached in those terms."[24] Besides, mid-level diplomats only consisted of a few regionalists at the upper policy levels who argued that analysis should take into consideration regional factors. Some of the clearest thinkers were George Ball as well as former China desk diplomat and later Secretary of State Dean Rusk, Senator J. William Fulbright and Secretaries of State William Rogers and Cyrus Vance.

Globalists viewed Gamal Nasser, Hafez Asad and many other Arab nationalists as under the direction, or at least the inspiration, of Moscow. However, regionalists saw Arab nationalism as an outgrowth of the historical forces but were divided on the quality of Nasser's leadership. Some viewed him as a modernizer and his neutralism a defense against Soviet influence, while others saw Nasser as a threat to valuable allies like Saudi Arabia. Almost all, however, agreed on the primacy of his position in the region. For Middle East hands, the United States must work with or at least not alienate neutralists. But for globalists like Dulles, Nasser was an errant pawn on the chessboard, neither black nor white. For Secretary of State John Foster Dulles, it was precisely his inability to make Nasser into a dependable client that generated anger toward Cairo.

For the Middle East hands, globalists erred by ignoring the underlying regional factors, which triggered crises and gave Moscow new opportunities.

From the globalist perspective, Middle East hands underestimated the most sinister threat: communist expansion. For regionalists working in the Middle East, Washington made policy decisions based upon the logic of the Cold War but ignored the regional origins of problems and the potential consequences.

Globalists like Henry Kissinger argued the United States should move slowly in step-by-step diplomacy (which he called "the peace process"). Journalists like Joseph Kraft and Robert Kaplan have praised Kissinger and other such advocates as "the peace processors" for their deliberately slow approach. Those peace processors might be more correctly termed "piece processors" for their lengthy, piecemeal strategy to dealing with the smoldering and periodically explosive Arab–Israeli conflict, which only grew in complexity as time passed.

Within the State Department George Ball was a vocal advocate of the regional view and saw progress in peace negotiations as an imperative to avoid the risk of a US–Soviet conflict, like when American forces went on high alert during the 1973 October War: "The most serious danger faced by the two nations [the United States and USSR] is that they may be propelled into a confrontation neither desires by their involvement in the affairs of third countries."[25]

The refusal of both Israelis and Palestinians to compromise prolonged and complicated the struggle for a solution. In 1973 the PLO was recognized by the Arab League as the sole legitimate representative of the Palestinians, and then Israel refused to engage in negotiations with the PLO. In 1975 Israel insisted on (and received) written assurances that American diplomats would not meet with the PLO. This froze the peace process for nearly twenty years.

From the view of the Middle East hands, the failure of the United States to achieve a peace settlement left America in a vulnerable position. Earlier, during the 1967 Six Day War, the USS *Liberty*, an intelligence-gathering ship, was attacked by Israeli warplanes with 34 Americans dead. During the October War in 1973 the United States resupplied the Israeli Defense Forces, triggering the oil embargo that ravaged the US economy and left a half million Americans unemployed.

State Department personnel have been among the casualties of the conflict since its inception in the 1940s: the first FSO murdered during the Arab–Israeli conflict was US consul Thomas Wasson, shot by a sniper as he emerged from Jerusalem peace talks in 1948. Of the 53 Middle East hands in this study, five died violently while fulfilling their duties and two other non-Arabists were murdered in the region. David Newsom's career experience illustrates the variety of violence a Middle East hand could face: in May of 1948 he was confronted by demonstrations in Karachi protesting US recognition of Israel; in December 1952 his office in Baghdad was burned; in 1967 he evacuated 6,000 US citizens from Libya during the Six Day War; and he was targeted for assassination by a Palestinian group.

After interviewing many of the Middle East hands, I find Newsom's experience not exceptional but typical. Most of those FSOs who served in the region suffered near escapes, shootings or had their embassies burned, bombed or attacked by mobs. Newsom pointed out that US foreign policy suffered most in the Middle East: "There have been more evacuations of US citizens out of Arab countries than out of any other part of the world. More Arab countries have, at one time or another, broken relations with the United States than any other group of nations. More American diplomats have been killed in the line of duty or threatened with violence here than in any other region of the world."[26]

Moreover, attacks on other embassy personnel in the Middle East escalated through the 1970s and 1980s. Within the span of little more than a year during Israel's invasion of Lebanon a number of attacks were made on American installations and diplomatic personnel: Embassy Beirut was bombed with 63 dead on April 18, 1983; Embassy Kuwait was bombed on December 12, 1983; diplomat Leamon Hunt was murdered on February 21, 1984; and Embassy Beirut was again bombed with eight dead on September 20, 1984. Additionally, the Beirut Marine barracks attack killed 241 armed forces personnel on October 23, 1983, and Malcolm Kerr, president of American University of Beirut and former MEAP instructor, was murdered on January 18, 1984. All of these events occurred during Israel's invasion of Lebanon, Operation Peace for Galilee, between June 6, 1982, and January 1985. In reviewing his decades of experiences in Beirut, Middle East hand Richard Parker concluded that "what is remarkable is that we are not worse off than we are."[27]

Moreover, for all the effort it took to become area experts, the Middle East hands often felt their influence on foreign policy was negligible. Ambassador Hermann Eilts, a veteran of three decades in the State Department, observed that not only had they failed to influence policy but even after reaching the State Department rank of assistant secretary for NEA few were rarely allowed to present their views on policy: "I am struck by the few occasions on which an expert officer […] has been able to get directly to the president of the US, and, on some occasions, how rarely he has been able to get to even the Secretary of State." Eilts argued that the "great expertise and institutional memory that our government has does not get to the top."[28]

Despite investing enormous time and energy in training Middle East specialists, policy makers did not listen to them, and they were further undercut by a campaign to discredit them. Middle East hands suffered professional attacks from all sides. In the early years a loose federation of groups known as the Conference of Presidents of Jewish Organizations organized pro-Israeli lobbying in Washington. It was later superseded in 1951 by the most effective lobby, the American–Israel Public Affairs Committee (AIPAC). In this era the AIPAC conducted a successful campaign to garner support for Israel in Congress and to undercut those it deemed Israel's critics, while simultaneously conducting a program of opposition research to track Israel's critics and publish information on them in a weekly newsletter called "Activities." An internal memo described AIPAC's influence on American foreign policy: "There is no question that we exert a policy impact, but since we work behind the scenes and take care not to leave fingerprints, that impact is not always traceable to us."[29]

In 1983 AIPAC published a book-length study, *The Campaign to Discredit Israel*, which included a list of 40 individuals that AIPAC deemed "anti-Israel," some of them State Department Middle East specialists and others even American Jews.[30]

AIPAC's think tank, the Washington Institute for Near East Policy (WINEP), established in 1985, has worked to present not only the Israeli view but to undercut any opposition. WINEP has published a series of papers on US policy that are often highly critical of the State Department. In 1984 WINEP announced the publication of *The Errors of the Arabists*, but when the author inquired to AIPAC in 1995, she was told that it had never been printed. WINEP has also provided a number of high-level advisers to the White House who have filled the upper ranks of US Middle East policy making: Dennis Ross, US envoy to the Israeli-PLO talks; Richard Haass former NSC adviser to President Bush; and Martin Indyk, who was appointed ambassador to Israel, although not yet a US citizen. Historians John Mearshimer and Stephen Walt have examined the development of AIPAC and its impact on policy making in *The Israel Lobby and US Foreign Policy*.[31]

How has the critique of American Arabists developed? The most well-known article, "Those Arabists at State," was written by Joseph Kraft in 1971. Kraft, a journalist, interviewed a number of Middle East hands in Washington and abroad. As his first rhetorical question, "Are the Arabists, as many supporters of Israel assert, still hostile to the Jewish state?" reveals, when deconstructed, his assumption is that they have always been hostile. Kraft implied Harry Truman's recollection of the old Orientalists applied to the new generation: "Some among them were also inclined to be anti-Semitic."[32]

In Kraft's second question, "Do they, as not a few White House men believe, still try to shape policy in ways contrary to presidential interests?" Kraft frames the issue from the White House view and reiterates that they "still" busily "shape" policy. Kraft does not debate whether the Arabists had US national interests in mind when offering advice. It is an exaggeration to suggest that any mid-level diplomats could "shape policy" contrary to the will of an American president.

Kraft does cite the observation of the Egyptian ambassador to the United States, Mustafa Kamel, who had said that the NEA bureau "is manned by a lot of tired Arabists who have lost whatever influence they ever had."[33] Kamel's comment is a more realistic view of the amount of influence that the Middle East hands exerted in Washington.

Kraft argued that the central tenet of Arabist thinking was that "the Arabs represent an opportunity for the US; Israel is a headache" and that they "set stock in what Arabs think and do and have," notably oil. This ignored the fact that the Middle East hands were charged with protecting American interests and advising the government. America has economic linkage to a region that is a valuable market (170 million customers have equated to an opportunity for corporations like Pepsi, Coca Cola, General Motors, Ford, Bechtel and others). American investments in oil (ARAMCO in particular) have a direct relationship to the domestic economy: if production is disrupted, the United States suffers not only the penalties of high energy costs but also the loss in oil profits that would have been invested by foreign nationals in government securities. The economic impact is undeniable.

Before the 1973 Arab oil embargo Middle East hand James Akins, in charge of energy planning for the White House, warned that the United States was becoming vulnerable to the threats of the Organization of Petroleum Exporting Countries (OPEC) regarding an embargo, but his warnings went unheeded even after he published an article in *Foreign*

Affairs. When Akins's warnings came true, *Forbes Magazine* heaped criticism on Akins in an article entitled "Don't Blame the Oil Companies: Blame the State Department."[34]

What Kraft called a "basic bias" and hostility to what he termed "Zionist influence" was in fact putting American interests first. The Middle East hands were not bound by a fascination with an "exotic" Arab world nor blinded by a hatred of everything Israeli. For Middle East hands American interests could be damaged when caught up in the Arab–Israeli conflict and suffer for it. This had a great potential to hurt the American economy, lead to anti-American terror and be exploited to great advantage by the Soviets.

Yet, decades after the Orientalists were replaced by the Middle East hands, the new group continues to be smeared with the old negative stereotype. The images created in the first half of the twentieth century still prevails. In 1993 Robert Kaplan's *The Arabists: The Romance of an American Elite* offered a fresh salvo of the old critique.

The Orientalist stereotype arose during the years of British hegemony in the Middle East and is still used against modern area specialists to undercut their ideas. The visual images never die but are continually resurrected. In 1971 Joseph Kraft's article had a full-page portrait of Lawrence of Arabia in Arab dress as a key illustration, literally casting an Orientalist shadow over the modern Middle East hands in photographs taken during Kraft's interviews. Later an Israeli newspaper recycled the images: each diplomat's head was severed from the original photo and set in a painting where the diplomats, dressed in flowing Arab robes, flanked Lawrence of Arabia. A quarter of a century later, Robert Kaplan used the same montage for his book at a time when Middle East hands spent their careers in pinstripes, laboring in the concrete confines of heavily fortified embassies. The image of men in flowing robes survived, even if they had to be painted on.[35]

When the *Atlantic Monthly* ran a feature article to introduce Kaplan's book, it was entitled "Tales from the Bazaar." The title page, in Arabic-style script, opened with a provocative question: "Whose side, some wonder, are our Arab experts on? Is that an unfair question? A report on diplomacy in Araby."[36] The tone that Kaplan assumed in the article echoes the phonetic possibilities of his title, "Tales from the Bizarre."

Both Kraft and Kaplan seem to assume American diplomats were looking out for Arab interests. Middle East hands have long pointed out that they favored neither Arab nor Israeli positions but regarded what was in the American national interest as the basis for US foreign policy. James Akins observed: "The Arabists have insisted that American interests in the Middle East must take precedence over those of any other country."[37]

Kaplan himself repeatedly used the Orientalist term "Araby" throughout the book, but certainly no diplomat would use the word "Araby." Yet it is a clever device to link modern American diplomats to the past. Kaplan's most provocative question, "Whose side are they on?" reveals his preconceptions. In its introduction to the piece, the *Atlantic* editors defined "Arabist" and summarized Kaplan's approach: "The term 'Arabist' has acquired a deeply pejorative connotation in America's political lexicon, referring to a diplomat in the Arab world who has 'gone native' and in the process lost sight of US interests. The State Department's Arabists were criticized most recently for diplomatic blundering that preceded the war with Iraq. They have been accused for decades of animosity toward Israel." Before even reading the article, the reader is informed that Arabists are by definition diplomats who do not place America's interests first, have been "blundering" and regard Israel with "animosity." Kaplan interviewed, but confined to the sidelines in his article and book, the three Arabists who have all held the most influential post, assistant secretary for the NEA (Richard W. Murphy, Edward Djerejian and Robert Pelletreau). None fit the Orientalist stereotype. They were neither the sons of missionaries nor had been oilmen but were professionals who had completed rigorous training and had risen through the ranks. Kaplan neglected these more important (and more representative) area specialists who lacked the Orientalist trappings.

Howard Teicher, a former National Security Council staffer, authored a book questioning the expertise of the Middle East hands and their reluctance to move the United States into a closer military alliance with Israel. In *Twin Pillars to Desert Storm: America's Flawed Vision in the Middle East from Nixon to Bush*, Teicher criticized State Department opposition to the proposition that Israel was a potential military asset. Teicher envisioned closer military and strategic cooperation between Israel and the United States in the Cold War but found his efforts to implement this alliance ran against the "conventional wisdom" of Middle East hands. Teicher observed they have thus prevented US–Israel "combined operations," which would bring US Armed Forces into Israeli ports and bases: "The Arab–Israeli conflict had for too long been manipulated by Arabists in the national security bureaucracy to prevent military relations between the United States and Israel which would enhance strategic American interest in the Middle East." Middle East hands countered with the argument that any joint US–Israeli military operations against an Arab country would have serious ramifications.[38]

Teicher argued that they did not base their area knowledge upon academic training: "Most of these government Arabists based their Middle East expertise on their tours of service in Arab countries, rather than on academic, research-oriented study."[39]

In fact, Middle East hands had invested significant time in training compare to government personnel dealing with foreign policy. In "The Socio-Educational Composition of the CIA Elite: A Statistical Note," Rhodri Jeffreys-Jones compared the educational levels of CIA employees with other government officers dealing with foreign policy. Comparing the biographies of 70 CIA employees with a control group, Jeffreys-Jones found the CIA held fewer first degrees as well as doctorates. On the question of whether "the CIA's analysts were monoglots," he found that 7 percent of the CIA had studied abroad compared to 25 percent of the control group, defined as drawn from area experts employed by "State, Defense, and the Export-Import Bank, etc."[40]

Teicher's critique focused on the diplomats' lack of training, and he appears to be unaware of the MEAP. He argued his own expertise came from "years of studying the history, politics and culture of the peoples of the Middle East, together with the practical experience I gained working in the US government." In a section on his role on Robert McFarlane's negotiating team in Lebanon during 1982–83, Teicher spends pages describing his dealings with Walid Jumblatt and at the end describes his farewell: "I told him I was interested in learning more about the Druze […] I knew that he had lived in India for some years and was a leader who inspired his followers through spiritual charisma as well as bravery. Jumblatt smiled, rolled his eyes, but demurred."[41] Perhaps he demurred because it was not Walid but his father, Kamal Jumblatt, who had made his reputation as a mystic through extended visits to India.

Teicher portrayed the Middle East hands as untrained, although most possessed an equal (often superior) level of education compared to other officials dealing with foreign policy. After paragraphs of stereotyping their intellectual and analytical poverty, he described Ambassador Robert Pelletreau as "one of the most fair, intellectually honest and open-minded Arabists with whom I would ever work." Teicher acknowledged Pelletreau's Yale law degree and fluency in Arabic but did not mention his two long periods in the MEAP, which were composed of an additional year and a half of language-and-area training beyond his other degrees. Pelletreau is not atypical of the Middle East hands.[42]

In 1975 the instability in Lebanon and especially Beirut led the State Department to close the training program in Beirut. Scholar R. Bayly Winder observed that American students could no longer explore the region as they once had: "A generation of young scholars has now moved into the academy without ever walking on the campus of the American University of Beirut [...] the scope of their view of the area has been egregiously narrowed."[43] After 1975, Americans were no longer free to explore Lebanon, Iran, Iraq, Syria and Libya and other regions.

How did America get into this situation? The second half of this study will examine how America coped with the challenges presented in the Middle East. It will examine the advice given by the Middle East hands and their role through 1975. Asian scholar John King Fairbank commented that the attacks on America's China specialists by Senator Joseph McCarthy, linked with the effectiveness of the China lobby, resulted in a foreign policy disaster and "unrealistic thinking" in Washington.[44] Many Arabists found US policy reflected "unrealistic thinking" and responded as academically trained professionals would. Richard Curtiss, a United States Information Agency (USIA) Middle East specialist, recalled that they were "patriotic American FSOs [who] [...] steeped themselves in knowledge of the area so that, *while they might be ignored, they could not be refuted* when they spoke out to correct American public misperceptions of the area, its peoples, and their problems."[45]

Middle East hands often found Washington unable to comprehend how deeply contemporary events were rooted in the distant past. Israeli Prime Minister Golda Meir recalled how Zionists viewed the establishment of Israel as the end of a 2,000-year diaspora and the incredible tragedy of the Holocaust. They were determined to hold onto territory to ensure unbreachable security. Meir argued that subsequent generations have the same goals: "[T]hey are totally committed to the development and security of the State of Israel [...] it is essential that there be a Jewish state where Jews can live as Jews, not on sufferance and not as a minority."[46]

Arabs also argued they had right on their side and refused to abandon their determination to hold onto the Promised Land. In *The Crusades Through Arab Eyes*, Amin Maalouf pointed out that many events are deeply rooted in the past: "[O]n the eve of the third millennium, the political and religious leaders of the Arab world constantly refer to Saladin, to the fall of Jerusalem and its recapture. In the popular mind, and in some official discourse too, Israel is regarded as a new Crusader state."[47]

People who speak in millenniums take the long view, while American policy makers sought easy solutions and both Arabs and Israelis considered their battle over "the much promised land" as a fight to hold onto what was theirs.

Explaining such complex issues to policy makers is difficult, as Hermann Eilts observed: "Issues such as those of the Middle East are too complex, are too deeply rooted in history, are too psychological in nature, to be boiled down into one or two simple paragraphs."[48]

The Middle East hands based their advice on the American national interest. Explaining complex situations rather than reducing them to a simplistic Cold War clientism, as well as pushing for a comprehensive peace settlement, placed them at the center of the conflict. Theirs was an unpopular perspective, which was held by a small group of area experts who suffered professionally and personally in trying to carry out Washington's directives. But, they were not partisans of either side; the national interest was their paramount priority, and they carried out their diplomatic responsibilities with good intentions. It was not malevolent diplomacy.

Chapter One

THE ORIENTALISTS FADE AWAY

American diplomats of the interwar era, referred to here as Orientalists, were the staff of the former Bureau of Near East Affairs (NEA). The hallmark of the group was that they possessed some kind of so-called area experience. Most often this meant they had lived in the region and knew some Arabic. The only Americans with such experience were usually the children of missionaries or oil company employees.

The Orientalists held deep convictions about American policy, its relationship to the people of the Arab world and, as British and French colonialism faded, the region's potential as an American partner. The Orientalists worked to retain good relations between the Arab world and the United States and took a vocal, high-profile role in advocating their foreign policy views. Their claims to expertise were often based on having lived or worked in the Middle East and their personal contacts with the political elite. Most Orientalists began their work during World War I and then rose to prominence in the interwar period. A few were drafted into the State Department late in life to serve as area experts during World War II.

Evan Wilson joined the NEA as the Orientalist era ended and recalled it was still "a sine qua non that its personnel should have experience in the area." This began in 1909, and Wilson recalled that "it was made a departmental requirement that the division be staffed by officers who had served in the Near East. This policy was still being generally followed when I joined the division in 1943."[1] The requirement was not academic study, but personal life experience.

In the interwar era there were no courses on modern Middle East politics and very few books on contemporary social issues or history. The study of the Near East was solely undertaken by the realm of anthropologists who often approached the region from an archeological perspective.

There were no schools in which to learn modern Arabic in the United States during the interwar period. The first professional organization for area experts, the Middle East Institute, was established in 1947, and the first organization for academic specialists, the Middle East Studies Association, was founded nearly two decades later in 1966. University-level courses in Modern Standard Arabic (MSA), rather than ancient forms of the language, only emerged in the United States after the instructors of the Foreign Service Institute (FSI) moved into academia. FSI's Dr. Charles Ferguson brought MSA to Harvard in 1955 and then to Stanford University in 1966. The first MSA textbook, written by two FSI instructors, was released in 1968.[2]

When Orientalists raised their voices to protest America's approach to dealing with British Mandate Palestine, they were drawn into a bureaucratic battle with President

Truman. They tried to maintain support for a United Nations plan to resolve the conflict and opposed Truman's decision to recognize the new state of Israel. Even as they presented their arguments, their diplomatic replacements were being trained by the US FSI.

Truman forced the Orientalists out, and, like General MacArthur, most faded away before Truman left office in 1953. Of the very few who held on, most were transferred out of the NEA. The consequences of opposing Truman's policy and the ousting of the Orientalists, as well as Senator McCarthy's harsh attacks on the State Department's other controversial area experts, the China Hands, were vivid examples of the fate diplomats faced in Washington's treacherous political currents. Those who succeeded them learned from their experience.

What made Near East Orientalists different from others in the State Department? Evan Wilson joined the State Department in 1937 and was told that the NEA dealt with "questions that often have little or no resemblance to the problems of Western nations." Wilson felt this left them open to criticism: "It gave rise to accusations that the officers dealing with the Palestine problem tended to side with the Arabs against the Jews [...] and allegations that some of the officers in question were anti-Semitic."[3] The NEA was a small, inbred world, populated exclusively by men who felt that they possessed a special understanding of the Arab world and wanted to retain good US ties to it. Moreover, the area experience requirement almost guaranteed that they brought along some political or religious baggage. And, since the staff was so small, it was easy to become a big fish in that small pond.

In 1937 *Harper's Magazine* examined the various State Department area desks and concluded the Near East Division "is not often marked with excitement [...] our relations with these people are not important."[4] Wilson referred to another comment made with "an attitude of condescension"; after he was posted to Cairo in 1938, a friend said: "The Near East! Nothing ever happens there."[5]

In the 1930s, American oil exploration and investment increasingly focused on the region. Historian John DeNovo observed that Americans firms began to challenge the British throughout the Gulf: "By 1939 increasing numbers of Americans were coming to work in the oil regions and the companies were making huge capital outlays." By 1940 America had dispatched its first minister to Saudi Arabia and an ambassador in 1946.[6] By 1944 the argument over Palestine in Congress had begun in earnest, and the Near East staff joined in the highly charged debate. Wilson found himself at the center of a maelstrom.

The typical desk officer at the NEA was much older and more seasoned than Wilson. Most had been born in the nineteenth century and had worked for the State Department since the Wilson administration. They saw the United States as different from the colonial powers in the region, as a disinterested arbiter with no colonial ambitions. That philosophy fit perfectly with the obligation of public service inherent in the missionary community and their sense of noblesse oblige.

Historian Philip Baram examined the 1919–45 NEA staff and found it was dominated by people he termed "middle managers," who inculcated their policy viewpoint in their subordinates. Baram concluded this was a male world of officers who were "insulated and inbred, elitist" and who hired like-minded associates and then apprenticed them to the system. Baram found most were "white Protestant males [who] shared a remarkable homogeneity and common mindset [...] most had a private school background, and many were from the south." Between 1919 and 1945 Orientalists stamped their policy views on their juniors, as Baram found that there was power in that core group and "the same very small group of middle managers held sway."[7] Why? Many missionary families had literally invested their lives in the Arab world, and their sons joined the State Department to protect the links forged by their ancestors. They knew of the area's commercial potential and the value of its oil reserves. Moreover, Orientalists wanted the United States to tap the reservoir of goodwill established earlier by generations of American missionaries.

The first generation had been Christian proselytizers who concentrated on religious conversion, but their successors focused on educational endeavors in the hope of establishing pro-American capitalistic and democratic values. They built universities to inculcate the Wilsonian values that they held dear and to establish a pro-American sympathy among the new Arab elite. These efforts led to the founding of US-sponsored institutions like the American University of Beirut, the American University of Cairo and other higher education institutions in the Middle East. Many graduates went on to study in America and returned to the region as the first generation of Western-educated professionals in medicine, the sciences and technology.

Since few Americans knew anything about the Middle East, those who knew the languages and had lived in the area derived a certain power from their knowledge. Edward Said, in his landmark book *Orientalism*, argued that Orientalists in the European foreign ministries built up an entrenched power that "translated" the Arabs and the mysterious "Orient" to their governments. The term "Orientalism" refers to the set of beliefs and the attitude toward the region that adopted them. In essence Orientalists, whether European or American, saw themselves as the only persons who could translate the remote and mysterious region.

Furthermore, Said criticized the power imbalance inherent when Orientalists traveled abroad and used their knowledge of Arabic and the region to rise to power in Britain's Foreign Office. British Orientalists were part of the institutionalized powers-that-be, or rather powers-that-were. People like T. E. Lawrence and Gertrude Bell dominated the British government's Arab Bureau. Bell's dramatic career, related in Janet Wallach's biography *Desert Queen*, describes how she literally drew the borders of Iraq and Kuwait and had the power of the British Empire to establish and maintain them.[8] Often these Orientalists lived as expatriates and wrote memoirs vividly relating their adventures in asserting colonial control over the region's peoples and assets.

When Britain did begin to professionalize its Orientalists, it was too late to rescue their waning power in the British Mandate or the larger region. The British Empire was shrinking after World War II, British Mandate Palestine was in crisis and London's confidence was shaken. A modern Arabist training school was established in the region in 1944, the Middle East Centre for Arab Studies (MECAS) at Shemlan, Lebanon, in an old missionary outpost. In a history of British Arabists, historian Leslie McLoughlin observed that the training school began with "the deterioration of Britain's position in the Arab world" and that the new rivals were the Soviets and the Americans. He noted, "For the British there began a period of adjusting to the vastly enhanced power of the United States to intervene in Arab-world affairs." Furthermore, MECAS became known as "the school for spies" among Arabs. The first director of the school appointed Aubrey Eban, a brilliant student of Hebrew and Arabic, as chief instructor in 1944. He later took the name Abba Eban and became the first foreign minister of the new state of Israel. The school remained in the hills above Beirut until it closed in 1978.[9]

In the United States a lack of knowledge, not just among diplomats but throughout the larger society, affected policy. In 1979 John King Fairbank, dean of America's China Hands and a renowned linguist and historian, argued that Americans had little or no understanding of some geographical regions and this complicated the process of making foreign policy. Fairbank complained that since America did not have "England experts," therefore "[i]t is rather primitive to have a China expert [...] the so-called experts are merely people who have spent some time specializing, and they can begin to give approximate answers. But that mere fact indicates how ignorant everybody else is, which is a serious problem."[10] Thus, for Fairbank, it was ignorance of these areas among the general populace that led to complications.

Fairbank's comments illustrate the key problem that faced State Department area experts, whether Orientalists or Middle East hands. While they worked to understand the region, they had to explain it to politicians and policy makers who knew nothing of the historical, political or religious forces at work in the region. American Orientalists were neither well known nor given the kind of authority that was inherent in the British imperial system. Instead American ignorance of the Middle East was used to great advantage by those who opposed State Department initiatives. Opponents could translate events to create a conventional wisdom that area experts found difficult to oppose.

Perhaps the most effective lobbyist for Israel as the British mandate collapsed was President Truman's former haberdashery partner, Eddie Jacobson, who convinced Truman to meet with Dr. Chaim Weizmann. Truman resented the arguments made by the State Department and called the Near East staff "striped pants conspirators." He told his sister in March 1948: "Someday I hope I'll get a chance to clean them out."[11] He did. Before he left office Truman had removed or forced most of the Orientalists to leave.

Who were these Orientalists, and how much did they resemble Britain's? The most famous, William Eddy, was a dramatic figure. Born the son and grandson of missionaries in Lebanon in 1896, he became a hero during World War I and served in American intelligence during World War II. Eddy was fluent enough in Arabic to serve as Franklin Roosevelt's translator with the Saudis and was later made America's first minister to Saudi Arabia. Eddy's career began early. He first learned Arabic as a child in Lebanon, then went to Princeton University until World War I interrupted his studies. He joined the Marine Corps, fought at Belleau Woods (where he was gassed by the Germans) and returned as a decorated war hero. He completed his doctorate at Princeton in 1922 and, still barely in his twenties, became head of the English department at the American University of Cairo; he then left for a series of college presidencies in America.

In 1941, already 45 years old, he again volunteered for the Marine Corps and served as chief of the Office of Strategic Services (OSS) in North Africa (1942–43), where he plotted an uprising of North African Arabs and Berbers. Eddy only reluctantly gave up the plan after the Joint Chiefs of Staff opposed it. He won the Navy Cross, Distinguished Service Cross, two Silver Stars, two Purple Hearts and the Legion of Merit. His heroic role and his fluency in Arabic were recognized by Roosevelt, who made him his personal adviser and interpreter for negotiations with King Abdul Aziz Ibn Saud in 1944. Baram observed that Eddy was "probably the nearest thing the United States had to a Lawrence of Arabia." One MECAS veteran wrote, "His practically native Arabic was invaluable in his work with OSS [...] it made him a very rare bird indeed, able to press his case directly with officials who knew not a word of English." After Roosevelt met with Ibn Saud, the British Arabist Mr. Grafftey-Smith arrived to speak with him and found Ibn Saud's speech "was not easy for me to understand, being a mixture of the classical [...] and the beduin locutions."[12]

Eddy built his career at a time when very few Americans had ever visited the region, and even fewer had ever lived there. He acknowledged the sacrifices made by generations of his own family, which bound him to the region. "Our parents and our grandparents are buried there [Lebanon]; many uncles and aunts gave their lives in missionary educational work." In a 1950 speech, he pointed to the work of missionary families building goodwill for America in Lebanon and concluded: "I'm proud of that kind of American effort."[13]

Eddy, then a consultant on TAPline (trans-Arabian pipeline project), which built oil pipelines across the region, praised "American commercial companies" and the State Department who together "labored unstintingly and unselfishly to promote mutual interest and goodwill in the Near East." He viewed these three spheres as linked: the missionary community, American commercial interests and the State Department. Eddy highlighted the difference between the Europeans and the Americans. Americans came not as colonialists, but for "the mutual benefit and development of the resources in a partnership."[14]

In contrast, British Arabists of this era were employed by a government that was busy administering an empire in the Middle East, including British Mandate Palestine and substantial responsibilities in Egypt and the Gulf region. According to McLoughlin, London's Foreign Office began a training program in 1943 that supported the British military and imperial responsibilities. The demands of the empire shaped how Britain trained their Arabists and how they viewed the Americans. Diplomats like William Eddy were on the other side of what McLoughlin termed "a bitter struggle for influence in the region within Saudi Arabia between Britain and the United States," and "Britain's diplomatic Arabists [were] locked in mortal (but invariably polite) combat with their American colleagues, and increasingly against American Arabists."[15]

The uniquely American approach of Christian endeavor, capitalistic economic development, as well as American democratic and capitalistic values promised development and modernization for the Arab world. This idealistic approach promised to benefit the Americans as partners in the region's development and prosperity, as well as promising more direct access to the region's vast resources and its commercial markets. America would replace the discredited colonial dominance of Britain and France.[16]

But his idealistic plan went awry, and William Eddy witnessed its unraveling. It all went wrong when Roosevelt met with Ibn Saud in 1945. This was a meeting of giants on neutral territory, aboard a navy ship in the Great Bitter Lake, perhaps an apt analogy for US–Arab relations over the next decades. Eddy coped with the collision of cultures as Ibn Saud's retinue decamped to the ship's fantail for fresh roast lamb and diplomacy. The meeting was to deal with the issue of Palestine and to outmaneuver the British. Roosevelt arranged the meeting with little advance notice to London. When Churchill learned of Roosevelt's plans to meet with Ibn Saud, King Farouk of Egypt and Haile Selassie of Ethiopia, he demanded similar meetings. Eddy recalled, "Nothing Churchill could say to Farouk would remove his hate for the British." Afterward Ibn Saud quietly informed Eddy of his disappointment with his meeting with the British, beginning with the food, which "was tasteless," and "there were no demonstrations of armament, no tent was pitched on the deck; the crew did not fraternize with his Arabs; and altogether he preferred the smaller but more friendly US destroyer."[17] In cultural matters the American approach was working quite well, but this was more than a friendly visit. A key objective was Roosevelt's need to find a refuge for hundreds of thousands of Jews scarred by the genocide of nearly seven million in the Holocaust.

Eddy worked hard to bridge the gulf. Roosevelt tried to pressure Ibn Saud into an agreement regarding the immigration of at least one hundred thousand Jewish refugees to Palestine. This was stalemated by Ibn Saud's insistence that Arab tradition would have the loser in battle (the Germans) repatriate them. Eddy described the king's response as "prompt and laconic: 'Give them and their descendants the choicest lands and homes of the Germans who had oppressed them.'" In response to repeated requests by Roosevelt, finally Ibn Saud stated firmly: "Make the enemy and the oppressor pay; that is how we Arabs wage war [...] What injury have Arabs done to the Jews of Europe? It is the 'Christian' Germans who stole their homes and lives. Let the Germans pay."[18]

In the end Roosevelt pledged to take no action regarding Palestine without first consulting with the Arabs. After Roosevelt's death, as minister to Saudi Arabia, Eddy made a determined effort to convince Truman to stem what he called "the deterioration of American political interests in the Near East." In desperation he organized a dramatic proposal to have all the US ambassadors to the region meet with Truman as a group. They arrived for an October 10, 1945, meeting only to find themselves, as Eddy recalled, "kept idle in Washington for four weeks" by Truman.[19] When they finally reached the Oval Office, ambassador to Lebanon and Syria George Wadsworth informed Truman that "the whole Arab world is in ferment" over the issue of Jewish immigration but that Arabs needed US treaties of friendship and technical advice for economic development. The group observed the implications of alienating the Arabs, advising Truman: "If the US fails them, they will turn to Russia and will be lost to our civilization." They also warned Truman that the region could become a US–Soviet trouble spot: "There need be no conflict between us and Russia in that area." Truman cryptically responded that he "would like these countries to turn toward both Russia and the United States." As to Palestine, Truman responded that he "simply couldn't answer at the present time" and would discuss the matter with the British. Truman reiterated that both he and Roosevelt "had given assurances that the Palestine problem would not be disposed of without full prior consultation." According to the meeting transcript Truman concluded: "Palestine would probably be an issue during the election campaigns of 1946 and 1948 and in future campaigns." According to Eddy, Truman closed by connecting his decision to political considerations: "I'm sorry, gentlemen, but I have to answer to hundreds of thousands who are anxious for the success of Zionism; I do not have hundreds of thousands of Arabs among my constituents."[20]

Eddy was deeply angered by Truman's position and resigned a year later. He returned to work for the Arab–American Oil Company (ARAMCO) and later its pipeline subsidiary, TAPline. Historian Hugh Wilford, in *America's Great Game*, observed that Eddy had connections to the CIA and later sent unsolicited letters on policy issues to Secretary of State John Foster Dulles warning of the decline of the US position.[21]

In May 1951 Eddy wrote George McGhee, arguing against a proposed $150 million aid package to Israel, which he hoped would be "a dead duck." McGhee, a former oilman, responded: "We appreciate your cogent views […] and are always glad to have your considered counsel."[22] But one wonders just how welcome his advice became over time.

Many of his generation perceived that their sacrifices to build a positive image for America in the Middle East were being squandered. Their missionary connection gave diplomats of Eddy's generation a unique view: they were intensely patriotic yet caught between two distant, often polarized, cultures. One ambassador who grew up as the son of missionaries observed: "Perhaps it's because when you're born abroad, and brought up largely with foreign children, you tend to become a super-patriot. You are convinced that your country has to be the best place there ever was […] there was also the ethical feeling that a missionary son has: It is not only a duty to serve others, but an honor."[23]

The Orientalists possessed a privileged knowledge of the Arab world, yet as Americans they strongly identified with the United States. They had literally invested their lives in linking America with the Arab world and viewed Truman's decisions as having destroyed their lifelong investment in the region. Orientalists had, literally and figuratively, translated the Arab world to a generation of policy makers, but the message did not get through. They hoped the area would emerge from colonialism, modernize and adopt American democratic (and capitalistic) principles and that its partnership with America would benefit Washington as well. In the post–World War II era, it was a vital region for American policy, as a source of oil for Europe and to replace American oil reserves.

Prominent among the oilmen who worked in the State Department was William Yale, who was one of the leading Orientalists of that era. Yale was born in 1887 to a wealthy and prominent family in Dobbs Ferry, New York. He graduated from Yale Scientific School and worked for oil and shipping companies in Cairo. He knew French and learned some Arabic on the job. His family connections won him a place as an adviser to President Wilson at the Versailles Conference. Yale joined the King–Crane Commission, an advisory panel that journeyed through the region to gather information and formulate proposals on the disposition of the collapsed Ottoman Empire. Yale's views differed from his companions, and he wrote his own minority report that was literally locked away. He had been unhappy with the majority position and wrote repeatedly to his father to express his concerns. Yale took the penname "Benjaminus" and sent letters to his family with the express purpose of having them reprinted in the New York newspapers as reports from the field, which he hoped would shape public opinion to reflect his own views.[24]

Yale felt the United States must oppose the British and the French mandate proposals that would institute colonial control over the area. His ambitious plan was to create an "American mandate," preferably in Armenia, to build a model pro-Western Christian state. He dreamed large and planned to divide the Muslim world by creating what he called "a strong independent (Christian) country [...] which will break up the unity of the Eastern world." He was determined "to see [the] solidarity of Islam interrupted by a strong Christian Power in the Near or Middle East." Yale's letters reveal an air of desperation, a feeling that he alone could properly reshape the region to America's advantage. He was also in secret contact with Wilson's opponent, Senator Henry Cabot Lodge. Yale informed his father in April 1919: "We are letting Senator Lodge know" of their plans, but he cautioned that the information was "being furnished him 'on the sly,' that is to say that neither he nor anybody is else is to know exactly the source from which it comes, but it emanates from us." His father was asked to find out the "reaction of the Senator" and to discern the Republican position.[25]

Yale's letters illustrate not only an independent approach but also a willingness to work behind the scenes to shape (or even subvert) presidential policy. Much like Eddy, Yale's effort was the work of a man on a mission in the style of Lawrence of Arabia. After leaving government service in 1919, he returned to work in Egypt and then taught at the University of New Hampshire. During World War II, he returned to State Department Policy Planning and became involved in the fight over the British mandate in Palestine.

Baram acknowledged Yale had "a strong emotional and intellectual interest in Jews" and held "strong sympathies" and many personal contacts in the community of non-Zionist Jews in America. Yale was, however, very hostile to Zionism and hoped to activate Jewish anti-Zionists in his efforts. In September 1942 Yale had suggested that the NEA contact prominent anti-Zionist Jews to generate a "popular front" against the Zionist Organization of America. The plan was never undertaken because the NEA decided such activity would reflect badly on the State Department.[26]

But earlier, as the British mandate over Palestine ended, Yale drafted policy papers, as he struggled to make the Solomonic split involving two peoples and one, much promised, land. Yale recalled the State Department's compromise plan in 1945 offered "a national communal Jewish government, a national communal Arab government, for continued Jewish immigration, and for large-scale economic development of the water, land, and mineral resources of Palestine." Yale favored a United Nations trusteeship that would divide the land and create an interim period of separation. Yale recalled the president "jettisoned" the plan by proposing 100,000 European Jews be allowed to enter Palestine. Twenty years later Yale bitterly recalled Truman's decision: "Perhaps in some dim future *shalom aleichem* and *aleikom salaam* may mean peace for both Arabs and Jews, but such is not likely to be the case as long as American politicians believe they can win votes by doing justice to one group at the expense of injustice to another."[27]

Older, tired and disillusioned after working on the peace settlements for two world wars, Yale resigned. Like Eddy, Yale later had a misty connection with the intelligence community, and some link to Allen Dulles's CIA, but his connections with the State Department were severed in 1957.[28] All of his passionate efforts to reshape the region failed not once, but twice: first in 1919, and again in 1948.

Another missionary son whose career is illustrative of the path many followed into interwar diplomacy was Edwin M. Wright. He was born in Tabriz, Iran, in 1897, the son of American missionaries and trained in divinity studies at Wooster College and McCormick Theological Seminary; he then earned a master's degree from Columbia University in ancient history and languages.

After a career as an educator in Iran he returned to the United States in 1938 to teach at Columbia. At the start of World War II, he joined the OSS and then organized Persian, Turkish and Arabic language broadcasts for the Voice of America. Like Eddy and Yale, he linked academia, intelligence work and diplomacy at the NEA. Wright recalled how few Americans there were with such expertise when he became a member of the Near East wartime staff: "The OSS put out a general request to find people who knew about the Middle East [...] there were only six people in America at that time (of American parentage), who could read or write Persian. I was one of them. Practically all of us got dragged into the government [...] a few from archaeology, a few missionaries' children, and a few from business."[29]

So, like Eddy and Yale, Wright was another Orientalist who answered the call. After settling at the Department of State's NEA desk, he became deeply involved in the debate over the UN partition plan for Palestine. As staff assistant to Loy Henderson, Wright ran afoul of American Zionists. Wright tried to ride out the furor, but two of Truman's advisors, David Niles and Clark Clifford, regarded him with suspicion. In November 1947 Niles returned a package that Wright had sent to President Truman, unopened, with the notation "President Truman already knows your views and doesn't need this" written on it.[30]

Wright was transferred out. After his exile from Policy Planning, it was rumored that Truman had personally singled out Edwin Wright for removal. Wright briefly became a visiting lecturer and leader of a two-month training seminar for the State Department, government and personnel of the armed forces from 1956–60. Wright's academic training was in ancient history and theological studies, but that approach led him headlong into a debate of biblical proportions. Wright organized the tour with a substantial portion spent in Israel, a quarter of the eight weeks. During this time he was accompanied by an Orthodox rabbi appointed by the government of Israel. Wright's penchant for making repeated references to historian Joseph Campbell's work on ancient prereligious myths caused tension. The rabbi argued with him, and eventually the group began to question the contending parties. Wright later retired to Ohio and died in the early 1980s.

These Orientalists shared certain elements in common: many were born in the missionary community or were connected with the oil industry. None of them had academic training in the modern political history of the region, and their policy positions often referenced their personal experience and investment in the region. They carried with them a deep emotional involvement in American foreign policy, which led them to great lengths to try, unsuccessfully, to personally shape it. While later generations of regional specialists had their careers invested in the region, for Orientalists, they had their lives invested in it. Their close personal connection to the Arab world led them to conclude that US policy, in particular support of Zionism, damaged US interests. They were willing to try almost anything to change it.

There is a very strong element of single-mindedness in their efforts and a common thread to their lives: they were convinced that America could reap great benefits in the Middle East but feared losing what gains had been made. The clashes with Truman in 1945–48 left the Orientalists profoundly frustrated.

Very few managed to remain in the NEA, and their usefulness was tarnished, not only in Washington but among the Arabs. In a meeting with King Faisal of Saudi Arabia in 1956, George Wadsworth, who had confronted Truman, alluded to their fate, telling Faisal that both he and Loy Henderson had been "promoted to be Ambassadors in order to get us as far away as possible from Palestine!" In a misstatement of historic proportions Wadsworth told Faisal, "We were old crusaders together in the battle for Palestine." The Arab king coolly responded: "Sometimes a crusade is not always successful."[31]

The Orientalists fought what they called "the battle of Palestine" with missionary zeal to secure influence in the area, Arab goodwill and to secure US access to Middle East oil. They envisioned Americans working with Arabs as partners, not as imperialists, to exploit the region's wealth. This, they hoped, would secure the long-term investment made by American missionaries and their families.

But Truman changed the division of the NEA forever. The missionary sons were ousted, and the continuity of the influence that Baram observed between 1919 and 1945 was shattered. No longer was there a group of long-term middle managers who apprenticed and inculcated junior staffers with their own values and agenda. Once the Orientalists were gone, there were no more missionary sons to take their place. Reforms in the hiring and promotion of State Department personnel transformed the staff of the NEA. In 1946 Congress passed the Foreign Service Reform Act to create a merit system for recruiting and promoting diplomats and to eliminate the old boys' network in the State Department. Diplomatic historian Robert Schulzinger has observed this "represented an attempt by professional diplomats to recapture the center stage in the making of foreign policy."[32]

The State Department sponsored an essay contest to spur fresh analysis and new ideas. Robert McClintock won with an essay on personnel policy that explained that "there is some dead wood, as in most human organizations, but in our better Foreign Service it should be chopped out before it floats to the top."[33] No one wanted the dead wood, those hired during the wartime manpower shortage, to rise to influential positions in the post–World War II era. The goal was a corps of new officers with specialized training in languages and economics whose skills would produce professional and objective political reporting. In the same era, with a wave of American investment in oil, the United States desperately needed more skilled officers at the mid-level and senior ambassadors to run the new embassies that would be established as British influence waned.

Who filled the gap during the transitional period? The State Department sent older, senior diplomats who were generalists as ambassadors to the Arab world. There were many senior officers who were skilled administrators and knew how to run an embassy and manage staff but had little area knowledge.

It did not take long to begin training junior diplomats, but it would take decades for them to reach the top. Even a decade after Truman cleaned out the NEA, there were few skilled senior officers remaining to serve. In 1958 a bestselling novel *The Ugly American* exposed the consequences of sending generalists, rather than area specialists, to Asia. William Lederer and E. Burdick called diplomats without language skills the State Department's "soundproofed" representatives. The book was, in the words of a *Washington Post* editorial, "a shot in the dark heard in every single American embassy around the world." The authors saw the Middle East as a particular weak spot in the Cold War: "In the whole of the Arabic [sic] world—nine nations —only two ambassadors have language qualifications."[34] Although the book was a novel, the statistic was factual.

Of all the US ambassadors in the Middle East only two were Arabists: Raymond Hare and Parker T. Hart. Both were careerists who had learned Arabic despite the difficulties and without a real training program. Their experience illustrates how difficult it was to become an area expert and also the perils of that position. Throughout their careers Hare and Hart were contrarians and held to the view that diplomats must constantly work at learning Arabic. In later decades, as the Middle East hands worked their way up the career ladder, they found both Hare and Hart to be mentors. William R. Crawford served in embassies under both officers and recalled that they were models who "served as an inspiration over thirty years to many of the rest of us who worked in the same area."[35]

Hare and Hart were the founding fathers of the modern Middle East hands. Parker Hart, slightly junior to Raymond Hare, worked with him in a series of posts, then succeeded him in a string of ambassadorships as both men rotated through nearly every embassy in the Middle East. Although both reached the top area post, assistant secretary of the NEA, they each held the post very briefly, neither longer than a few months, just before each retired. This is surprising since their accumulated area knowledge and language skill should have brought them to the top administrative post earlier in their careers and for longer tenures.

Both men viewed the missionary community as something apart from them. Parker Hart observed that missionaries who focused on education rather than proselytization were a valuable American resource. Hart noted "missionary educators" were "building schools, educating people and taking care of the sick. They were a resource that Ray Hare and I and others could draw upon with good results."[36] While the Orientalists who often came from missionary families identified closely with them, Hare and Hart saw themselves, and the NEA, as something separate.

They were also not of the social elite or the missionary community that had dominated the Foreign Service between the world wars. What was their background? Raymond Hare was born in West Virginia, the son of a fish hatchery supervisor, and grew up in Maine and later Iowa. He worked his way through Grinnell College by waiting on tables and was desperate for a job after graduation. Grinnell's dean suggested Hare take a teaching position at Robert College in Istanbul. Hare abandoned teaching for a position with the American Chamber of Commerce in Istanbul and then contacted the US consulate, took the Foreign Service exam and began his diplomatic career.

In the 1930s the State Department sent a few promising junior officers to learn Arabic in a three-year program at L'Ecole des Langues Orientales Vivantes in Paris. Washington hoped that the French might succeed in teaching Arabic to young US diplomats. Hare was totally exasperated with the slow approach taken by the French. His experience, as well as that of other American diplomats who attended the Paris school, embedded a negative attitude among senior State Department staff for decades. Hare quipped that the French approach was "more 'morte' than 'vivant,'" and the training in Arabic and Turkish "was more geared to learning *about* the languages than in their use." After spending three years at the expense of the State Department, Hare and fellow student James Moose confronted their professor, told him they still couldn't speak Arabic and challenged anyone in the class to read from an Arab newspaper. The professor responded with the verbal equivalent of a Gallic shrug: "You Americans are so practical!"[37]

After three years in Paris, Hare could not read or speak Arabic but found his French greatly improved. Once back at work, Hare studied with tutors at a variety of Middle East posts and eventually learned the language. Conversely Moose spent his career arguing against anyone else in the State Department attempting Arabic language training.

Parker Hart joined the State Department in 1938 and built his career on his talent for languages. Born in Massachusetts and educated at Dartmouth, he earned a master's degree at Harvard, then studied diplomacy at the Institute for International Studies in Geneva. Hart had an unusual talent for learning hard languages at a time when most American diplomats learned at most French. He developed skill in Arabic, French, German, Portuguese and Turkish.

Hart did not attempt the Paris program but instead swapped English lessons for Arabic with a Saudi and then attended the American University at Cairo. While working in Saudi Arabia, Hart became friends with Sulyman Olayan, later a multimillionaire contractor in the Saudi oil boom. Olayan taught Arabic to Hart for the modest fee of three riyals an hour. But after a lifetime of effort, Hart could still reflect upon "[m]y very weak Arabic."[38]

Only a very few American diplomats had the energy and determination to create and pursue their own private language program. Hare's perseverance and Hart's gift for languages made them exceptional. Their skill was a vital tool for modern diplomats, as Raymond Hare later observed, the object of language study was a means to understand the people and the region: "Language, even if your knowledge of it is only partial, is the most ready way into a culture."[39] As a senior officer Hart recognized that he needed to "jack up my Arabic"[40] before taking up a new post as President Kennedy's ambassador to Saudi Arabia. He received JFK's permission to spend three months in a special FSI program before leaving for Jidda. The State Department pressured him to drop the program and leave immediately for his new post. Hart finally forced his superiors to back down when he threatened to take the matter directly to President Kennedy. His persistence paid off.

Hart often used his knowledge of the language to monitor translations. During critical negotiations with the Saudi king over the Yemen civil war, an interpreter used the Arabic term "shart," which implied that JFK had set "conditions" the Saudis must meet. Hart understood the translator's choice of Arabic word and observed how it had "inflamed" the king. Hart intervened, telling Faisal in Arabic this was a "confusion over the meaning of words," and a different word was selected. Hart felt the word was "too legalistic, too sharp and jagged an edge for him [Faisal] to take [...]" His knowledge of Arabic had been critical as it "bridged over the crisis."[41]

Hare and Hart's approach to policy differed. Raymond Hare liked to call his approach quiet diplomacy, and the hallmark of his work was that it achieved results with little fanfare. In essence both were "organization men" of the 1950s and were content to labor within the system and conform to policy. Neither took a romantic view of the Arab world or had any personal connections to it. Moreover, both had lived and worked under conditions that gave real meaning to the term "hardship post." Hare found his post in Yemen during the 1940s as "unspeakably primeval," and Hart recalled when he and his wife arrived at their new home in Damascus that "we could hear the screams of people being tortured up the street."[42]

Hare grew increasingly concerned in the 1950s that American policy had become too closely identified with the British in the Middle East. Hare recalled that was the time when the United States was "forced to assume responsibilities which we had previously assiduously avoided." This led the United States to take on a new role "not out of desire to dominate, but primarily to maintain a Western position there."[43] Hare drafted the Tripartite Declaration, an early effort to reduce arms transfers into the Middle East, and for the remainder of his career, he worked to limit weapons proliferation and to promote what later became the "Food for Peace" program.

Abroad during much of the debate over Israel, Hare had not been deeply involved in the policy battle, but he happened to walk into the UN for a meeting in May 1948, unaware the United States had just recognized Israel. He was shocked, having thought Washington would support UN trusteeship, but Hare accepted the presidential policy and supported the American position.

When Secretary of State John Foster Dulles conducted a major shakeup of the State Department in 1956, *Time* magazine enthused about Hare as the new ambassador to Cairo: "He looks like Ronald Colman, has a profound knowledge of Arab society and economic life, but no previous ties with Nasser, hence symbolizes a fresh, new era of US-Egyptian policy."[44]

During the Cold War Hare feared that the United States increasingly assumed it had an unlimited ability to exert its will. He argued that America must realize that there should be limits on what the United States attempted to do in the Middle East. Regarding Communist subversion in the Cold War, Hare felt some of Truman's statements were "much stronger [...] than any policy that we have been able to engender."[45]

Both Hare and Hart were models for the Middle East hands and they stand apart, *sui generis*, from the previous generation of Orientalists. Their careers began as the Orientalists' era drew to a close. They embodied the ambitious careerist who labored to learn Arabic, served without complaint in hardship posts and war zones and carried out Washington's policy, whether they personally agreed with it or not. Their careers illuminate the inherent differences between the old network of Orientalists and the new generation of State Department professionals—the Middle East hands. Hare and Hart did not have a personal agenda and never tried to take control of policy. When the Middle

East hands saw problems developing, they worked to diffuse them. Most of all they saw themselves as part of the system and worked within the chain of command. They viewed their role as experts to be consulted, not individuals on a mission. Both survived by maintaining a low profile in a highly charged atmosphere, and Hare took pride in being called the quiet diplomat by the generation of diplomats who succeeded him.

Hare and Hart began their careers before the training program of the FSI was established. Thus they formed a bridge between two eras, and their mentoring of junior diplomats helped build a transition from Orientalism to professionalism.

Chapter Two

THE MIDDLE EAST HANDS EMERGE

The origins of the Arabic language training program of Foreign Service Institute (FSI) were in the wartime Army Specialized Training Program (ASTP), which was created in 1943 to provide a high-speed pipeline to get university-educated technical specialists into the American military. The ASTP trained young men in two dozen languages, including Arabic, and a variety of engineering and scientific fields.

In *Scholars in Foxholes: The Story of the Army Specialized Training Program in World War II*, historian Louis Keefer describes the testing and selection of the brightest candidates who might successfully withstand the pressure to complete 4 years of education in 18 months. From the outside the program appeared to be an easy way to avoid the fight, but Secretary of War Henry Stimson had established it to provide the expertise the army needed not only during the war but afterward in shaping the postwar world. Nevertheless the students marched to a series of humorous drill songs, including "Take down your service flag mother, Your son's in the ASTP, He'll never get hit by a bullet, While taking the square root of three." At its peak 200,000 soldier-students were in uniform, drilling and at their studies all day on 227 campuses. But the army repeatedly ordered the universities to release groups of ASTP students prior to graduation to meet their manpower needs.[1]

The ASTP became a laboratory for developing new methods of rapidly training Americans in the hard languages, especially in Arabic. When the ASTP was shuttered at the war's end, most of its Arabic staff were hired by the State Department to establish the new Middle East Area Program (MEAP). In addition, an estimated 80 percent of the ASTP students who survived the war used the GI Bill to return to universities. Both ASTP graduates and other veterans with language skills were targeted for recruitment into the State Department's MEAP.

The experience of one ASTP Arabic language student illustrates the challenges many of them faced and the impact of the military's manpower demands. Curtis Jones left Bowdoin College to volunteer to fight in World War II, and by early 1943 he was an army private enduring "the obstacle course, close-order drill, Neanderthal platoon sergeants, mind-deadening KP, and 5 a.m. sprints through the snows of Fort Devens." Jones heard that passing a series of exams and IQ tests might lead to a transfer into some new technical training program. He landed in the Moroccan Arabic program, although he recalled that "[f]ew of us knew that Arabic was a language, let alone that it had a Moroccan variant." The new program was directed by a new professor in linguistics, 25-year-old Dr. Charles Ferguson, who had just completed his master's thesis on the Moroccan Arabic verb and pioneered Arabic training in the US military. His methods reflected a bottom-up approach that began with learning the fundamental sound components of Arabic and put "special stress on mastering sounds unrecognizable to the untrained ear, sounds which are critical indices of meaning" in Arabic. Jones observed that "[s]ome Arabic-language aspirants never made the cut. But most made enough progress in the emission of genuinely Moroccan sounds in Arabic to prove wrong the language traditionalists" who were skeptical of the new methods. Curtis worked hard, but only the top four students were shipped off to a classified destination. Then they were shipped back to the university for no apparent reason. In October 1943 the entire ASTP Arabic class was shipped out, and the Arabic cohort found themselves in New Mexico awaiting "general duty in the Pacific Theater." Dr. Ferguson completed his doctorate in 1945 and later the same year was hired by the State Department.[2]

The ASTP may have been undercut by the army's desperate need for manpower to mount the invasion of Japan, but those who survived the ASTP and the war aimed for new careers.

After the war, Jones and his instructors moved to the US State Department to pursue peacetime careers in diplomacy. Many of the new Middle East hands who began their careers after World War II were veterans of the US military and the ASTP.

The first Middle East hands were different from the Orientalists in their social class and educational backgrounds, as well as in their path to a diplomatic career. Out of the more than one hundred and twenty US Foreign Service officers (FSOs) trained in Arabic by the State Department's FSI, not all subsequently chose to stay in the Middle East or qualified on the final proficiency exams. Out of this group I have identified 53 FSOs who completed the MEAP and subsequently formed the core of the State Department's division of Near East Affairs (see Appendix Brief Biographies).

The criteria for this study was that they must have completed the Middle East language-and-area training program between 1946 and 1975, and then held at least two posts within the region. The study omits those trained after the Beirut school closed in 1975, and any who did not complete their studies or soon left the bureau of Near East Affairs (NEA).

These were typically ambitious careerists, relatively junior FSOs and often veterans of the armed forces. They represented a broad swath of geographical, educational and class backgrounds. This runs counter to the typical NEA officer identified by Philip Baram in his study of the interwar State Department's Orientalists. It also runs counter to the stereotype put forward by Robert Kaplan who described modern Arabists a "courtly and WASP-ish elite," bound to the missionary philosophy and heritage of the British Arabists. Kaplan asserted American Arabists were imbued with a romantic fondness for Arabs and had a veiled agenda. He considered them "the most exotic and controversial vestige of the East Coast Establishment" who had joined the State Department to escape "the loss of quaint privilege, which accompanied the growth of the middle class and the suburbs after World War II."[3]

Rather than upper-class refugees, the post–World War II Middle East hands were from the rising middle class. They were often political science types, academically oriented and who often held advanced degrees in foreign affairs, languages or history and were ambitious careerists. They were drawn from diverse geographical and social backgrounds, but were predominantly persons with a strong interest in foreign affairs who also possessed significant language skills. They rarely brought Ivy League credentials and more often completed their educations after military service on the GI Bill. They did not necessarily have a background in Middle East affairs when they joined the State Department, but were attracted by the potential for advancement that the challenge of Arabic language-and-area studies promised. Others entered the program after the State Department began an internal recruitment program.

Why choose Arabic and Middle East training? In the highly competitive atmosphere of the postwar State Department, there was one region where the number of embassies, and therefore a greater number of job opportunities for the career-minded, virtually guaranteed rapid promotion: the Middle East. The Orientalists had been removed by Truman just as the Arabic program was established, and there was a vacuum waiting to be filled by those who could earn the language credentials. In addition, the State Department advertised these opportunities in its magazine, *American Foreign Service Journal*. The opportunities for skilled linguists were very evident.

The State Department desperately needed skilled Arabists and they made the career opportunities crystal clear to junior officers through a crash recruitment program. Anyone who had the talent and determination to complete the program was on the career fast track. Another factor was that political appointees, rather than career FSOs, were being assigned the coveted European posts. While the ultimate goal for any State Department careerist was an ambassadorship, an FSO might spend an entire career in European Affairs and never approach the rank of ambassador. Yet the opportunities for an Arabist were expanding, and were much better than in any other regional bureau. But the Middle East was a region filled with what the State Department defined as hardship posts because of their remoteness, harsh climate and challenging conditions, which affected not only the FSOs but also their families.

Many factors broke the continuity between the pre- and post-1946 staff at NEA, but most of all the training and promotion of area specialists destroyed the Ivy League old boys' network that had once filled the NEA with the well-connected East Coast elite. The new system required candidates to pass a battery of exams, and then meet tough language proficiency standards that had not existed before. This created an intellectual elite who could speak one of the world's most difficult languages and understand its most obscure region. After 1946 the State Department generalist, with no area training and often no language other than French, was passé.

The new MEAP had no antecedents in the State Department. While the State Department had developed Chinese, Japanese and Russian training programs in the interwar era, Arabic was so difficult to learn that the State Department sent its aspiring Arabists to a program in Paris (as discussed in chapter one). Few succeeded in learning any usable Arabic and that strategy was abandoned by Washington.

The development of the MEAP revolutionized the staff at the NEA because it the program differed from how the Russian studies and other programs were designed and managed internally. From the start the Arabic language program was run by an emerging group of scholars called scientific linguists and its area studies component was taught, for the most part, by academics from outside the State Department. No longer were amateur

Orientalists chosen from a small elite of expatriate Americans and then apprenticed to senior officers or "middle managers" inside the NEA.

The wholesale ousting of the Orientalists by President Truman removed both staff and management, and this was analogous to a university removing an aging department of undertrained scholars and replacing them with a group of young PhDs. The new Middle East hands had a more professional approach and lacked the ingrained missionary perspective of the Orientalists.

Since many were veterans of the armed services, rather than drawn from the world of missionary families, they were imbued with a different approach. As veterans they were disciplined to obey the chain of command and institutional loyalty and were more inclined to accept their orders and Washington's policy directives. Their sense of duty was not missionary's zeal but rather characterized by loyalty to the government and State Department. But, above all, they were committed to their careers.

The armed services connection was particularly strong not only because the State Department had taken over the Army's wartime language training program but also because so many young men in the late 1940s and 1950s had served in the military. When the ASTP was dissolved its director and many instructors became the directors of the FSI's MEAP just as the State Department was looking to hire veterans and skilled linguists. Many found their veteran status and wartime language training was the ticket to advancement in the peacetime State Department.

After completing the training program a graduate became the ideal candidate for promotion in the postwar State Department: an area specialist who held the new credential completion of the MEAP. The program was designed to blend training in Arabic with area studies and political reporting skills. Many who succeeded proved early in their careers that they were skilled political reporting officers and made themselves into the model area specialist who the State Department wanted to promote. The most important task for the Cold War–era State Department was to develop accurate information on the Third World, a critical area that few policymakers or politicians understood.

The program attracted a number of personalities, but not the dilettantes or "missionary, bird-watcher and Loy Henderson types" described in Robert Kaplan's *The Arabists: The Romance of an American Elite*.[4] Instead, the Middle East hands were serious, ambitious careerists who had earned credentials and many were the unusual person who could learn a hard language quickly. Almost the entire group held undergraduate degrees in fields relevant to foreign policy like political science, history or languages.

The Middle East hands generally fall into three personality types: political science types, linguists and technical types. Many FSOs, indeed the most successful, combine elements of more than one category.

The predominant group had training in international relations and might be described as political science types: Hermann Eilts, Donald Bergus, Earl Russell, Cleo Noel, Francoise Dickman and Richard Murphy. All had majored in political science, history or diplomatic studies in college, and most held advanced degrees from the new academic programs specializing in foreign relations like the School for Advanced International Studies or Tufts University's Fletcher School of Law and Diplomacy.

The career path of Cleo Noel is typical of this kind of diplomat. He was born the son of a shopkeeper in Oklahoma, worked his way through junior college and the University of Missouri studying botany, then history. He volunteered for the Navy in June 1941, and after the war used the GI Bill to pay for graduate school. While working on his doctorate at Harvard he took the Foreign Service exam on a whim and found himself channeled into the MEAP.

Most were attracted to a career in the diplomacy and international affairs, but not specifically to the Middle East. Francoise Dickman graduated from the University of Wyoming, received a master's from the Fletcher School, and went to work as a researcher for the Brookings Institution. He joined the State Department working in Latin American Affairs but switched to Arabic when he realized he could move up the career ladder faster in the NEA.

Some Arabists began their careers in other regions, for example, Hermann Eilts and George Lane both abandoned European Affairs. Earle Russell and Richard Murphy both left African Affairs for the NEA.

A second type was skilled linguists. While almost all in the study group possessed significant language-learning ability, some had already majored in language studies before joining the State Department. They saw the advantages to a career where their natural skills were the ticket to promotion, and advanced language training could be completed at government expense. Hume Horan, one of the top Arabic linguists, had advanced proficiency in four languages. He recalled the advantages of a State Department career over one in academia: "After graduate school, after all the grubbing for fellowships, assistantships, and grants, to be in Beirut, on a salary, plus living quarters allowance and diplomatic privileges, was to be in a sort of language student's Elysium."[5]

Others, like William Crawford and Rodger Davies, had foreign language degrees and fluency in multiple languages. Davies held an advanced degree in Hispanic languages and had been assigned by the Army to the ASTP Arabic program in the hopes that a skilled linguist could succeed where others failed. Later, as a junior State Department officer, he completed training in Arabic and Greek. Perhaps the brightest star was Norman Anderson, who earned high ratings in six languages, including Arabic and Russian, and by the end of his career became director of the language school and managed the MEAP.

Some of these language overachievers had training in both foreign affairs and languages. Their focus on graduate school reflects the developing field of international relations: Harvard graduated five of these FSOs, and the rest came from the School for Advanced International Studies, George Washington University, Columbia and the Fletcher School of Law and Diplomacy as well as some state universities. Very few had studied abroad, not only due to the disruptions of war but also because most were not independently wealthy or even upper class.

Others were focused on technical or scientific fields: Andrew Killgore and Robert Pelletreau each completed law school and were State Department lawyers when they recognized the opportunities for advancement in Middle East area specialization. Marshall Wiley held an MBA and a JD before joining the State Department and had worked as an economics officer. Heywood Stackhouse held an MBA and had worked on economic issues in Latin American before studying Arabic. Stackhouse mastered Hebrew, French and Spanish and spent his career in the Middle East, including a post in Tel Aviv and was later director of the Office of Israel and Arab–Israeli Affairs.[6]

Technical types often applied their blend of skills to diplomacy: James Akins was trained in economics and had been a science teacher before he joined the State Department. He mastered three languages, including Arabic, but he drew upon his technical background when he was put in charge of the White House Office of Energy Planning. Richard Parker's degree in agriculture and mechanics from Kansas State was very useful when the State Department assigned him to oversee plans for the East Ghor canal project to irrigate the Jordan River valley.

George Curtis Moore possessed a remarkable blend of almost all of these types. In high school Moore excelled in both the sciences and language and began premed at USC, but his career was interrupted by wartime service as a Navy medic. He then earned a master's degree from USC's School of International Relations and joined the State Department where his language skills made him a prime candidate for the Kreis Resident Officer program. This program channeled junior officers through an intensive course in German and assigned them at the county, or "kreis," level in Germany. The objective was to effectively monitor German politics during the postwar era to prevent a resurgence of Nazism, as well as to encourage the development of democracy. Noel and other State Department linguists served under the US High Commissioner's office, monitored West Germany elections and tried to ensure that neither Nazis or Communists dominated German politics.

Journalist Robert Kaplan has implied there was an agenda among those Middle East hands whose careers began in Germany: "It is noteworthy that [Talcott] Seelye and his colleagues, after a living experience in post-Hitler Germany when the ashes of the Holocaust were still warm, requested postings in the Arab world [...] It is impossible to know their inner motivations."[7]

In fact, their motivation was career advancement. The State Department's Kreis program offered two exceptional career advantages: at the time, the late 1940s, it was the only fully funded bureau of the State Department due to Washington's Cold War focus on West Germany. The crash program had the ability to promote and assign diplomats into the field in a matter of weeks, and it paid much higher than normal salaries. FSOs from every region would be interested in those opportunities, but they had to have the ability to tackle a new language and learn it quickly.

Talcott Seelye recalled the financial and career advantages: "The salary was about 40% more than we would have gotten starting out as FSO-6's [entry-level positions]" and "in those days you sometimes waited two and three years between the time you passed your written exam and got your appointment." Ambitious careerists vied to get into the Kreis program and then switched to Arabic training when the German assignments ebbed and Arabic emerged as the fast track.[8]

As was stated earlier, the typical Middle East hand was an aggressive careerist, did not come from the East Coast elite and most often possessed a proven ability to learn foreign languages. Their profile was more academic and far less aristocratic than their predecessors at the NEA. Their collective profile also runs counter to what Phillip Baram found among the 1919–45 era Orientalists: before World War II the NEA staff were mainly drawn from private schools and Ivy League colleges and they were often from the East Coast elite or from Southern origins.

Instead the Middle East hands were military veterans from middle class origins, with proven language skills and academic training in politics, history, law or economics, most often at public colleges and American universities. Hard language training requires a person with a sense of adventure, a determination to overcome challenges, as well as the skill and self-confidence to rapidly master a difficult challenge.

Military service also shaped them: first their reliance on the GI Bill was a means for many who might never have afforded university training to enter the middle class and made them a better fit for the command structure of the State Department. Military service also prepared them for coping with the hardships and difficult conditions stationed in diplomatic hardship posts overseas. Many ASTP veterans were viewed as prime candidates for recruitment into the MEAP.

The personality type of a typical Middle East hand also reflects their military experience: 28 of the 53 identified in this study had served in the Army, 10 in the Navy and 4 in the Air Force. It is interesting that not one person in the study group was a Marine Corps veteran. The archetype of the Orientalist had been Marine Major William Eddy, the hero of two wars. Perhaps this reflects the different values and temperament of the post-1946 group: no longer was the ideal a "gung ho" Marine, prepared to rush headlong into a dangerous situation or act alone.

Two transitional FSOs working in the Middle East, Raymond Hare and Parker Hart, had been in the State Department when the war began, and thus neither served in the military per se, although Hare spent much of the war in Cairo as British and American forces struggled to stop the Nazis. Parker Hart spent 1944–45 working to secure a US air base at Dhahran in Saudi Arabia.

Veterans of the Vietnam War are underrepresented in the group. In the late 1960s the severe shortage of specialists in Asian languages, especially Southeast Asian languages, forced the State Department to alter its recruiting priorities. Promising linguists were recruited for a crash program in Vietnamese.

Raymond Hare, one of the two most senior Middle East hands, might have had his own son become a fellow Arabist, but Paul J. Hare's career was rerouted in 1964. While still a junior consular officer in Tunis, he received what he described as "a sudden dispatch" transferring him into Vietnamese language training. When asked if he had any choice, he responded: "No option [...] it sounded like it came from [President] Johnson himself."[9] Paul Hare did not get another Middle East post until 1981, as political affairs counselor in Tel Aviv.

Thus, the ASTP and the GI Bill created opportunities for veterans seeking upward mobility. These factors combined to create a more mature and educated pool of potential diplomats after 1946. Since the Middle East program had large numbers of positions to fill, these efforts to professionalize diplomacy had the most profound effect on the NEA.

The origins of the Middle East hands were not from the old East Coast elite, but were quite diverse. The largest number from a single state were from New York (six), Massachusetts (five), followed by California (four) and the District of Columbia, Iowa and Ohio with three each. But, if the population density of the top-ranked states is taken into account, there is no truly dominant state. But, if analyzed on a regional basis, a pattern does appear: many were drawn from a swath of mid-Atlantic states, with heavy representation from the West Coast and Midwest.

The one underrepresented region was the South. Only two Middle East hands came from there, which is particularly curious since Philip Baram's study found that the Orientalists were predominantly Southern. When I asked Alabaman Andrew Killgore about this, he responded that few Southerners in the 1940s were aware of the Foreign Service as a career. In addition, a study of the origins of Russian language specialists noted that many interwar Southern universities and high schools lacked programs in Russian, and the origins of 1950s Soviet specialists "has been western public schools and eastern private schools." While schools were slow to develop Russian studies, they were even more reticent to invest in Arabic in the interwar era. China hands had been largely drawn from the missionary community. In more general terms, of the 58 State Department personnel identified as "notable ambassadors" only 3 in the postwar era were from the South.[10]

Once more, by geographic origin, the Middle East hands were at odds with the traditional stereotype of the Ivy League, East Coast elite diplomat. As we have seen, changes in State Department hiring and recruitment show that after 1946 Middle East hands were trained, not born. Rather than hiring Arabic-speaking American expatriates and making them into diplomats, the Foreign Service recruited a more representative group and selected the most promising linguists from a pool of skilled candidates, many of whom were veterans.

In terms of racial and gender diversity, the group was almost entirely white and male. This reflects the hiring practices of the State Department. Moreover, even after a small number of African American men built successful State Department careers, there was an ingrained reluctance to hire, retain or promote women. In addition, the State Department fought a series of class actions lawsuits, the Palmer cases, well into the 1970s.

In 1960, a time when African Americans found advancement in the State Department very difficult, Terrance Todman began his career as the first black Middle East hand. Todman was a talented linguist in Arabic, French and Spanish. Many African Americans resented the State Department's determination to channel them into assignments in Africa. Todman spent his first tours in Tunis and Lome, then to ambassadorships to Chad, Guinea and Costa Rica. Todman's rising star led him to move beyond the NEA and into a string of increasingly important posts: assistant secretary of state for Inter-American Affairs, ambassador to Spain, Denmark, Argentina and finally to the highest rank, career ambassador. Todman, like many who studied Arabic, found it the key to advancement, but, as a model for diversity, Todman's career accelerated when the State Department finally moved to diversify. Todman chronicled his struggles in an interview titled "Being Black in a 'Lily White' State Department."[11]

For the few women in the Foreign Service the battle was to stay in. Male FSOs were allowed to marry, even if they chose to marry a foreign national, with only minor restrictions. If a woman FSO married, however, she was told to resign from the Foreign Service, a policy that forced women either to sacrifice marriage for career or career for marriage. This policy remained in effect until it was overturned by a class action lawsuit in 1971. Since it remained a personnel policy for so long, it skewed the gender composition of the State Department and the NEA staff well into the 1980s.[12]

The effect of this policy is evident in the average length of a female diplomat's career: in 1922 the average was 3.5 years. By 1931 not one woman remained in either the Foreign or Consular Service. In 1934 a decade after the first woman entered, one official commented, "It is the opinion in the Department that the Foreign Service is not a suitable place for women. No one says this publicly, but it is a fact." That misogynist attitude prevailed for decades and seriously damaged many careers. Change came only after a series of class action lawsuits begun by Alison Palmer and the Women's Action Organization in the State Department forced the promotion of women in the 1970s and 1980s.[13] Ironically, when Washington was forced by a court decision to recruit women area specialists, they resorted to reappointing former careerists who had been forced into retirement decades earlier. Many who had been forced out were invited back since their language skills and area experience remained highly valued. The State Department needed women who could be rapidly appointed to high visibility positions in order to prove that the old policies had been discarded. But language skills could not be quickly replicated, hence the strategy of bringing women out of retirement made more sense than training new ones in a drive to demonstrate change.

This does not mean that the State Department's senior officers wanted more than a few highly visible women to be groomed for ambassadorships. In 1961 less than 10 percent of the State Department's diplomats were women (300 out of a total of 3,700), and, even after efforts to promote them, as late as 1990, they only represented 24 percent.[14]

Facing the 1964 election, President Lyndon Johnson was looking for a woman to appoint to an ambassadorship and asked Secretary of State Rusk to nominate one. The transcript of a phone conservation on January 20, 1964, reveals President Johnson demanding Rusk immediately give him the name of a woman he could appoint: "I want to get some real women ambassadors [...] 'cause these women will run me out." Rusk tentatively responded, "We've got an FSO." When LBJ asked who she was, Rusk responded, "Gee, I don't know." Not a promising start for women's advancement.[15]

Some did advance, but few within the chronology of this study. The competition for seats in Arabic training courses made it easier to exclude women between 1946 and 1975. Only Winifred Weislogel and April Glaspie succeeded in completing the Middle East training in this era. Both chose to remain unmarried to protect their careers. Weislogel, the first woman Arabist, had impressive credentials including a master's degree but struggled to get into MEAP training. She eventually was given a slot only to find it was in a small branch program in Morocco, the Tangier Arabic program. She later became deputy chief of mission in Togo.

The first to attain ambassadorial rank was Glaspie, who joined the State Department in 1966 with a master's in international relations, then began the MEAP in 1972. After years of language training and nearly a decade of field experience, she was assigned to Cairo, the most prestigious American embassy. During Kissinger's shuttle diplomacy, Glaspie and another woman MEAP graduate, Elizabeth Jones, were given an additional task beyond their regular duties: Henry Kissinger's laundry. Their special assignment came about when Kissinger complained his shirts had too much starch. Despite the humiliations and hard work, Glaspie served in a series of tough posts. Her command of Arabic enabled her to move up the ranks, but her career ended with her toughest and most controversial assignment as ambassador to Iraq (1987–1990) dealing with Saddam Hussein.[16]

There was an additional complication for women Arabists; an informal State Department policy was applied in the Islamic world: women were very reluctantly posted to Muslim countries, in particular the Gulf region. This policy was overturned by a class action lawsuit in 1970.[17] A handbook on protocol blithely summarized the position of women FSOs: "Very few of them have husbands, which simplifies the matter of precedence and seating at table." The author asserted it was not Americans who had a problem with women as diplomats, since "the idea is rather quickly accepted at least in western countries."[18] Senior American officials asserted that Muslim host nations would never accept American women as diplomats. This canard was used for decades to keep women area specialists from posts in the Middle East.

American women who worked in countries where Islamic law was in force found the problem was American opposition. In Pakistan Jane Abell-Coon termed her cultural position as "[t]he third sex […] their [the Pakistani's] social ideas didn't apply to me [nor] their expectations of me as a woman."[19] When she applied for a post at Bombay, the outgoing ambassador wrote a three-page letter to the new ambassador listing "all the reasons why a woman could NOT do consular work in Bombay." Consular work entailed such mundane chores as dealing with American sailors who got in trouble and tourists who needed help or died in the host nation. Abell-Coon surmised the ambassador objected to the idea of a woman dealing with "shipping and seamen," the tough work that entailed jail visits to the incarcerated sailors to arrange their release.

Tours of duty in Saudi Arabia did pose unique problems, as women came under restrictions against driving cars, etc. In reality, not all of the difficulties came from the Arab world; many female Arabists had to struggle against the ingrained attitudes of senior American policy makers and their senior officers overseas. For these reasons, during the span of this study, women Arabists were quite the exception to the rule.

To understand how Middle East hands made their way up the career ladder, it is important to examine their typical career path. Many chose to become Middle East hands when they realized that they could get ahead by learning Arabic. As a junior diplomat stuck in a low-level job in Australia, Richard B. Parker carefully reviewed the number of posts available for the four hard languages and concluded: "Arabic offered the most possibilities." Parker recalled Arabic was a way to more interesting work and "[t]he only way I was going to get out of administrative work." Others made similar discoveries. Heywood Stackhouse decided between Russian and Arabic: "I made a cool calculation […] I counted up the posts where Russian was the language. There were two. I counted the number where Arabic was the language. There were 24. I became an Arabist."[20]

Another on a similar path was William R. Crawford. The son of two college professors, he was intrigued by a Foreign Service career. He discussed his plans with people he knew in the State Department and was informed that skill in hard languages was the key to the fast-track: "I asked people and they said 'You know you have got to be prepared for ten years of doing things not that interesting—administrative, consular work.' And I said, is there any way around that? Someone said, 'Become a specialist [...] and have a language that nobody else has—become a Language-and-Area specialist.'" When Assistant Secretary of State G. Lewis Jones gave a lecture on the Middle East to the incoming class of junior officers, Crawford volunteered for a post that would get him into Arabic specialization: "I said, 'Mr. Jones I'd like to go to Saudi Arabia'—and he looked at me as if I was out of my mind." Crawford had volunteered for what he admitted was "[t]he worst post in the Foreign Service" in the hope it would move him ahead of his peers.[21] Crawford's move paid off when he was assigned to Saudi Arabia as a political reporting officer and later was one of the first Middle East hands to become an ambassador.

George M. Lane, with a degree in French and a master's in diplomatic studies, applied for Arabic while working in European Regional Affairs. His superiors, as he recalled, were "absolutely appalled" that he had chosen to abandon "what they considered *the* track in the Foreign Service." In the post–World War II era political appointees increasingly claimed the plum ambassadorships as political rewards. Decades later, Ambassador Lane concluded, "The people who took Arabic guessed right [...] if I had stayed [...] [in] the European channel, I never would have been an ambassador."[22]

The two who reached the top most quickly became the model for those who followed. Richard W. Murphy, born in Massachusetts and with degrees in history and anthropology, joined the Foreign Service in 1955 after a stint in the US Army. He was sent to Salisbury, Zimbabwe (then Rhodesia), but felt his career had stagnated. He wanted to become a political reporting officer, which he saw as the route to the top. Some political reporting posts were labeled as language-designated positions (LDPs) and gave special preference to area specialists. LDPs vastly improved the chances of promotion and many of these posts were only open to the small group of budding area specialists. Murphy recalled how he decided: "I was not committed to Arabic had no genetic or academic reasons. It finally came down to the least constricting language in terms of future assignments—we had a dozen posts. As mercenary a choice as that."[23]

The decision to try area specialization quickly paid off: the State Department sent Murphy for training in international studies and then to the MEAP at Beirut and finally to Syria for specialized dialect training. Murphy was assigned to a political reporting post in Syria and later became liaison to the United Nations negotiating team on the Yemen Civil War.

In 1967 he was a political reporting officer in Jordan when the Six Day War broke out and was left behind when nonessential embassy personnel and families were evacuated. Murphy sat in the blacked-out embassy writing reports as the Israeli Air Force conducted air operations overhead. By 1971 he became ambassador to Mauritania in the midst of a tragic drought and organized a US airlift to ship emergency food supplies. As ambassador to Syria he attempted to reestablish relations in 1974 and laid the groundwork for an AID program and also the evacuation of Syrian Jews, although he was unable to interest Henry Kissinger in opening negotiations over the Golan Heights issue. After the embassy in Beirut was bombed, leaving over sixty dead, Murphy led the investigation and managed yet another American evacuation. From 1983–89 he served as assistant secretary of state for the NEA and was the first Middle East hand, after Hare and Hart, to reach that position.

The career of Hermann Frederick Eilts was typical of Middle East hands. He became the prototype of the fast-track careerist and was careful to emulate Hare's quiet diplomacy. His career took off the fastest, as Eilts became the youngest ambassador in the entire Foreign Service. Born in Germany, his family immigrated to America, and he grew up in Scranton, Pennsylvania. His original plan was to study diplomacy at the Fletcher School and planned on a State Department career in European Affairs. His plans were altered first by a stubborn professor at Fletcher who insisted Eilts accept a graduate assistantship that required he learn Arabic, and secondly by the approach of World War II, which interrupted his academic studies. Like many of his colleagues, his path to NEA was indirect.

He retained a palpable touchiness on the subject of learning Arabic, and in Kaplan's book, *The Arabists: The Romance of an American Elite*, he downplayed his pre–State Department study of Arabic: "The Foreign Service gave me a language test, which consisted of asking me to count to ten in Arabic. Having counted correctly, I was pronounced an Arabist."[24] In fact he held a master's degree from the Johns Hopkins University's School for Advanced International Studies in Middle Eastern studies and continued Arabic training at the University of Pennsylvania.[25] Eilts already had significant training when he joined the State Department. Unlike the stereotype of the Arabist who picked up his area knowledge on the job, Eilts and many others brought significant academic training to the Foreign Service.

On his first assignment overseas Eilts learned firsthand the risks of working in the Middle East. En route to Baghdad he was prevented from entering the city due to an outbreak of cholera. So the State Department assigned him to the consulate general in Jerusalem to await further orders. He arrived in 1948 just as the Arab–Israeli conflict exploded into war. Consul General Tom Wasson was fired upon as he emerged from truce talks.[26] Three consular officers were shot in a four-day span in May 1948, and on the same day Wasson was shot, Menachim Begin announced that the Irgun had "sentenced to death" every British member of the Arab Legion. UN negotiator Folke Bernadotte was assassinated later that year.[27]

Eilts, aware the Orientalists were literally under fire in Jerusalem while those in Washington were being ousted by Truman, was also wary about being perceived as pro-Arab. To position himself as aware of both sides' concerns, Eilts fought for a post in the embassy at Tel Aviv: "I wanted very much to get a tour of duty in Israel; I felt that this was critical to an image of wanting to be fair on Arab-Israeli issues." The State Department refused to post an Arabist to Israel. Undersecretary Averill Harriman sent Eilts to Libya instead to take charge of critical negotiations for the Wheelus Air Base. Eilts protested that his position at Tel Aviv was set but Harriman insisted and Eilts recalled that "He just turned off his hearing aid and said 'You're going to Tripoli.' Therefore, the Tel Aviv assignment was out. I didn't like Tripoli." Later Eilts encountered Harriman who reminded him: "You could never have gone as ambassador to Saudi Arabia if you had gone as DCM in Tel Aviv." Eilts's career had been rerouted from a path that he argued would have given him "[t]he image of seeing both sides by direct experience." But there was a positive side: "From a career point of view probably not going to Tel Aviv turned out to be in my interest. I was one of the youngest ambassadors to Saudi Arabia, as a matter of fact, to anywhere."

The highpoint of his career came in 1978 when Eilts later served as a senior advisor to President Carter during the negotiations between Menachim Begin and Anwar Sadat at Camp David. Ambassador Eilts, along with Ambassador to Israel Samuel Lewis and William Quandt of the National Security Council as well as CIA intelligence specialists advised Carter on the negotiations. Although Eilts was then a former ambassador to Saudi Arabia, he felt his cautions regarding what the Saudi government would support were not heeded. He also encouraged Carter to invest more time in negotiating the language of framework. Eilts viewed Carter as pressuring Sadat to make more concessions than Eilts thought the Saudi government would support.[28]

The one Middle East hand who was privileged to work on the major presidential peace initiative also witnessed its failure. Eilts had spent a lifetime building expertise, but his counsel was ignored with catastrophic effects for American policy. That failure, however, harkens back to Middle East hand Don Bergus's 1956 appraisal that there was "no royal road to peace" and any comprehensive Arab–Israeli peace agreement would require both sides to compromise.

In conclusion, after Truman ousted the Orientalists there was a significant gap of expertise at NEA that was eventually filled by a corps of trained professionals who understood the languages and the history of the Middle East. The wartime ASTP program was the place where new language training techniques were developed to teach Arabic. It marked the transition between the Orientalists and the post–World War II professionals who built their career after 1945. In addition, ambassadors Raymond Hare and Parker Hart mentored these junior officers and set an example of institutional loyalty and quiet diplomacy. For both men a diplomat must support presidential policy and work within the chain of command. Quiet diplomacy stressed this low-key, low-profile approach, and the Middle East hands understood US influence, and the Middle East hands understood what was feasible in the region during the Cold War. They encouraged Washington to use diplomacy to avoid conflict and cautioned against exerting military force in the region to avoid overt political alliances.

The new Middle East area specialists reflected the demographic changes in the post-1946 State Department and in American society. The State Department, and especially the NEA, became far more middle class and diverse. Middle East hands possessed significant academic credentials and took pride in their professionalism. Most of all they were organization men committed to work within the State Department chain of command and not against it as the Orientalists had. Their ultimate objective was not to reshape American policy but to serve their country and advance their careers.

Chapter Three

LANDFALL: LANGUAGE TRAINING IN BEIRUT, 1946

A very small contingent landed on the beach at Beirut, Lebanon, in November of 1946: Dr. Charles A. Ferguson, a State Department scientific linguist, and two young State Department diplomats, William Sands and Donald Bergus. All were army veterans and just beginning their State Department careers. The task was to establish the first US program to train diplomats in Arabic and to create a corps of Middle East language-and-area specialists.

Despite a brief retreat back to Washington to reorganize, in its first decade the school established a program that could rapidly train Americans to speak Arabic. But the results were limited: from 1946–52 training was a brief, six-month introduction to the Middle East and Arabic, sometimes conducted in Beirut and at other times in Washington, DC. Only later in the Cold War was it permanently settled in Beirut and expanded into an intensive multiyear course.

This era was filled with fits and starts, landfalls and retreats, ambitious goals and setbacks. In the first decade the State Department was deeply committed to the effort but soon its limitations were apparent. There was a long struggle to get Congressional funding to improve it. Six months of Arabic training was not enough time to develop useful skills. Moreover, the companion area studies course lacked resources.

The Cold War competition with the Soviets was increasingly a factor garnering support from Congress and the Eisenhower administration. At best in this era the program periodically turned out a handful of graduates who were in great demand but not yet fully fluent. In the end, Cold War fears that the Soviets were training specialists in Arabic to a much higher standard set off fears of what I would term the Cold War "linguist gap."

The State Department also aimed to deal with the people of the Middle East and the developing world directly in the so-called shirt-sleeved diplomacy and to erase the stereotypes of monolingualism from the popular press. American diplomats would no longer be the striped-pants "cookie pushers" at receptions but instead professionals who knew the area in which they served, talked to "the man on the street" and understood the nuances of regional politics.

The Senate investigated language skill levels in the State Department, and William Lederer and Eugene Burdick's novel *The Ugly American* focused popular attention on the problem. Washington's Cold War anxieties intensified concerns about the lack of language skill among American diplomats. Only after a decade of struggle, in 1957, was the Arabic program fully funded and quadrupled in size.

Arabic training met resistance among senior American diplomats to releasing junior staff for months and then years of Arabic training. In 1946 the enormous changes wrought by World War II led to demands for change. First, the US Congress passed the Foreign Service Act of 1946, which mandated the State Department improve the skills of American diplomats by better recruitment, competitive promotion and modern training. Second, the Middle East was recognized as an area vital to American interests, and the State Department desperately needed Arabic linguists and area experts to communicate more effectively than the Soviets.

During the war the Army Specialized Training Program (ASTP) developed a new method of quickly building speaking skill (as discussed in chapter two).[1] When the ASTP was disbanded at the end of the war, the State Department seized the opportunity and hired the ASTP's resident language genius, Dr. Henry Lee Smith, as director of all language training. He brought along most of his staff to the new Foreign Service Institute (FSI) in Washington.

American diplomats were relying upon native speakers, often foreign nationals, to act as conversational intermediaries and to translate documents and newspapers. This raised concerns not only about the quality of the translations but the trustworthiness of the intermediaries. While it would continue to be necessary to use native speakers for technical translations, the postwar objective was to form a core group of skilled political reporting officers who could gather their own information and monitor native translators. No longer would American diplomats sit silently and rely solely upon native speakers for communication.

Historically speaking, the State Department's first attempt to train an Arabist in the region began in 1826 at Algiers. The consul general, William Shaler, had argued with the State Department for years that the only way to learn such a difficult language as Arabic was to begin very early in life and to live in the area. Shaler requested an American child be sent to the consulate to be raised as a native speaker. The Department of State refused. Shaler then turned to his family, requesting a young nephew be sent to him. They refused. The only alternative was to find a skilled Arabic linguist. Eventually the State Department sent William Hodgson, who held a master's degree and had studied Turkish and Arabic. He continued his studies in Arabic, and later he served as a treaty negotiator and diplomat.[2]

The lesson of Hodgson's success was then abandoned by the State Department for 120 years. Training linguists in the region worked, but it was expensive and time-consuming. Then, as now, training older, senior officers as linguists did not work. They could not learn hard languages with any facility and often resisted spending the time. Moreover, the training had to be done overseas, since students cannot be pressured to develop hard language skills unless constantly forced to use the language in what today would be called language immersion.

The innovator was Dr. Henry Lee Smith Jr., who claimed he could teach anyone to speak any language. As a newly minted PhD in his late twenties, Smith combined an academic career in New York with a 1939–40 radio program called "Where Are You From?" The show featured Dr. Smith who was challenged by members of the audience to guess their origin based on hearing them speak only two or three words.

According to the *New York Times*, he was correct 80 percent of the time. During the war Smith was put in charge of the ASTP and brought his language learning methods. His knack for publicity was also appreciated by the army: Smith became the boy wonder of the ASTP, interviewed by *Time* and photographed by *National Geographic* as he recorded language training records that were shipped to soldiers around the globe. Years later Smith reprised his "Where Are You From?" radio program as a television show.[3]

In 1946 Smith had the power to organize a global training program for the State Department's diplomats. Smith proclaimed the goal of the Foreign Service Institute (FSI) was "to deal with all the principle peoples of the earth in their native tongues."[4] That proved harder, especially in Arabic, than even the irrepressible Smith thought.

His system of learning by listening was called the "audio-lingual method." The key was to hear native speakers, then repeat what was heard and continue the process until use of language became natural through what he called "guided imitation," meaning the student would carefully imitate the sound of a language rather than learning to read it from a book. The student was taught a series of phrases that were to become so ingrained that verbal responses became instinctive and natural. His system did develop accurate speaking in months, not years, using rote memorization, but there were limits. This method became the standard used in university language labs where record players or tape recorders intoned the voices of native speakers.[5]

A downside to this approach was that language learning involved four skills: hearing, speaking, reading and writing, but only the first two were addressed. Smith's method skipped over reading Arabic script by substituting a phonetic bridge language. The written text was in a phonetic transliteration. Graduates of his six-month crash course could speak the language, but they could not say too much nor could they read anything.

While the United States adopted Smith's new method, the British retained the old grammar-translational method, which emphasized tedious study of Arabic script and reading Classical Arabic. Generations of British Arabists were trained on Reverend Thatcher's *Grammar of the Arabic Language*, first published in 1910 and still in use until 1965.[6] Arabic script, like Cyrillic (for example, Russian and Slavic) and Sinitic (Chinese and Japanese) scripts, offers no clue to an English reader of the sound of the text. More important, once the 28 consonants in Arabic script have been learned, they shift into four different forms based on their position within the word. The complexity of sounding-out Arabic was made more difficult by the nine vowels that might or might not be written in the script. These were challenges that made it impossible to quickly teach reading and writing skills.[7] Thus, American program's goal was speaking/hearing and not reading/writing.

Middle East hand Richard W. Murphy studied in Beirut, while the British operated their program at Shemlan and recalled, "They had the edge on classical Arabic and the written product, because they were trying—in the fifties—to turn out men who would help run that end of the empire, East of Suez."[8] The British objective was to administer their empire, not to chat with the man in the street, so reading was important. They needed to deal on a government-to-government (or government-to-colonial entity) basis. George M. Lane, who also completed the American program at Beirut, observed the difference between a British and American first-year student would be that the British students could read street signs and menus, while the Americans could communicate with Arab speakers in colloquial Arabic using simple phrases and order a meal.⁹

From the start the Americans focused on a people-to-people approach, but that more democratic approach was literally pedestrian. The FSI met their initial objective without understanding the vast social distinctions in spoken Arabic. Middle East hand Rodger Davies finished the FSI's program of what he described as "intensive FSI brainwashing" in 1948: "In those days at FSI, 'language was what is spoken on the streets.' I learned my lessons well." Perhaps too well. Posted to Damascus in 1949, Davies paid a call on the Syrian chief of protocol, and on the way out, his interpreter cautioned him to refrain from speaking Arabic until they could "work on his accent." Davies recalled: "He said I spoke like the man who swept up horse manure in front of the Beirut Embassy."¹⁰ It was as if Henry Higgins had found Eliza Doolittle, and instead of teaching her upper-class British English, he had used her to train the Foreign Office's diplomats in the Cockney dialect of the London streets.

In his famous 1956 Suez speech Egyptian president Gamal Abdel Nasser moved freely from high classical Arabic into low colloquial Arabic and back again. Dr. Charles Ferguson, a professor of Arabic studies at the FSI, was the first to describe the phenomena of using two vocabularies and linked this behavior to social and educational standing. He described the "leveling" of Arabic speech by the listener "diglossia."¹¹

The political implications were important, since Nasser showed he could appeal to the masses using low Arabic, while holding their respect by switching to the high classical form. American diplomats, who were taught the lower form of colloquial speech, realized in the field they had learned a manner of speaking that markedly lowered their status. When native Arabic speakers realized the Americans did not speak in an educated manner, they lowered their own speech to the Americans' level.

Worse yet, the effort to teach the regional dialects, rather than the modern form of Arabic used on radio broadcasts in the 1950s, presented another problem. Diplomats found the Lebanese dialect they learned at Beirut did not extend very far. A diplomat who sounded good in Beirut found it hard to make himself understood in Kuwait, had to make some adjustments in Cairo and was all but deaf and mute in Rabat or Baghdad. When a branch FSI Arabic school opened in Tangier, Morocco, its first graduates quickly found that Tangerine Arabic was useless outside Morocco.

The real success story was the Soviet program, a long and extremely rigorous program that started in the schools. Anecdotal reports of Soviet efficiency were revealed in *The Ugly American*, and led to Senate Foreign Relations Committee investigations that showed the United States really was far behind their Cold War rivals.¹²

The key difference was that the Soviet system was able to select its students at a young age, some as early as 17, and then put them through a half dozen years of language training. Afterward they were trained as diplomats. Language training in Moscow reflected the demands that could be made under the Soviet system in a very well-funded program, whose graduates were far superior in Arabic skill.

It was not unusual for an American to find his Soviet counterpart working in the Middle East possessed two or three times as many years of training. Richard Murphy recalled the graduates of the Soviet program were top notch: "The ones they grabbed right out of university and put into a finishing school in Arabic were excellently trained." The Soviets invested more than five years to train an Arabist, while the United States struggled for a decade to fund a two-year program. Another reason for the Soviet success was, as Murphy observed, the Soviets did literally "grab" their promising linguists. The FSI had to recruit them.[13]

In 1986 a State Department team, led by Middle East hand Monteagle Stearns, visited Moscow's State Institute for International Relations and found their rival's method far superior. Stearns described the system as "unabashedly elitist," but that their investment in "facilities [were] superior to those at FSI."[14] In the 1950s the United States was only beginning to understand the emerging "linguist gap" and the Soviet edge in Arabic.

It is important to understand the Middle East underwent vast political and economic change brought by the end of colonialism and the oil boom. All of this resulted in social and linguistic changes. For centuries Arabic had been rooted in the written script passed down in the Classical Arabic of the Koran. With the advent of mass media, especially radio broadcasts, spoken Arabic had to bridge the enormous dialectical differences. One language linked millions of people at a variety of educational and cultural levels from Morocco to Indonesia.

American linguists argued over how to deal with this newly emergent form, first called "Radio Arabic," and later codified as Modern Standard Arabic (MSA). The FSI made radio monitoring skills a standard part of training, as MSA emerged as an Arabic Esperanto.[15] Just as American regional accents dissolved as television exposed the country to a standardized pronunciation, Arabic underwent a profound change.

The American program needed to recruit people who were capable of developing an advanced level of proficiency. The question was how to identify those capable of becoming both linguist and diplomat? The answer was to recruit a large pool of candidates and select only those who possessed proven ability to meet the challenge.

Throughout this decade there were plenty of diplomats who recognized the potential for advancement and volunteered for Arabic. The State Department became increasingly selective, revising and elevating the entrance standards. Later they developed an outcomes assessment, which functioned as a testing and rating system that graded their skills. This professionalized the corps of Middle East hands. The FSI also became the gatekeeper into what became a skilled, credentialed profession. Moreover, the general broadening of recruitment, sometimes called the democratization of State, was accelerated and magnified in the NEA because so many junior officers were needed as the American presence expanded in the 1950s and 1960s. Like a Wild West land rush in American history, the language frontier was wide open, and these were the pioneers who would stake their claim in the hopes of building a career.

The phenomenal expansion of Middle East posts occurred in two waves: first the number of posts doubled in the postwar era with an explosion of Arab nationalism and petrodollars, and then expanded again after 1968 when the British began to withdraw from the Gulf region and another group of Arab states became independent nations. While political campaign contributors fought for political appointments to coveted European ambassadorships and displaced career FSOs, most of them did not vie for Middle East ambassadorships. Due to the difficult conditions and the fact that most of the consulates and embassies were defined as hardship posts, there was no competition from political appointees. The State Department could select from its corps of Arabists for the expanding list of new embassies in the Middle East.

State Department recruiting stressed the career advantages of area specialization. They soon had a large pool of candidates vying to get in, but the intensive program was predicated upon a low student–instructor ratio, so there was a limited number of seats available. The FSI method worked intensively with each student in small groups. The size of the school was severely circumscribed for two reasons: Smith's method was designed for classes of a half dozen students working with one native speaker. During the 1950s there were also severe budgetary limitations that restricted funding for the program in its first decade. This made competition for those six seats in each course very intense.

Arabic not only meant rapid promotion but a chance to avoid perhaps a decade of administrative work. Other hard languages did not offer the same opportunity; Russian was overstaffed. Only a few Chinese specialists were needed, and Japanese posts were limited. Arabic posts were expanding and the exit of the Orientalists left a manpower shortage.

Producing Arab linguists takes time, and it was decades before they would become senior officers but most reached the top far ahead of their peers. Arabists became a valuable commodity. Decades later when many opted for early retirement, *The Stearns Report* noted: "The cost of losing a hard language officer this year may only become fully apparent several years hence. Like deforestation, the depletion of language skill eliminates assets that require years to replenish."[16] But, in 1946, the FSI was planting trees.

The MEAP attracted those willing to make short-term sacrifices for long-term gains: a commitment of up to two years of intensive study and then a string of hardship posts. The rewards were substantial: one of the first graduates became the youngest ambassador in the Foreign Service (Hermann Eilts assumed the position of ambassador to Saudi Arabia at age 33). Many began their careers as political reporting officers and rapidly reached responsible positions.

Of the 53 in this study group, 37 became ambassadors.[17] They achieved their ranks through rigorous training that defined them as professionals and transformed the NEA from an aristocracy into a meritocracy.

But in 1946 they were off to a rocky start. Senior officers, often generalists with little language training, were unwilling to release their junior officers for a short period of training. Older officers knew the difficulties of hard language training and had little confidence the new techniques would work for Arabic.

Volunteers were recruited in *American Foreign Service Journal* (later *Foreign Service Journal*), which served as the connecting link for diplomats abroad and at home. It was an important forum for the debate on the shift from generalist to area specialist.

A special essay, "Language Training for the Foreign Service and the Department of State," opened the first phase of recruiting for language-and-area training in 1946. This was a combination of sales pitch and recruiting drive for the new language program and was followed by a spate of articles supporting the emphasis on area specialization.

Any ambitious young officer need only glance at the July 1947 issue to make a reasoned guess as to where his future lay: on the cover was a photo of the Ras Tanura refinery in Saudi Arabia with a feature article, "Oil in the Near and Middle East," and another "Should the Foreign Service Officer Specialize?" by Frank Hopkins from the FSI. Of course, the answer to his rhetorical question was yes. Hopkins wanted to allay any fears about the pitfalls of specialization and claimed "a new day has dawned" for language training. He outlined the scope of the program, concluding on Arabic: "The Department means business."[18]

Anyone with wartime ASTP training or experience in the Middle East was actively sought out. Dayton Mak recalled that the program had few volunteers in its first year: "A notice came out that the Department was going to set up a school for Arabic language studies [...] so I applied for Arabic language training, and bingo, I got it. People weren't pounding at the doors to take Arabic language training."[19] Another member of that class was the *rara avis*, a diplomat with a graduate degree in foreign languages (Portuguese) and a graduate of the ASTP's Arabic program. With that experience on his record Rodger Davies was sought out for the Middle East program: "I became an Arabist by pure fluke."[20]

Throughout this period the director of the FSI envisioned a future when "[i]t will not be the [area] specialist who is an anomaly, but the officer who has never bothered to acquire any real specialized competence." He concluded the future was in the hard languages and the payoff might be an ambassadorship: "The direct line of advancement will be through the acquisition of special knowledge and difficult skills." To drive home his point he drew a sports analogy, comparing the generalist to a utility player "good enough to be a useful auxiliary, but not expert enough at any position to play on the first team." It was clear the "first team" equated with the ambassadorships.[21]

The State Department stressed this was a new model of American diplomat and sought to override the objections of senior staff. Another offer was circulated requesting that volunteers respond directly to the FSI offering junior officers a way around their supervisors. Curtis Jones recalled the tenor of that time: "I entered the Foreign Service in 1946 much impressed by the word coming out of Washington that the postwar diplomat would be a new breed—not the effete Ivy Leaguer of former years—but a concerned public servant who would mix freely with other nationalities and speak their languages like his own." Jones had served in the army and been trained in Moroccan Arabic, but while he was eager to volunteer, one person stood in his way. After he was given a place in the 1948 class, but just before he left Addis Ababa, an old veteran of the Paris Arabic program came to inspect his post. James Moose related vivid memories of his own "frustrating experience" learning Arabic and told Jones he did not believe any American diplomat could learn it. Jones recalled Moose saying: "Why then, he asked, did I propose to waste my time and the taxpayers' money at FSI?" Mak returned to Washington and later learned that the FSI inspector "had marked me down for studying Arabic to escape the 'real work' of the Service, such as keeping the accounts and issuing visas."[22]

Moose's reaction reflected two things: first the skepticism among senior officers that any Arabic training method would be effective, and second, the belief among many older diplomats that all they needed was a native translator. Either James Moose or George Wadsworth, depending on who is telling the anecdote, coined a well-known Orientalist platitude on what the young Arabist would find when he finished his studies: "Arabic is the key to a door. When you open it, you find nothing."²³ For the Arabists this was a new proverb.

Although experienced administrators, many senior officers working in the Middle East during the late 1940s and 1950s were generalists with little foreign language skill. The Orientalists had been ousted in the bureaucratic warfare over recognition of Israel or had retired. Senior officers who served as assistant secretary of the NEA in this era were almost never Arabists. In those days generalists ran the embassies, because the Orientalists had been driven out. Some Washington desk officers did not even have working experience in the region of their responsibility. Those in the field who only spoke English or French were limited in their political contacts with persons who could communicate in those languages. In the postcolonial world that severely limited their ability to gather information.

The downside to serving in the Middle East was the harsh reality of living there. Recruiters for the program argued air travel would "make the unhealthy or remote post less hazardous" and that there would be "more responsible work and more rapid promotion." Still, the remoteness, harsh climate and lack of medical care could not be ignored. Parker Hart recalled the heat in Saudi Arabia: "We tested the radiation temperature from the tarmac […] it was 154 degrees."²⁴ Medical care for a sudden illness might mean a risky evacuation to Beirut's American University of Beirut medical center or Cairo. Those with families had to face exposing their dependents to these same hardships and health risks. In some hardship posts, political instability and violence might lead to the evacuation of dependents or even the requirement, at times, that children not reside in-country.

Some who completed Arabic language training chose to transfer out when faced with the reality of living for decades in a series of hardship posts. To ensure that candidates knew what they would face after the training program, the FSI added a new requirement: all students must first complete a tour of duty in the area before being assigned a seat in the Arabic program. The rule was so stringently enforced that in 1951 Talcott Seelye, born in Beirut to American educators, was required to take a post in Jordan before being admitted to the course.²⁵

One of the first graduates of the program, Hermann Eilts, found that this requirement also made young officers assimilate more easily to life in Middle East posts: "They obviously had an interest in the area and were not going around bitching that it was hot." There was also a marked advantage in training diplomats who already had begun developing their political reporting skills, Eilts pointed out: "When we began to get the first people from the FSI in Beirut, some were good, some were not so […] [but] they certainly were a lot better than those who were coming to us from the FSI in Washington who were generalists."²⁶

Shortly after joining the State Department, William R. Crawford volunteered for a hardship post in Saudi Arabia: "They were desperate to get anyone, any warm body, to go to this benighted post [in Jidda, Saudi Arabia.] It was in many ways terrible, terrible, terrible: physically, climactically, totally." While still in his 20s, Crawford was promoted to be in charge of Jidda's political reporting.²⁷

At first the FSI took both young war veterans and senior diplomats who hoped to restart their careers but soon found that older diplomats could not learn Arabic. The ideal candidate was less than 30 years of age, with prior experience in a language training program.

In 1946 the Beirut program began as a six-month crash course focused on speaking skill via rote memorization of simple phrases. Dr. Charles A. Ferguson studied the structure of Arabic and developed the program in the field, using native speakers, whom FSI called "native informants," to provide continual, exacting repetition of local dialect forms of speech.

The native informants were primarily drawn from second-generation Arab-Americans or Arab graduate students in Washington area universities. Some of their life experiences were remarkably similar to the FSOs. They were most often in their 20s or early 30s, military veterans, born in the United States and skilled in languages. One native informant, George Makdisi, was studying for a master's degree in modern European history and considering a diplomatic career while supporting himself by teaching at the FSI. Dr. Ferguson, aware that Middle East studies would soon expand into academia, advised Makdisi to "forget about [the] Foreign Service and study for a Ph.D. in Arabic." Makdisi eventually became a professor at Harvard and the University of Pennsylvania.[28]

Did the native informants have a political influence on the Middle East hands during their training? Those who worked in the Washington program were nearly as Americanized as their charges. In this era their contact was brief, and very few Middle East hands could later recall the national identity or even the names of their tutors. This would change after the program lengthened when in Beirut, and they spent much more time working together.

Dr. Ferguson had been a director of the ASTP training programs in Japanese, Arabic and Bengali. His first FSI student, Donald Bergus, recalled: "Dr Ferguson was himself a newcomer to the area and had no particular political view."[29] In 1946 the program did not include area studies, but Ferguson struggled to teach them some basics about regional culture.

There was almost no political history, because Ferguson taught culture through the study of Arab proverbs. Proverbs reveal embedded social attitudes, and one study has identified them as "[t]he quickest way to understand a people or a culture." From the Arab point of view, proverbs are seen as "one of many sturdy bridges that need to be spanned between Arabs and the West so that Westerners would begin to realize that the Arab World has worthwhile things to export other than just oil and dates." The writer, a minister in the Kuwaiti government, placed them among the highest forms of Arab literature.[30]

Ferguson was under severe time constraints with only weeks to introduce his students to a complex culture and focus their energies on the language. He encouraged them to research the meaning of Arab proverbs and to turn their work into scholarly articles. He took a serious, academic approach, as did his students. Many Middle East hands had attended graduate schools and therefore took a research-oriented approach to their studies. Dayton Mak researched the origins and meaning of 40 proverbs, "Some Syrian Arabic Proverbs," published in *Journal of the American Oriental Society*. These proverbs offered insight into attitudes deeply embedded in the region's culture and served as an aid to understanding cultural differences. For example, some provided rueful commentary on social inequalities: "If you have no power over the hand, kiss it and pray for it to get broken." Others were political in nature, in view of the massive shipments of grain aid that the United States would make during the JFK years: "Chaff of your country rather than Crusader's (foreign) wheat." Other Middle East hands also published their research in refereed journals: Rodger Davies wrote "Syrian Arabic Kinship Terms," Arthur Allen authored "Some Iraqi Proverbs and Proverbial Phrases" and Hermann Eilts wrote book reviews and an article on Yemen for *National Geographic*.[31]

Ferguson began to develop his own training materials since there were no English–Arabic textbooks for the audio-lingual method. Later he and his successor at Beirut, Ernest McCarus, developed the first series of FSI Arabic and Kurdish materials. But outside the FSI, the British implemented the MECAS training program, and many universities still used *Thatcher's Arabic Grammar*, which contained such lines as "The Sheik's daughter has flashing eyes"—hardly useful phrases for diplomatic work. Some British MECAS students met in what they called "Thatcher's Club."[32]

In this phase of the American program's development, Ferguson scrambled to teach useful skills. One student summarized the result as such: "The course was only six months long, but we ended up with a pretty good basic knowledge of street Syrian-Lebanese Arabic." Pragmatically speaking, the program achieved Smith's objective; they could converse in simple phrases, but they were far from becoming interpreters or translators. The studious among them listened to Smith's recordings at night and carried pockets full of vocabulary cards. Even as the 1980s FSI's new FAST course in Arabic pointed out, even a short introduction to Arabic would "cushion culture shock and bolster student confidence in handling day-to-day situations."[33] Certainly those objectives applied to earlier efforts as well.

Harrison Symmes found they only had a very limited vocabulary: "A colleague went through a year of training and ended up in a post in the Arab world. Bill Stoltzfus, who was another good Arabist, passed through that place and later came down to Kuwait where I then was, and said 'Do you know, Mr. X is the most fluent person in Arabic I've ever heard on ninety words.' That was the kind of thing we were doing in the Arabic training program."[34]

Dayton Mak analyzed the difference between his early efforts to learn Arabic in a half year, as contrasted with the longer course: "When it moved to Beirut and then they made it a two-year course–they really learned it. We learned street Arabic, kitchen Arabic. What we knew, we knew very well, but not much."[35] Kitchen Arabic would allow you to order a meal in a restaurant or tell the consulate cook what to make for dinner, but little more. After six months of intensive training they could open a simple conversation or manage to order food. Most Middle East hands returned to Beirut to advance their level of Arabic proficiency or learn new dialects for their next post.

Since the FSI did not have the staff to offer advanced training, the most promising students were given the chance to attend specialized programs at the new School for Advanced International Studies or the University of Pennsylvania. Those chosen usually had prior training to build upon, among them Hermann Eilts, who recalled, "In this first decade the FSI simply could not muster that level of area training." He completed a graduate-level program in language, culture and history that he found "Clearly very useful for someone who would spend the rest of his life, or much of the rest of his life in the Arab world."[36]

The Cold War Linguist Gap

These were difficult times, as Senator Joseph McCarthy launched bitter attacks on the loyalty of American diplomats and made demands for security investigations that paralyzed the Foreign Service. Investigations of American diplomats in Asia, suspected of sympathizing with communism, resulted in the removal of most State Department China hands.

In 1954 the Wriston Committee investigated hiring and promotion policies and found a lack of language expertise, especially in Arabic. The report concluded, somewhat archly, that more Arabists were needed: "It is no secret that the linguistic competence of American overseas personnel is not as high as it should be."[37] America did not have enough Arabists.

The Wriston Report also suggested sweeping changes to expand the training and promotion of area specialists. The State Department was criticized for not "making room for specialists." While area specialists should have been promoted, generalists held onto the upper ranks. The Wriston Committee demanded the logjam at the top be broken, describing the usefulness of the generalist as a "nineteenth century theory" and that "[s]pecialization has become so vital an element in the day-to-day conduct of diplomacy [...] that to allow the 'generalist' to preempt all but a small segment of the FSO category is to deny American diplomacy full flexibility and depth." Furthermore, the Wriston Committee demanded the State Department "open its ranks to a large number of people with a high degree of specialization" and do it promptly.[38]

The State Department created a new incentive, the Language-Designated Post (LDP), as a career reward and then calculated the number of new Arabists it needed to fill those posts. In 1959 the State Department needed 231 new Arabists. At the time they only had 39 at "working" proficiency, 16 in training, and therefore a shortfall of 159. At six students per classroom, working fulltime, that would require staff to run 26 more sections. The State Department planned to double the number of Arabists within two years but that would take time and money.[39]

The Wriston Committee also recommended that training be upgraded: "The [Foreign Service] Institute be given a status equal to that of the war colleges; that the faculty be recreated at once, and the curriculum revised; and the direction be committed to a man of first class ability." The new FSI director was Harold B. Hoskins, a skilled public relations person who had the talent to garner congressional support.[40]

Hoskins, the son of American missionaries and an Arabic speaker himself, firmly believed that American diplomats must learn about the region and speak its languages: "We might remind ourselves of the old Arab proverb, *Kull lisan insan* which can be translated as 'Every new language is a new soul." He concluded, "It is hard, if not impossible, to really know a country well without knowing its language."[41]

Hoskins was determined that new American diplomats "really know a country well" and aimed to make Smith's original dream, of diplomats trained overseas, into a reality. Smith realized he would be forced to compromise on the dream of intensive study abroad, "The ideal condition for learning a foreign language is the intensive course taught by a bilingual technical linguist in the country to which the language is native. Since this happy state of affairs hardly ever exists, in practice recourse must be had to various successive approximations to it."[42] Although "various approximations" had been the rule in the past, now the goal was to move the school back to Beirut. Hoskins argued, "Language is never taught in a vacuum, but always as part of the total cultural behavior of a national group or society." In other words, the goal was immersion into the language as well as the culture itself. Intensive hard language training overseas would produce true professionals.

When Hoskins took over in 1955 he made two things clear: change was coming, and he had the support of President Dwight Eisenhower and Secretary of State John Foster Dulles.[43] As director of the FSI Hoskins made a major address, which outlined his program to create "more effective American representation in the Middle East." He focused on how American diplomatic and commercial interests were linked and observed that the Arab–Israeli conflict was America's "main liability" in the region, observing that it "affects adversely the attitude of either the Arabs or the Israelis or of both toward practically every US activity in the region, be it governmental or private in nature." He went on to warn there was a Cold War opportunity for the Soviets, who would use their language edge "to confuse and weaken the alliance of free peoples." Hoskins concluded the solution to the Communist threat was to train more area specialists.[44]

He observed that American missionaries had inculcated American ideals to a generation of Middle East professionals who were "American-trained" but not necessarily pro-American. He pointed out many were "among the extreme Nationalist groups that are critical of American foreign policy." He wanted diplomats who understood the "cross-cultural problems" of working in the region. FSI soon offered advanced senior seminars, with area specialists as guest speakers, on issues such as "The Significance of Middle East Oil in World Economy." More important for the future of the area studies component, he proposed the program be based at the American University of Beirut.[45]

Hoskins used the prevalent Cold War anxiety to generate presidential and congressional support. He did not have to exaggerate the Soviet advantage in hard language expertise. Alarm over what I would term the "linguist gap" was at its height in the United States and was focused on Arabic. The competition with the Soviets in weapons, science and technology now extended to communicating as well.

The first effort to close the linguist gap was to triple the length of the program. Students would spend six months in Washington and then a full year of language-and-area studies in Beirut. Although it sounded workable, the two-stage approach was expensive and still did not close the gap. It took significant time and expense to transport students overseas and to support them in Beirut. The added complication that the regional post they had left must be filled by a substitute for a year and a half only magnified the problem. The program drew its best students from the posts where the manpower shortage was most acute and substitutes hard to find.[46]

The program could now demand a higher standard from the candidates it chose to admit. FSI required prior "demonstrated ability" in language learning, either in the wartime ASTP or university training. FSI instructors interviewed prospective Middle East hands to test their language ability because the tough new program made failure more likely and the heavy recruitment of applicants made it possible to raise entrance standards.

Andrew I. Killgore had learned German as a State Department lawyer under the Kreis program in postwar Germany and later volunteered for Beirut. He was tested by a professor of German and by Frank Rice, head of the Arabic program. Killgore was quizzed for a half hour before being accepted, but there was no seat available in the course, but then he heard a slot had opened up. Killgore turned to Ambassador Parker Hart, whom he called "[t]he grand old man of the Arabists [...] the most prestigious one," then director of the NEA. Killgore recalled that "[a] young officer who was serving in Nairobi applied for the course some months earlier [...] his boss at the consulate general said 'I will support you in this, but if your successor is not physically on the spot, present, working, when the time comes—you are not leaving.' And the guy was cruel enough to do him out of that job."[47] The senior officer was well aware of State's manpower shortage, but Arabist Parker Hart got Killgore into a seat in Beirut.

One of the most successful students passed through the program twice. Richard Parker became the first Foreign Service officer and nonnative speaker to achieve the FSI's highest rating in Arabic. Parker got a head start while in the field: "I had been studying Arabic on my own in Jerusalem, at my own expense with a local tutor, and had made some progress." He had heard negative reports about the Beirut program and was not entirely convinced of its effectiveness, but Parker knew he would succeed: "I had been asked to comment on my interests in Arabic training, and had said I had heard mixed views about the competence of the FSI in teaching this language, but I was confident of my ability to learn it in spite of the FSI, if that became necessary."[48] By 1961 the *Biographic Register*, a State Department publication listing the professional resume of every FSO, included the ratings of all who earned a minimum S-3 or R-3 and their language training. The Introduction noted that "[t]his signifies that the individual has been tested by the Foreign Service Institute and has received proficiency ratings of at least S-3 and R-3 in the language(s) shown."[49] Parker's S-4/R-4 meant he had earned the highest speaking and reading scores for a nonnative.

Thus any candidate for promotion could be evaluated on the basis of demonstrated expertise.

Parker had a knack for languages and attended the Beirut school in 1953 and returned in 1961 to reach an advanced level of proficiency, then continued working throughout his career to improve his skills. Later Parker admitted the method worked, "I liked the FSI technique. The constant drills and rote learning process which I think is the only way to learn that language." Yet for Parker regional dialects remained a challenge. After leaving the Beirut school he was assigned to Jordan on the Eric Johnston Plan for allocating the limited water supply. He found he could not communicate effectively: "I hadn't been there a week when this message came in concerning the negotiations [...] and it said 'Please call this to the attention of the Prime Minister immediately.' The Ambassador was out of town and the DCM [Deputy Chief of Mission, the ambassador's senior officer] was out of town [...] and I had to deliver this message to the Prime Minister who didn't speak any English."

Armed with the English text sent from Washington, Parker went to the prime minister's home and applied his Lebanese–Palestinian Arabic: "I started a sort of sight translation of this message. He said, "Just wait a minute, wait a minute—We can't do business that way." I was speaking colloquial Arabic. He said 'I'll bring my son out–he reads English' and his son came out and he translated it— interpreted it—into what we now call Modern Standard Arabic—which was unknown to us. This term had not been invented yet."[50]

William Crawford also struggled to shift from one Arabic dialect to another: "I worked very hard with a Yemeni tutor to try to convert it [Lebanese colloquial] to Yemeni." Crawford was then transferred to Morocco. "Five years later I tried very hard to convert that to Moroccan Arabic [...] I went and put myself through three or four months at FSI which was by that time in Tangier—to pick up some Moroccan Arabic. I did pick up some Moroccan Arabic, but in the process smashed my Syrian/Palestinian/Lebanese Arabic." Crawford concluded that teaching regional dialects was wrong: "I think all of us came to the conclusion that what they ought to be teaching was Modern Standard Arabic—which is what really Nasser and the Egyptians brought into being as the language of radio and television and the newspapers."[51]

Both Parker and Crawford encountered the new form of Arabic that radio had created and that served to bridge regional dialects. The program's key objective, since Hoskins enunciated it, had been to communicate with the peoples of the world in their own languages, but the FSI had underestimated the difficulty of rapidly transforming an English speaker, no matter how skilled a linguist, into an Arabist.

The school hit its nadir in 1954 when the director, Dr. Ferguson, resigned to teach at Harvard University's new Center for Middle East Studies. Talcott Seelye was stranded in Beirut without a director or any direction but designed his own program to learn the local dialect. "I was interested only—primarily—in speaking." He focused on this because he believed, "You had to be able to speak to people and relate." But when Seelye landed in Kuwait he found his accent was a problem: "Whenever I opened my mouth a Lebanese pronunciation or expression somehow slipped into my articulation." Seelye developed a novel means of retraining, which also developed information for his political reports: "I had an employee who was garrulous and he spent late afternoons in the *majlis* (parliament) downtown [...] So he'd come in every morning, first thing I'd sit down for half an hour, and he'd talk about what he picked up. So I had a chance to be exposed to hearing Arabic and talking to him and also picked up the gossip. A nice combination." Arabic could be used to gather information for political reporting in new ways. The *majlis* is a traditional forum, analogous to a legislative body, and some governments use that term to describe their legislative bodies.

Michael E. Sterner attended sessions of the *majlis* (parliament) in Cairo. His investment paid off in a way he could not have anticipated. A young Anwar Sadat noticed Sterner in the gallery and through that means Sterner built a relationship with Sadat long before he reached prominence.[52]

Arabic skill also was concrete evidence that American diplomats were different from the British and French. Local political leaders took note, but such skill required constant practice. Seelye discovered what happened if he did not practice his Arabic: "I was assigned the unenviable task […] to inform King Faisal, then on a visit, that the US was about to give Israel surface to air Hawk missiles—the first major arms deal with Israel. I thought perhaps my fluency in Arabic would somehow temper this bad news, but of course this was not the case." Seelye recalled that in spite of the bad news, "[t]he king was very gracious," but Seelye was only the message-bearer. The king could signal his displeasure with the political message to others. But a few years later, as chargé in Jidda, Seelye was again called upon to make a presentation to King Faisal. This time he received a mild reprimand: "I had occasion a second time to visit the king on official business, and this time apparently my Arabic had begun to erode somewhat, because after I had finished making my presentation to the king, he said to me […] [in Arabic] 'Mr. Seelye, where did your Arabic go?'"[53]

Skill in any hard language is valued by those whose language has been learned, but well-spoken Arabic was more than a sign of education. Educated skill in Arabic signified cultural status in the Arab world as well. As it is the religious language of the Quran and Islam, this American use of it meant even more. Seelye found the quality of his Arabic was more notable than the content of his presentation.

Area studies, however, was not yet integral to the program. Parker recalled: "We never really did have, as I recall, a structured course in Arabic studies—politics or anything else. It always seemed to us rather hit and miss." Area experts were hard to find and Parker was not happy with the special lecturers: "[E]ither the anthropologists had discovered linguistics or the linguists had discovered anthropology—I'm not quite sure which—but the two of them were lecturing to us." One had done research on the Navajo language, but "he was not a very effective lecturer […] we didn't appreciate it." Parker met another with an equally arcane approach, "He had this three dimensional model of a culture, and what happened to you when you came in contact with it."[54]

FSI needed a metric for the program and began a testing program that rated diplomats on a four-step scale. As Crawford recalled, there were dire career implications: "We had a couple who could just not possibly learn Arabic. Because it all depends on the triconsonantal root, and unless your ear could get tuned to that, you'll never learn it, you'll never hear that right. So a couple of us really emerged with pretty close to interpreter-level Arabic."[55] Others did not. Skill ratings became part of each FSO's personnel record and factored into the promotion process. It was no longer simply completion of the program but a high-skill rating that promised promotion.

All of this was driven by Washington's fears of communist subversion in the Middle East and the drive to give American diplomats an edge over the Soviets. Ironically, at the same time the British moved in the opposite direction. They rejected area specialists in favor of generalists. A decade after abolishing the old Levant Consular Service and promoting generalists, in April 1956 London acknowledged their reforms had serious ramifications. The old rationale had been that "[e]xperts trained in the specialized services had become so very expert, had specialized so narrowly, that they had lost all balance."[56] Just months before the Suez Crisis, the British found themselves shorthanded: "The supply of officers with thoroughly expert knowledge is running out."[57] The British realized their error. The mid-level officers were gone, but London had few to take their place at a critical pass. In addition, the Americans were expanding the consulates and embassies in the region. MECAS had originally been established with the goal of "the acquisition of a living language" according to a 1944 document, but the program's organizers focused on the longer and more difficult task of training reading and grammar due to the administrative needs of empire.[58]

The American program's biggest challenge became obtaining funding, because it cost much more than the old method. One critic of the audio-lingual method examined the expense of teaching six students to a class, ten hours a week, for six months while employing a school director and a native informant, as 15 times more expensive. Although the Senate Foreign Relations Committee demanded better Arabic linguists, the House Appropriations Committee slashed FSI's budget. The roadblock was the chairman of the appropriations committee, John Rooney, who made headlines by repeatedly reducing FSI's budget from $1.2 million in 1953, to $768,451 in 1954 and $907,143 in 1955.[59]

In the spring of 1958, with Rooney's budgetary axe a looming threat once more, FSI director Harold Hoskins went on the offensive. Hoskins, accompanied by top State Department officials Christian Herter, Loy Henderson and Henry Wriston (author of the *Wriston Report*) lunched with President Eisenhower to appraise him of the situation.

A report in the *New York Times* pointed out: "Despite his obscurity, [Rooney is] one of the most powerful men in America, in a negative way, so far as US foreign policy is concerned." The *New York Times* concluded that after meeting with the FSI group, Eisenhower "was sincerely disturbed, and even angry." The president told the FSI team he was "interested" in Rooney and "offered to do something about talking to him." Ike's "hidden hand" ended Rooney's reign of budgetary terror when he dispatched Secretary of State John Foster Dulles and CIA director Allen W. Dulles to appear before Rooney's committee. They made headlines by requesting the restoration of budget cuts, although it took three hours of closed-door testimony by the head of the CIA to break the logjam.[60]

James Reston of the *New York Times* opined that when the Secretary for Defense would "ask for another billion" in funding he had no problem, "but let Mr. Dulles ask for a million to replace poorly qualified pork-barrel ambassadors with well-qualified professionals, or let him ask for a few hundred thousand to run three language schools or train his top Foreign Service officers and he is in for a protracted debate." CIA director Allen Dulles told the Senate Foreign Relations Committee of the "pressing need" to stay ahead of the Soviets in languages.[61]

Increasingly, Cold War anxiety that the Soviets were far ahead in language skills, or anything else, took precedence over the more idealistic argument that American diplomats should be able to converse with other peoples in their native tongues. It was a contest to win "the hearts and minds" of the Third World by verbal persuasion, and Washington feared America was losing. Just as the launch of Sputnik prompted National Defense Education Assistance loans for education, so Cold War fears prompted funding for Arabic studies.

A 1958 study by Dr. Menahem Mansoor of the University of Wisconsin reported, "only twenty-three American colleges and universities offer instruction in Arabic," and there were "fewer than thirty qualified instructors of Arabic in the US." That same year Dr. Ernest McCarus took over the FSI program and credited "the stimulus provided by Sputnik" with having a "far reaching and permanent effect on the character of area studies in this nation."[62] With the evidence on their side, the Dulles brothers made their Cold War strategy clear and Congress responded.

The fear that America was trailing the communists in anything caused intense anxiety in Washington. Jacob Ornstein called it "the languages race." While JFK's missile gap argument in the 1960 presidential race proved to be an exaggeration, it helped him win the presidency. But the linguist gap was not an exaggeration.

As Ornstein recalled, the evidence had begun to accumulate: "A diplomat returning from Libya [...] reported that the Russians moved into that country with a mission of fifteen Arabic–speaking diplomats. The United States mission had only one language officer, who was shortly thereafter transferred to a post outside the Arabic-speaking world." Worse yet, Ornstein noted some embassies were forced to rely upon, and trust, foreign nationals for translations: "To be so heavily dependent upon foreign translators, upon whose accuracy and reliability supervisors are often unable to check, or where sensitive materials are concerned, is obviously undesirable." The linguistic shortcomings of our ambassadors were aired in Congress and Senator Leverett Saltonstall began referring to diplomats as "[o]ur most promising overseas task force." The point was, like any task force, Middle East hands had to be supported by their government.[63]

Middle East hands saw another kind of change coming: the English- and French-speaking elite, remnants of waning imperialism, were on the decline. London's control over British Mandate Palestine had ended in 1948, and their position in the Persian Gulf waned as Arab nationalism grew. Middle East hand Earle Russell explained the political implications in the 1950s: "We need to build up good personal relationships with the new leaders of the Arab world, and to do that the Department needs men who can speak Arabic."[64]

In 1957 an FSI linguist proposed that Arabic be reclassified as a world language, like German and French, because it was the native tongue of so many persons. In fact it was the native tongue of 65,000,000 people and the religious language for 250,000,000 around the globe.[65] In the early years of the Cold War, it became clear there were important reasons for America to train Arabists. The days of the old colonial-educated Arab elite, with whom American ambassadors once amiably chatted in French and English, were numbered. In the next two decades (1957–75) the FSI program would produce a new generation of professionals.

Chapter Four

FILLING THE COLD WAR LINGUIST GAP: THE MIDDLE EAST AREA PROGRAM IN BEIRUT

The most productive years of the language-and-area training program at Beirut were between 1957 and 1975. In this period the program was expanded, received more funding and trained the majority of the Middle East hands. Foreign Service officers (FSOs) who completed the Middle East Area Program (MEAP) possessed the credential that promised career advancement to the top posts. In a frantic effort to fill the expanding need from Morocco to Iran, the Beirut school developed new methods to train specialists who would report and advise on a region deemed vital in the Cold War. Its goals were simple; as the school's director told students, after two years they would have "the ability to read newspapers and a certain modest fluency in everyday conversation."[1] Earle Russell aimed to learn enough "to talk to them in their own language," and his rationale in 1955 was simple: "The US can no longer afford to rely solely on French and English speaking contacts in the Middle East." Furthermore, Russell argued politics had changed: "The Arab states are independent and extremely touchy about anything that could be mistaken for imperialism. We need to build up good personal relationships with the new leaders of the Arab world, and to do that the Department needs men who can speak Arabic."[2]

The MEAP's new director, Dr. Ernest McCarus, developed a new curriculum based upon Modern Standard Arabic (MSA) and forged close links to the American University of Beirut (AUB) that resulted in the MEAP. The establishment of the MEAP at Beirut was central to the development of the worldview of these American diplomatic professionals. The object of the program was twofold: first, teach diplomats to speak enough Arabic to communicate and, second, provide them with area studies training so they could function effectively as political and economic reporting officers.

The Foreign Service Institute (FSI), inside Embassy Beirut, was at the center of the American diplomatic community, as well as in the city that was the commercial and financial center of the Middle East. The embassy was adjacent to the most visible symbol of American goodwill for a century: the AUB. The language students found themselves at the nexus of the intellectual, economic and political currents of the Middle East. Dr. James A. Snow, an FSI Arabic linguist and later the school's director, described its central position: "Beirut was then a transport hub—people were coming through all the time to see the current crop of students […] It also served as an informal networking process and support group." Snow saw the school as the model for language training and "for developing professionalism [...]"³ The embassy was frequently the site of regional meetings for American diplomats, and mid-career officers joined the Beirut course for refresher language training.

For the citizens of Beirut this was also a peaceful and prosperous time, one described the atmosphere as "[t]he Golden Years of Lebanon, which lasted until the end of the 1960s—a period of hope, intercommunal harmony, economic expansion and intellectual florescence."⁴

Diplomats from the course quickly became the core staff in the State Department's recently expanded division of Near East and South Asian Affairs (NEA) and served in embassies across the Middle East. Investment in Middle East specialization paid off, as Ambassador George Lane recalled: "The people who took Arabic guessed right [...] There are lots of guys [...] who never got to be ambassadors because they were in Europe. But, if you were in the Middle East, if you were an Arabist, you had a very excellent chance."⁵

This window of career opportunity opened because of the reluctance of political appointees to seek ambassadorships in the region, largely because most Middle East assignments were classified as hardship posts. Second, as the British dominance in the Persian gulf receded, a number of new US embassies opened in the newly independent nations. The British retreat from "East of Suez" was announced in 1968 just as American specialists reached the prime of their careers, as Lane recalled: "Suddenly the number of missions doubled—not just posts—but the number of embassies. So the number of openings for ambassadors went way up."⁶ A total of nine new American embassies were established and needed ambassadors.

The long-promised reward of career advancement came with increased personal risk. By the 1970s, as US policy became more closely identified with support for Israel, the Americans became enmeshed in an increasingly more anti-American climate.

The Beirut school aimed to build a foundation of language skills and area training that was to include area studies, which covered the political, economic, religious and historical background of contemporary events.

The training program shaped their worldview. It is therefore important to explore what they were taught, what they experienced, and how it shaped their careers. The State Department's hyphenated usage of the phrase, language-and-area training, signified the philosophical linkage between the two academic fields of linguistics and area studies.

The director of the program in 1958, Dr. Ernest McCarus, was part of the new group of post–World War II scholars that historian Thomas Naff argues shaped the "evolution of Middle East studies in the US" and their approach "split away from the traditional paths of Orientalism." He identified their salient traits: "They were all well-traveled, broadly educated and linguistically sophisticated [...] some being fluent in six or more languages." Naff found these linguists were mostly military veterans and came to the Middle East specialization by chance.⁷

McCarus was the ideal person to direct the MEAP for a number of reasons: he was a linguist with expertise in a number of languages, including Japanese and other "hard languages," he was a veteran of the wartime Army Specialized Training Program and he had written a textbook codifying MSA. Most importantly he was a firm believer in language immersion that would force students in a foreign environment to accelerate their learning.

Area training was expanded as both a team and individual experience. The FSI launched an eight-week "flying tour" to introduce students to a broad spectrum of Middle East leaders, with visits to commercial and industrial centers. The program's capstone was an individualized "solo flight," which forced language students to prove they could use their skills to survive, gather information and build knowledge. These trips required each student to submit a plan with specific objectives and write a report afterward detailing what they learned. Most students were well aware that they must develop significant skills if they were to function in remote posts where they might be the only American with any skill in the local language.

Dr. McCarus also had to guide his students in their pursuit of area studies at the AUB. Neither McCarus nor senior State Department staffers provided the bulk of the area studies training. This diverged from past State Department practice, as Orientalists had been trained by senior officers.

Historian Philip Baram found in his study, *The Department of State in the Middle East 1919–1945*, the earlier generation had been inculcated with the policy views of the "middle managers" in the old NEA. Soviet specialists, described by Daniel Yergin in *Shattered Peace* and Hugh de Santis in *Diplomacy of Silence*, were influenced by senior officers who ran the training program at Riga, Latvia and influenced how those specialists viewed the Soviet Union.

Unlike Sovietologists and the old Orientalists, the Beirut school's directors were linguists, but not always Arabic specialists. In the original plan Henry Lee Smith argued the school's director must be an expert in the science of language learning, but not necessarily in the specific language under study.[8] McCarus, although at work on research in Arabic and also Kurdish, began his career as an army specialist in military Japanese.

McCarus concluded his students should learn MSA first and then develop a regional dialect. He explained the blend of skills required: "MSA is a universal form of Arabic learned in schools across the Arab world, it is opposed to dialectical or colloquial Arabic of which there is a particular variety for each community and differs according to region and such social factors as religions, socioeconomic status, etc." He saw the goal for his American charges was to know both: "For a non-Arab to be said to 'know Arabic' he or she must master both MSA and any colloquial dialect." The British attempted to split the difference and meld together the colloquial forms into one "dialect" at their Middle East Area Centre for Arab Studies (MECAS), but later a MECAS student recalled critics said they had taken the 18 dialects of Arabic and created a nineteenth.[9]

But MSA promised to bridge all the differences because it was the product of Arab-language broadcasters facing the same challenge to bridge dialects. MSA emerged in the 1950s as a Middle East "Esperanto," which was understandable across the region and was often termed "radio Arabic" by Americans. Egypt's Gamal Nasser had used radio as a very effective tool for political mobilization, and it was his ability to reach across the Arab world.

American diplomats saw firsthand the power of Nasser's ability to communicate and the power of his nationalist message: Michael Sterner observed that even "in a far off place like Aden [...] you could walk from place to place in town and not miss a word [of Nasser's Voice of the Arabs broadcast] because every radio in the entire town was tuned in." Such incidents illustrated the power of Nasser's nationalist message. Sterner concluded: "One could speculate [...] this would be a tide that would affect western interests."[10]

This impelled the Beirut school into a rapid linguistic revolution of their own: to find a way to rapidly and effectively teach MSA to Americans. The British established a school high in the mountains above Beirut in Shemlan, and the Americans established theirs in the heart of downtown Beirut at AUB. Each approached the language differently because they demanded different skills from their diplomats.

The Americans focused on teaching oral communication so that US diplomats could talk to the "man in the street." The British focused on not only speaking and listening skills but reading and grammar. A 1958 British monograph on "modern written Arabic" opened with this declaration: "As the fundamental grammar of written Arabic has hardly changed at all during the last thirteen centuries [...]"[11] Yet in those same years the United States scrambled to cope with a revolution expressed in language and driven by linguistic as well as political change.

The first published studies of "radio Arabic" were done by the first FSI Beirut director, Charles A. Ferguson and his students. They examined Nasser's means of communicating with (and appealing to) various Egyptian social classes.[12] Later Ernest McCarus wrote texts on Arabic, both MSA and Kurdish dialects, and produced a series of textbooks for the school. James A. Snow, under his tutelage, defined MSA grammar for English speakers in an FSI guide, *Modern Written Arabic*, and later became the school's director.[13] The American objective was to deal with the Middle East in contemporary terms, not Orientalist terms, and meet the demands of using Arabic in the field.

McCarus forged closer ties with the AUB so that students could attend courses at the university and use its library. Language classes were conducted in the morning at the embassy, and then the FSOs walked to the nearby AUB campus for afternoon area studies classes separate from the regular AUB student body.[14]

McCarus also viewed Arabic proverbs as a useful means to teach cultural values and to explore social attitudes. As Dr. Ferguson had done earlier, McCarus continued to use Arabic proverbs to develop an understanding of culture and language. FSOs were taught to memorize and research the literal and figurative meanings of proverbs. George Lane recalled, "It's just like learning poetry in some other language or songs, and a wonderful way to learn something about the culture."[15]

The entire modus vivendi of the MEAP was to teach Arabic to working diplomats so they would no longer be what a critic had termed "our soundproofed representatives." There were important reasons for developing such skill. Knowing Arabic gave American diplomats broader access to the people of the region and a sense of control over their surroundings. It helped them to gather information, monitor translations, safeguard themselves in dangerous situations and see that the intent of their message was accurately communicated.

Arabic was a safeguard for a diplomat in the field, and there could be tragic implications for those without such skills. Secretary of State Henry Kissinger selected Francis Meloy, a skilled diplomatic, but a non-Arabist, as ambassador to Lebanon in July 1976.

Meloy had a reputation for dealing well with tough situations and had just come from posts in the Dominican Republic and Guatemala. He arrived in a Beirut riven by civil war and divided by the Green Line, a de facto separation between warring factions. Shortly after a contentious presidential election Kissinger urged Meloy to "show the flag" by delivering his credentials to the newly elected Lebanese leader, Sarkis, rather than the current office holder. On his mission Meloy, his aide Robert Waring, and their driver were taken hostage and murdered. Kissinger recalled "Meloy's death hit me hard. Not only had I sent him on the mission that cost him his life, I also felt personally responsible for assigning him to Lebanon in the first place."[16]

During the subsequent investigation Waring's successor, Middle East hand Talcott Seelye, found that the embassy had a communications link between the driver and the backup security car. The second car had been waved off by the driver, in Arabic, as it approached the dividing line, allowing Meloy to continue without guards. The ambassador's car disappeared shortly beyond the crossing. Seelye concluded that had Meloy spoken Arabic, he would have understood that his security detail had been dismissed and might have been able to deal with the situation: "Meloy did not know a word of Arabic—it was a great mistake to send somebody out, particularly at a critical time, who did not know the language."[17]

Working in the Middle East built a practical awareness of the risks and disabused them of any romantic visions of the region. Middle East hand William Brewer: "The fact of the matter is that many of us Arabists have reason to mistrust the Arabs more than other Americans because we have served among them. Some of us have been mistreated by them."[18] Brewer pointed out that some had careers damaged when Arab leaders requested they be recalled to protest US policy. Moreover, as attacks on American diplomats increased their fellow Middle East hands who had to step into crisis situations. Brewer replaced two colleagues assassinated in the Sudan. Talcott Seelye stepped into a similar situation in Beirut followed by Richard Parker and George Lane. William R. Crawford replaced Ambassador Rodger Davies who had been murdered inside the US Embassy in Cyprus in 1974. Brewer pointed out their goal was to protect "US interests in that part of the world."[19]

Even while at the school they were enmeshed in crises. Michael E. Sterner arrived in the fall of 1958 just after the US Marines landed to stop the civil war, and he and his fellow diplomats in the Beirut school were sent out to gather information for the embassy: "The students had an opportunity to look into the causes of the conflict, to talk with the Lebanese in a way that political officers could not [...] we were constantly meeting with the political officers because we were a resource that they could draw on."[20]

Although Arabists have been stereotyped as ignorant of Israel and Israeli interests, it is important to understand that the program introduce them to the entire Middle East, not just the Arab world. Sterner described his visit to Israel: "We met people who were genuinely warm and hospitable, and, of course, we got an exposure to the other point of view. Certainly we came away with the impression that Israel was an extraordinarily vibrant, and in those days, a very strong place. There was enormous conviction that they were a frontier land and it was imbued with idealism [...] although lasting only two weeks, also had a good deal of impact."[21]

During his career Sterner spent considerable time working in Israel during peace negotiations to implement the Sinai II Disengagement agreement.

Israel became, in the words of one MEAP trainee, "almost required" as a solo travel destination. Charles Cecil visited two kibbutzim and spent more than a week on his own in Israel.[22]

There was also a more formal immersion program, known as "the family stay," which forced students to live in an Arabic-only environment.

There was also an FSI field trip, which was an eight-week seminar on Middle East issues, conducted as a teaching tour of the region. In 1959 the group spent a week in Israel. For a few promising Arabists, special arrangements were made for more advanced language training. Ambassador Richard W. Murphy spent his last weeks of immersion in a Syrian village to prepare him for a post in Damascus: "I was very lucky because I went straight from living in a mountain village in Lebanon for the last two months of the course to living in the northern Syrian center in Aleppo—where Arabic was the most widely spoken language [...] So I was immersed in it, and it really was not a matter of choice."[23] These trips were not vacations and being immersed in the region might pose significant risks, as some students found out.

During an extended journey in remote mountain regions of Lebanon, Earle Russell was arrested on the suspicion of being an Israeli spy. He had chosen to travel by donkey through the mountains and rode into a village, Qornayel, carrying two cameras, which aroused the suspicions of local officials. They took him into custody where he was faced with the challenge of explaining his way out of the tangle in Arabic to a group of non-English speakers. They were in no rush to call his embassy and questioned his claim to being a diplomat: "You say that you are an American diplomat. But what American, let alone a diplomat, rides around the country on a donkey?" When the man in charge contacted Lebanese security, he archly concluded his list of his suspicions: "And, he speaks Arabic."[24]

Earle Russell was the epitome of the so-called shirt sleeve diplomat. He was a World War II veteran, skilled at languages, with degrees from the University of Michigan and George Washington University. After posts in Addis Ababa and Tunis he and his wife were sent to the FSI Beirut School, and featured in the *Saturday Evening Post* article, "We Love the Foreign Service Life." His wife Beatrice wrote a memoir of their experiences *Living in State* in 1956, which related their adventures in remote posts throughout the Middle East and North Africa. Their goal was, in her words, to support US foreign policy as it was "engaged in the much more complicated struggle for men's minds."[25]

Russell, sometimes with his wife, traveled on long journeys into remote areas to gather information for his embassy: in Ethiopia they undertook a 1,200-mile trip, in Beirut he attempted the donkey-back journey and made another trip around Tunis. After a few brushes with terrorism in Tunis, his wife wrote that such events "remind us that our American passport is no guarantee of safety."[26]

In 1971 Earle Russell was on duty in Morocco when he received notice of his promotion to deputy chief of mission in the embassy at Senegal. Russell decided to make the 2,567-mile journey to Dakar by car across the Western Sahara. He and his family did not arrive when expected. Eight days later their car, which had broken down, was spotted by an aerial search team. All survived except Earle, who died trying to save them.[27]

Richard Parker recalled, "We were stunned. Earl was so strong and experienced in outback travel that we had not thought to question the wisdom of his travel plans."[28] Only a few years earlier in 1966, Edward Peck, a self-described "experienced Sahara traveler" took off from Oran, Algeria, across the Sahara by following a track rather than a road and using his Arabic to ask for directions. He could discuss conditions and request information, but along the way Peck's car cracked an oil pan. He was picked up by a passing truck loaded down with US AID wheat. The villagers offered to use human power to unload the wheat and to put the car onto the truckbed, if the Americans promised to leave the wheat shipment in their village. The deal was struck; the villagers unloaded the wheat, and Peck's sedan was trucked back to the consulate. He later recalled the elation of the locals who saw him off "cheering loudly and repetitively in Arabic and French, thanking America, still waving until lost to view." Despite the happy outcome for everyone in the village, there were other upheavals during his tour at Oran. The event included: "nine different mob demonstrations outside the offices and residence, evacuation of all other Americans, temporarily running our nation's only one-man post, and flying the only in-country American flag."[29] Peck became a lonely holdout in Oran.

Training Arabists was not just a matter of offering lectures in a sterile classroom. Their experiences forced them to manage the pressures and risks inherent in working in the field. Ambassador Richard B. Parker pointed to the demands of modern diplomacy: "We're not in an academic environment, we are in an operational environment, and the considerations we have to take into account are essentially political and economic and not academic."[30] Parker developed useful skills, like the ability to translate radio broadcasts from Arabic that might be the only means for an embassy to quickly get vital information. Andrew I. Killgore observed that even in Washington there were intense pressures on a desk officer: "Hell, they [Arabists] don't have time to be scholarly—things are coming at you from all directions."[31]

The ability to read Arabic was valued, but one that took enormous time and effort to develop. It might take more than two additional years. Eventually most MEAP students could skim the headlines and pull out the facts. Instructors handed out newspapers and gave students five minutes to summarize the headlines or played tapes of radio broadcasts and required students to translate the gist of the message.[32]

The State Department did make a major investment in training at least one Middle East hand in advanced skills, and his case illustrates how important and also how rare such skill became. William Rugh made the political analysis of Arab journalism his work. Rugh was allowed to pursue his studies through to a doctorate after he completed his training at Beirut in 1964. He earned a master's degree from Johns Hopkins University and a doctorate from Columbia in 1967. His two major works, *Arab Perceptions of American Foreign Policy during the October War* and *The Arab Press: News Media and Political Process in the Arab World* examined Middle Eastern perceptions of, and reaction to, American foreign policy.[33]

In *The Arab Press* Rugh observed there are 18 separate nations in the region and the Arab press reflected that complexity. The media in each state "respond[s] in many ways to their environment [...] [it] can only be understood in terms of the economic conditions, cultural milieu and political realities of the societies they serve." Rugh analyzed both the way in which local news was reported and how American policy was transmitted through the Arab media.

The Middle East hands were focused on the political complexities within the region and could be called "regionalists," with their perspective on foreign policy shaped by their highly specialized area knowledge. The regionalist approach stressed the need to understand the differences between Arab states and to understand the unique political situation in each.

Rather than assume a homogeneous "Arab mind," Rugh concluded the Arab media "varies considerably from country to country." He cautioned that "neither the media nor their environments can be understood properly without reference to the other." Rugh illustrated his point by citing news reports of the *same* discussion at an Organization of African Unity meeting, drawn from three different Arab news services: in Morocco, the headline was, "We must control our resources to liberate Africa"; in the Sudan, "Soviets congratulate Sudan"; and in Algeria, "New Step to Liberate Palestine."[34]

It is important to understand why the United States was willing to invest the time to train a small subset of Middle East hands to the highest level. They needed a few diplomats who could analyze Arab reactions to US policy through an understanding of the nuances of language but could not invest so much time in training for all of them.[35]

In a subsequent study of the role of Arabists as Public Affairs officers, in *American Encounters with Arabs*, Rugh described the impact of "soft power" through Fulbright exchange visits, Arabic broadcasts of the Voice of America and public diplomacy.[36]

In times of crisis expertise was vitally important. Rugh's examination of the October War in 1973 concluded "The Arabs saw the US as having a strong pro-Israeli bias," and the Arab press reaction revealed a "deep suspicion" about American motives. He observed that the Arab press underestimated the importance of the US–Soviet Cold War conflict and instead "saw all of these American moves as calculated only to help their Israeli enemy, not as part of the American global strategy [...] intended to prevent WWIII." Rugh pointed out that American motives were not well understood by Arabs and "fluctuate[d] considerably [...] a changing mix of positive and negative elements" but concluded that Cairo's leadership "set the tone." Rugh concluded American motives were not well understood by Arabs, and American intentions were very different from Arab perceptions of them.[37]

While in Tunisia, Talcott Seelye opened the paper to find his photograph prominently displayed, while he "wondered what I was doing on the front page," he noticed the Arabic caption: "Giscard d'Estaing." Seelye figured the paper had confused the file photos while announcing the French president's visit to Tunis, but reflected: "I wonder to this day if the French knew about it, because they didn't read Arabic."[38] Fortunately that situation was more comic rather than tragic.

In 1967 a group of Arabists wrote a memo critiquing the program and summarizing its limited accomplishments over two decades: "Of approximately 120 officers trained by FSI in Arabic since the early 1950s, only 10 of us have been test-rated at the S-4/R-4 level, only 7 at the 4 level in one or the other; and only 33 at even the 3–3 level—a total of 50 out of 120 who have ever reached or exceeded the minimum level of usable language competence." When the Cold War "thawed" a bit in 1986, the Russians allowed a State Department delegation to visit their language school and the Americans found the USSR's investment went far beyond what Washington had ever made.[39]

Life in Beirut, at first idyllic and later tragic, shaped the Middle East hands into a group with a strong sense of pride in their hard-won skill and service to their country. The program became a rite of passage, which set them apart from others with pretensions of Middle East area expertise. It also placed them in the center of the volatile Arab–Israeli conflict and waves of anti-American violence.

The Golden Era: Area Studies at Beirut 1957–75

The most dramatic change in this era was the expansion of the area studies component during the Cold War. Only fragmentary details of the program on the campus of the AUB have survived, but something of its approach can be extrapolated from studying the program's instructors and their contemporary writings.

The goal was to develop a sophisticated understanding of the region. For this the Beirut school drew upon well-known scholars from America and the AUB. The AUB was a microcosm of the Arab world. Its undergraduates were drawn from across the Middle East, included Christian and Muslim students, and women comprised nearly a quarter of students. More importantly, their politics reflected the increasingly militant, often leftist or Marxist, political viewpoint of a generation that had grown up listening to Nasser's nationalist message.[40]

AUB had been founded a century earlier by American missionaries to educate Arab youth. The university's motto, "So that they may have life and have it more fully," embodies that goal. It was established to inculcate American democratic and capitalistic values in the Arab world and to build up a wealth of goodwill. Wilsonian idealism, in particular his phrase self-determination, was a key part of this message. American policy makers were increasingly viewed by AUB students as having abandoned Wilsonian ideals. The AUB faculty struggled with the gulf between the ideals it promoted and the reality of American Cold War foreign policy. Americans, whether diplomats or educators, found themselves in a defensive mode.

Most AUB professors were sympathetic to Arab nationalists; however, most represented an older, more conservative generation, who advocated a moderate nationalism. They had often completed their graduate studies in the United States and developed close ties within the American academic community. After the Six Day War in 1967 and the prominence of the American role in Vietnam, AUB students were increasingly alienated by American foreign policy.

Hisham Shirabi recalled that when he was an undergraduate in the 1940s AUB was populated by wealthy, youthful Arab elites "devoid of critical thought about whatever we read." Shirabi began his own political transformation during his graduate studies at the University of Chicago in 1948 and returned to AUB in 1970 as a visiting lecturer. He found that senior faculty were critical of his Marxist views, and they were shocked when he referred to "the post-Christian era."[41]

Lebanon was destabilized as the refugee camps were once again flooded by Palestinians after the 1967 war and again following the 1970 Black September uprising in Jordan. The tenuous demographic and political balance in Lebanon collapsed, and Beirut became a dangerous place rather than the "Switzerland of the Middle East" as it had once been advertised.

In the late 1950s Beirut was a cosmopolitan center for the Americans to explore, the AUB's faculty was composed of the most noted Arab intellectuals and its five libraries housed the region's largest collection of English and Arabic materials. Richard Murphy attended the AUB where a variety of area studies courses offered: "Everyone I knew gravitated, certainly, towards Near East history, that was where you had some very good—the best—professors."[42]

Courses in Middle Eastern history, politics and religion were organized by American and Arab professors, such as Malcolm Kerr, Zeine N. Zeine, Nicola Ziadeh, Nabih Faris, Constantine Zurayk and others to build the area studies program.[43] After completing the MEAP's introductory survey, the FSOs were free to select other courses. In 1960 the program included historical lectures by Nabih Faris on the Quran, Nicola Zayidi on "Basic Concepts of Islam," Kamal Salibi on "Islam and Christendom during Medieval Times," Zeine on the Ottoman Empire and another Faris course on "The Arab Awakening."[44]

The diplomats of this era were allowed to plan their own course of study. By the 1960s the goal was to use area studies to achieve a more thorough and practical knowledge of the Middle East. Beirut offered a special opportunity to learn the language and travel throughout the entire region from a central base: they could easily travel into Syria, Israel, Jordan, Iraq, Egypt and the Gulf with a concomitant exposure to a variety of nations with divergent interests.

Journalist Robert Kaplan has portrayed the AUB's increasingly radical atmosphere after the Six Day War as the product of the AUB's administrators, concluding: "But, in a way, they had it coming to them. By openly encouraging Arab nationalism and seeking a student body not just from Greater Syria, but from all over the Arab world, they had over the decades unwittingly made the AUB a battleground for Arab politics [...]"[45]

The AUB community, and its student body, was evolving in these decades. But its faculty's commitment to democratic values and free speech left them little choice but to tolerate its expression. War and the presence of large numbers of refugees, further radicalized the student body. Many of its students were from families that had been made refugees by war. Their lives and livelihoods were so disrupted in 1967 that the school had to forgive some indebtedness for tuition. Rather than a school for radicals, the AUB was pro-Western in orientation and struggling to weather the turmoil. Many professors were viewed by their own students as excessively accommodationist or insufficiently radical.[46]

As for course content, the MEAP dealt with Islamic and Ottoman history with a focus on modern politics.[47] Instructors represented the moderate wing of Arabism and Arab nationalism, although many had been the leading Arab nationalist thinkers of an earlier generation. While some were Christian and others Muslim, those who studied Islam did not espouse fundamentalism or political Islam as it developed in later decades. Moreover, even those who made a career of studying Islam were often Christian Arabs.

Some faculty were Americans, for example, Malcolm H. Kerr, the son of two American professors at AUB and a Presbyterian educated at Princeton and Harvard. His research focused on contemporary Middle East politics and Classical Arabic. In sum, the MEAP staff was a complex blend, decidedly friendly to America but not necessarily in sympathy with American foreign policy.

How did the faculty view the US role in the Middle East? Almost all of them had been trained in American graduate schools and had lived in the United States for at least a part of their lives. Most had vivid memories of the conflict over the British Mandate in Palestine and the founding of Israel. Perhaps their one common principal was a belief in Arab nationalism and also the power of modernization. The remainder of their beliefs regarding the role of Islam and their historical interpretations of Arabism were diverse.

One professor in the MEAP, Zeine N. Zeine, instructed Americans in the history of the Ottoman Empire. Zeine did not regard the Turkish Ottoman influence over the Arabs as completely negative but instead examined the counterinfluence of Arabism and Islam upon the Turks. In *The Emergence of Arab Nationalism*, he stated, "The principal theme of this study [...] [is] that Arab nationalism in its genesis and growth has been inseparable from Islam."[48] In his view Islam was a force that remained strong despite Ottoman control over the Levant. Zeine debunked the prevalent view that Arabs suffered under the Ottomans for four centuries, but instead argued "Ottoman rule protected the Arab world and Islam from foreign rule and encroachments for nearly four hundred years." He also cautioned his readers not to ignore the role of Islam. His auditors might have taken from this course an awareness that Islam had "gone underground" in the Ottoman period, but remained a powerful, unifying social force.

Zeine pointed out that Arab civilization was not extinguished by its occupiers, and language was "their most cherished and precious heritage, after Islam." He also argued that language had Arabized the Turks, who adopted Islamic Shariah law and consequently its language. Islamic universities trained the Ottomans in Islamic law and eventually the sultanate adopted Arabic names and its battle flags bore Islamic mottos. For Zeine what bound the Ottoman Empire together "was undoubtedly Islam."[49] The Islamic dimension of Zeine's argument would have made clear to FSOs the potential power of Islam. For Zeine, Arab nationalism began in the seventh century, not the twentieth, and was rooted in the rise of Islam. He rejected the splintering of nationalism and secularization, but found "dynamism" in Islam, a power upon which Arabs must rely, in time of "spiritual crisis."[50] From a historical viewpoint, according to Zeine, whenever the Arab world was severely challenged, its response had been an Islamic resurgence. FSO Charles Cecil commented that even in 1995 Middle East hands needed to understand that "[t]he Quaranic arguments being used by fundamentalist leaders [...] so that we can reply to them."[51] Rather than creating "Islamophiles," the MEAP raised their awareness of the political trends that would become powerful, dangerous forces during their careers.

Nabih Amin Faris, another MEAP instructor, was educated in the West and worked as Princeton University's curator of Arabic manuscripts until he joined the American Office of War Information during World War II. Afterward he became a professor of Arab history at AUB.[52] Like Zeine, Nabih Faris drew connections from the Islamic past to Arab nationalism and saw "the Islamic idea" as more powerful than "the Arab element" in politics and society. Faris focused his research on the Arab Revolt during World War I. In a 1957 essay, Faris pointed to fragmentation after the war as the primary weakness in the Arab world but laid the blame for their subsequent problems in both "the work of imperialists" and "the Arabs themselves." Rather than excuse the Arabs and blame the West entirely, Faris stressed internal Arab political weakness and the power of Islam as factors in their political decline.

The emphasis on area studies built a regional perspective that clashed with the global perspective that prevailed in Washington. Bipolar Cold War axioms, which placed the Soviets as the inspiration for any number of Middle East events, were too simplistic to entirely explain regional events. Middle East hands understood the historical forces behind events, but, unfortunately, policy makers like John Foster Dulles, Dwight Eisenhower, Richard Nixon and Henry Kissinger viewed the Middle East as a chessboard where Moscow moved its Arab pawns.

As early as 1946, Faris had called for the formation of "a United Arab States" to link the Arab world into a powerful combination. In the wake of the Suez Crisis, Faris felt that "[t]he setbacks suffered by the Arab world would not have taken place if it had been united." Nasser had tried but failed to unify the Arab nations, but Faris argued that unity remained their "ultimate hope." Faris felt neither the West nor religion would save the Arab world, but a very broad nationalism would prevent what he termed the "'Balkanizing' of the Arab World." In 1957 he argued that the challenge came from "the imperialists and Israel," but he remained deeply pessimistic. Creating that broad unity was only "a remote prospect." Faris's AUB colleague Malcolm Kerr dissected how that experiment failed when Nasser attempted to create the United Arab Republic in *The Arab Cold War*.[53]

Perhaps the most famous and intellectually influential AUB professor was Constantine Zurayk, who lectured on the role of Islam in the Arab world. Dr. Zurayk, born in 1909 Damascus, was a Greek Orthodox scholar with a master's degree from the University of Chicago and a doctorate from Princeton. He had taught at AUB before World War II and then served as the Syrian representative to the United States and to the United Nations. After abandoning his diplomatic career, he returned to teaching, and he was appointed as AUB's president from 1954–57. Zurayk struggled to hold the AUB together in a time of conflict. He recognized parallels between American unrest over Vietnam and "[t]he deep-seated and sweeping rebellion in the minds and hearts of Arab youth," which divided his campus. Like many American college presidents, Zurayk found his own students had rebelled against political injustices and against their professors as well.[54]

Zurayk carefully blended Christian and Muslim references in his addresses to the student body and over time made Islamic references much more overt. His addresses reveal a certain intellectual pattern in his approach to the religiously mixed student body located in a nation with eight major confessional bodies and numerous sects. As a minister might, he always opened his discussion with a quotation from the Bible, then added a reference from the Quran. In 1955 his graduation address began with a quotation from Corinthians; he continued with the Quran's Surah 33, "The Allies" and closed with Walt Whitman.[55] His eclecticism reflects the mix of religions and ideologies on the AUB campus and within Lebanon.

Zurayk was perhaps the most blunt and clear-minded critic of Arab failures in the 1948 Arab–Israeli war. His best-known work, *The Meaning of the Disaster* or *Ma'na al-Nakbah*, was written after the war to explain why the Arabs were defeated. Zurayk defended their claim to Palestine, but laid the blame directly upon the Arabs themselves, in particular their leadership. After the Six Day War in 1967 he wrote a similar analysis, but by then his Arab audience was less willing to accept the critique.[56]

Zurayk made no excuses for the Arabs, which was an increasingly unpopular stance. Many older faculty faced that dilemma, as younger Arab intellectuals were alienated by US actions.

The Middle East hands were trained by the Arab intellectuals who had pointed out Arab failings and who had not heaped all of the blame on the West. The strongest formative factor in shaping their outlook was the area studies program. They were also exposed to escalating anti-US hostility. On the fringes of Beirut were the Sabra and Shatila Palestinian refugee camps and the lush downtown was surrounded by rapidly growing slums filled with the poor. Palestinians were a visible presence in Jordan and the West Bank where reporting on the camp conditions was a part of some FSOs' duties.[57]

Middle East hands did not hold the United States responsible for the plight of the Palestinians, and many have observed that Palestinian leadership repeatedly failed to effectively make their case. Middle East hands recognized Palestinian failings, as Michael Sterner observed: "I thought the Arabs were plenty responsible for their own failings, in many ways quite aside from American policy [...] There is much more that Arab leadership could have done for themselves." When the Near East training tour visited Cairo, George Lane witnessed the plight of the refugees: "The really sad thing about the refugees is not so much their physical surroundings or diet [...] but their psychological situation. They are constantly being told that it's only a matter of time before they can return to their old homes, while in fact I see no possibility that any more than a token number will be taken back by the Israelis, and then only if they agree to go and colonize the central Negev." Lane cited the Palestinians' failure to create political institutions: "The Arabs totally misplayed their hand, they refused to compromise when they could have, and they could have created a Palestinian state anytime between 1956 and 1967. But they didn't—they allowed Jordan to annex the West Bank."[58]

Arab failings, in particular their political and military unpreparedness, had led to neglect in prosecuting their case through the Arab League, the Arab Office and other organizations. Professor Zurayk recognized the Arabs had a just cause in their claim to Palestine, but felt they lacked a sense of nationalism, unity and progress. Without the will to modernize, abandon feudalism and separate religious organizations from the state, then resistance to Zionism would fail. He noted the Arabs had already had their "awakening," but failed the test. Moreover he recognized the tactics used to resist the British as the mandatory power were ineffective when confronting "a group which believes in its right to the country" and had mobilized world opinion on its side.[59]

For Zurayk and many Arab nationalists, Islam was recognized as an integral part of the region, but they sought first and foremost to modernize society. This required a separation of the religious from the national, and to emphasize "the positive and empirical sciences," which would turn Arabs away from what Zurayk termed the "benumbing fancy and insubstantial romanticism."[60]

Zurayk was not a radical, but instead a pro-Western nationalist in a time when leftist Marxism was the dominant trend. He cautioned against an Islamist theocracy, but in fact over the next decades many secular states would find themselves challenged by the unifying power of Islam. Even conservative Islamic states like Saudi Arabia, Bahrain and Kuwait were challenged from within by fundamentalist elements. The Middle East hands who heard Zurayk's arguments understood the complexity of a culture where politics and religion were intertwined.

Zurayk had pessimistically prophesied in 1948: "Even if we succeed in establishing a united state [...] one day we will wake up and, lo! all of Palestine will be in the hands of the energetic, militant Zionist minority [...] if we should fail and partition should become a reality [...] we shall fall easy prey to the expansionist Zionist power." It was the Israeli determination and energy that he recognized as the defining factor in their success in establishing a state.[61]

It is important to remember the AUB faculty, especially those working with the MEAP students, represented the first generation of Arab nationalists, and by the 1960s their views were often rejected by a younger Arab generation who increasingly supported emergent radical elements. Harold Hoskins, a State Department administrator and the son of missionaries, commented in 1956 that American missionary efforts at AUB might have unexpected results: "We cannot claim that our educational efforts have created only pro-American sentiment [...] They use the freedom of speech that we advocate to criticize the US freely."[62]

Radicalism grew in the refugee camps inside Lebanon and Jordan. George Habash, a Lebanese Christian, began life in the refugee camps, was educated as a physician in the AUB medical school, but was radicalized by the string of Arab defeats. He abandoned medicine, adopted Marxism, and founded the radical terror group, the Popular Front for the Liberation of Palestine.

Malcolm Kerr symbolized all of the good hopes of the AUB effort, and also its links to America and academia. His fate in many ways paralleled that of the Middle East hands. Kerr taught political science at the AUB and in the MEAP. He later became a professor at UCLA Berkeley and director of the Gruenbaum Center for Near East Studies. He increasingly turned his attention toward American foreign policy and authored a Rand Corporation study on Middle East policy.

Kerr suffered the consequences of being drawn into the Middle East conflict when he was appointed as personal adviser to President Carter for Middle East issues; his wife recalled that "extremist members of the California Jewish Defense League [...] set fire to our car one night" outside their California home.[63] It would not be their last encounter with violence.

Kerr remains the most intellectually accessible of the MEAP instructors because he wrote about US foreign policy from an American perspective. The Middle East hands, as professional diplomats, did not publicly critique American policy, and to survive in the Foreign Service they had to support American policy whether or not they saw it as wise. But Kerr, as a scholar and analyst of American policy, can be understood as sharing similar experiences in the region and intellectually akin to the Middle East hands. If the Middle East hands were free to critique American foreign policy, then they might have expressed similar opinions.

Kerr described the 1860s as a time characterized by "[t]he disintegration of political and social authority in the northern half of Lebanon," which brought the end of feudalism. Kerr irreverently assessed the diary (and its author) as writing with "a semi-literate mixture of Lebanese colloquial and formal literary language, full of bad grammar and spelling." But he used the text as the starting point for a serious discussion of the roots of sectarian conflict from the perspective of a Lebanese, which also considered the impact of the British and French maneuvering.[64]

His work was a good background for his subsequent examination of Lebanon's twentieth-century disintegration. His knowledge of the complexities behind Lebanese politics was passed to his FSO students, and they would also learn from his decades of expertise.

Journalist Robert Kaplan compared Kerr's knowledge of Arabic to that of Jerry Weaver, an amateur Arabist whom Kaplan argues "never formally studied Arabic, but he picked it up [...] [and could] communicate with Arabs as well as Malcolm Kerr could."[65] Hardly. Kaplan casually rationalizes how easily such skill might be "picked up." One of Kerr's fellow students at Princeton University, Charles Issawi, recalled when Kerr arrived as an undergraduate his command of Classical Arabic was so advanced Princeton assigned him to the doctoral-level course. Although he had lived in the region, Kerr developed his skills over years of graduate training and research. As the Middle East hands' experience at Beirut illustrates, such expertise came at great cost. It took years to earn their credentials and more work to maintain them.

Kerr's task, as an academic, was to make Middle East events comprehensible to the students he trained and to the Washington politicians he sometimes advised. That was the task faced by the Middle East hands—to make complex events comprehensible to policymakers. This was complicated by the fact that most officials in Washington knew little about the region and often did not wish to deal with its complexities.

Middle East hand William Crawford observed that their training and area experience together combined to provide them with a claim to bureaucratic legitimacy. Crawford recalled: "[I] had a degree of expertise which was unchallengeable by anybody in the NSC.." He had served as a political reporting officer in a number of posts, then was ambassador to Cyprus and later Yemen. He concluded: "Nobody [in Washington] was going to be a specialist in Yemen and nobody else had that degree of Cyprus experience that I had."[66]

But their area expertise was not always appreciated. Secretary of State Henry Kissinger told aides he could not understand the reports from Beirut. President Richard Nixon appointed L. Dean Brown, a State Department generalist, as ambassador to Lebanon. Brown recalled Nixon and Kissinger's opinion of area specialists: "They don't understand a word of it [Arabist reporting]." For the two policymakers, according to Brown: "It's all too long and too complicated." Nixon told Brown what kind of reporting he wanted from Beirut: "Keep me informed" but with the modifier "I don't want that State Department garbage."[67]

While Kerr understood the complex roots of modern sectarianism, he sometimes had to use analogies to explain it. Kerr's study of the Beirut elections in 1960 clearly explained why Lebanon was inherently volatile: "lacking the safety-valve of a wider national political scene, political life goes on in a parochial atmosphere and the full attention of politically-minded persons is directed to affairs which are necessarily local." The nation's population was comparable in size to some American cities: "Lebanon in this sense is a Brooklyn or a Baltimore cut off from the US, with its own armed forces and its own seat in the UN, a hothouse of local issues without even the ventilating currents of New York City, let alone Washington."[68] A decade later Kerr remained pessimistic: "Since WWII, there have been some seven civil and international wars, twenty forcible overthrows of government, half a dozen assassinations of heads of government, and a constant drumfire of more petty violence."[69]

He found the volatility in the Palestinian refugee camps analogous to African American unrest in America. And, like black anger, which had exploded in rioting that year, "Israel, to the Arab radical, is Alabama and South Africa and the Chicago slum rolled into one. And we liberals, who say we want to help [...] we are the Mayor Richard Daleys." While this was written 20 years before the first Intifada or Palestinian uprising, there are distinct parallels. Kerr had warned there was an intense and increasing anger toward both Israel and the United States, which would boil over, as he concluded "more diplomatic difficulties" were on the way.[70]

Moreover, Kerr argued that the continuation of the Arab–Israeli conflict and the status quo of the refugees would lead to renewed conflict. In a 1969 RAND study, he argued these problems were of "a long-term nature" and they "bear the imprint of June 1967." The result was, according to Kerr, "The exacerbation rather than the amelioration of the strife."[71] In other words, unless the Arab–Israeli conflict, and the issue of the occupied territories, was not defused then conflict would reignite. Only a few months later, the War of Attrition between Egypt and Israel began and less than three years later the October War.

In his 1972 presidential address to the Middle East Studies Association, Kerr chose as the topic "The West and the Middle East: The Light and the Shadow." Kerr assessed how decades of Western influence had negatively affected the development of the Middle East, the intensification of anti-Americanism, the crisis of US foreign policy and the targeting of Americans for vengeance.

Malcolm Kerr drew his theme from Arnold Toynbee's observation that a shadow is cast by the West over the developing world and that the West is rarely conscious of the impact it has on those nations. Kerr asked his audience to consider "has the progress of an autonomous civilization been blocked by the western impingement?" Would "the challenge of the west" be viewed as a threat? He drew a balance sheet on the impact of the positives and negatives the West had brought to the region during the Cold War: "sound finances and improved irrigation and the Suez assault in Egypt, the unification of Jerusalem and the demolition of Arab homes in Palestine and USIS Libraries and PL 480 and Phantom aircraft." He closed with a reference to Toynbee: "This being the picture, should not we turn our head and move out of the light before our victims 'stagger to their feet and stab us in the back?'"[72]

Kerr saw how good intentions had failed to bring about the desired results. He questioned the fundamental assumptions upon which postwar US policy had been based and pointed out how badly the US position had eroded. Many Arabs were radicalized and the target of their anger was America.

Exactly one month to the day after his address, Middle East hands Cleo Noel and George Moore (the US ambassador and his deputy chief of mission at Khartoum) were taken hostage and murdered by Palestinians intent on avenging Israeli and US actions during the Jordanian civil war. However, Middle East hands had known all along that the Palestinian refugee issue would one day explode, and had repeatedly advised Washington to defuse it. Kerr had also feared that the United States was becoming a lightning rod for Arab anger. Those inside the State Department, however, found making their voices heard difficult and that dissent was risky.

Kerr argued that Nixon should work toward peace in his second term and urgently warned of an oil embargo. Kerr cited the warning of US vulnerability given months before by Middle East hand James Akins: "[He] and others are well aware of the rising bargaining strength and skill of OPEC." Akins's concerns had been brushed aside, yet a few months later OPEC launched the oil embargo.[73]

In 1980 Kerr explained the dilemma in which many Middle East hands found themselves. In his book *America's Middle East Policy: Kissinger, Carter and the Future*, he argued the US view of the Middle East was skewed by a clash between regionalists and globalists. Kerr identified the regionalist view with George Ball and other State Department officials who looked at the local causes of conflict. What might be called the globalist or Cold Warriors' school of thought viewed events through the Cold War "balance of power" model, as did President Eisenhower, his Secretary of State John Foster Dulles, as well as President Nixon and his National Security Adviser (and later President Gerald Ford's Secretary of State) Henry Kissinger. Kerr argued Washington was not likely to factor in the regionalists' concerns because the Cold War generated "unacceptable levels of controversy and confusion," which forced each President to turn "back (with or without much conviction) toward the conventional wisdom."[74] But this stalled any hope for resolution of the conflict.

Moreover Kerr argued Washington should make a realistic assessment of the price of not pushing peace negotiations forward. He pointed out, as would many Middle East hands, American interests had already suffered: "Far from getting a free ride from the Arabs [...] [America] has been paying heavily for the unresolved conflict in many large and small ways."

Kerr summarized the consequences: "The radicalization of half a dozen Arab regimes, the strengthening of their ties with Moscow, and their hostility to the US; the destruction of Lebanon; the suspiciousness and resentment of a whole generation of Arab intellectuals." Moreover other allies had distanced themselves: "The reluctance of US friends [...] to cooperate in regional defense planning; the boycott of a large number of American firms; the continuing risk to which American commercial interests and oil supplies are exposed; and the expenditure during the past decade alone of some $20 billion in military and civilian aid to Israel and Egypt."[75]

The Middle East hands' warnings also failed to find a response. Moreover, Kerr acknowledged that such concerns "have traditionally meant more to American ambassadors in the field, and to the professional Middle East specialists in the State Department" rather than to presidents and other policy makers.

Conversely globalists, especially "strategic analysts, Sovietologists, military planners, and others who predominate on the staff of the NSC," discounted the regional aspect and emphasized the Soviets as actors in a Cold War conflict.[76] As the National Security Council assumed more direct power within the foreign policy process, it attracted former CIA analysts, Soviet specialists and military types (notably Robert Komer, Eugene Rostow, Joseph Sisco, Zbigniew Brzezinski, Robert McFarlane and others) with this global perspective. It was these globalists who had influence and shaped Middle East policy rather than the trained corps of area specialists in the State Department. Kerr concluded, "[Globalists] have an inherent advantage in the long term in influencing American Middle East policy over the Regionalist school."[77]

Middle East hands might earn the highest diplomatic ranks, but their policy advice had very little influence or impact. American presidents ignored their warnings that the United States must find a way to broaden the peace process, even as they warned that America must defuse the conflict or face an erosion of its position.

Malcolm Kerr had predicted in 1975 that it was "conservative realists" who would move the peace process forward: "If progress toward peace is made, it will not be negotiated between the likes of Martin Buber and King Abdullah but between such men as Yitzhak Rabin and Hafez Asad."[78]

In 1993–94, it was Rabin who signed agreements with the PLO and Jordan. In 1999 Asad began negotiations with Ehud Barak on the Syrian and Lebanese front. Rather than prescience, both Kerr and the Middle East hands relied upon their knowledge of the area and a realistic assessment of the political situation. Their regionalist perspective was based upon academic study as well as their accumulated knowledge of its history and internal politics learned while working in the region.

The Middle East hands, like Malcolm Kerr, argued that American foreign policy should deal with the festering Arab–Israeli conflict as part of a comprehensive peace settlement. It was not a pro-Arab position but reflected a recognition that American interests were at risk and more radical forms of anti-Americanism were emerging.

Kerr warned of the Arab "perception" of Americans and the "shadow" that American foreign policy had cast. They warned that despite good intentions US interests were at risk and they were the focus of anti-American hatred. Many Middle East hands felt that US policy could have been more effective. Ambassador David Newsom questioned whether American interests might have been better served by US policy.[79] Implicit in his argument was the belief that their advice represented an alternative course that might have better served American interests.

The thrust of Kerr's argument was that the Cold War conventional wisdom overwhelmed the regional nuances. The policy that Washington promulgated reflected what Undersecretary of State George Ball termed "unrealistic thinking." Despite having made a tremendous investment in developing a corps of area specialists, Washington rarely heeded their advice. By 1973 the decline of the Beirut program was in sight. The Middle East hands had begun to fill the openings and the manpower shortage was over, violence made young State Department officers reluctant to volunteer for Arabic training and needed Asian linguists to deal with the Vietnam War.[80]

In the fall of 1967 veterans of the Beirut school led by FSOs Richard Dawson and Hume Horan drafted a memo requesting changes, having observed that Arabic training was attracting fewer junior officers. After the Six Day War, the United States was forced to close some embassies over security concerns. In October 1967 their memo summarized the situation: "The days are over when Arabic was the language of the newest, most politically active frontier of the Foreign Service. The frontier has closed."[81] Their allusion to historian Frederick Jackson Turner's famous phrase meant that, like the American West, the golden era of opportunity was over.

Ironically the Middle East hands found themselves living on a dangerous frontier. The State Department had promoted Middle East area specialization as the path to career advancement. But by 1967 skilled area specialists found themselves struggling with anti-American hostility, mobs attacking embassies, bombings, hostage takings and assassinations.

The Beirut school was rocked by conflict. Rioters targeted the US embassy, and Dr. James A. Snow and his class of Middle East hands watched the mob smash and burn their cars in the embassy parking lot. Across the region, embassies, consulates and United States Information Agency (USIA) libraries were attacked. The USIA libraries, built throughout to promote American values and a positive American image, were often attacked by anti-US mobs. Lebanon began a new descent into civil war by the mid-1970s, and in 1975 Dr. Snow determined it was no longer safe for the Americans to even walk outside the embassy. The Beirut school was shut down and relocated to Cairo, but was thereafter markedly reduced in size.

In 1976 the US ambassador Francis Meloy, his aide Robert Waring and their driver were murdered while attempting to cross the "Green Line" dividing war-torn Beirut. The Israeli military intervened in Lebanon, first in 1978 and again in 1982. Beginning in 1982, a series of kidnappings targeted Americans: the CIA station chief, journalists from CNN and the Associated Press, as well as the staff of the AUB, Beirut University College and the Lebanese International School. Twenty years of civil war was worsened by Israeli and Syrian military interventions. War and sectarian violence killed hundreds of thousands of Lebanese and drove a significant portion of their population into exile. MEAP veterans would return to Beirut, no longer a center for travel but the center of conflict, and try to defuse the conflict later in their careers.[82]

President Reagan twice sent US troops into Beirut as part of a peacekeeping force to ease out the Israeli and Syrian forces and also a withdrawal of Palestinian fighters. In October 1983 a car bomb killed 241 US Marine and Navy personnel at their Battalion Landing Team headquarters at the Beirut airport. A few months earlier, in April 1983, the American Embassy was bombed with sixty-three dead and over one hundred wounded. Ironically, Richard Murphy, who had graduated from the MEAP in 1959, was assigned to manage the evacuation and lead the investigation of the embassy bombing.

After AUB president David Dodge was kidnapped, the university appealed to Dr. Malcolm Kerr to return to Beirut and save the institution. As the new president of the AUB, Kerr struggled to cope with the political and social upheaval as Israeli, Syrian, PLO and Lebanese forces battled in the city. Kerr struggled to continue with his campus surrounded by warring forces, warplanes bombing civilian areas, the AUB's hospital stressed beyond its limits by an influx of civilian casualties and the AUB's faculty and students at risk. In January 1984 Dr. Kerr was murdered on the campus by unknown assailants. He died representing American interests in the region, in much the same way as the Middle East hands he had trained.[83]

In the 1990s Middle East hand Richard Parker was asked to reflect upon what he would have preferred the United States had done over the past half century. In response, Parker observed, "We would have wished to avoid, and could have—the blowing up of our embassy in Beirut, the slaughter of our Marines there, the hostage problem in Iran, having Iran be instrumental in the destruction of one presidential administration and threaten another."[84]

Then Parker continued to cast backward to the broader patterns of American policy in the Middle East: "I would add our failure since 1945 to come to terms with Arab and Iranian nationalism, our inability to deal successfully with the problem of Palestine, and our over-identification with regimes and rulers that too often have legitimacy problems." He noted many issues could have been handled better, and therefore the United States would have avoided some costly tragedies. He concluded: "What is remarkable is that we are not worse off than we are."[85]

Ironically, the United States had trained a corps of area specialists to advise Washington, but their policy recommendations and warnings were often ignored for Cold War reasons or domestic political considerations. Dr. Kerr highlighted the political forces at work and his fear that US interests would suffer further damage. The graduates of the Beirut school received Arabic language training and area studies, but another factor in their development was the impact of anti-American hostility and violence. The reality of working in the region became a tragic factor, which only intensified over the decades. The Middle East hands risked their lives to represent America and their worldview was not the product of a romantic vision but a reflection of the hard political reality.

Chapter Five

"THE DEPARTURE OF KINGS, OLD MEN, AND CHRISTIANS": THE EISENHOWER YEARS

During the Eisenhower presidency Middle East hands began to work their way up the career ladder working in embassies and consulates where their Arabic language skills and area expertise were badly needed, as well as in the State Department's regional desks in Washington, where they replaced the older generation of generalists. When Foreign Service officer (FSO) William Brewer left Washington for language training in Beirut in 1947, he stopped to ask the desk officer for Lebanon what it was like to live and work there. The officer-in-charge of Lebanese affairs told Brewer he did not know because "[t]he closest I've been to Beirut is Addis Ababa."[1] A decade later Brewer conducted a review of the experience of the desk officers at the Bureau of Near East Affairs (NEA): the 1947 staff had a combined total of five years of Middle East area experience. A decade later Brewer's colleagues had a total of 110 years of area experience.

The challenge of developing area expertise was highlighted in the *Wriston Report*, a study of State Department personnel. Some staff had remained in Washington posts working on policy for an area they had only read about. Others worked abroad by relying mainly on contacts with the English or French-speaking elites (a particular problem in the Middle East). These generalists were able administrators in embassies but were limited in their ability to do political reporting.

In 1954 Middle East hand Raymond Hare was appointed inspector general of the Foreign Service and charged him to carry out the *Wriston Report* reforms. He and Parker Hart, another skilled Arabist, were then the only senior Arabists at the administrative level in the Eisenhower years, but neither was appointed to the top post of assistant secretary of NEA by Eisenhower although the position was open several times. Eisenhower first relied on a brigadier general, Henry Byroade, who had experience during the occupation of Germany and who then ran the Bureau of German Affairs. Ike later appointed George Allen, a generalist with experience in Iran, Yugoslavia and Nepal. In 1956 he chose William Rountree, a former treasury budget clerk and lend-lease administrator, who had some experience in Palestine and the wartime Middle East Supply Center. But Rountree spoke no Arabic. Eisenhower's final opportunity led him to select G. Lewis Jones, another generalist. This reflected Ike's Cold War focus, as he appointed administrators at NEA who were neither area specialists nor diplomats but whose Cold War views matched his own.

His special envoys to the Middle East were men like Eric Johnston and James Richards who struggled to deal with complex regional issues but lacked regional knowledge. Historian Salim Yacub has observed Eisenhower's reliance on these envoys was "standard administration practice," and noted CIA agent Miles Copeland's referred to them collectively as "Great White Fathers."[2]

Early in their careers Middle East hands rotated through regional posts: Hermann Eilts served in Aden, Jidda, Sanaa and Baghdad and then became Dulles's personal aide at the Baghdad Pact negotiations. Donald Bergus served in Baghdad, Jidda and Beirut and then became desk officer for Israeli–Jordanian affairs and later adviser to NATO on NEA. In 1957 he drafted the NEA's post-Suez Crisis policy paper.

Middle East hands generally rotated to a new post every two years and were not assigned to any one post for long. There was always concern that diplomats might develop "localitis," the dreaded diplomatic disease that occurs when an FSO identifies too closely with his host country.

Middle East hands tried to fit their area knowledge into a larger policy framework to promote initiatives that might benefit America's vital national interests: herein summarized as the Beirut Axioms (see epilogue). They focused on two key areas: the simmering Arab–Israeli conflict and the rising tide of Arab nationalism. They understood the historical roots of conflict, which led them to urge an American role in reaching a comprehensive settlement of borders and the refugee problem. They emphasized the need to use diplomacy to protect American access to the area's oil, military bases and trade.

The dominant Cold War view emphasized marshalling client states, fear of communist subversion of Arab states and a growing pressure to align the US position with British policy. Middle East hands advised a moderate course that did not hew to the British line, counseled restraint in arms sales and encouraged generosity with food aid. They did not, however, have the power to alter the conventional wisdom in Washington. They certainly could not mitigate the Cold War worldview that permeated the Eisenhower White House.

Realistic discourse on Communism was also inhibited by McCarthyism, which peaked in this era and which took a dreadful toll in the State Department. Middle East hands were well aware of the fate of the China Hands, feared being denounced as "red" or insufficiently anticommunist. Washington's outlook always placed the fear of communist subversion uppermost. Anyone seen as deviating from that view risked their career. In 1952 Senator Joseph McCarthy launched attacks against the former Secretary of State George C. Marshall, and Eisenhower feared risking an open confrontation, even at the price of abandoning a valued mentor. Ambassador Joseph C. Green, who knew John Foster Dulles at Princeton and as Secretary of State, recalled that when Foster addressed the Foreign Service he told the audience, "I believe that most of you are loyal." Green recalled, "The effect of that one sentence can easily be imagined. It was repeated from Washington to all the posts of the Foreign Service abroad and made a most deplorable impression."[3]

In this period Israel was an ally, but what became known as the special relationship was not fully developed. The US–Israeli relationship did not have the closeness that was later exhibited, and there was no military partnership since the United States was not then Israel's arms supplier. Washington was unwilling, and perhaps unable, to move Israelis to deal with the issues stemming from the 1948 war: borders and refugees. Additionally, the British position was dramatically weakened by the Suez Crisis, and its Arab clients were an aging generation whose links to imperialism left them in disrepute in the new age of nationalism. Secretary of State Dulles moved American policy more in concert with London. British neocolonialism, Israeli intransigence and Arab nationalism all threatened the favorable US position in the Middle East in the Eisenhower years.

The World According to Dulles

While some have argued Dulles's attitude toward Nasser hardened over time, it is apparent from the record of his first visit in 1953 that his view was firmly set from the start. Anticommunism was central to his approach and led him to underestimate the explosive potential in the region.

Dulles had a background in law and foreign affairs and the formidable reputation of being the third Secretary of State in his family. His siblings added to his power base: Allen, as director of the Central Intelligence Agency (CIA), and his sister Eleanor who worked in State Department economics and intelligence posts as well as Berlin affairs. American diplomats were concerned about the brotherly closeness of the CIA and State Department chiefs. Ambassador to Jordan Joseph C. Green argued that it led to "the development of the CIA into something way beyond what was intended." During morning conversations over breakfast each kept the other informed of what they were doing, but Green feared that "[n]o one in the Department beyond the Secretary knew about many of the things the CIA was doing." Green argued that this allowed the CIA to conduct operations in the Middle East with a freer hand: "If informing the Department of State had meant informing the Department of State in such a way that four or five people knew what was going on, many of those things could never have been done."[4]

Foster was not shy about flaunting the family legend. On his 1953 trip to Lebanon the official memorandum notes that Foster opened his remarks to the Lebanese minister by announcing: "On the personal side [...] his sister had lived in Beirut for two years and that his brother was active in affairs which also were of considerable interest to Lebanon." The CIA chief and former Office of Strategic Services agent, Allen Dulles had indeed been "active" in the region for decades and believed he knew the "Orient" well. From 1922 to 1926, Allen had been in charge of the State Department's old Near East desk and had met T. E. Lawrence at Versailles. They reportedly remained in touch.[5]

Allen Dulles was an Orientalist from what might be called the Lawrence of Arabia school of diplomacy. He also retained close ties with the old generation of Arab monarchs who would be swept away by the rising tide of Arab nationalism. Both he and Foster were extremely ill-suited to understand the rising tide of Nasserism or the unpopularity of leaders who had cooperated with the British and French. Neither could appreciate the Middle East hands' emphasis on quiet diplomacy as the CIA ran covert operations from inside the American embassies, often without the full knowledge of the embassy staff or Washington.

Moreover, John Foster Dulles's determination to contain "godless Communism" led him to overlook the nuances. The Middle East hands were not too fond of their taciturn secretary. Hermann Eilts returned from Istanbul on the same plane as the secretary, and later recalled that he chatted with another diplomat about Islam, "[T]o my surprise and gratification, Dulles who was right across from me, put his cards down and just turned around and just listened for a half hour or so, and I like to think he got something out of it." Evidently, so did Eilts, who received a special promotion a month later. He became Foster's aide for the Baghdad Pact affairs and worked to support a policy that many of his peers felt was ill-conceived. Eilts might have been chosen by the secretary as a Middle East advisor, but Dulles made his own policy. Talcott Seelye feared Dulles would "pull Iraq out of the Arab mainstream," and he gave Nasser "justification" for other actions. Seelye recalled that the Baghdad Pact "certainly was Dulles's pet."[6]

Richard Parker found Dulles difficult to work with and cold: "We respected and admired his abilities as a lawyer, as a drafter, as a politician. But as a human being, he didn't have much appeal to us." After working an entire evening interpreting between Dulles and a Saudi prince, Parker was addressed twice by the secretary, saying only hello and goodbye: "I could have been a telephone instrument in his hand as far as that was concerned." On the policy side Parker felt Dulles viewed Nasser "as a Soviet puppet." For Parker and his peers that raised concerns because "on the working level [we] thought that was wrong," and many at NEA disliked "his attitude that neutrality was immoral." Parker argued, "The Soviets were always our bête noire [...] all sorts of things we did were justified as being something to prevent the Soviets from taking the area over." Parker also observed that Dulles emphasized the Cold War view, which put Middle East hands in a difficult position since it was "almost impossible to disagree with Washington."[7]

Harrison Symmes argued Dulles was unable to deal with Arab nationalism because it was inherently neutralist. Dulles's anger was rooted in a combination of hostility toward Bandung-era neutralism and a bipolar worldview: "To him neutralism was a sin. You were either for us or against us. So Nasser was one of the chief sinners of the world." Symmes viewed Nasser as "an extreme nationalist" but felt that the United States "should find a way to deal with him."[8] For Secretary Dulles there was no modus vivendi with Nasserist neutralism, Arab nationalism or communism.

Soviet Ambassador Anatoly Dobrynin arrived in Washington in 1952 at the height of what he described as "anticommunist and anti-Soviet hysteria." While Stalin's death in March 1953 offered an opportunity to defrost the Cold War, no break came. Dobrynin described Dulles as Eisenhower's "principal cold warrior" and "an additional cause of uncertainty and worry" for the Soviets. Dobrynin saw Dulles as "[a] moralist every bit as committed to capitalism and the Christian religion as Molotov was to the ideas of Marxism-Leninism." Dobrynin pointed out that the Dulles–Molotov meetings were "[a] dialogue of the deaf *and* the blind."[9]

During his May 1953 tour of the Middle East his fundamental misunderstanding of the problems presented by a group of senior Orientalists (including Major William Eddy, then employed by TAPline, and a group of American missionary educators: Dr. Park Johnson, Dr. William Stoltzfus and Dr. Alford Carleton) was on display. They warned Dulles of the deterioration of American interests and expressed concern that ties to

Israel were dangerous. The Orientalists warned that there was a different Cold War in the Middle East with Israel "against whom the Arabs are conducting a cold war of much greater importance to them than the cold war against Russia." They advised Dulles that Arab resentment of Israel was the central issue. They feared "Arabs have lost faith in disinterested help from America" and "No Arab leader can stick his neck out to collaborate with the West." They were also concerned when Dulles dined in Jerusalem with Israeli officials. Tel Aviv was then the Israeli capital, but Israel had made claims on Jerusalem (then a divided city). Arabs saw the dinner as supporting those Israeli claims. Stoltzfus suggested tensions among Palestinians in the United Nations (UN) refugee camps might be relieved by a US offer to absorb "[a] token number […] to show our good will."[10]

Dulles was aware of the refugees' plight. During his visit to Jordan, Joseph C. Green the ambassador to Amman, overrode the plans of the British commander of the Arab Legion, Sir Patrick Coghill. The embassy motorcade had been scheduled to travel through the Jericho refugee camp at 70 miles per hour, but Green insisted it travel more slowly "[s]o that Foster could see the refugee camp and get some impression of it."[11] The Palestinians applauded as Dulles passed through the camp where they had been living since 1948.

Despite the firsthand experience, Secretary Dulles told the Orientalists that the administration would do "[w]hat is good for the US" but not undertake what he termed "a pro-Arab policy." The irony, from the viewpoint of the Orientalists, was that they were convinced they were arguing for a pro-American policy. Dulles pointed out their ideas would work against the British and that "[i]t would be impossible, therefore, to have both a pro-UK and a pro-Arab policy." His linkage of US policy to the British was not to be formally announced until early 1956, but here was evidence that he was determined to shore up the British Foreign Office's ill-fated policy. There was an immediate, and volcanic, reaction by the Orientalists; but Dulles ignored it. On the issue of a peace settlement, Dulles only offered to "consider some form of guarantee against Israeli expansion" and opined that "formal peace is not possible in the near future." He closed by cryptically observing that time would ease the situation and "better results would be likely if the Egyptian stumbling block can be removed." Whether he meant the difficulties negotiating over the Suez Canal or had made a more threatening reference to Nasser was left unstated.[12]

In Lebanon Dulles emphasized the security America provided against the predominant Soviet threat when he told President Camille Chamoun that "in the larger sphere of global relations the US wields the balance against Soviet Russia. If that shield were removed, the Arabs would really have something to worry about." Chamoun was not worried about the Soviets showing up in Beirut anytime soon, but did fear the Israelis and his political rivals. His minister informed Dulles "The Soviets were succeeding very well" by playing the Israel card and the US should defuse the issues of "boundaries and Jerusalem" or the Soviets would exploit it. Dulles continued to harp on Soviet aggression: "We must express real concern when we hear Arabs say there is no communist threat, merely the threat of Israel and the imperialist powers."[13]

This remained the fatal flaw in his approach, and it came back to haunt him. In 1958 Chamoun appealed for CIA help to win the 1958 election against his leftist rivals and then played upon Dulles's fear to paint them as communists. Ike landed the Marines to protect Chamoun's regime. Dulles insisted on British access to Suez and sent a message to Nasser via the Chamoun channel: "If Egypt is unwilling to cooperate for the defense of the free world, she probably will not have her independence for long. This type of nationalism is as dead as imperialism."[14]

Although Dulles believed Arab nationalism was dead, it was not, and neither was neutralism. Ironically, Egypt did come under attack three years later when Israel, Britain and France tried to recapture the canal and oust Nasser in the Suez Crisis. Conversely, Middle East hands saw the British star on the wane and were disinclined to hitch American interests to it. Instead Dulles aligned the United States with London in an ill-fated partnership.

Eisenhower also heard a negative image of the State Department from Vice President Richard Nixon who vented his own hostility toward American diplomats. After an overseas trip he told Eisenhower that "an astonishing number of them have no obvious dedication to America and to its service." Nixon argued they were political partisans: "[M]ost of these men had been appointed to the career service during the New Deal years and consequently they felt no loyalty to the present government." Nixon continued to state that these diplomats hoped they would "never have to go back to the US." Ike later recalled Pat Nixon was even "more emphatic than Dick in her expressions of belief that there was a very great deal of this kind of feeling and thinking in the Foreign Service."[15] The Eisenhower administration, from the secretary of state and CIA director to the vice president, were fighting the Cold War in the Middle East without a clear understanding of the forces at play within the region.

The Middle East policy initiatives under Eisenhower can be divided into three phases: First, 1953 to 1955, when the Eric Johnston Plan to allocate Jordan Valley water was proposed; second, the period of the Suez Crisis and its aftermath, from 1956 to early 1957; finally, 1957 to 1959, when the Richards Mission was launched to implement the Eisenhower Doctrine, a commitment to fight communism in the Middle East.

The Eric Johnston Plan

Eisenhower and Dulles took an indirect approach to the Arab–Israeli conflict by seeking to deal with the issue of water without first settling the fundamental issue: to define the borders obliterated by the collapse of the UN partition plan and the Arab–Israeli war. The fate of an estimated 750,000 Palestinians stranded in UN refugee camps since 1948 remained unresolved.[16]

Ambassador to Jordan Joseph C. Green sent a cable to Washington summarizing the problem. He argued Zionism is "the issue in this country," stressing the relationship with Israel had created "deep-seated distrust of [the] US and its motives." But the real complication was "480,000 refugees from Palestine in Jordan with no (repeat no) present hope of integration or removal creates a special aspect of Israeli question here." This received a terse, one-sentence response, shot back by NEA's John Jernegan in cablese: "WLD (would) appreciate UR (your) specific suggestions re alteration policies and attitudes mentioned final sentence URTEL (your telegram) 238."[17] Washington did not want to hear a call for tackling the tough problems.

Behind the scenes Secretary Dulles launched a secret peace effort, together with the British, called Operation Alpha, which failed. Historian Salim Yaqub detailed the problems: the Eisenhower administration had joined Britain in pursuing "a major diplomatic initiative, Project ALPHA, to achieve an Arab–Israeli peace settlement." But both Egypt and Israel "reacted cautiously," while Nasser sought "a more robust solution to the twin problems of Israel and the [Baghdad] pact."[18] He then demanded a US arms deal and turned to the Soviets. By early March 1956 the deal was dead and shortly thereafter the United Kingdom, Israel and France launched the Suez War.

The Eric Johnston Plan thus became Eisenhower's high profile effort to calm the region and to use water allocation as a way to solve the problem. Yet, without defined borders it was unlikely that water allocation could succeed.

In his briefings with Eric Johnston, Dulles stressed the link between water and refugees. More arable land was the key to making the refugee problem go away. Unstated in this premise was that the Palestinian refugees from the 1948 war, having spent half a decade in the UN refugee camps scattered around Israel, might have enough water to survive where they were and thus remove the need to be returned to their homes. This would eliminate the need to pressure Israel to repatriate or compensate them, and with the thornier issues inherent in defining Israel's borders. From the Israeli perspective, any settlement to allocate water would limit their future access of additional supplies to foster their growth.

Eric Johnston was ill-suited to launch the initiative. He was neither an Arabist, nor even a diplomat. He had been the head of the Motion Picture Association, president of the US Chamber of Commerce and sat on the Tennessee Valley Authority (TVA) advisory board.[19] The TVA had drawn up a Middle East replica of its original project for the United Nations. Dulles wanted Johnston to travel throughout the region and sell the plan. But even Johnston's own staff of water experts had cautioned the plan was created "without considering political factors or attempting to set the system proposed into the national boundaries."[20] Thus it would divide the Jordan River based upon engineering principles, but with no political calculus in mind. It was highly unlikely that people living in a desert region, and technically in a state of war, would choose to share vital water resources.[21]

Middle East hand Talcott Seelye cabled Washington with an outline of "Jordan's mood on the eve of Johnston mission." He explained that another high-profile American mission that year (Dulles's visit had been the first) "risks serious repercussions […] if it becomes clear that mission […] offers little better than collaboration with Israel on Jordan-Yarmuk waters." Moreover, the Jordanians viewed the water as belonging to Syria and Jordan, not Israel. The key issue was the refugees, and this meant any US initiative must be part of a "larger, overall political settlement." Otherwise Jordanians would reject the plan as "further evidence of US subservience to Israel" and "exacerbate anti-Americanism to point of no return." In conclusion Seelye stressed Johnston must offer "a more substantial quid pro quo," withhold the plan or "sound out" the Jordanians before attempting to publicize it. Two days later on October 15, 1953, Johnston, citing Seelye's cable, sent a telegram to Assistant Secretary of State Henry Byroade, informing him he would withhold the TVA plan and make preliminary visits to each capital to avoid "arbitrary rejection [from] all quarters."[22] Perhaps Seelye's cautions had some effect at the start.

Over the next night Israeli commandos staged a dramatic raid on Jordan that demolished the village of Qibya and parts of two other villages. Seelye sent a cable that noted the attack had been timed to coincide with Johnston's planned arrival and an Israeli attempt to divert the Jordan River. These events left any hope of Jordanian–Israeli cooperation, in Seelye's opinion, "dashed to smithereens." The raid had been planned and carried out by General Ariel Sharon's new commando group, Unit 101. Historian Isaac Alteras described Unit 101 as an elite volunteer group of "talented guerrillas, scouts and nightfighters," which killed 66 Jordanians, "every man, woman and child" in Qibya, dynamited 42 homes, the school, the mosque and then "turned their fire on the cattle."[23]

Ariel Sharon, mindful of the vital importance of water, later wrote: "The matter of water diversion was a stark issue of life and death." Historian Howard Sachar argued that the Johnston Plan finally collapsed when Israel began its own diversions in 1955, then "[t]he Syrians mounted tentative efforts to dam the sources of the Jordan." But Israel halted the work: "Syrian and Lebanese engineering teams began the construction of diversion canals several miles within their own frontiers. They did not get far. Israeli artillery promptly shelled and destroyed their bulldozers."[24]

Johnston, armed with a plan based on hydrology, not political reality, found it difficult to deal with three riparian states that were at war and held conflicting claims on the water and the land. The plan remained unpopular in Jordan because it would replace the Yarmuk project, which Amman favored, as well as give far too much water and recognition to Israel. In Syria, where the plan had less direct consequences, Eric Johnston cabled "the door remained open" but acceptance hinged on Israel's "compliance with UN Resolutions." In Lebanon, the reception was "more realistic and favorable than anywhere else" with "clear evidence of interest" especially when the possibility of "Israeli territorial concessions" to permit refugee resettlement were raised. Lebanon's delicate sectarian balance had been skewed by the arrival of waves of Palestinian refugees and the possibility of reducing the presence of the camps was welcome. Israel was not warm to the plan because they viewed it as limiting their potential by reducing their present share of the water and the cross-border raids further complicated the situation.

Johnston convened the embassy staff in Amman, including Seelye and Miles Bunger, who had drafted the embassy's original Yarmuk proposal. Seelye recalled Johnston "asked for our unvarnished views," urging them to "speak out." Seelye recalled the embassy staffers told Johnston there was little "prospect of solving the Arab–Israeli problem through economic means," and it was "a political issue and had to be resolved in a political way." The next day the Jordanians made a "flat refusal to discuss any plan for use of Jordan waters other than Bunger scheme for Yarmuk."[25]

In Israel Eric Johnston found there was a desire to transform the plan in such a way that Israel could expand settlements in the Negev desert. Israel made a series of demands that Arab governments could not accept: to double the water allocation, to add Lebanon's Litani River into the scheme (a river wholly within Lebanese boundaries and outside the original plan) and to multiply the electric allotment Israel would receive by a factor of seven. During negotiations Israel continued to demand a doubled allocation.

By late October of 1953 Israeli Minister Pinhas Lavon announced the Johnston plan was "designed to stunt our growth."[26]

Eric Johnston had been warned by many Middle East hands that his plan was unworkable and even cautioned by the TVA staff. For Dulles, the failure of the Eric Johnston mission led to a disenchantment with diplomatic solutions. There seems to be a linkage between his disappointment over Johnston's failure and his efforts to "punish" Nasser. While the State Department worked with Johnston, the CIA ran covert operations in Iran and Syria to remove politicians they deemed as unfriendly, further discrediting the United States in the Arab world. Historian Hugh Wilford has detailed a number of secret CIA initiatives, largely run by agents Kim Roosevelt, Miles Copeland and Wilbur Eveland, in *America's Great Game: The CIA's Secret Arabists and the Shaping of the Modern Middle East*. One such operation played out to the detriment of Ambassador Henry Byroade in Cairo, who arrived at a reception for Eric Johnston, unaware of the CIA's secret machinations: "Now, having had no intimation that Kim Roosevelt was even in Egypt, the ambassador was treated to the sight of the senior CIA officer walking into the room arm in arm with the prime minister, laughing at some private joke." Wilford argued that Nasser played the "crypto-diplomacy" game very well and that it became the Eisenhower administration's "preferred method for dealing with Middle Eastern leaders, and Kim Roosevelt [was] the chief crypto-diplomat."[27]

NEA issued a paper after Eric Johnston's initial effort entitled "Trends in Israel Policy toward the Arabs," which pointed out the diplomatic collapse was based on "Israel's demand for complete control of the Jordan River" and a "sudden series of broader incidents perpetrated by Israel" in which 20 Arabs were killed in Gaza, Arab Bedouins and their flocks were shot in the El Auga DMZ, the Qibya attack, as well as the Banat Ya'qub water diversion. The paper stated that "[t]he Israel[i] actions have tended to nullify the Johnston mission."[28]

Most Middle East hands in the field and at NEA placed the refugee issue as paramount in solving the Arab–Israeli conflict. In 1955 the NEA, with input from Raymond Hare, outlined a proposed list of the "Principal Elements of Settlement" and sent the policy paper to Secretary Dulles:

a. Permanent recognized boundaries
b. Security on the border [...] control of infiltration
c. Termination of Suez Canal restrictions and [...] Arab secondary boycott
d. Agreements on repatriation and resettlement of refugees
e. Agreement on compensation of Arab refugees
g. A free port at Haifa for Jordan
h. Agreement on the Unified Development of the Jordan Valley.[29]

It is important to note that the Jordan water plan came *last* in the minds of those at NEA. It was boundaries, border issues, the Suez conflict and refugees that needed to be resolved. Without defined borders there was no way to allocate the water resources. In related documents the authors noted that Israel strongly desired overt security guarantees with either the United States or United Kingdom, and the plan promised little for Egypt—a "relatively limited supply of 'carrots'" as they termed it.

After Johnston returned to Washington he claimed the Embassy Amman staff were "disloyal" including Ambassador Green. All except Seelye were removed. Seelye was told by the new ambassador that Bunger had been transferred "because the Yarmuk Dam project didn't fit into the water sharing plan (Johnston's)," and another FSO was sent to Newfoundland "to cool off." Seelye was told he would stay because they needed "some continuity."[30]

It was a harsh lesson for a careerist. Dissent, no matter how realistic (or even if it had been requested), had a high price. It took four decades until Seelye's analysis was proven correct. Dealing with water issues had to be preceded by a political settlement because of the inherent need to define borders before dividing resources. The first water agreement was reached 43 years later in 1996. The Israeli–Jordanian–Palestinian Authority water agreement was signed in Oslo three years after the adoption of the Declaration of Principles as the start of a political settlement.

The Johnston mission, however, triggered a new round of fighting in October 1953. Syria, which had claims on the waters of the Jordan River, was confronted by Israeli forces who invaded the area with earth-moving equipment. The Israeli government sent forces into the United Nations demilitarized zone between Israel and Syria at the Jisr Banat Yacub bridge (Daughter of Jacob Bridge) and used bulldozers to divert the Jordan River away from Syria into Israel.

In recounting the collapse of the Eric Johnston Plan historian Isaac Alteras summarized: "Israel's water diversion project [...] would scuttle a unified plan for the use of the Jordan river waters by all riparian states." The reference to a unified plan referred to the Johnston Plan.[31] Syria appealed to the UN. This raised the question of how the United States would vote as well as whether Johnston's plan would survive.

Middle East hand William Brewer, then the political officer in Syria, cabled reports on events inside the DMZ and monitored the cable traffic on America's diplomatic efforts in the UN Security Council. Although a resolution had been drafted to condemn the Israeli water diversion, at the last moment the American representatives added new language to weaken it. Brewer recalled: "Embassy Damascus objected, this in effect undercut the entire resolution." But Brewer found that no one in Washington (or at the US UN office) wanted their input: "For our pains we were simply cut out of the final exchanges of telegrams with the (State) Department. The next text was put to a vote—and was promptly vetoed by the USSR." Brewer saw this as a turning point for Soviet influence. The Soviets had made a substantial gain: "This Soviet action represented Moscow's first overt move to improve its position with the Syrians and led to close Syro-Soviet collaboration by 1957." Most Middle East hands viewed the refusal to keep the original text as a gift to Moscow. Brewer argued it was a serious error that ran counter to Eisenhower's Cold War goal: "We did ourselves no service by thus offering the Russian an opening to move into the Near East." After the Israelis staged yet another Gaza raid, which also coincided with Johnston's mission, Richard Parker argued that most Middle East hands "saw this sort of action by the Israelis as the vector of Soviet penetration in the area."[32] The Soviets had been handed an opportunity by the Americans.

The Johnston mission failed, not because of the embassy staff were "disloyal" but because all parties would have to make sacrifices. The secret CIA operations further disrupted Johnston's stop in Cairo as well as the ambassador's standing with Nasser while attempting to promote it. Syria and Jordan had no interest in a plan that allotted them some water but less than they already had within their borders. Israel saw it as giving them some water but limiting their future growth. No one was prepared to share water while there remained unsettled boundaries and conflict on those borders.

Yet, to the end Johnston maintained his was "the only logical and equitable approach," and argued the water "belongs, in some part, to all of them." But he was no longer dealing with the Tennessee Valley but with the international conflict over the Jordan valley waters. Historian Howard Sachar felt that "in the light of Israel's raid at Gaza the Arabs manifestly could not trust the Jews to carry out a water agreement in good faith." But underneath it all, the real problem was that it "implied Arab recognition of the Jewish state [...] and would have fostered Israel's growth and development."[33] Notably, for Sachar, the plan would secure rather than limit Israel's water resources. Just before the Arab League debated whether to support the plan in February 1955 Israel launched another raid into the Gaza Strip and any possibility of a water agreement evaporated.

Turning Point: The Suez Crisis

The position of France and Britain in the region was contracting. French control had dissipated after 1943 in Lebanon and 1946 in Syria and they were embattled in Algeria. London had abandoned British Mandate Palestine in 1948 but attempted to remain influential in Iraq, Jordan, Aden and the Gulf Emirates, where oil and geostrategic influence were at stake. Conversely, American oil projects had developed on the partnership model, typified by the Arabian American Oil Company (ARAMCO) in Saudi Arabia, and the US military had expanded its global presence with base agreements in Libya, Turkey, the Gulf and elsewhere.

Middle East hands saw the American role as divergent from the old colonial model, but increasingly the Eisenhower administration pushed for British–American linkage on Middle East policy. This ran against the prevalent current of Arab nationalism and neutralism.

In May 1956 Dulles informed his ambassadors in the Middle East that "while differences may arise" between the United States and the United Kingdom, the nations were "two allies." He made clear that they were coordinating their approach in order to prevent "third countries" from "play[ing] one country against the other." He pointed out that the Foreign Office would be touting this closer connection in the Arab world: "It is understood confidentially that British chiefs of mission in the Middle East have been instructed to stress, in their dealings with third parties, the general agreement existing between British and American policies." Dulles also informed them: "The Department believes that American officials, in their conversations with representatives of third countries, should emphasize the similarity of US–UK interests" Dulles mildly qualified his statement by acknowledging there might be times that the United States should "avoid identification" with the British.[34]

The key "third party" in all of this was Egypt. The Revolutionary Command Council in Egypt, known as the Free Officers, had taken power through a coup only a few years earlier in 1952. Gamal Abdel Nasser had continually pressured the British to withdraw from their military bases and the Suez Canal as the expiration date on the agreement to use those installations neared. Nasser, himself the architect of a coup, was deeply suspicious of another, inspired by the British.

In 1956 "the descent to Suez" began when Secretary Dulles, miffed with Nasser's high-profile role at the 1955 Bandung conference of nonaligned nations, his criticism of the Baghdad Pact and purchase of Czech arms, abruptly cut all US support for the Aswan Dam project. The British followed suit. The Aswan project had been designed to control flooding in the Nile valley, provide cheap hydroelectric power and speed modernization throughout Egypt. The American and British rejections of support torpedoed international funding for the project.

Nasser's stock with Eisenhower and Dulles, already low, sank further. Dulles had approved Operation Omega to use the CIA to undermine Arab nationalism. A different approach was recommended by the State Department, which set forth a more moderate proposal to clip Nasser's wings: "Plan of Action: Immediate Measure to be Undertaken against Egypt" in March 1956. The plan urged that the United States delay export licenses for arms, negotiations on Aswan and CARE shipments and "continue to delay pending Egyptian requests [...] PL 480 [wheat]." It also suggested the British slow their withdrawal from Suez.[35] The operative word for the Americans was "delay"; in each case the NEA proposed stalling, not stopping. While NEA struggled to temper the Dulles approach, they could not change his overall strategy.

Nasser abruptly nationalized the Suez Canal on July 26. This placed the transit through the strategic canal under Egyptian control, deprived British and French investors of income and promised steady stream of user's fees would flow into Cairo's coffers. The British demanded the canal be placed under international control to avoid any Egyptian control over the strategic waterway. Dulles struggled to coordinate an international canal users' organization because Suez was the route for oil tankers from the Gulf to Europe. If closed, then tankers headed to America would be forced to transit around Africa.

Behind the scenes Britain, France and Israel began planning a joint attack on Egypt in a series of secret meetings. On October 29, 1956, Israel attacked across the Sinai, and on October 31 Britain and France opened air attacks on Cairo. Prime Minister Anthony Eden's aide, Evelyn Shuckburgh, recalled that "the Americans were not consulted, the United Nations was flouted." Shuckburgh mused he had spent years trying to deal with Egypt but was appalled Eden would invade. Ironically, Eden had been a Foreign Office Arabist earlier in his career. On November 1 Shuckburgh stated, "We think A. E. has gone off his head. What can be done? [...] thinking of all I have done to get us *out* of Suez, now we are going back."[36]

The plan was made without consulting Eisenhower despite Dulles's efforts to advertise the close linkage with Britain earlier that year. This made Eisenhower's shock at the British involvement even greater. In his October 31 television address Eisenhower observed the British, French and Israelis were "among our allies," and although they regarded the canal as their "lifeline," he argued, "We believe these actions have been taken in error. For we do not accept the use of force." His stand was based on international law, not sympathy for Nasser. Dulles looked no more warmly, probably much less so, upon Nasser.

The attack imperiled Eisenhower's imminent reelection, but he publicly demanded the Israeli, British and French withdraw and secretly pressured London with a threat on their currency in the global market. The British and French complied by November 6, but Israel only left the Sinai, while its forces remained in the Gaza Strip.

In February 1957 Ike conferred with Dulles and US UN representative, Henry Cabot Lodge, to press for an Israeli withdrawal. In his memoirs he stressed that world opinion could not accept the Israeli occupation of Gaza, even as leverage to gain access to the Strait of Tiran. Ike refused to allow Israel to "defy the UN" but insisted they "withdraw unconditionally" in order to "expect the support of the rest of the Free World." Ike informed Israel they should not continue "an occupation in defiance of the overwhelming judgment of the world community."[37]

Eisenhower did not force Israel to withdraw at the behest of the Middle East hands. The policy was made at the highest levels and did not even include the assistant secretary of the NEA. Richard Parker recalled Dulles was "calling all the shots" and had taken the role normally filled by the area specialists. Parker perceived Dulles had decided that "he is the desk officer and he's doing the work, and he's writing it."[38] Middle East hands had no input.

With his address on Suez, Eisenhower had markedly raised America's stock in the Arab world by calling for a complete Israeli withdrawal, but the White House feared Nasser would emerge more prominent. In December, Dulles continued his Cold War chess game to sign up clients in mutual defense agreements that would unite American client states against the Soviets. He closed a meeting by informing them that the State's "long term objective" in the region should be "to get all the Arab states together," but the United States should first take "a preliminary step to exclude and thus isolate Egypt and Syria as a means of diminishing Nasser's influence so that he could not aspire to take over leadership of the larger group."[39]

Middle East hands abroad found the Arab reaction to Eisenhower's speech marked a wave of pro-American sentiment. In Kuwait, Talcott Seelye enjoyed finding the United States regarded as "really the shining light at that point." The British, who controlled Kuwaiti defense and foreign affairs, were resented, and the Kuwaitis were not ready to let the United Kingdom's political agent forget it. He and Seelye sat at a public parade that, to their surprise, featured "a little mock battle showing these guys attacking the British at Suez, at which point the British political agent stood up and walked out." Seelye proudly noted "at that point we were doing all right."[40]

Middle East hands were concerned that the United States might fail to take advantage of this remarkable upswing in pro-American sentiment. Washington did fail to exploit it. In a message to the NEA in late 1956 William Brewer argued that Washington must move right away while "American prestige is high" in order "to fill the vacuum created by the declining influence of the British and the French." He hoped that Washington would "use this negative asset for positive policy" or else "the Arabs will turn more than in the past to the USSR."[41]

The Eisenhower Doctrine and the Richards Mission

The remainder of Eisenhower's term in office, however, was absorbed with pressing Middle East states to choose sides in the Cold War, and to develop a foreign policy that was both anticommunist and antineutralist. In March 1957 he announced the Eisenhower Doctrine. It was based on three "simple and indisputable" facts: the Middle East was "prized more than ever by International Communism," the Soviets would "use any means to gain their ends" and finally the "free nations of the Mid East" needed and wanted US assistance. He asked Congress to support a strategy of economic aid, military aid and armed force. The key phrase was "to secure and protect the territorial integrity and political independence of nations requesting such aid against overt armed aggression from any nation controlled by international communism."[42] In practice this would prove to be a blank check guaranteeing US intervention.

Eisenhower was determined to garner preapproval from Congress for any future military action and got it. The White House was ready to use the Sixth Fleet for any operation they deemed fit the doctrine. Ike told Congressional leaders this was needed to halt the Soviets, and Dulles went as far as to call it "a first step prior to a complete departure from international Communism."[43]

But Eisenhower still had to sell it to Israel and the Arabs. It was overtly anticommunist, but it was also constructing a thinly veiled anti-Nasserist alliance. Historian Salim Yacub argued that the Eisenhower Doctrine "could help a conservative regime consolidate domestic power and move closer to the West, it could not prevent a radical regime from consolidating its own power and moving closer to the Soviet bloc." Yet despite the "enormous prestige" garnered by Ike's Suez address, it failed to overcome "the political weakness of the United States in the Arab world." In the end Arab leaders "were loath to be seen as doing America's bidding."[44]

Ike chose former South Carolina Congressman James Richards as his personal emissary, yet another non-Arabist, non-diplomat. Dulles gave Richards his mission's objectives: "to deter communist military adventures and to maintain an atmosphere of calm confidence on the part of area states." Dulles cautioned that some might ask how these proposals related to "non-communist aggression in the area and to such area problems as Palestine and the Suez Canal" but these were to be dismissed as "intra-area problems" outside of his mission.[45] Again the Cold War logic ignored serious concerns within the region.

Richards was warmly welcomed when he arrived in Libya, Iran and Iraq. But by turns Libya's King Idris, Iran's Shah Reza Pahlavi and Iraq's Nuri al-Said each were deeply disappointed when they discovered the small size of the aid package. Nuri pointed out he was already spending 60 percent of his budget on defense and needed more "to hold off a Soviet attack." Evidently Eisenhower desired "more bang for the buck" in his foreign aid budget for the Northern Tier, which he viewed as a bulwark to keep the Soviets out of the region.

As news of the limited amounts Richards offered spread throughout the region his receptions became progressively cooler. Syria and Egypt delayed allowing him to even land in their countries, which Richards resented as "not compatible with dignity of this mission." His visit to Israel was a disaster, undertaken when the White House became aware of a "very strong feeling on the Hill that he should go," since omitting Israel would "jeopardize" Congressional approval of the aid package. Richards found Israel only interested in whether a threat from an Arab state would be covered by the Eisenhower Doctrine and then refused to issue a joint communique. Historian Isaac Alteras has observed this would have alienated the USSR and might "jeopardize the chances of large-scale Jewish immigration." David Ben-Gurion and Abba Eban forcefully argued for a compromise Knesset Resolution to avoid a more overt snub, and it finally passed with nearly half of the voters abstaining.[46]

The one place where the Richards Mission might have had a positive effect was in the Yemen where there was real potential for Soviet gains, but it failed because Richards mishandled the offer. Months earlier CIA director Allen Dulles had briefed Eisenhower on Soviet arms flowing into Yemen. Consul William R. Crawford, a Middle East hand, was told to gather intelligence and found the British had been using airpower to suppress a rebellion among the desert shaikhs. The shaikhs in turn had appealed to their brother, the Imam in Sanaa. Earlier they had expressed their complaints to the ambassador in Saudi Arabia George Wadsworth. He described the air raids as "barbarous," reporting the British planes were even "buzzing" ARAMCO installations staffed by Americans.[47]

NEA had been aware the Soviets had met with the Yemenis and offered military aid to resist the British in early 1956. But after Suez, Moscow saw a new opportunity. In January 1957 NEA reported that the USSR "appears to have been stimulated by their desire to 'raid the Aden Protectorate.'" The British had made the situation worse by continuing because it now involved not just Aden but Sanaa, and through them the Soviets. Sanaa was committed to defend the Adeni shaikhs, even without an air force or modern arms, but the Soviets had appeared with generous offers. NEA was forced to admit that Yemen was "the only place [...]where the Soviet Bloc has made successful inroads."[48] A decade later as the British prepared to leave Aden it was the Soviets who collected the political victory when South Yemen emerged as a Marxist state.

Secretary Dulles found reports of Soviet activity "worrisome" and had Richards diverted there. Richards tersely cabled a baseball analogy, noting he was "[p]laying in tougher league now—batting average hit slump." Richards had indeed struck out. He resented how the Yemenis were "obsessed with what they call 'aggression' by British on southern frontier." He was surprised to find it was "far more alarming [...to them] than communism." Richards resented being told by the Imam they might take Soviet aid "as result of attacks by other countries." The British, not the Soviets, were the problem in Yemen, but that did not fit with the Cold War vision of Eisenhower and Dulles.

Richards's offer of $2 million in road-building aid met with approval, until the Imam Ahmad found the United States had offered $200 million to the "Arab big four" and angrily calculated: "Only one percent of the $200 million has been offered to Yemen." Then he walked out. Richards also reported William Crawford had found "24 Russian and Czech technicians" were in the country. Richards reported Yemen was the one site where the Soviets were making gains, but claimed that "[t]he Imam is playing into the hands of the Russian technicians and Russian policy."[49]

By August 1957 NEA had prepared a report on technical aid that began, "We have for several months considered Yemen one of the most critical areas of the Near East." That realization had come far too late. The role of Richards in the Yemen was a perfect example of what was wrong with Cold War analysis and Washington's reluctance to see how linkage with London could harm American interests. The problem was British colonialism. Ironically, the Soviets did succeed in Yemen but by default. Richards and Dulles simply could not comprehend that the Yemenis would turn to the Soviets when they perceived that the British were the more immediate threat. Middle East hand William Crawford was instructed to make "more frequent visits for longer periods" to the remote area, but Aden was already lost. In Yemen, British actions opened the way for the Soviets to fish in troubled waters. Most importantly, the United States was unwilling to talk tough with the British about their continued harassment of the Adeni tribes. Eisenhower had again sent an envoy with no regional experience and a blinkered anti-Soviet perspective that mirrored the conventional wisdom in Washington. In both cases, the Johnston mission and the Richards mission and the Middle East hands' opinions were overlooked, and their opinions based on area expertise were brushed aside. Twice the Dulles team had struck out by adhering to the logic of the Cold War.

Soon Secretary Dulles's already punitive attitude toward Nasser took another turn when he devised a water diversion plan of his own. In 1957 he requested that Middle East hand William Lakeland study "the feasibility of diverting the Nile to the Red Sea in order to cut off Egypt's water." Lakeland regarded the scheme as rather wild and managed to supply Dulles with "ample data to indicate that it would not work." William Brewer, desk officer for United Arab Republic (UAR) affairs, recalled Lakeland had been ordered to develop, not a plan "to improve US–UAR relations but rather […] on a plan to make them worse." Brewer wanted to normalize US–UAR relations but could not until after Dulles retired.[50]

The Soviet relationship with Nasser was based on desperation, not on political affinity. Nasser feared and suppressed Egyptian communists.

Cairo's treatment of the Communist Party became an issue during a volatile April 1958 meeting between Nikita Khrushchev and Nasser. On the morning after their first meeting, Nasser confronted Khrushchev over his references to the Egyptian Communists and commented that if Nasser was "to follow a socialist path he could not be anti-Communist." When questioned about it the next day Khrushchev blamed the interpreter to shield himself.

During the heated exchange Nasser repeatedly told Khrushchev he had heard him and the Soviet premier repeatedly denied it. As tensions rose, Khrushchev finally turned on his interpreter with a threat: "No, no, if he makes a mistake in such an important affair, we must make him into a piece of soap." The anecdote, vividly recounted by Nasser's aide Mohammed Heikal, ends with the interpreter "sweating with fear" and Nasser, who is alarmed by Kruschev's extreme reaction, attempting to pass it off. Nasser was very likely unaware of the fate of many of the interpreter's Arabist colleagues: between 1918 and 1972 more than three hundred Soviet Orientalists, many of whom were Jews, had been secretly imprisoned or executed.[51]

There was fundamental incompatibility between Cairo and Moscow, but Nasser managed to accept Soviet aid while crushing Egyptian Communists. The paradox of the Cold War was that Khrushchev saw Nasser as too anti-Communist, while John Foster Dulles saw him as a client of Moscow, and both attacked his neutralism. In November 1957, a Soviet official pressured the Egyptians to choose: "Non-alignment is a myth. Egypt must decide to choose an international camp if it is seeking real force [...] we will strengthen you and defend you."[52] Whenever Washington refused aid, Cairo had no choice but to look to Moscow.

After the Suez Crisis, the Middle East situation was shifting so rapidly it had made earlier US policy papers obsolete. In 1957 a new assessment of policy was to be made. Middle East hand Donald Bergus was selected to draft the document, and, as he recalled, "see it through the process up to President Eisenhower." National Security Council document, NSC #5801, "Long-Range US Policy toward the Near East," reveals the conflicting viewpoints inside Washington.[53]

There was no agreement between the National Security Council (NSC) and the Departments of Defense and State over how to proceed in 1958. Defense argued for a US initiative either "by the US directly or through the UN or through a third party" to get "a peaceful and equitable settlement." The State Department, on the other hand, proposed that the United States "constantly explore the prospects and possibilities" of a US effort "to persuade the Arab states and Israel to work toward a settlement." This wording reflects the Secretary of State's reluctance to work with Nasser.

In an NSC meeting a few days later Dulles openly acknowledged the Eisenhower administration "had gone further in trying to moderate the policy and position of Israel, and to show greater sympathy for the Arabs, than any previous administration." Yet he refused to back a peace effort as the priority. The Defense Department supported it since "certain courses of action [...] simply could not be followed from the domestic political point of view." Dulles noted that even the Soviets were wary of openly threatening Israeli sovereignty and continued that "we are in fact reduced to following the old British formula of 'muddling through.'" Dulles conceded, both State and Defense "had been in agreement that the establishment of Israel [...] would inevitably lead to the situation in the Near East which now confronts us. Nevertheless, the warnings and advice of the Departments of State and Defense had been ignored."[54] It was more than he had acknowledged previously and perhaps more than Bergus and the Middle East hands might have expected to hear.

The opening proposition upon which the entire long range plan was predicated—"NSC #5801 attempts to reflect the undisputed position of Free World leadership in the area held by the US and our greater involvement in intra-area affairs"—must have sounded a bit overblown even before the events of that summer. By the middle of 1958 the Middle East was in crisis. The Baghdad Pact had been denounced by the Soviets as "a British prison for the Arabs." This was used very effectively to heighten anti-US and anti-British sentiment. Evelyn Shuckburgh observed that the Russians were "slanging the Baghdad Pact [...] and they take the very words out of the Egyptians' mouths [...] They are getting very skillful at this and bidding for a power position in the area."[55]

The second US proposition dealt with Arab unity and argued that it was in America's interest to "encourage constructive efforts […] to create indigenous strength." This rang hollow, since it was to be limited to Jordan, Iraq and Saudi Arabia—disunited and weak allies. It was an admission that the United States had given up on other nations although it did not openly acknowledge communist gains. The paper avoided the word nationalism while it grudgingly acknowledged that neutralism was "a permanent factor in the Near East political arena."[56] It was January, but by July Eisenhower would face another major crisis.

Richard Parker, assigned to the State Department's Iraq desk, was awakened at six in the morning on July 14, 1958, by an urgent phone call. He had been on alert to a possible coup in Jordan and was deeply concerned, terming the situation "very shaky," but the message received was not what he had expected. "I got a call from the telegram duty officer," and he said, "Mr. Parker, there's been a revolution in Baghdad." I said, "You mean, Amman." He said, "No, Baghdad." Parker scrambled down to the State Department and found the officer-in-charge was on leave: "I was all alone. Stuff started coming in from everywhere. The dimensions of the thing gradually became clear to us, we realized what a terrible disaster it had been for American and British policy in the area." Reports showed the entire pro-Western alliance was dissolving under a series of anti-Western, nationalist revolutions. Lebanon began to fall apart before Parker's eyes that same day. Although Ike had pledged to defend any Arab state threatened by communism, Parker saw events were being interpreted in light of the Eisenhower Doctrine's anticommunism and laid the blame for the crisis on CIA tampering in Lebanon's complex and fragile politics: "President Chamoun of Lebanon cashed the blank check we had given him earlier under the Eisenhower doctrine. He was fighting a small scale rebellion in his country. A rebellion which we had helped arrange by helping him rig the election the previous year in a scandalous way. This was all coming apart and something had to be done."[57]

Later that day CIA director Allen Dulles appeared at the White House to brief Eisenhower and the NSC. Eisenhower announced at the outset that "this is our last chance to make a move. We cannot ignore this one." Dulles, always focused upon the Soviet angle, asked rhetorically, "What will [the] Russians do?" Ike, obviously incensed, argued: "From [a] strategic point of view, Israel ought to declare war on Egypt!!"[58] Cooler heads prevailed, and the meeting adjourned until the afternoon.

Then Ike met with a congressional delegation during which Speaker of the House Sam Rayburn "asked if these developments are in fact mostly civil wars." To which Ike responded that "they have that appearance but we know they are fomented by Nasser under Kremlin guidance. But the danger to all the West to be cut off permanently from Middle East oil is terrible."[59] The bottom line was that the conflict endangered the secure flow of oil to American allies.

Rayburn had a point. In fact the events were "mostly a civil war," but Eisenhower's anxieties magnified Nasser's role. The next morning Ike said: "The present incident comes about by the struggle of Nasser to get control of these [oil] supplies—to get the income and the power to destroy the Western world." By evening, the NEA's director, Stuart Rockwell, told Richard Parker the decision had been made to land marines in Lebanon.

Parker went home feeling physically ill and "much depressed." He did not think the landing had much chance of success: "It had no business working, but it did."[60]

The decision was not based upon NEA's advice, as Parker recalled, but instead on Allen Dulles's CIA briefing memo presented at the White House. Parker found it "a very superficial document" but "was probably instrumental in our decision to land the troops." He tersely stated, "People at the top do not know much about the area, they have no time to listen to specialists [...] Policymakers need a practical recommendation in two short paragraphs."[61] And, the CIA provided it.

Ironically, CIA covert operations had helped create the situation. Historian Hugh Wilford observed that the key CIA agents were moving out just as Lebanon descended into chaos: in late 1957 Kim Roosevelt left for private business; early in 1958 Archie Roosevelt was assigned to a post in Spain. Their aide Bill Eveland found that there was "a changing of the CIA guard over the Middle East." Vice President Nixon, whose low opinion of the State Department was already well known, called Dulles to discuss the Beirut landings late on July 15 and commented: "McC[lintock] changed his mind and the Sec said he tried to stop them from landing. N[ixon] indicated the need for people who can stand up better than that."[62] Ambassador Robert McClintock had barely avoided a disastrous confrontation between American and Lebanese forces, as he later reported: "intelligence had reached me that all available Lebanese artillery and tanks were lined up on airport road with orders to fire on advancing Marine column. (I did not know at that time, but later learned, that Lebanese Air Force had been ordered to take to the air and to fire on American forces)." McClintock then collared Lebanese Forces General Chehab and inserted them both between the two sides. McClintock was relieved that they had "avert[ed] what would have been a first class political defeat for the US if Lebanese armed forces had engaged the American Marines."[63] But later McClintock forgot this brush with disaster and became a proponent of similar interventions.

A week later, with the circle of pro-US nations much reduced, Dulles told Ike that Arab nationalism was like "a flood which is running strongly. We cannot successfully oppose it, but we can put up sand bags around the positions we must protect [...] Israel and Lebanon and [...] the oil positions around the Persian Gulf." He warned that the Soviets were "seeking to incite the floods."[64] This analogy reveals Dulles's globalist view of events as a Soviet-inspired disaster of biblical proportions. In fact, floods are uncontrollable events, but ones that grow out of regional factors like topography and rainfall—not summoned up by the communists.

Conversely, Middle East hands saw events as the logical outgrowth of having ignored the festering regional problems that had been dealt with in a heavy-handed manner that boded ill for the future. William Brewer recalled that Middle East hands "were opposed to the idea of the landings at the time they took place, as we felt this was a return to gunboat diplomacy which had been practiced by the British in the nineteenth century." The United States had linked their policy to the British and then adopted their operational methods. This was bound to be resented in the Arab world. Brewer saw the Arab reaction as "very alert to the roles and position of the great powers" and acknowledged that the landings had brought some calm, mainly because the power of the US Sixth Fleet had been made manifest.

Talcott Seelye, reviewing the Cold War decades, recalled: "The automatic reflex of Washington normally is, when there is a crisis in the Middle East, to do two things: you announce that you have alerted the 82nd Airborne Division and you announce you are moving the Sixth Fleet."[65] That pattern began with the Beirut landings, but it remained alive for Deputy Undersecretary of State Robert Murphy. He requested the US Navy supply him with a chart indicating the Sixth Fleet's day-to-day schedule.[66]

For Middle East hands, especially senior Arabist Raymond Hare, it was not the landings, but the lessons learned in the aftermath that boded ill. Washington's confident Cold War analysis of the Beirut landings was very different from the concerns worrying the Middle East hands. They felt the landings had annihilated any pro-US sentiment gained by Eisenhower's insistence on an Israeli withdrawal from the Sinai and Gaza.

Quiet Diplomacy or Send in the Marines

Washington took a lesson from July 1958: the Sixth Fleet was an effective means to display American power and the marine landings, or limited intervention, was a pattern that could be useful elsewhere. The Middle East hands drew very different conclusions: Arab states perceived the United States as a threat, building a coalition of obedient pro-American states in a defense pact was intensely resented by many Arabs and trying to suppress moderate nationalist movements would only bring in the radicals. The old regimes who cooperated with the British, the French and the Americans were doomed.

Although the Americans never fired a shot on the beach in Beirut, a real war broke out inside the State Department as cables were fired back and forth between Ambassador Robert McClintock in Beirut and Ambassador Raymond Hare in Cairo as each tried to define the lessons to be learned from the limited intervention in Beirut.

In January 1959 McClintock, a generalist and non-Arabist, argued the landings had "wider strategic implications," which had created "a highly salutary effect in a global sense as well as in regional application to the Middle East." McClintock's cable resonated with the Cold Warriors in Washington when he pointed out that the "Kremlin changed course four times in four weeks" and the landings had punctured the "myth of Soviet superiority." McClintock was the archetype of the generalist with experience in Panama, Japan, Chile, Finland, Sweden, Washington, Brussels, Cairo, Vietnam, Cambodia and India before becoming ambassador to Lebanon. He felt Arabs were now aware that "what US can do in Lebanon it can do elsewhere."[67]

Hare, as a Middle East hand and experienced regionalist, argued McClintock had misread the outcome. Hare argued the landings had "produced profound shock to UAR." Nasser had taken off on a "frantic trip from Yugoslavia to Moscow," but for Hare that was not necessarily a good thing. Moreover, he warned the Sixth Fleet was now a "very real and somewhat menacing element." The operation had succeeded, but Nasser had a "fundamental lack of confidence in the west." There were lasting geopolitical implications: "Possibility US military intervention in area will henceforth be constant factor in calculations (of) UAR and USSR." He cautioned that "conditions in Lebanon of (a) special character which do not [repeat not] obtain elsewhere within area." Hare's repetition of "not" in cable language signified his emphasis on that point. This was a key implication for him, and he closed by cautioning "a few random rifle shots [...] could have gravely jeopardized our enterprise."⁶⁸

Raymond Hare refused to accept the Cold War view. He worked with NEA's deputy, Armin Meyer, to develop a small-scale program to rebuild US-Egyptian relations. This proposal promoted a benign form of economic aid, eschewed overt military action and undercut Soviet influence by ending Nasser's dependence on Soviet wheat, but it could only be attempted once Dulles had withdrawn from the scene.

Hare suggested that the United States should create a "constructive discussion with Nasser [...] attempting [to] establish some less noxious relationship." He suggested Robert Murphy be sent as a special envoy. Hare, whose father worked for the Maine Bureau of Fisheries, reached back into his past and compared Nasser to a trout and Murphy to the angler: "I believe [we] should continue cast fly over him from time to time in order [to] maintain some sort of contact [...] suggest that consideration be given to having Murphy drop in here [...] He is adept political angle and possible he might get real strike where we have previously tended get nothing but annoying nibbles and sometimes have lost bait in bargain." Murphy arrived in Cairo that August, as Hare had requested, but found Nasser's mood "hypersensitive" and reported that "his blood pressure was still high." Nasser opened the meeting by informing Murphy of Dulles's "personal antagonism," and the remainder of Murphy's meetings was dominated by Nasser's anger over what he read in the American press, in particular the "cumulative effect of adverse criticism of UAR and himself." Furthermore, Nasser told Murphy that "he was especially steamed up by several articles in [the] last issue [of] *US News and World Report*." Murphy got a few words in when Nasser assured him Egypt would adhere to neutrality. He took pains to point out the USSR's "sensitivity" to Egyptian needs and how its aid was sent "without strings," and he advised the United States "to take a page out of the Soviet book." The issue of Israel was consigned to a brief comment at the end.⁶⁹ It is clear from Murphy's report that Dulles's demonization of Nasser had serious consequences. Hare failed to convince Washington when he argued that confrontational tactics had actually weakened the American position.

The following spring Hare warned against a repetition of the landings since the "odds against successful repetition would be very high." Richard Parker reflected on the lessons drawn from the limited intervention in Beirut and argued, "You can draw a straight line from Lebanon to our involvement in the Dominican Republic and in Vietnam." He also felt that Washington erred when they attempted to apply it elsewhere: "It was not a precedent for other places."⁷⁰

Eisenhower and Dulles had few options by 1958 because they viewed the Middle East as part of the Cold War chessboard and had aligned America with the British who were deeply unpopular with Arab nationalists. These factors contributed to the decline of US interests. Despite substantial gains made during by Eisenhower's principled stand over Gaza withdrawal, the US position had steadily declined. By 1958 it hit its nadir as Iraq, Jordan and Lebanon simultaneously descended into anarchy, and it seemed no pro-Western government would be left. During the crisis, Henry Byroade, the former head of NEA, warned Dulles: "The Arab Middle East will certainly see the departure of kings, old men and Christians from positions of leadership long before the revolution there has reached its fulfillment. I assume that our policy thinking has recognized this state of affairs." Byroade argued that the United States must "remain flexible enough to live with and work with [...] the new type of leadership that seems bound to me to come to the Middle East, and which I believe we are virtually powerless to prevent." Dulles told Byroade this course was "the best calculated to preserve our influence in the area."[71] Dulles never realized the "kings, old men and Christians" could no longer be propped up and never saw there were limits to America's ability to control events and he remained inflexible.

Raymond Hare recognized the US–Egyptian relationship needed to be rebuilt, and he carefully used quiet diplomacy to lay the groundwork for an improved relationship: "You have got to make an initial effort to understand who Nasser was and what made him tick." He found Nasser's origins as the leader of a conspiracy, the Free Officer's movement, planted in him a fearful, suspicious nature that was magnified by the British efforts to bring him down: "He was suspicious."[72]

Reshaping the American relationship with Egypt would be very difficult, but Hare worked with NEA's Armin Meyer in Washington to establish a program that would ship surplus grain to Egypt for almost no cost. The plan was designed to build a bridge of goodwill with Egypt, which Parker saw could create a "gradual easing away from boycott toward accommodation." He saw an opportunity in late 1958: "The anti-Nasser fervor dimmed somewhat with the departure of Dulles [...] and the realization that the policy of confrontation was leading nowhere."[73]

Secretary Dulles had first been stricken ill at the height of the Suez Crisis in November 1956 and hospitalized. The White House released word that he would fully recover, but by April he was dead. Meanwhile, Christian Herter, Dulles's personal choice, was appointed as Secretary of State. Herter was a faint echo of Dulles, the dynamic Cold War warrior, but Herter allowed NEA to attempt a modest rapproachment with Cairo. Ike seemed to find some new flexibility to shift his policy when suddenly cut off from his anticommunist alter ego.

NEA recognized the changed atmosphere. Nasser was most dependent upon bartering Egyptian cotton to Moscow for Soviet wheat. Meanwhile Egypt was unable to feed its ever expanding population. The United States, however, was overstocked with surplus grain and congressional representatives from farm states favored US aid exports of American wheat. For years Dulles had refused any suggestion of wheat aid being sent to Egypt. Earlier, in an attempt to break the deadlock, King Saud had carried a message from Nasser to Washington requesting wheat. But Parker Hart found that "[h]e [Saud] couldn't budge Eisenhower any more than we could from Cairo." Hart witnessed the negative effects of the White House refusal and the advantage Moscow gained from offering Soviet aid: "Nasser therefore gave him [Saud] a very cold reception and said, 'We got our wheat from the Soviet Union. I'll send you pictures of it.'"[74]

In the aftermath of the Faisal–Nasser blowup, Radio Cairo's "Voice of the Arabs" focused new hostility on the Saudis. It was especially ironic since the CIA had provided Nasser with everything to build the radio station. Historian Hugh Wilford observed the CIA decision to provide the gear and technical training to Nasser's regime "would return to haunt it a few years later, when Cairo became the Arab world's main purveyor of anti-American propaganda."[75] Nasser skillfully used radio to communicate with not only Egyptians but to position himself as a leader of the nonaligned movement.

Hare's quiet diplomacy succeeded in improving the situation through an offer of PL-480 wheat aid. Some of the Middle East hands called Hare's plan the "three-stage rocket" to build a new relationship with Egypt. In Cairo Mohammed Heikal, confidant of Nasser and editor of *Al Ahram*, had his own three-stage description of what Egypt's experience during the Dulles years: "seduction—punishment—containment." After the wheat deal was secured Heikal described the new turn in the US–UAR relationship: "there was a breathing space in affairs between the two countries."[76] Hare cabled his support for the wheat aid package to Washington, comparing the change in policy to tennis champion Bill Tilden's famous maxim: "Never to change [a] winning game but always change [a] losing one." He pointed out the key effect would be anticommunist as it would "reduce [UAR] dependence" on the Soviets for wheat. In selling the idea he observed, "This is not [a] mere wheat deal but [a] transaction in fundamental foreign relations."[77]

In retirement the mild-mannered Hare recalled how easily it could be done since the United States had wheat "running out of the bins" and could sell it to Egypt for what he called "wooden nickels"[78] or Egyptian pounds. Under Hare's plan the UAR paid only for the cost of shipping the wheat, in Egyptian pounds, as a face-saving transaction. It was a highly effective move against Soviet influence, and, unlike military aid, did not threaten Israel. Hare argued this would have "broad appeal." John Badeau, Hare's successor in Cairo, recalled the wheat aid "gave rise to a sort of honeymoon period."[79]

In the spirit of the season Hare signed the deal on Christmas Eve 1958. The most important aspect of the offer, his son Ambassador Paul J. Hare has argued, was that it erased UAR dependence on the Soviets: "Moreover, he [Raymond Hare] knew that US wheat would undercut Egypt's trade with the Soviet Union, because the Egyptians had been selling their long staple cotton in exchange for Soviet wheat."[80] At very little cost the United States had improved their relationship with Egypt and reduced the Soviet role in the Egyptian economic equation as well.

In his study of the economic aid program William Burns pointed to this first contract as a "far more reliable means" to improving relations with Egypt than our other technical aid and quoted Hare's observation: "We could at least begin to try to bury the hatchet underneath all of this American grain." They did bury it. Ike met Nasser briefly in New York in late 1960. Heikal recorded how Nasser thanked Eisenhower for putting "your principles before your friends" at Suez. Ike recalled Nasser "hoped Africa would not become a battleground for the East–West Cold War" and insisted that Egypt would not "surrender to Communist domination." In the first year, US wheat represented 24 percent of Egypt's grain imports, and a year later rose to 66 percent. This strategy remained viable through the Kennedy years as Food for Peace, keeping Egypt quiescent. Undersecretary of State Chester Bowles quipped that it would lead Nasser to "forsake the microphone for the bulldozer."[81]

Washington wanted Nasser busy constructing a new Egypt rather than using radio to criticize the United States. The PL-480 wheat program, established through the initiative of Hare and the Middle East hands at NEA, did improve American relations with Nasser and laid the groundwork for JFK's Food for Peace initiative.

For the Middle East hands America had to capitalize on the goodwill brought about by Ike's principled stance during the Suez Crisis and then use foreign aid to win friends. After that base of trust was built, they could work to defuse the refugee and border issues that had festered since 1948. The approach of Eisenhower and Dulles pushed for big results through flawed initiatives, the Eric Johnston Plan and the Richards Mission, which failed because the envoys did not understand regional concerns and dismissed the advice by area experts.

Eisenhower was challenged by the tumult of anti-Western revolts in July 1958: the Iraqi Revolution, civil war in Lebanon and the near collapse of the Jordanian monarchy, which proved that Dulles's strategy to construct an anticommunist alliance in the Middle East was not viable. Middle East hands used quiet diplomacy and argued Washington should avoid linking US foreign policy with London because of the Suez Crisis. Dulles might have steered around the rockiest issues if had he heeded their counsel.

The second stage of Hare's "three stage rocket," would be launched much later. Deputy Assistant Secretary of State Armin Meyer had toured the Palestinian refugee camps, while working on the wheat deal in 1958–59, and recalled that visit "made a particular impact on me," especially when a UN official warned that the camps were "cesspools" in which "poison abounds and nothing but demoralized and deformed human mentalities will emerge."[82] Meyer returned to Washington determined to put forward an initiative to resolve the Palestinian refugee problem, but his proposal fizzled. In 1961 he was ready to launch the second stage of the "rocket" with an appeal to President John F. Kennedy.

Chapter Six

QUIET DIPLOMACY IN ACTION: THE KENNEDY AND JOHNSON YEARS

John F. Kennedy was the first president to make clear he intended to make effective use of his area specialists. He told Secretary of State Dean Rusk that Arabic language specialists should be appointed to Middle East posts. When considering candidates to be ambassador to Libya, Kennedy voiced his concern that one candidate did not speak Arabic: "We should appoint ambassadors primarily who have a knowledge of Arabic." JFK voiced concerned about the thin line of expertise: "Do we have a sufficient number of officers to maintain this practice?" Regarding appointments to Israel, Kennedy proposed that the deputy assistant secretary of Near East Affairs (NEA) Armin Meyer be nominated as ambassador to Israel because, as Meyer recalled, "What Kennedy had in mind was to send a professional diplomat well versed in Arab world affairs to emphasize regional realities to the Israelis."[1]

JFK wanted a particular type of area specialist, and he wanted more from them. In his January 1961 State of the Union address Kennedy announced his administration "recognizes the value of dissent and daring" in those who chose public service careers.[2] In April 1961 the *Foreign Service Journal* featured an editorial "Daring and Dissent," which reiterated JFK's message to American diplomats in the State Department's professional journal.[3] Then, in May 1962 Kennedy gave a spirited address to the American Foreign Service Association, telling them that America's diplomats: "Should be the best, in language, in knowledge, in experience." The second part of his message was even more direct. The president demanded to hear "evidence of dissent and controversy"[4] in their political reporting. But these Foreign Service officers (FSOs) had survived the Orientalist purges at NEA and Senator Joseph McCarthy's attacks on the China Hands. They were committed to supporting policy but also to career survival. One adage echoing down the State Department hallways encapsulated their experience: "There are bold FSOs and there are old FSOs, but there are no old, bold FSOs."[5] Kennedy aide Arthur Schlesinger pointed out that area specialists had learned under Eisenhower to stop "telling Washington what they really thought and consecrated themselves to the clichés of the Cold War."[6]

But Kennedy thrived on debate and wanted to be surrounded by dynamic advisers, and he appointed a number of East Coast intellectuals as top White House aides, especially in the National Security Council (NSC). The men he chose came to be known as "action intellectuals," a mix of professors, technocrats and advocates of modernization theory and limited military interventions in support of an activist foreign policy. In a 1967 article for *Life Magazine* Theodore H. White noted this "brotherhood of scholars forms the most powerful community in our society." These included McGeorge Bundy, a Harvard professor of government who became JFK's special assistant for National Security, Walt Whitman Rostow, also a special assistant, and Robert McNamara as Secretary of Defense. Historian John Dumbrell saw them as encompassing Kennedy's key advisers who came to dominate policy making. Kai Bird identified McGeorge Bundy and his brother William as two key action intellectuals who had powerful influence over foreign policy in *The Color of Truth*. Bird notes how Mac Bundy grew impatient with the details of diplomatic reports, "So he took to summarizing tedious State Department cables with one-liners that amused the president." Bundy quickly determined Secretary of State Rusk was a weak competitor, and Bird noted that soon "Bundy's shop was running circles around Rusk's State Department." Perhaps the full implications were unclear to Kennedy but former Secretary of State Dean Acheson attended a cabinet meeting on the Berlin crisis and "was astounded that White House aides were making foreign policy instead of the State Department."[7]

At the State Department there was a belief that a low-key approach would produce results for the NEA, but working against the State Department in the bureaucratic battles was mild-mannered Secretary of State Dean Rusk, who seemed incapable of protecting State's turf when challenged by the NSC or CIA. He was no bureaucratic infighter. Rusk rarely spoke aloud in cabinet meetings and remained a reticent, inscrutable figure nicknamed "buddha." Arthur Schlesinger could not fathom "the enigma of Rusk," referring to him as the "silent secretary." Rusk's gentleness, bordering on diffidence, put State at a disadvantage.

Israeli Ambassador Abba Eban discreetly described Rusk: "He was never numbered among the Americans whose powerful enthusiasms were aroused by Israel's statehood and by our subsequent policies." For Eban it was Rusk's loyalty to his superiors that made the difference: "his fidelity to the presidents under whom he served was absolute. All three of them—Truman, Kennedy and Johnson—were friends of Israel."[8]

To manage the NEA, Kennedy appointed an academic and area specialist on South Asian issues, Phillips Talbot. He had joined the State Department as a lateral entry in 1961 and held the post through 1965. He and his deputy, Armin Meyer, worked well with both the Middle East hands and JFK. Meyer recalled: "I think the policy of 'quiet diplomacy' and 'normalization of relations' with Nasser was a good one. Happily, the Mideast was not on the front pages of American newspapers. We called it a period of 'relative tranquility.'"[9]

The transition from Eisenhower to Kennedy began with the launch of the first stage of the foreign policy "three-stage rocket" in December 1958 with the PL-480 wheat program, then transformed by JFK into the Food for Peace aid program. The second stage began in 1961 with an effort to normalize relations with Egypt's Gamal Abdel Nasser. Foreign Service officer (FSO) William Brewer worked to organize an international effort to reopen the damaged Suez Canal to oil tankers. Normalization, however, was to be limited to reopening the canal and cultural exchanges. This was consonant with the Middle East hands' Beirut Axiom to improve relations within the region while not making overt alliances.

The third stage that the NEA proposed was to dissolve the Palestinian refugee camps with negotiations through the Joseph Johnson Plan. Finding a way to solve the refugee problem and get Palestinians out of the United Nations Works and Relief Agency (UNWRA) refugee camps, which were identified as a key source of radicalization, was the key objective of Middle East hands like William R. Crawford, who helped draft the Joseph Johnson initiative. The Johnson plan may have been America's best method to forestall political radicalism and violence.

As JFK increasingly relied upon his National Security Council staff, especially action-oriented operators like Robert Komer, a new force began to take a dominant role in Middle East policy.

Kennedy was so focused on the region that Arthur Schlesinger termed him the "Secretary of State for the third world." He also recalled JFK knew more about the Middle East "than most of the officials on the seventh floor of the State Department."[10] While that sounds exaggerated, in view of how firmly generalists were entrenched at the highest levels, it had some legitimacy.

Kennedy's approach was made clear by his 1960 statement on Algeria and the Third World: "Call it nationalism, call it anti-colonialism [...] the word is out—and spreading like wildfire in nearly a thousand languages and dialects—that it is no longer necessary to remain forever poor or forever in bondage." JFK was not hostile to Cold War neutralism and pointed out that "some who call themselves neutrals" were friends of the United States, while other neutral nations were "unremittingly hostile." He would draw distinctions between them and not condemn them all, as Dulles had. Kennedy realized the power of such movements in 1962; he noted that they must be accommodated, since "[t]hose who make peaceful revolution impossible will make violent revolution inevitable."[11]

The Arab world welcomed the diminution of overtly Cold War rhetoric. In his study of the nonaligned movement, political scientist Cecil Crabb quoted an African proverb: "When two elephants fight, it is the grass that suffers." Arab leaders focused their East–West concerns between Maghreb and Mahrib, which describes the East–West nexus from Morocco to the Arabian peninsula. They had no desire to be collateral damage in a US–Soviet fight at a time when America installed nuclear weapons systems in Central and Southern Europe, Turkey and elsewhere. Major American air bases were established in Saudi Arabia and Libya, which required good relations with those countries.

Middle East hands emphasized a more democratic and activist approach on the local level, in what they termed "shirt-sleeve diplomacy," to converse with a broader cross-section of people and use their language skills to gather information beyond the routine embassy contacts.

Earl Russell went on a series of hazardous information-gathering journeys from a variety of posts. Hermann Eilts negotiated the Wheelus air base lease in Libya, then Richard Parker worked to win Congressional approval of the agreement, which secured access to an airbase the Pentagon deemed critical for Cold War military readiness.

At this time the American–Israel Public Affairs Committee (AIPAC) emerged as a potent lobbying force. AIPAC's founder, Isaiah L. Kenen, stated the organization was established "to lobby the Congress to tell the President to overrule the State Department." A succinct description of how AIPAC operated in that era. Their publications targeted the Middle East as AIPAC developed substantial clout in the 1960s.[12] The result was that

Middle East hands realized they must walk a very thin line in their policy recommendations. The line was situated between what they perceived as America's national interests and what was politically feasible in Washington.

The Israeli lobby made the Middle East hands aware of its political power. JFK's director of Arab-Israeli Affairs, William R. Crawford, was assured of his own inconsequence by Israeli lobbyists: "They'd just say, 'We know Crawford, that you're opposing this. We respect your point of view as a conscientious one, but we have ours, and we know we're going to win.'" It was one thing to claim victory, but he realized, "They would win." He thought the United States would not transfer tanks to Israel, but later found the tanks had been secretly diverted from NATO stocks in Europe by "a presidential directive unbeknownst to the Department of State." The frustrations were palpable. Crawford recalled: "I ended up with a duodenal ulcer. It went away fairly quickly after I stopped working on Israeli affairs."[13]

Jewish voters had supported the Kennedy campaign in 1960, and he had garnered 80 percent of their votes. After the election JFK moved to address Jewish concerns, and their continued support became his concern. Israeli diplomat Mordechai Gazit points out that Kennedy offered "support [for] the security of both Israel and her neighbors" in May 1963 and reaffirmed the commitment in a letter to Israeli Prime Minister Levi Eshkol in October. Historian Lewis Paper calculated that "on nineteen different occasions […] Kennedy reaffirmed a pledge to Israel to help defend her in the event of an attack by the Arab nations."[14] JFK also promised, via his aide Meyer Feldman, the Sixth Fleet to guarantee Israeli security.

When Israel was under international pressure to have its secret nuclear facility at Dimona inspected, JFK arranged for US scientists to inspect the reactor rather than the International Atomic Energy Agency (IAEA).[15]

Israeli diplomat Mordechai Gazit has claimed that Kennedy's meeting with Golda Meir in 1962 was not made with an eye toward the 1964 election, but it is obvious JFK factored it into his political calculus. He prefaced his December 1962 remarks to Meir by saying, "[W]e should think of the future and especially of the next year or two." While the special relationship quotation is often cited, the second part is less well noted: "[W]e cannot afford the luxury of identifying Israel […] as our exclusive friends […] and letting other countries go." After listing water problems, border issues, refugees, and Hawk missiles as challenges, JFK asked Meir to recognize that their "partnership produces strains for the US in the Middle East."[16] Middle East hands feared an overt alliance with Israel would drive Arab neutrals into the Soviet camp.

The NSC staff made bold suggestions to Kennedy, often based upon little area knowledge. NSC adviser Robert "Blowtorch" Komer took the lead in making policy on the Yemen War to the point that JFK began referring to the conflict as "Komer's War." Middle East hands found Komer too ready to shoot from the hip. Phillips Talbot's deputy at the NEA reported on Komer's behavior during a presentation on Iran: "[H]e pounded the table and said, 'The time has come for us to do something even if our better judgment tells us it's the wrong thing to do.'" Komer's many memoranda and his oft-expressed opinions were in constant circulation, whereas documents drafted by Middle East hands were less influential.[17]

Even Komer's influence on Middle East affairs had its limits. In December 1963, he continued to urge US intervention telling McGeorge Bundy to tell the new president that the United States was "probably in for real trouble there." Historian Warren I. Cohen noted that despite the trouble Nasser caused and the fact that "[e]verything Komer feared would happen, did happen, with minimal consequences for the US," LBJ, Bundy and Rusk "[m]ay not have known how to get out of Vietnam but they knew better than to involve the United States in Yemeni affairs."[18]

In bureaucratic battles, the quiet diplomacy of Raymond Hare and Parker Hart, mentors of the Middle East hands, was no match for JFK's action intellectuals. Komer subtly undercut the NEA when, on the eve of a critical meeting with Golda Meir, he advised JFK: "State may have too big a menu for you to take up with Golda." Top NSC posts were staffed by Cold Warriors who focused on blocking the Soviets, and many, like Komer, had CIA connections as well. Michael E. Sterner recalled there was always a group who used the Cold War alone as a framework for analysis, and "people who saw the Middle East as basically a chessboard over which US and Soviet pieces were being moved."[19]

Vice President Lyndon Johnson's dislike of Egyptian leader Gamal Abdel Nasser was well established early on, and LBJ saw Israel as an underdog. In 1956 Senator Johnson opposed any Israeli withdrawal from Egypt, telling the State Department that it was time they realized "we can't deal with this Colonel [Nasser]." Historian Steven Spiegel concluded: "As President, LBJ was ill at ease or even hostile in meetings with the Saudis; and he was no captive of big oil."[20] It seems a blend of Old Testament imagery and Texas history led him to regard the Israelis as pioneers fulfilling Biblical prophecy and the Arabs as an impediment roughly equivalent to the Mexicans in old Texas.

As Vice President LBJ toured the Middle East in 1962, on his way into Beirut with US Ambassador Armin Meyer, Johnson halted his limousine and jumped out to shake hands. As Johnson greeted folks at a melon stand on the outskirts of Beirut, Armin Meyer pointed out that the Shatila refugee camp stood directly across the street. LBJ plowed into the camp shaking hands and repeating his support for the "integrity and independence" of Lebanon. Meyer recalled how LBJ "walked through the whole camp, chatting in a kindly manner with the poor souls living in such squalid conditions." The *New York Times* put LBJ's photograph at the melon stand on page one but made no direct reference to the Shatila camp. Instead it termed Johnson's stop "another handshaking sortie into a cluster of workers' homes" on his way to "the Mediterranean beaches and Miami-style hotels" of Beirut.[21]

Quiet Diplomacy in Action: The Joseph Johnson Plan

The first focus of quiet diplomacy was Nasser. The Middle East hands agreed that an inwardly focused Egypt meant a quiescent region. One of the major challenges was to keep Nasser's nationalist fervor within Egypt. Arthur Schlesinger recalled that Kennedy hoped Nasser would "concentrate on making progress at home rather than trouble abroad."[22] Middle East hands aimed to achieve such ends through quiet diplomacy. For his part Nasser responded that he intended to put such problems "in the icebox."[23] The

Middle East hands supported JFK's view, and they all wanted Egypt to stop causing problems in other countries like the Yemen. It worked, for a while.[24]

Earlier Nasser had reacted to Dulles's establishment of the Baghdad Pact and circled the Arab wagons by creating the United Arab Republic (UAR). Rather than fence in the maverick, the Middle East hands proposed that Kennedy correspond with Nasser, work to reopen the Suez Canal so as to secure the oil supply route to the United States and supply Egypt with American wheat so that it would not need to barter with Moscow. In the regional framework, Middle East hands supported an initiative to solve the refugee problem. Combined, these ideas built upon the Beirut Axioms: an effort to resolve the critical issues, avoid close alliances and promote what was in America's national interest.

Near East Affairs proposed to JFK that he initiate correspondence with most Arab leaders, most notably Nasser. The goals were to build a better relationship and avert negative reaction to upcoming US–Israeli talks. The NEA was concerned in early 1961 that Kennedy's scheduled May 28 visit from Prime Minister David Ben-Gurion might reinforce the perception that JFK was pro-Israeli and proposed a series of letters to Arab leaders to allay these fears. Historian Herbert Parmet portrayed the letters as "consistent with the best traditions of surreptitious State Department overtures to the Arab world," which were then "unmasked" by a Jordanian leak to the *New York Times*.[25]

Rather than a surreptitious effort by the Middle East hands to sneak one past Kennedy, the suggestion was made in a memo that argued that "the proposed letters will be helpful in our launching of the new approach to the Arab refugee problem" and acknowledged that "we have little doubt [...] these letters will leak to the press," either in the United States or the Arab world, and noted "we would concur" in their publication. In fact, the official format for the letters closed with "White House has no plans [to] publish this text but has no objection should GUAR [Government of Egypt] desire to do so." Phillips Talbot pointed out the president had wanted "money in the bank" with the Arabs, and the letters were designed to achieve that goal.[26]

On May 10 a telegram went out from the NEA that observed that they were "keenly interested in any measures which will minimize adverse reactions to Ben-Gurion visit" and concluded that JFK's letters be "cast in warm friendly tones." They noted in their message that other regional neighbors should be informed "otherwise Arabs apt to allege PCC move 'hatched' by Ben-Gurion and President in their talks."[27] In other words, the Palestine Conciliation Commission (PCC) effort, the forerunner of the Joseph Johnson Plan, might be tainted in Arab eyes as a US–Israeli plan if it was not relayed beforehand. The letters were drafted in anticipation that they might see the light of day and Meyer requested, and received permission on May 23, to advise Israeli ambassador Avraham Harman to inform Ben-Gurion.[28] The letters were not a secretive plot but aboveboard and approved at each step.

The correspondence focused on three points: first, the United States would aid the Middle East states "to control their own destiny," then to look "for solutions to disputes" and finally to support Food for Peace and other development aid. It concluded that the "underlying tensions" of the Arab–Israeli problem needed to be solved and the United States was willing "to help resolve the tragic Palestine refugee problem on the basis of the principle of repatriation and compensation."[29] It also endorsed the PCC and UN efforts on the refugee issue.

The JFK letter hit the newspapers, first in Amman, and then the *New York Times* on June 26, 1961. On the same day Ben-Gurion's ministers "declared that party's opposition to opening the gates to mass repatriation [...] the Arab nations had plenty of room for settlement of the refugees."[30] Then the Saudis weighed in negatively. Five days later Kennedy angrily wrote to NSC adviser McGeorge Bundy, "The reaction has been so sour" and demanded to know "what they hoped to accomplish and what they think we have now accomplished."[31] Rusk wrote a response defending the letters and pointing out that much of the reaction had been "in the devious Arab mind." Rusk argued the letters "may forestall the successful implementation of increasingly extremist moves by the Arabs."[32] Kennedy remained particularly upset by an insulting Saudi response and Meyer felt the letter "was still rankling the President months later."[33] This boded ill for the launch of the Joseph Johnson Plan.

The Kennedy correspondence continued with four more letters sent to Nasser and a continuing stream to Saudi Arabia dealing with substantive issues. Although Israeli diplomat Mordechai Gazit has argued that JFK's correspondence was impersonal, "His letters to King Faisal to Saudi Arabia, for example, were drafted by others and signed by him unchanged."[34]

This does not fit with the recollections of the Middle East hands involved. In a June 29 White House meeting with Parker Hart and other US ambassadors, Kennedy told them "to develop personal contacts on every possible level," and Hart requested permission to convey JFK's "personal regards to the King of Saudi Arabia and to the King of the Yemen."[35] Kennedy agreed. Hart, as ambassador to Saudi Arabia, was deeply involved in shaping the presidential exchange with King Faisal, especially during the Yemen war. Hart recalled the demands: "I'd be getting up at 3 o'clock in the morning to answer a message and finding that it contained a personal message from President Kennedy to Faisal." Hart personally tweaked the English before it was translated into Arabic to make Kennedy's intent survive the transition into the more flowery forms expected in Arabic diplomatic correspondence: "I would try to dress it up with some phrase which when translated into Arabic would make it graceful."[36]

Hart saw JFK's effort as having a particularly positive effect in the Arab world, one that built an important connection to an important ally: "Kennedy did, from the very start of his administration, make a big effort to establish a warm, personal connection with every chief of state in the Middle East." Middle East hands understood how this initiative was received by Arab leaders, as Hart explained, "This was a very important thing to do, particularly in the Middle East where personal relationships count for so much."[37] FSI Beirut graduate Richard W. Murphy arrived in Jidda to assist Hart.[38]

Armin Meyer realized the letters' impact when he arrived as ambassador to Lebanon in late 1961: "They facilitated what was for me a very pleasant environment in which to become an Ambassador." Meyer's appointment sent a key proponent of quiet diplomacy to Beirut to replace Robert McClintock, the strongest proponent of the 1958 Marine landings.[39]

There was a larger strategy. William Brewer, desk officer for Egyptian affairs, was given the job of "restoring normal relations with Egypt," which meant reopening the Suez Canal, jammed with the rusting hulks of two dozen sunken ships in the Suez Crisis. The closure had spurred the construction of larger oil tankers with deeper drafts that could carry oil around the treacherous horn of Africa. But in order for supertankers to transit the canal, it had to be cleared and deepened. This would make the oil supply route more secure and dramatically reduce transport fees, all of which benefitted the American economy.

An earlier UN effort to open the canal after the Suez War ended when British ships were to be brought in, and Nasser balked at having the United Kingdom present. Brewer located an American dredge, the world's largest, which belonged to the Army Corps of Engineers. He arranged for the dredge to be transferred; General Wheeler, commander of the corps, supported the project. Brewer lobbied Congress for an international loan to pay the expenses. The International Bank for Redevelopment made the loan, and the work got underway. Brewer explained that Middle East hands were *not* making the effort "because we thought the Egyptians were so wonderful. But simply because we didn't see there was any particular need to penalize the Egyptian government unduly." He concluded: "it was very much in our interest, and in the interests of all maritime powers, to get the canal functioning again." When Armin Meyer asked what would happen if normalization went further, Brewer cautioned: "My hunch is that the Egyptians will then ask for arms." Both concluded the United States was not prepared to go that far, and Brewer remarked, "It would be a mistake to try and move beyond that stage [...] you would raise expectations."[10] Nevertheless they faced tough opposition from the Israel lobby in Congress, and Meyer suggested NEA send a letter to all members of Congress explaining their position. Congress supported the plan and the loan. The Middle East hands' efforts, through quiet diplomacy, created a better relationship with Egypt. Meyer emphasized the quiescence and that NEA's Nasser policy "worked very nicely." Meyer also observed: "During that period (1958–61) there were no breakouts of hostilities of any kind out in the Middle East."[41]

The refugee problem remained the critical issue. Both Meyer and Assistant Secretary Phillips Talbot were deeply concerned in 1961 that the refugee camps might become the "focal points for a very strong mood of discontent." Meyer recalled how the NEA saw the spring of 1961 as the time to attempt a solution: "We had been able to convince the Kennedy Administration that the best course of action in the Middle East was to work on the refugee problem; everything else was relatively settled. Israel existed; everybody realized it. The Arabs knew it. The armistice lines were in pretty good shape at that time."[42] During the Eisenhower era Meyer had visited the camps and was told of the explosive potential if refugees remained there for generations. He recalled being told years earlier by the Indian director of the UN mission to the camps: "As long as these refugee camps exist, they are like cesspools. Poison abounds and nothing but demoralized and deformed human mentalities will emerge from them." Meyer later recalled, "This made a dramatic impression on me."[43]

There was also the expense of keeping the Palestinians in the UN refugee camps, which was almost entirely paid for by the United States. It had already cost Washington in the period from 1948 to 1961 more than a quarter of a billion dollars according to JFK's adviser Meyer Feldman. Congress complained to Middle East hand Hermann Eilts that there was "[n]o light at the end of the tunnel." The cost for 1961 alone was over $23 million, but Eilts managed to shift part of Egypt's PL-480 wheat aid to the Gaza Palestinians and thereby limited the short-term costs. But Eilts recognized it could not continue indefinitely as the refugee population expanded and the rationing system broke down. The refugee population was growing and so was the complexity of the problem.[44]

Meyer, Eilts and Crawford drafted a proposal to Kennedy that urged action to prevent "repercussions highly detrimental to the interest of Israel, the US and peace in the Near East." Beyond that looming threat, they observed it was unlikely that Congress would continue funding 70 percent of the UN refugee bill.[45] Action needed to be taken on the problem of a million displaced persons living in squalid conditions since 1948. As Meyer saw it, "The only real issue that kept stirring up the Arab–Israel problem was that of the refugees in the camps and outside the camps as well."

For the first time, an American president heeded the Middle East hands' warnings and moved to grapple with the issue—but warily. The State Department nominated Joseph Johnson, a skilled international expert from the Carnegie Endowment for Peace, to carry forward the initiative. He was teamed with Middle East hand William Crawford, who had significant experience working on Arab–Israeli and Israeli issues. It was Crawford's job to draft material for Joseph Johnson and Dean Rusk and serve as State's adviser and liaison in developing the plan.

Crawford recalled it was the State Department, not the White House, which initiated the effort to solve the problem. The original proposal was a result of NEA's lobbying of Rusk and JFK. Armin Meyer recalled he and Talbot brought Joseph Johnson to the White House: "After hearing Johnson's full explanation, Kennedy said, 'This seems to be such a good idea even Ben-Gurion should appreciate it. Mike [Feldman] you go out and talk to BG and see if he won't agree to this.'"[46]

The Johnson effort grew directly from the Middle East hands' conviction that eliminating the refugee problem was central to ending the Arab–Israeli conflict and defusing future violence. It was an integral part of their hope to keep the region quiescent.

Joseph Johnson was skilled in diplomacy and international affairs having served as Rusk's chief in 1946 at what later became United Nations Affairs.[47] Crawford saw Johnson as a good choice since it was important to "vest the leadership of that effort in a very prominent American," and Johnson was "one of the best Americans of his era: moral, liberal, understanding, shrewd and graceful." Their partnership worked well with each handling a side of the paperwork: "Joe drafted all correspondence to the PCC. I did the purely internal US Government paper."[48]

Israeli concerns were also factored in. Crawford was committed to Israel's security: "I had always taken [...] as an article of faith that during the span of my career—one of the principles that the US was very solidly committed to was the existence of the state of Israel." He had also negotiated Arab–Israeli issues: "I worked on the Jordan waters problem, on the Arab refugee problem, so I spent many years on precisely that." He described his career-long objective as "[e]fforts—continued efforts—to help Israel be accepted in the Middle East."[49]

The Joseph Johnson proposal was based upon implementation of UN Resolution 194, which had been drafted after the 1948 war. The aim was to achieve it via quiet diplomacy with little fanfare. The language of the UN resolution called for the refugees to either be returned to what had been Palestine or to be compensated and resettled elsewhere: "The General Assembly [...] Resolves that the refugees wishing to return to their homes and live at peace with their neighbors should be permitted to do so at the earliest practicable date, and that compensation should be paid." Furthermore it specifically instructed they be aided to "facilitate the repatriation, resettlement, and economic and social rehabilitation of the refugees and the payment of compensation."[50] The plan was to return only some refugees and compensate the rest, thus erasing future claims.

This was no easy task because demographic considerations were important. Crawford saw the plan as a "controlled, carefully-screened implementation of Resolution 194, designed to make sure that in no given year would the process get out of control and result in Israel's being swamped." Crawford drafted a presentation in August 1962, which called for JFK to "launch a plan designed to insert the first 'thin edge of the wedge' in seeking a solution." He stressed it was quiet diplomacy in action: "The result of more than a year's quiet but intensive effort."[51]

In the proposal Crawford argued that the United States must "break [a] fourteen-year deadlock" and prevent those who might use the refugee issue to "'Algerianize' the Arab–Israel dispute." There was also an economic benefit, since Congress had complained about that the continuing expense of the US contribution, projected at $25 million, and steadily rising. Crawford argued if the plan worked the expense would end, and if it failed there was a basis to "disengage" from the obligation.[52]

He concluded that the initiative was built upon JFK's correspondence, an assent from Ben-Gurion and a year "of quiet discussions" with both sides. While a negotiated settlement was "manifestly unattainable" at the time, the plan involved "backing into the problem in small steps,"[53] which would establish a UN headquarters to privately question a thousand refugees. Refugees would be asked, in a two-step process, whether they wanted to return and where they wanted to live, either in Israel or another nation. Israel could veto any returnee. There was also financial leverage since only in the case they settled outside of Israel would they receive compensation. Israel would pay 40 percent of the plan's expense, while the United States and the Arabs would pay 30 percent each.

The plan listed "Anticipated Israel Objections": first, they did not want to take any back but would consider 100,000 to 150,000 if the rest went elsewhere. Second, controls were built in, and the United States would generously support the expense and provide security guarantees. Here Crawford reiterated the plan put full control over the number of refugees with Israel, and that they could opt out entirely if Arabs did not accept the rest. He also suggested "a secret bilateral assurance"[54] that the United States would not support any overwhelming repatriation.

The "Anticipated Arab Objections" surrounded "the absence of any prior [Israeli] commitment" to repatriate, "the plan's clear recognition of Israel's existence and sovereignty" as well as the key clause that refugees would only be compensated if they resettled outside Israel. Crawford concluded that the plan was "the most practical, impartial course, offering [the] greatest real advantages to each side." The timing of the pending

Hawk arms sale to Israel was taken into consideration. Crawford's draft closed by warning that problems might arise "as the result of Israel's planned water withdrawals from the Jordan system and the possibility that the US might supply missiles to Israel." For the United States "our prestige will be high," and if the United States discharged its "moral responsibility," it could then "gradually disengage" from the problem.[55]

Secretary of State Rusk was reluctant to risk any of Kennedy's political capital on the plan. He wrote later that other Arabs would "slit their throats" if the Palestinian refugees did not exercise their claim to return.[56] He was unable to deal with a golden opportunity to resolve an onerous international problem that area experts feared would only get worse. Crawford acknowledged Rusk was involved during the negotiation process: "Johnson, with me at his side, would come in periodically and report to Rusk." Although Crawford admired him personally, he concluded that Rusk did not give the plan enough support: "He was certainly not a crusader for this plan."[57]

When the final plan was presented to Rusk by Crawford, he was shocked to watch Rusk write a "lukewarm endorsement" on the paper.[58] Crawford later mused it was this "faint endorsement" that allowed JFK to blink when faced down by the Israeli lobby. In a 1988 interview Crawford recalled that Johnson had not been present and only learned of Rusk's note years later.[59]

While the Johnson Plan was being presented to Kennedy other events put the NEA initiative in jeopardy. In August of 1962 JFK ordered his envoy to Ben-Gurion, Meyer "Mike" Feldman, to negotiate for Israeli acceptance of the Joseph Johnson Plan with Ben-Gurion and Golda Meir at the same time that he offered them the Hawk anti-aircraft missiles.

On August 9 Crawford drafted a memo that warned Feldman about the linkage: "Our resolve on the *quid pro quo* is firm and remains firm." The outlines of the quid pro quo stated clearly that Ben-Gurion must cooperate with the Johnson Plan for the weapon system to follow. Crawford continued, "We judge Ben-Gurion to be increasingly confident he will get the Hawks and perhaps even a security guarantee" and then might "risk non-cooperation in, or sabotage of, the refugee plan." Crawford stressed Feldman must convince Israel that "[w]e are not bluffing" and that the United States would withhold the missiles. Ben-Gurion ended all hopes for success when he announced he would refuse "to allow Israel to be destroyed from within."[60]

Unbeknownst to Crawford and Talbot, Robert Komer of the NSC staff had already undercut JFK's support and suggested a different strategy to Feldman. Komer lobbied JFK aide McGeorge Bundy: "Mike [Feldman] is very goosy about [the] Johnson Plan [...] and would like to start disengaging." Komer urged Bundy to "emphasize" to JFK not to "disengage too quickly [...] let someone else torpedo it." Komer concluded, "I've suggested Mike plug same idea with Israelis. Why should they get out in front on wrecking Johnson Plan; let Arabs take the onus."[61]

In September 1962 the Israeli Knesset passed a resolution that ended any hope for the Johnson plan: "There can be no returning the Arab refugees to Israeli territory and the only solution is their settlement in the Arab states."[62] After that Johnson remained convinced that publication of the plan had ultimately killed it. Phillips Talbot felt Arabs saw the Johnson Plan as "an excuse to provide for the further arming of Israel."[63] Despite the resolution the Hawk sale was completed. Mordechai Gazit, chief of staff for the Israeli prime minister, argued that Feldman had made an "attempt to trade the good news about the Hawks for Ben-Gurion's promise to continue to cooperate with the UN Commission's Arab refugee initiative."[64]

Historian Herbert Parmet moderated the connection between Feldman's offer of the Hawks and the Johnson Plan by claiming they were "peripherally related." The timing of Feldman's joint proposal made the linkage clear. Crawford's memo, unavailable when Parmet did his research, makes it clearer. Feldman later argued that the ultimate failure was due to the fact that "the State Department had gotten together with Johnson while I was in Israel to, as I saw it, make the plan slightly more favorable to the Arabs." Parmet concluded that its demise served "as evidence to the Israelis of a friendship that Kennedy had formed." Secretary Rusk blamed the failure on "Arabs [who] were unwilling to agree to any figure for the return of Palestinian refugees that was within Israel's capacity to accept."[65]

Joseph Johnson, in a 1964 article, said his effort had been "fascinating, frustrating, and, at times, infuriating." But he was convinced there was an innate reluctance on both sides: "neither side will—or perhaps even dares—subscribe publicly to a formal agreement acceptable to the other." He predicted that in any settlement there must be a willingness "to compromise since neither side would 'get what they want.'" But, he warned that Israel might "take possession of the whole west bank of the Jordan," which happened less than three years later. He also laid much of the fault for its failure on "how active and effective Israel's friends can be in supporting her cause." Johnson was particularly concerned when Don Peretz, an academic who had family in the Israeli government, said that the premise that the refugees were "the principal obstacle to peace" was not the case. Peretz argued younger refugees would "seek normal lives," implying they had not pressed to return to Palestine, concluding, "[W]e must reconcile ourselves to seeing it [the Palestinian refugee camps] continue for a generation or more." Conversely, the Middle East hands foresaw the consequences of that scenario, and those concerns drove the NEA's initiative.[66]

Middle East hands were left to deal with the consequences of the demise of the Joseph Johnson Plans. Armin Meyer recalled: "Less than two years later [1964] the PLO was founded." He opined, "[I]f we could have gotten those refugees out of those camps and made them productive members of society, we would have, to use Joe Johnson's phraseology, 'dissolved' the refugee problem, thus thwarting what has since become the formidable 'Palestinian problem.'" Meyer argued it was in Israel's best interest "to get those refugees out of the camps, emphasizing that they were going to be nothing but trouble for Israel."[67] He had said that if the refugees were given a range of options, not just a right of return to Israel, many would accept compensation and resettle elsewhere, thus dissolving the UNWRA refugee camps.

In a 1990 interview Meyer looked back over decades of radicalism and violence to recall: "I think we could have been spared all this terrorism business and other miseries if we had gone ahead with that project at that time."[68] William Crawford saw the collapse of the initiative as directly linked to the growing regional frustrations that exploded in 1967 and further complicated a settlement: "If it had not been scuttled, there would not have been a '67 war, and the whole face of the Middle East would not have been changed."⁶⁹

The camps did become the breeding ground of radicals—the "cesspools" that the UN official had warned Meyer about. Subsequent generations of Palestinian refugees mired in the camps eventually became the terrorists who staged the 1970 Black September uprising in Jordan, destabilized Lebanon until it sank into prolonged civil war, attacked American embassies, murdered ambassadors, hijacked planes, took the Israeli Olympic team hostage and continued for the next decades to wage a war against both Israeli and US interests.

In December 1962 Kennedy was told by Komer that "[o]ur policy to date toward Israel has been one of all give and no get."⁷⁰ JFK admitted to Israel's Foreign Minister Golda Meir: "We have not made any progress on the Johnson Plan and that is gone." Kennedy then referred to "the special relationship" between America and Israel. In response Meir told Kennedy they had no territorial claims: "Israel is perfectly prepared to live within its present borders [...] doesn't want more land [...] doesn't need [...] Jordanian sand." She stressed that the return of any refugees would "make an Algeria out of Israel." Kennedy obliquely raised the issue of nuclear proliferation at Dimona, asking Meir to consider "our problems on this atomic reactor."⁷¹ In both cases the United States had no leverage. Dimona was well on its way to completion without IAEA oversight. Moreover, there was to be no Israeli signature on the Nuclear Non-Proliferation Treaty; the Johnson Plan was dead, and Israel had the Hawks.

Turning Point: The Johnson Presidency

Less than a year later, on November 22, 1963, assistant secretary for the NEA Phillips Talbot sat in his office watching the grim aftermath of events in Dallas. He was joined by Middle East hand Curtis Jones, who realized it spelled the end of Talbot's career, "I think that Talbot knew right then and there that he was on his way out." Jones felt JFK's passing meant the Middle East hands' window of opportunity had closed: "With the advent of President Lyndon Johnson [...] Middle East policy did almost a 180 degree turn." Jones, who succeeded Brewer on Egyptian affairs, saw that it marked a turning point: "Our policy of dealing with Nasser was dead." In 1965 LBJ assigned Talbot to Greece, and Jones asked for a transfer. He was sent to Aden, at a time when anti-US sentiment ran so high that the NEA's George Moore shipped Jones a bulletproof vest. Jones survived, but later Moore was murdered by the Palestinian Black September group.⁷²

President LBJ was deeply suspicious of his area specialists and unable to keep any assistant secretary for NEA for long. Kennedy's NEA chief, Phillips Talbot, left in September 1966. Senior Middle East hand Raymond Hare held the post for a few months before retiring. Worse yet, Johnson left the key advisory post empty as war loomed in 1967. Then in April 1967 he transferred a nonarea specialist, Lucius Battle, to be ambassador to Cairo (his first Middle East post) after an explosive exchange with Nasser and then appointed him assistant secretary of the NEA as war loomed in the Middle East.

The contrast between Kennedy and Johnson reflects the differences in their view of the region. Kennedy relied on linguists and area specialists while Johnson sent Battle, a non-Arabist who opposed PL-480 wheat foreign aid to Cairo, as the program came up for renewal. Johnson appointed Harrison Symmes, a Middle East hand and a vocal opponent of King Hussein, as ambassador in Amman. At the height of the 1967 Egyptian crisis Johnson decided to select Richard Nolte, a non-Arabist who was not trained in diplomacy, to Cairo.

The NSC expanded the influence even more so under LBJ. The NSC was characterized by William Crawford as "a duplicate Department of State in the White House." Late in the LBJ years, journalist Joseph Kraft reported that Johnson had circulated an Arabic text, drafted for the president by NEA's Middle East hands, to outsiders to find out "What it really meant."[73]

Although JFK trusted his area specialists, Lyndon Baines Johnson was suspicious of Nasser and Arabs, as well as Arabists. LBJ left the diplomats outside of the policy process and made personnel changes that further shunted them aside. He replaced Kennedy's choice for ambassador to Cairo, an academic and Arabist linguist John Badeau, with Lucius Battle. Johnson went far afield in selecting a non-Arabist who had never held a post in the Middle East, nor even visited an Arab country. Battle was welcomed by Nasser aide Mohammed Heikal, and upon his arrival, Heikal asked whether he had "spent any time in the Middle East," to which he received a negative reply. Battle recalled, "He then asked whether I spoke any Arabic. I again said: 'No.' He then said: 'Thank God!' again." Heikal explained to Battle his preference: "The Americans who think they speak Arabic don't really speak Arabic. When they start, they begin to think that they can put themselves in our place and think and feel the way we do. We don't understand ourselves; how can an American possibly do so?"[74] Or, perhaps, Heikal was concerned that the State Department's area experts understood both Arabic and Arabs too well. But Nasser's relationship with Battle went rapidly downhill.

Tensions rose in Cairo over the Congo crisis, and by November, according to Heikal, it was Congolese students not Cairenes who burned the United State Information Service (USIS) library on Thanksgiving Day. The USIS libraries were built as goodwill gestures around the world that offered American literature and access to pro-US information.

The embattled Battle was sitting home celebrating the holiday when the Marines called to inform him that the embassy was under attack. Battle made a bold move: "I walked to the Embassy [...] The Marine barracks were on fire, as was the library. I walked very slowly and the mob let me go through. The Marines were all lined up behind the door [...] They yelled at me to run, but I thought that if I did that, I would be killed [...] The crowd waited long enough for the gate to swing open so I could get through. Then it went back to rioting again." Battle later protested that the Egyptian police and fire services had reacted too slowly. Nasser expressed "his deep regret" and told Battle that he "would give a thousand books in his own name for the library and he would give us a new building."[75]

Events soon took an even more dramatic turn. On December 18, 1964, Egyptian fighter jets shot down an American civilian plane over the Egyptian desert. The plane had failed to file a flight plan, was the same model Israel had recently used to make intelligence-gathering flights over Cairo and refused to land when requested. Battle realized, "The whole incident seemed perfectly explainable after the story had been told, but it didn't at the beginning." The fact that the plane belonged to Mecom Oil Company, whose owner John Mecom was a close personal friend of LBJ, did not help matters. The death of the American crew created, as Battle concluded, "A terribly unpleasant situation." With incredibly poor timing, Dr. Stino, the Egyptian minister who handled foreign aid issues, requested renewal of the PL-480 wheat program. Battle explained there was doubt the program would survive and later admitted he had not handled the meeting well: "I was quite rough with Dr. Stino. I was served some orange juice, but didn't stay for coffee—that was a signal of how upset we were."[76] While the issues of beverages sound minor, the snub caused by refusing a fundamental cultural tradition signaled a very sharp American rebuke. Stino feared Egypt would suffer a budgetary crisis and was crushed by Battle's message. Stino relayed the spoken as well as the implicit messages to the premier, who told Nasser, presumably emphasizing the negative aspects of Battle's visit. Nasser then attacked the United States; as recounted by journalist Mohammad Heikal, Nasser addressed an Egyptian crowd: "The American Ambassador says that our behavior is not acceptable. Well, let us tell them that those who do not accept our behavior can go and drink—and then he asked them: 'From where?' And they shouted, 'From the sea!'" Nasser went on: "And if the Mediterranean is not enough to slake their thirsts they can carry on with the Red Sea." Then Nasser sent a direct message to LBJ about the value of the aid against Egyptian independence: "What I want to say to President Johnson is that I am not prepared to sell Egyptian independence for thirty million pounds or forty million pounds or fifty million pounds."[77] Middle East hand Richard Parker was appalled: "Few utterances could have been better calculated to upset a Washington already infuriated [...] The Americans never got over it, and it continued to rankle in spite of the efforts of diplomats on both sides." Parker concluded the use of wheat and debt rescheduling had been used by Congress and the president "as political levers" to control Nasser, and by summer of 1965, "the decision had been made to keep Nasser on a short leash."[78]

In September 1965 Raymond Hare, new assistant secretary for the NEA, was not happy to find the wheat aid program, which he had arranged seven years earlier, in deep trouble: "The first thing that was on my desk as a problem was this damn PL–480 wheat [...] Congress liked to kick things around like that." Nasser was quite aware that the carrot was now a stick. Lucius Battle cabled a report of his last visit with Nasser in March 1967, noting it was dominated by a "thirty minute tirade" in which Nasser announced "UAR would not respond [to] US pressure." Worse yet the wheat that was to quiet the situation and pry Egypt out of the Soviet orbit now rankled Nasser: "He had gone to bed each night disturbed that UAR dependent on US for food and had resented each item in American or world press reminding UAR that five out of each eight loaves of its bread were provided by US." Despite the hunger Nasser said he would not approve any wheat deal "in [a] manner that appeared [to] be begging on knees." Battle did not include in the cable, but recalled later in his oral history, that he asked Egypt to withdraw their request: "So when I made my farewell call to Nasser, he withdrew his request for aid. I told him that I wanted the record to show that he had given up on the issue before I had done so."[79]

Battle was then elevated to assistant secretary for the NEA by Lyndon Johnson. Thus, a person who could not get along with the Arab world's most prominent leader was placed in overall control of State's Middle East bureau at a time of heightened tension in March 1967.

When Nasser vented his anger, he might have had in mind an Arab proverb, drilled into students at the Foreign Service Institute's (FSI) Beirut school and the subject one Arabist's research: "Chaff of your own country rather than Crusader's [foreign] wheat." The message was that Arabs would rather rely on the poor produce of their own land than rely on better grain provided by foreign powers. It echoed the Egyptian distaste for the coercive use of foreign aid offers whether by Moscow or Washington. Richard Parker concluded the whole Lyndon Johnson strategy toward Egypt, "where Nasser was a bad boy," was misguided: "It was an attempt to use aid as a political weapon. And, it did not work."[80]

Admittedly Nasser was not easy to work with. Parker recalled maxim of Malcolm Kerr, an FSI Beirut instructor, about the difficulties of negotiating with Nasser: "Doing business with Nasser was like trying to change a tire on a moving automobile." William Brewer commented that the best the Middle East hands could do in such circumstances was "preventing some bad thing from happening, [rather] than in achieving any positive good. But, on the other hand, if you can prevent something bad from happening, the situation is not made any worse."[81] Middle East hands might prevent things from going wrong, but under Battle's command, they were powerless to improve the worsening situation.

Then as Battle arrived in Washington the Egyptian–Israeli conflict heated up. Battle's replacement as ambassador to Cairo was a political appointee Richard Nolte, an academic who had written about Egypt. Nolte was delayed in getting to Cairo. Battle informed him that "Egypt was about to blow up" and advised him to read the cable traffic and get to Cairo. Nolte spent two weeks in London, and as he stepped off the plane in late May 1967, he answered a reporter's query about the situation with the offhand response, "What crisis?"[82] Before Nolte could present his credentials, Israel attacked Egypt and the Six Day War was on. At a time when the United States should have had its most skilled diplomatic representatives working to avert war, the post at Embassy Cairo was in transition.

After Battle left, Richard Parker, political affairs officer in Cairo, could only meet with a member of the Foreign Ministry at his own diplomatic level to discuss embassy evacuation plans. He cabled to Washington the overconfidence of the UAR official who said Egypt was "ready for war but was not seeking it." Parker warned, "It almost seemed UAR was seeking war." In his cable Parker queried whether "Goal appeared be [the] elimination [of] US influence from Middle East as much as it did to strike a blow against Israel," the Egyptian responded that he, "did not argue with thesis [...] his manner cordial but grim."[83]

On May 27, 1967, a cable did go out under Nolte's name, which observed, "His [Nasser's] only area of miscalculation may be his estimate of Egyptian military capabilities vis-a-vis Israel, and even there we may be in [for] some surprises."[84] The biggest surprise was for Nolte. He was recalled before he even presented his credentials. Nasser severed diplomatic relations.

Twenty-five years later Parker recalled how Nolte "arrived in the midst of the crisis and never caught up. That was unfortunate for him personally, but it was also unfortunate for US interests, because personal communication at the top was impossible."⁸⁵ Lower level diplomats could not arrange a meeting with Nasser. Parker found the embassy political officers could only struggle to do everything they could: "an enormous load fell upon David Nes and myself" with Battle gone and without an experienced Middle East hand as ambassador. Parker described the problem of having "a political appointee," without diplomatic training, suddenly thrust into a difficult diplomatic situation: "[W]ith absolutely no government or Foreign Service experience at all [...] it was sort of like sending Hanson W. Baldwin (a military commentator) out to command a division in Vietnam." Parker and Nes busied themselves evacuating embassy staff and burning embassy files. The files had to be shredded then hauled up to the embassy roof to a device that resembled a cement mixer and was loaded with flammable liquid. In their haste, while the embassy officers were burning shredded files on the roof, the burn barrel exploded. Parker recalled: "A great column of fire went up. The fire department was there in a matter of minutes. They thought the embassy had been hit, and the war was on, the Israelis were bombing, and everybody thought we had taken a hit of some sort."⁸⁶

With war imminent, Israeli diplomats tried to convince Washington that it should support Israel. Israeli Ambassador Avraham Harman met with Secretary of State Dean Rusk on June 2. After their meeting Harman was told by Supreme Court Justice Abe Fortas: "Rusk will fiddle while Israel burns. If you are going to save yourselves, do it yourselves." That is an interesting turn on the phrase Rusk had coined for LBJ to use with Abba Eban a week earlier: "Israel will not be alone unless it decides to go alone."⁸⁷

It was not only Rusk's lack of a commanding spirit at the helm but the bureaucratic atmosphere within the White House and the bureaucratic competition that left the State Department unable to deal with the crisis, although they struggled to avert a war. In particular, tensions between the NSC staff and the NEA remained high. At the same time the NSC refused to accept evidence presented by George Ball and others at the State Department that NSC's perception of US public opinion on the Arab–Israeli issue was seriously flawed.

The aftermath of the war was a disaster for the Middle East hands. During the fighting they had worked while under fire during the air war and were under siege on the ground as angry Arab mobs, who believed the United States had actively supported the Israeli surprise attack, attacked American embassies. Within days the Suez Canal was again blocked, this time for seven years, and diplomatic relations were severed by most of the Arab states. Thus, Middle East hands were sidelined as the NSC took over as Johnson's advisers. Everything the Middle East hands had accomplished in the Kennedy years—rebuilding the Nasser relationship, reopening the canal and trying to resolve the refugee crisis as a first step to peace—was obliterated.

On June 8, 1967, the Israeli Defense Forces attacked a US Navy intelligence-gathering ship, the USS *Liberty*, off the Israeli coast near Gaza. There were 37 US Navy personnel killed and 171 injured. Ambassador to Israel Walworth Barbour strongly supported the Israeli position and cabled Washington the same day with an unusual rationale for silence on the subject: "Israelis do not intend [to] give any publicity to [the] incident. Urge strongly that we too avoid publicity. If it is US flag vessel its proximity to scene conflict could feed Arab suspicions of US–Israel collusion."⁸⁸ It is curious that he presented such an argument. An Israeli attack on a US ship would not be taken by the Arabs as evidence of "collusion" since, logically, allies do not attack each other.

The controversy revealed Johnson's commitment to Israel. Despite strong US evidence to the contrary, LBJ argued the Israeli attack was accidental and mitigated the death toll: "We learned the ship had been attacked in error by Israeli gunboats and planes. Ten men of the *Liberty* crew were killed and a hundred were wounded. This heartbreaking episode grieved the Israelis deeply, as it did us." Johnson, a Navy veteran, reduced the number of US dead from 37 to 10, and the injured from 171 to 100. Historian George Lenczowski pointed out this was far less than even the Israelis acknowledged. US Navy sources reported 37 dead and 171 wounded, and Israeli sources 32 or 37 dead. Secretary of Defense McNamara excused that Israeli forces had strafed *Liberty's* lifeboats, remarking: "These errors do occur."[89]

Secretary of State Dean Rusk boldly stepped forward to issue a strongly worded protest to the Israeli ambassador. Rusk's "American Reply to the Israeli Apology" termed the attack "quite literally incomprehensible" and concluded that it "must be condemned as an act of military recklessness reflecting wanton disregard for human life." He requested Israel "take disciplinary measures" against those responsible and said the United States expected compensation. For his troubles Rusk triggered an "Israeli rebuttal to the American response," which said the United States could give "timely information of the approach of US vessels to shores where the Israel Defense Forces are in authority." Rusk did not believe it was an accident, stating in his memoirs, "I didn't believe them then, and I don't believe them to this day. The attack was outrageous." Rusk recalled he had always assured Arabs that "they needn't fear Israeli territorial expansion."[90] Rusk had repeatedly offered American assurances for nearly a decade: "Throughout the sixties the Arabs talked continuously about their fear of Israeli expansion. With the full knowledge of successive governments in Israel, we did our utmost to persuade the Arabs that their anxieties were illusory." Furthermore, Rusk recalled Prime Minister Levi Eshkol's June 5 radio address had stated Israel had "no territorial ambitions." Rusk noted: "Later in the summer I reminded Abba Eban of this, and he simply shrugged his shoulders and said, 'We've changed our minds.' With that remark, a contentious and even bitter point with the Americans, he turned the United States into a twenty-year liar."[91] That was the turning point for American diplomacy. By allowing Israel to continue to occupy neighboring states, the United States became, in the eyes of those it had previously reassured, a 20-year liar.

Rusk and LBJ might have made more use of their Middle East area experts, avoided delays in sending an ambassador to Cairo, as well as appointed skilled diplomats to such an important post in the midst of a crisis. Embassy Cairo should have had access to top Egyptian leaders and events so that conflict would have been mitigated by a knowledgeable area specialist who could have handled the diplomatic maneuverings and more forcefully presented the case against risking war.

The last point rests upon the evaluation of what triggered the crisis. A series of Soviet reports in May 1967 warned Egypt of Israeli troops massed on the Syrian border. Israel denied this, and it appears they had not done anything. However, it triggered an Egyptian buildup in the Sinai and Nasser's demand to remove UN peacekeepers. These actions challenged Israeli access to the Strait of Tiran and resulted in an Israeli attack on Cairo, then Syria and Jordan. Richard Parker examined the Six Day War in his book, *Political Miscalculations in the Middle East*, concluding there was no buildup and that Egypt was mistaken to believe the Soviet reports.[92]

Aftermath of the Six Day War

After the situation blew up at dawn on June 5, 1967, Israel quickly established itself as the dominant power, defeating in turn Egypt, Jordan and Syria. Egypt's Sinai Peninsula, Jordan's West Bank, East Jerusalem and Syria's Golan Heights were captured. The immediate human consequence was that tens of thousands more Palestinians became refugees or came under Israeli occupation. Lyndon Johnson did not press Israel for even a partial withdrawal.

Although JFK had promised that the United States would aid Israel "in case of an invasion," the situation was far different in the summer of 1967. According to Mordechai Gazit's account, Kennedy wrote, "The United States has a special relationship with Israel in the Middle East really comparable only to that which it has with Britain […]" and "[…] in case of an invasion the US would come to the support of Israel." Clearly American policy took a new turn under Johnson, who told an Israeli diplomat following Kennedy's death, "You have lost a very great friend, but you have found a better one." LBJ sent aid to Israel after it had launched, rather than suffered, an invasion.[93] His words and actions confirmed the United States would support Israel and tolerate much within that alliance.

When the administration weighed the fallout from the Six Day War and the American position on resupplying arms to Israel, Harold Saunders wrote to Walt Rostow in July 1968 to express concern over a Gallup poll that indicated only 10 percent of Americans favor any "general, not necessarily military action" in support of Israel in case of a war. Saunders wrote: "I'm surprised that only 10% of Americans would even favor general support for Israel and fewer urge that we be peace-makers. But I'm astonished that Americans 59–24 oppose even sending arms to Israel. Neither result seems consistent with the noise level in Congress or the political assessment we operate from." A *Time-Louis Harris* poll in May 1969 produced similar results. When respondents were asked "If Israel were in danger of being overrun by Soviet-aided Arabs would you favor sending US troops?" There was a 9 percent positive response.[94] Saunders further undercut the message by stating that "George Ball put Gallup up to asking these questions." Ball, although not an Arabist, had a strong reputation as an independent thinker on diplomacy. Ball argued Israel should make compromises rather than risk another war and reiterated his thesis in *Foreign Affairs*.[95]

Saunders concluded by trying to dismiss the hard evidence placed before him and Rostow: "I suppose it's possible to doubt the validity of Gallup's sample."[96] Saunders seems totally incapable of acknowledging the US public might not operate from the political assessment that underlay the assumptions he and Rostow brought to policy making.

The State Department's public affairs office found a pattern had appeared in their public opinion data, as early as June 2, 1967. Dixon Donnelley, assistant secretary of state for public affairs, wrote to Secretary Rusk to inform him that of the mail received 17,440 letters between May 29 and June 1 on the Arab–Israeli crisis: "about 95% favored support of Israel, 4.5% opposed American intervention in the crisis and 0.5% supported the Arab cause." He concluded: "Close to half of the total showed evidence of being the product of organized campaigns—form letters, stereotyped cable texts, etc. One striking note was the large number of identically worded messages from the same city, indicating a highly effective and well-organized campaign."[97]

When the White House received 17,440 letters in a five-day period and then five days later exactly 17,445 more letters arrived, suspicions were raised. Donnelley observed: "The proportion of form mail and identically worded telegrams remains high." This was forwarded to NSC adviser Walt Rostow with a cover letter suggesting they be passed to the White House Press Office.[98] Considering Lyndon Johnson's well-known sensitivity to polls, it was important to accurately assess just how strongly (and in which direction) the winds of American public opinion were blowing.

United Nations Resolution 242

American foreign policy was presidential policy. US ambassador to the United Nations Arthur Goldberg informed Israeli ambassador Abba Eban, as Eban later recalled, "to draw sharp distinction between what the President had said personally and what I had heard from other sources. The American choices were now so grave that only the presidential commitments mattered."[99]

While some have argued it was after the June War when Israel decided to hold onto its enormous territorial gains, but that is not evidenced in the reports sent from the American Embassy in Tel Aviv on June 7. Ambassador to Israel Walworth Barbour cabled to Washington the exultation among Israelis at their victory and that Israel "will insist" on "conclusion of final peace treaties" and "must have firm, accepted frontiers on all sides." He cautioned that, "despite the heady atmosphere of victory and the temptation this may provide for expansion," they would "remain with their present borders." However, in detailing what he judged to be the end result he pointed out Israel would want to "take and hold onto" the Sinai, Sharm el Sheik, and "an appreciably widening of the narrow belt between Jordan and the sea," as well as what Barbour termed "some improvement [...] on the northern Galilee front." With the war still in progress Barbour concluded the Israelis would go as far as the Suez Canal "but not cross it" and "secure the West Bank up to the Jordan bridges." As to Nasser, they would like to see "his disappearance." Barbour concluded: "I believe the Israelis can be expected to accept nothing less."[100] The second Barbour cable of June 7 was entitled "Israeli View of Middle East after War." It reported a dramatic meeting between the embassy's Deputy Chief of Mission (DCM) and an Israeli. The Israeli presented the war as a "smashing victory [which] had pricked Nasser's bloated pretensions and undercut Soviet ambitions in the entire area." He went on to inform the embassy that "Britain too had cause to be happy for pressure on Aden was now relieved." The American countered by relating the view from the embassy "at [the] moment US lives and property in area were in danger, oil to west is being cut off, Suez Canal was closed to US, relations with Arab nations being severed, access to area sharply limited, possibility strong leftward swing in Arab politics." Undaunted, the Israeli stressed what he wanted "to get across was that with Israel on verge stunning military success opening up brave new world for Israelis and ourselves."[101]

Most of the Arab world, convinced by Nasser's charge of American collusion with Israel, broke relations. The Middle East hands would have to deal with the consequences of closure of the Suez Canal, severed diplomatic relations with numerous Arab states and expanded areas of occupied territory (and new refugees). In the days and weeks after hostilities ceased, America's Middle East hands should have been negotiating peace but were instead closing their embassies. The Israelis told Barbour's DCM the "most important message" was that the US government and its friends "should do nothing to limit Israel's victory and thereby fruits of peace they and we would gain." LBJ did not limit the victory by demanding a withdrawal, but there were bitter "fruits of peace." Barbour also advised that Israel had "hard information a pogrom against Jews planned for Beirut" and "it cannot stand idly by." Barbour concluded by telling Rusk to "inform Lebanese government [at the] soonest."[102] With that Barbour relayed an Israeli warning that Israel might attack a fourth Arab nation.

Secretary Rusk suggested Barbour make "[the] strongest presentation of dangerous situation" and requested a "vigorous plea for Israeli acceptance cease-fire and immediate public notice this action." He had been receiving a string of pleas from Ambassador Findley Burns in Amman, which mounted as Jordanian desperation became apparent. A flash telegram (high priority) was sent directly to Tel Aviv from Amman pleading for a cease fire and that cease fire to "remain secret temporarily if King is to maintain control." Richard W. Murphy, then political reporting officer in Amman, sat in his embassy watching the Israeli air force in action: "They landed a missile in the wall of the King's office, which was quite a success, but I assume, an accident. Nobody's that accurate—it is June of '67 after all. They landed one out at his palace [...] they took out the airport [...] it was a little reminder that they had and were ready to use highly skilled people and good weaponry."[103]

The resupply of Israel with American, rather than French and German arms, signified an important enhancement of the US–Israeli special relationship. From that point forward Israel would build close ties to the US defense industry and receive military aid from Washington.

The consequences of the war were felt at every embassy in the Arab world. The unflappable, phlegmatic Hermann Eilts observed America's closest ally, Saudi Arabia, believed the United States had worked with Israel: "Unfortunately, earlier US pronouncement on Gulf of Aqaba has already convinced most Arabs that USG [US government] is pro-Israeli." Eilts had spent June 6 making a strenuous defense of US neutrality to the Saudi Foreign Ministry while Cairo's broadcasts accused the United States of aiding Israel. Eilts said Saudi radio was repeating the "latest Cairo broadcast of alleged Israeli confession [that] US aircraft involved." Rusk responded with a circular to all posts to "meet with appropriate members of your host government for the purpose of countering Nasser's Quote big lie. Unquote."[104]

What would be Washington's response? On June 7, 1967, NSC adviser Harold Saunders sent a memo to McGeorge Bundy that presented "The Agenda." Saunders opened with a belated acknowledgement of what the NEA had argued for decades: "Refugees must be the nub of a settlement. The Arabs' reason for waging the holy war is to win the right of the refugees to go home." What would be Saunders's recommendation? "Action: The Joe Johnson plan is still the best working base"[105]—a tragic admission for the NSC to make five years after their own staff had undercut the plan.

That does not mean there was any consensus to pressure Israel. An "eyes only" memo directed to the president from adviser John P. Roche asked rhetorically: "Whose State Department is it?" He quoted from Isaiah—refuse favor to the wicked—and argued LBJ should "collect the domestic bonus that will fall in our lap" rather than "alienate Jewish support." His uppercase rationale argued: "The Arabs have to hate us and the rougher the Israelis are on them, the more they will hate us NO MATTER WHAT WE DO." In that Roche was correct; as Israel became "rougher," the United States found itself increasingly the object of intense Arab hostility. On State, Roche commented: "I was appalled to realize that there is a real underground sentiment for kissing some Arab backsides."[106] In the first weeks of June any critique of Israel went underground and remained there. Roche said what he felt as well and what was the dominant view in the Johnson White House.

The United Nations was central to dealing with the aftermath of war. LBJ shaped the UN debate and the US position vis-à-vis the Israelis and Arabs, as his US UN staff shaped United Nations Resolution 242. This new basis for negotiations was hammered out between July and November of 1967 in New York, and it was approved by the Security Council. Resolution 242 established the "land for peace" formula, which became the basis for future negotiations.

As it became apparent that there would be no American demand for full withdrawal, as had occurred after the Suez War, the Arabs met in Khartoum. From the Arab view there remained a strong rejectionist attitude, based upon their claim to the entire territory. Over the decades their inability to abandon at least some part of that claim severely damaged their cause. In August 1967, the Arab League met in Khartoum, demanded full withdrawal from the occupied territories and issued a communique: "No peace with Israel, no recognition of Israel, no negotiations with it, and insistence on the rights of the Palestinian people in their own country."[107] Their response became known as "the three noes of Khartoum."

Israel's senior diplomat, Abba Eban, was appalled by the first draft of the UN resolution and called it "one of the most embarrassing discussions which the US and Israel had ever held" because he felt the draft signaled "we were in serious trouble." Why? The draft called for "all parties to the conflict to withdraw without delay their forces from the territories occupied by them after June 4, 1967."[108] This meant immediate withdrawal. Moreover, if ratified, it might have forced the United States to support a repeat of its pro-withdrawal stance of 1956.

In response, Eban argued with US UN representative Ambassador Arthur Goldberg, claiming he should not support the US–USSR draft text, which called for all parties "to withdraw without delay" to the June 4 lines. Eban felt this would give up "all the results achieved in the past six weeks of common struggle." He also viewed this as inimical with statements by both Johnson and Goldberg, particularly LBJ's of June 19, which described such a withdrawal as "a prescription for the renewal of hostilities." In that speech LBJ dismissed the idea of "an immediate return to the situation as it was on June 4."[109]

Eban recalled how he "pointed out that if this text was presented and voted on, Israel would find herself in the tragic position of having to flout a joint American-Soviet proposal endorsed by the General Assembly." He also characterized the United States as having "detached itself from Israel and allied itself to the Soviet Union without prior consultation." With that statement Eban put LBJ on notice that Israel was prepared to follow her own vital interests, not a policy drafted by Washington. Eban saw it as "a Soviet-Arab-American alignment against us," but Israel was saved from rejecting the draft when the Arabs shocked everyone by rejecting the Goldberg–Gromyko text against Soviet advice. This was a cause for much rejoicing by Eban: "We could not conceal our relief."[110] It also illuminates the fact that both Israel and the Arabs did not act as obedient client states and never took on subservient or even predictable roles. Israel saw the proposed text as ill-conceived and a threat to all they had militarily accomplished. The Arabs refused to accept anything but immediate and unconditional withdrawal.

In October Eban and Johnson met for the first time since before the war, and Eban recalled that "[h]e [LBJ] was now firmly resolved not to weaken the position which he had outlined on June 19." Johnson informed Eban that "[a]n 'edifice of peace' would have to be built."[111]

When debate renewed in November on Resolution 242, the US–USSR draft was history. The US position was now closely aligned with Israel and the Soviet with the Arabs. Goldberg argued the June 4 lines were not original borders but armistice lines, and the postwar lines merely ceasefire lines. Eban concluded that Goldberg was presenting "for the first time" the US support for a text that was for Israel, in Eban's words, "a doctrine of territorial revision."[112]

The Goldberg variations on the border issue concluded: "Since such boundaries do not exist, they have to established by the parties themselves as part of the peace-making process." In 1981 Arthur Goldberg admitted that the final text "neither command nor prohibits territorial adjustments [...] although it 'tilts' in favor of adjustments to ensure secure boundaries for Israel." With that the US diplomatic effort had created what Eban termed "a perceptible loophole for our cause." American diplomat Richard N. Curtiss observed: "Arab signatories cite the French text's call for withdrawal from 'the territories occupied' while Israelis cite the English text's 'territories occupied.' The Arabs say Resolution 242 specified that Israel must withdraw from *all* occupied territories, while the Israelis say it leaves the extent of the withdrawals to be negotiated."[113] It made all subsequent negotiations, and hence the US position as arbiter, much more complex.

The resolution's preamble, drafted by Lord Caradon, stated that the UN was "Emphasizing the inadmissibility of the acquisition of territory by war." Despite that clear intent, the English and French text were open to interpretation. The French text read *"retrait des forces armées Israéliennes des territoires occupés lors du récent conflit,"* while the English read "withdrawal of Israel armed forces from territories occupied in the recent conflict." In French the preposition *"de"* and the article *"les"* are combined: *de + les = des*; such a contraction is translated: "of the, from the."[114]

Lord Caradon, observed the omission "was deliberate [...] If we had put in the 'the' or 'all the' that could only have meant we wished to see the 1967 boundaries perpetuated in the form of a permanent frontier." Richard Curtiss noted Arabs used the French to call for withdrawal from "all the occupied territories," while Israelis argued that omission of the English definite article "the" left the extent of withdrawal indefinite. Curtiss observed, "The ambiguity of the two versions is not accidental. Authors of the resolution had decided that this was the only way to secure the agreement of all parties to Resolution 242." Goldberg defended the English text: "The French and Russian texts differ, but it was the English text which was voted upon." However Riad's successor El-Zayyat noted that "there was no such absence in the equally authentic French text" and quoted political scientist Guy Lacharriere's observation that the French text was used by some voting in the Security Council.[115]

Israeli ambassador Abba Eban concluded that the UN resolution "could not be described as an Israeli victory, it certainly corresponded more closely to our basic interests than we could have dared to expect from the UN a short time before." The final text set the terms of any future bargain: land for peace. Israeli withdrawal was to be exchanged for Arab recognition of Israel's right to exist, secure borders and free navigation through international waters.[116]

What was unexpected was that subsequent movement on withdrawal did not occur under UN representative Gunnar Jarring's mediation. Richard Parker noted that among Middle East hands "expectations were dashed by Arab unwillingness to give the sort of commitments Israel was demanding [...] and by decreasing Israeli interest in exchanging land for commitments of any kind." Deputy assistant secretary for the NEA Rodger Davies observed that Israeli intransigence was increased by a desire to hold onto the land, and "their appetite had grown with the eating."[117]

In a crucial way Rusk and Johnson were unlike Dulles and Eisenhower: they did not take a firm stand on Israeli withdrawal. Rusk, with years of experience on the Palestine question, should have been able to make a convincing case, but Johnson took the lead in opposing Eisenhower's pressure on Israel in 1956–57. Moreover, the US role in shaping the terms of settlement and Resolution 242 was based Johnson's input. The NEA did not work out the policy, but instead LBJ and US UN Ambassador Goldberg conferred.[118]

In considering the political distance between the United States and Israel, Rusk pointed out in his memoirs that "Israel is not an American satellite" and argued that distinction "is a point many Arabs unfortunately miss." And he was quick to add, "the opposite is true as well: The US is not an Israeli satellite, a point that Americans sometimes miss." However, Rusk admitted: "The Israelis prefer to gamble on doing things their own way, in the expectation that we will follow along." The complexity seems to elude him. Since the United States did follow along in the wake of the Israeli occupation and then supplied Israel with arms, Arabs concluded the United States was an Israeli satellite.

In September 1968 Parker translated how Nasser spelled out the three steps to take: *sumud, tahrir* and *nasr* or steadfastness, liberation and victory. In October Parker Hart, as assistant secretary of the NEA, took Parker along to meet with Mohammad Riad, Egypt's foreign minister, to discuss a series of artillery barrages against Israeli forces in the Sinai. Riad informed the Americans they "had not seen anything yet. There would be increasing incidents as long as Israel occupied Arab territory." Richard Parker recalled he and Hart "were impressed by Riad's firmness."[119] Months later the War of Attrition would begin. Nasser's three stages would culminate in Sadat's attack across the canal in October 1973.

In conclusion, Kennedy offered Middle East hands a chance to advance initiatives on solving the refugee problem and building better relations through quiet diplomacy. It did create a brief period of relative calm. Ultimately that was undercut by JFK's concern about Jewish support in upcoming elections. The Israeli lobby effectively weighed-in on the refugee issue and nuclear inspections at Dimona. Rusk's lack of support left the Joseph Johnson Plan a dead letter. Despite State's insistence on the quid pro quo, the Hawk missiles were delivered. As early as 1962, Kennedy had proclaimed the special relationship.

In retrospect, if the Joseph Johnson Plan had succeeded in ameliorating the refugee problem, the cascade of consequences might have been diminished—the radicalization of refugees, the formation and radicalization of the PLO and other Palestinian terror groups, the Six Day War and the subsequent conflict might have been mitigated. Their proposal could have avoided some of the consequences.

LBJ enlarged on both Kennedy's friendship with Israel and the disenchantment with Nasser. His promise to be "the better friend" of Israel literally underwent a fiery test in the opening of the Six Day War and the USS *Liberty* attack but emerged stronger than ever. Johnson supported Israel in the United Nations where the controversy over the text of UN Resolution 242 allowed Israel to maintain its occupation, and later settlement, of the territories.

Middle East hands had made significant progress through quiet diplomacy for a brief time but they represented only a very thin line of expertise and were forced to walk a very thin line. Their policy positions found little resonance with Johnson and were opposed by the Israeli lobby. LBJ marginalized Middle East hands by relying on nonspecialists as the NSC staff took a more dynamic role in policy.

Middle East hands opposed arms sales to both Arabs and Israelis, but Israel received Hawk missiles, tanks and advanced jet aircraft without providing the quid pro quo. After the Six Day War they were supplied with US equipment. These arms shipments created both an aura of Israeli invincibility and linked Israeli military actions with the US supplies.

Finally, the United States lost what Kennedy and Johnson paid so high a price for in Vietnam: credibility. By acquiescing in the Israeli occupation after the Six Day War, the United States became, in Rusk's words, "a twenty year liar." The Middle East hands' primary goal—a negotiated settlement and defined borders—was indefinitely suspended. This led Arab states to view US policy as permanently tilted toward Israel. The State Department was no longer central to policy making as the Middle East was locked in a state of hostility from which it struggled to emerge.

Ultimately their efforts were undercut by Kennedy's shift toward his "action intellectuals" in the NSC and his increasing reluctance to pressure Israel. Lyndon Johnson's deep distrust of his Middle East area experts further distanced them from the center of policy making. Nasser's adventurism in Yemen and the confident militarism of Israel after the Six Day War ended the brief era of good feelings in the Middle East.

Chapter Seven

KISSINGER'S ARABESQUE: THE NIXON AND FORD YEARS

In the Nixon and Ford administrations Middle East hands saw their investment in area specialization lead to career advancement, and they were poised to assume key roles where they might have shaped policy. Ironically, they arrived at the top just as Nixon and Kissinger made the Oval Office the center of Middle East policy making.

Middle East hands reached the top only to find a false summit, a mountaineering term that describes the quest to reach the top of a mountain, visible afar, but, because of a steep angle of ascent, the climber reaches the summit only to discover another looming above it. They had climbed the mountain, but never truly reached the top. They had not been, as one critic described them, the "secret drivers of America's Middle East policy since the end of World War II," but more in the Nixon era its victims.[1] Within a span of less than three years a wave of assassinations took the lives of five American diplomats in the region.

The Nixon White House resorted to secret diplomacy rather than the Middle East hands' quiet diplomacy. American foreign policy was bifurcated: Secretary of State William Rogers worked through normal diplomatic channels, while National Security Council (NSC) adviser Kissinger communicated via a "backchannel" sending different, often contradictory, messages to foreign leaders. Foreign governments quickly learned to ignore what came from Secretary Rogers or his State Department.[2] Later in the Nixon era Kissinger replaced Rogers as Secretary of State and retained his NSC post as well.

The Middle East According to Nixon and Kissinger

Richard Nixon always took special pride in his foreign affairs expertise. As Eisenhower's vice president he established his reputation by making frequently global tours to gather information and advised him during the Suez Crisis. He was visiting American embassies in the Middle East, in preparation for his presidential run, at the outbreak of the Six Day War. The policies that Nixon adopted as president did not reflect the practical counsel he had earlier offered Ike. An examination of the record in 1958, 1960 and 1967 reveals this disparity.

During a January 1958 White House debate on long-range strategy, Nixon argued that "anyone who has visited the Near East or studied the area must certainly have reached the conclusion that the major immediate problem there was the problem of the Arab refugees." He urged a direct approach: "Solution of the refugee problem [...] was the thing to concentrate on at the moment."³ But as president he declined to support the Rogers Peace Plan that dealt with the issue.

In 1960, Nixon met with Prime Minister Ben-Gurion and told him, "The Arabs were effectively using the refugee problem as a political weapon" and pointed out that Israel should defuse it "by making clear Israel's willingness to accept Arab refugees once a peace settlement had been reached."⁴ Although Nixon boldly identified the problem and was willing to voice his opinions in the White House and to the Israelis, he did not support his own Secretary's initiative.

In 1967, with the Six Day War literally hours away, on June 1, Nixon predicted there would be no war: "For war to result, a nation must both want war and have the power to wage it. In the Middle East those who want war do not have the power to wage it, and those who do have that power do not want it." His canny political instincts frustrated the press when they sought elaboration. One reporter recorded: "He later declined to identify which nations were which."⁵

Nixon's diplomatic instincts, however, were often negated by his political instincts. When Nixon and his aide Patrick Buchanan reached Morocco in 1967, they were guests of Ambassador Henry Tasca, who appointed Middle East hand George M. Lane as Nixon's interpreter. As the Six Day War began Nixon and the embassy staff gathered in the ambassador's residence to hear to an address by King Hassan. Unlike the majority of those present, who were intently focused upon the Moroccan response, Lane observed Nixon pacing back and forth: "Dick Nixon was walking up and down the living room saying, 'It's the Russians. It's the Soviets. They are behind this. It's the Soviets.'"⁶

This Cold War view was a recurrent pattern during his presidency. Nixon remained wedded to a Cold War analysis that viewed all Middle East events as caused by Soviet instigation. He viewed the Six Day War, Syrian intervention in the Jordanian civil war and Egyptian defense of the Suez Canal as parts of a Soviet plot and supported Israel's refusal to negotiate. Nixon later emerged as a strong proponent of Israel's continued occupation of Arab territory. He first said: "The destruction of Israel as a state is simply not going to happen" and then told reporters that he "did not believe any side in the Middle Eastern war was capable of a quick victory without massive assistance from a foreign power." A fortnight later in Tel Aviv, he announced: "Israel had a right to keep the places that served as springboards of aggression against her until a settlement insuring her security was reached."⁷

This Cold War perspective and Nixon's willingness to militarily support Israel was at variance with a growing segment of American opinion. In 1968 an opinion poll revealed only 10 percent of Americans favored US military support for Israel, and by the time Nixon had reached the Oval Office, a May 1969 *Time Magazine* poll indicated such support had dropped to 9 percent. Policy analyst Graham Allison observed that "the settled assumptions shared by postwar American leaders," in particular regarding the Cold War, were not shared by a growing segment of America and the lack of support for Israel was a primary indicator of the split. He summarized the axioms of the earlier generation: "The surest simple guide to US interests in foreign policy is opposition to Communism." Allison concluded the foreign policy view of what he called "young America" increasingly centered on the principle that "Opposition to communism is a misleading guide for US foreign policy."⁸

Nixon focused on the Soviet dimension of the Arab–Israeli conflict and always viewed the Soviets as key drivers of events: "The difference between our goal and the Soviet goal in the Middle East is very simple but fundamental," Nixon told Rogers. "*We* want peace. *They* want the Middle East."⁹ Journalist Seymour Hersh has concluded neither Nixon nor Kissinger could comprehend that "[t]he Russians were not behind every sand dune in the Middle East."¹⁰

Nixon's Middle East policy had conflicting objectives and perhaps reflected his conflicting emotions. Many of his private conversations in the Oval Office reveal a man with a deep-seated personal animosity toward Jews, who stood in marked contrast to his public words and his concrete actions to assist Israel. He did not owe his 1968 election victory to Jewish voters, having captured only 17 percent of their votes, and many of his most critical decisions on military resupply of Israel were made in 1973 well after his reelection. One Middle East hand recounted to Seymour Hersh how Nixon spoke to him, after Jordan's King Hussein left the White House and made a series of comments that "just sickened me [...] It was as if he thought since I was an Arabist and an Ambassador [in the Middle East] that I was some kind of a Jew hater." Israeli leaders grew to trust his deeds. Israeli Prime Minister Golda Meir informed Kissinger that Nixon was "an old friend of the Jewish people," which Kissinger remembered as "startling news for those of us more familiar with Nixon's ambivalences on that score."¹¹

Nixon's NSC Adviser, Dr. Henry A. Kissinger, was a native of Germany who fled with his family to America in the 1930s. He had served in counterintelligence during World War II and afterward was involved in secret anticommunist activities in Germany. By 1952 he was teaching at Harvard and advising the Eisenhower White House. He had excellent Cold War and conservative credentials as a member of the Center for Strategic and International Studies and as an adviser to the Central Intelligence Agency (CIA) and NSC on covert operations. According to Seymour Hersh, Kissinger's counterintelligence work after the war included "recruiting ex-Nazi intelligence officers for anti-Soviet operations inside the Soviet bloc." In 1954 he met Nelson Rockefeller while working on covert operations for Ike's Cold War Planning office and the NSC Operation Coordinating Board. His doctoral dissertation, *A World Restored: The Politics of Conservatism in a Revolutionary Age,* examined diplomacy at the Congress of Vienna, and in 1957 he authored *Nuclear Weapons and Foreign Policy* on the utility of limited nuclear war. Kissinger began the 1968 campaign as Nelson Rockefeller's adviser on Vietnam, but Nixon's transition team leader recognized Kissinger as "the most qualified card-carrying Republican around." He was adept at managing bureaucracy, but even he admitted he had difficult relations with his colleagues, and Kissinger himself quipped: "It took me eighteen years to achieve total animosity at Harvard. In Washington I did it in eighteen months."¹²

Although he knew little of the Middle East, Kissinger argued his approach was from the realist school and keyed to the Cold War. He wrote that his efforts in the peace process were "not a starry-eyed quest [...] but a method for conducting the geopolitical competition." Kissinger developed a strong affinity for Israel's Labor government and Prime Minister Golda Meir in particular. He recalled their relationship: "To me she acted as a benevolent aunt toward an especially favored nephew, so that even to admit the possibility of disagreement was a challenge to family hierarchy producing emotional outrage."[13] This closeness precluded the toughness required to push Israel toward a settlement and avert war. It ran counter to the Middle East hands' view that the United States should push for a peace agreement while avoiding the risks of overly identifying with other nations.

By the Nixon era the American–Israel Public Affairs Committee (AIPAC) had substantial influence and developed real lobbying power in Congress. They launched a highly effective program to expand Israel's share of the foreign aid budget and to marginalize the policy positions represented by the Middle East hands. In May 1975 AIPAC garnered the signatures of 76 Senators in support of renewed aid and commented that it had "vigorously countered" President Ford's call to "reassess" aid in the 94th Congress. AIPAC reported that they remained "confident that the 95th Congress will demonstrate the same awareness of the fundamental US interests by supporting a secure, viable Israel." By 1985 AIPAC could muster the support of 97 senators and a number of representatives opposing arms sales to Jordan. In contrast the National Association of Arab Americans, the Arab lobby, was founded in 1972 and was less effective. If political donations equate to influence, then the Arab lobby remained far behind. In one year, groups lobbying for closer US–Israel ties gave a total of $3.6 million to politicians, while National Association of Arab Americans donated $20,000.[14] AIPAC's highly effective think tank, the Washington Institute for Near East Policy (WINEP), made presentations to Congress and issued position papers, and its president, Martin Indyk, became a top NSC staffer. This put further pressure on policy makers in the State Department, as Indyk informed an interviewer that WINEP's purpose was "to counter Arabist views." Indyk was later nominated as ambassador to Israel, although not an American citizen and his citizenship had to be rushed through prior to his confirmation. Scholars John Mearshimer and Stephen Walt have examined the history and development of AIPAC in their study *The Israel Lobby and US Foreign Policy*, which notes AIPAC's effectiveness escalated sharply after 1967.[15]

AIPAC was deeply concerned that Nixon might push Israel into peace negotiations, according to assistant secretary of Near East Affairs (NEA) Joseph Sisco, it would raise "The great Israeli fear that an imposed settlement would occur."[16] The one person who might carry forward that initiative was Secretary of State William P. Rogers.

Rogers was a graduate of Colgate and Cornell Law School and Nixon's trusted friend. He had been a successful New York lawyer, a former Attorney General and advised Nixon during the Eisenhower-era slush fund scandal. Rogers was not a foreign affairs specialist, although he had made two brief missions to Africa for Eisenhower. One journalist's thumbnail sketch: "A frequent golfer and squash player, drinks little and does not smoke." Upon his nomination Rogers vowed "I'm going to do a lot of listening and reading in the next thirty or forty days." He saw part of his task was to "find some way to calm the volcanic Middle Eastern situation." His long experience as a lawyer and negotiator made him well-suited to the one region of foreign affairs that Nixon allowed him. Rogers said he was prepared "to play a subordinate role [...] I recognized he wanted to be his own foreign policy leader." During the transition Rogers told a State Department aide he would not fight for turf, but instead used a golf analogy, saying they would "'wedge out' what we could."[17] He underestimated that amount of drive possessed by his bureaucratic rival NSC adviser Henry Kissinger. Rogers was not up to the level of hardball that Kissinger could play.

In private Nixon had given Kissinger control over all foreign policy except the Middle East, but the NSC adviser began a crusade to win control over that as well. Kissinger told Nixon that Rogers was "an amateur." John Ehrlichman recalled Kissinger saying, "Rogers is stupid! Rogers is a danger to the world! Rogers is an amateur!" and threatened to quit unless Rogers was removed. He told Nixon that Rogers's work "was helping the Soviets." In his memoirs, Kissinger described Rogers as "an insensitive neophyte who threatened the careful design of our foreign policy."[18] Note the possessive denoting whose foreign policy was at issue.

Even Nixon found the Rogers–Kissinger rivalry taxing: "Kissinger bridled at my assignment in 1969 and 1970 of all Middle Eastern problems to Rogers. He felt that Rogers was influenced by the pro-Arab elements of the State Department." By Nixon's own admission, he and Kissinger viewed Rogers as under the control of "the pro-Arab elements" in the State Department, but Roger's peace initiative had been initiated at Nixon's behest. In his memoirs Nixon appears to have enjoyed the rivalry: "Kissinger felt that Rogers was vain, uninformed, unable to keep a secret and hopelessly dominated by the State Department bureaucracy." Conversely Nixon recalled: "Rogers felt that Kissinger was Machiavellian, deceitful, egotistical, arrogant and insulting."[19]

The new director of the NEA was Assistant Secretary Joseph Sisco, a Soviet specialist with a doctorate in Soviet affairs and Russian language studies. He began his career with the CIA, then transferred to the State Department's United Nations bureau and spent his entire career in a series of Washington posts.[20] He was not an ally of the NEA's area specialists, and his background in Soviet studies predisposed him to view the Arab–Israeli conflict from a staunchly Cold War perspective. His view clashed with the regionalist perspective of the Middle East hands. Sisco viewed the results of the Six Day War in Cold War terms, as "an important 'victory' largely because of the denial of opportunity to the Soviet Union" and "the Israeli action helped the interests of the US in the broader, big power context."[21] The Six Day War had closed the Suez Canal, led to severed US relations with many key regional powers and had taken an enormous toll on US political and economic interests.

Kissinger was no Middle East specialist when he came to the White House. He recalled that when he first heard "the sacramental language of UN Resolution 242, mumbling about the need for a just and last peace within secure and recognized borders" that he deemed it "so platitudinous that I accused the speaker of pulling my leg." He might have been surprised to learn the text, supposedly authored by Britain's Lord Caradon, had been drafted by Joseph Sisco a half decade earlier. Sisco in turn credited boss US UN representative Arthur Goldberg as "really the architect of Security Resolution 242." Sisco, then assistant secretary for International Organizations, recalled that "the language was developed by the US and for reasons of legislative tactics [...] we put (it) in the hands of the British as a sponsor."[22]

By early 1969 Secretary Rogers was determined to move forward on the basis of UN Resolution 242. Kissinger had a different Middle East policy in mind, a strategy of stalemate: "I thought delay was on the whole in our interest because it enabled us to demonstrate even to radical Arabs that we were indispensable to *any* progress and that it could not be extorted from us by Soviet pressure." But he overlooked the fact that no progress might radicalize Arabs, especially Palestinian refugees, and give the Soviets an opening. Middle East hands viewed progress on resolving refugee and border issues and a comprehensive settlement as priorities.

When Nixon entered the White House tensions were already escalating. Palestinian refugees had been radicalized by two decades of suffering in refugee camps and in July 1968 the Palestine National Covenant asserted: "The Palestinian Arab people possesses the legal right to its homeland […] armed struggle is the only way to liberate Palestine."[23] This was an abandonment of peaceful means to improve their condition. Yasir Arafat took over the Palestinian Liberation Organization (PLO) just as Secretary Rogers took office; Arafat made the cover of *Time* the week before Rogers. But the PLO was splintering and a variety of increasingly radical offshoots emerged: Al Fatah, the Popular Front for the Liberation of Palestine and Black September. The youth in the refugee camps now posed a formidable threat. Since the 1950s Middle East hands and UN officials had argued the camps must be dissolved or else a new generation of radicals would emerge, and in the 1970s they did.

Kissinger's Arabesque

One key maxim is that all foreign policy is presidential policy, and Nixon was determined to retain control over foreign policy rather than to delegate it: "From the outset … I [Nixon] planned to direct foreign policy from the White House."[24] His selection of Rogers and Kissinger was a means to that end. Rogers readily admitted he was a neophyte in foreign affairs and was not strong at bureaucratic gamesmanship. Nixon vested power in Kissinger and set the stage for an unprecedented White House takeover of State Department turf.

Secretary of Defense James Schlesinger described Kissinger's operating style: "Other people, when they lie, look ashamed. Henry does it with style, as if it were an arabesque." Kissinger used covert bureaucratic politics to create what was in essence an arabesque, defined as "a complex and ornate design."[25]

In the transition planning sessions of December 1968, Henry Kissinger won Nixon's agreement to expand the power of the NSC and create a parallel foreign policy apparatus in the White House. This would evade Senate oversight and magnify the influence of the NSC while it marginalized the State Department. Since the NSC adviser and his staff are not subject to Senate approval, although diplomatic appointees are subject to Senate confirmation, Nixon had a free hand to appoint ideologues to the NSC staff. Kissinger later asserted that his NSC meetings were protected by the president's "executive privilege" and he was not accountable to the Senate. The Pike Committee convened in 1975 to investigate the NSC, the Forty Committee and other White House groups involved in planning covert actions. Pike cited Kissinger for contempt, but the final report was suppressed by Congress.[26]

This effort immediately set off alarms at the State Department. Alexis Johnson, undersecretary for political affairs and the highest ranked career Foreign Service officer (FSO), had designed the interdepartmental regulations balancing the power between State and the NSC. During the transition Kissinger announced his proposal to eliminate that system, the one thing that maintained State Department leverage over the NSC. Johnson, termed it the "Kissinger/NSC takeover of State's interdepartmental functions." He realized that Rogers was "entirely unfamiliar" with the ramifications of the proposal. Before Johnson had returned from the inauguration Kissinger had Nixon's signature on an Executive Order that put the NSC in control. This erased the Senior Interdepartmental Group—Interdepartmental Regional Group system that Alexis Johnson established in 1966 to manage the policy papers flowing from State to NSC and the Pentagon. Diplomat Roger Morris warned State's head of SIG "You're going to get screwed, you're going to lose all kinds of power. We don't think this building should be cut out." Rogers did not fight it. Alexis Johnson noted that Kissinger regarded American diplomats as "determined to undermine him" and this fed into Nixon's "long-standing paranoia" about the Foreign Service. Kissinger then went further. He eliminated American area specialists from doing language interpretation for the White House and used foreigners to interpret (even on the China trip where he used Mao's interpreter). It was a reversal of all the Middle East hands had worked to achieve.[27]

The NSC plan was authored by Morton Halperin, assistant secretary for Defense and Kissinger protégé. Halperin suggested the use of National Security memorandums as a means to keep the State Department busy doing research rather than initiating policy. As an NSC staffer in the Nixon White House, Halperin codified his method of bureaucratic gamesmanship. The strategies he developed with Kissinger are defined in his book *Bureaucratic Politics and Foreign Policy*.

He recommended a "Machiavellian use of the press," the utility of press leaks and the manipulation of the bureaucracy as well as the president. Halperin defined the one indispensable trait of a Secretary of State as "the killer instinct," and its "key component [...] a drive for power." Halperin added that the Secretary must "display a temper," possess "chutzpah" and should use "the threat of resignation" to "politically embarrass" the president so he will "take their views into account." Among Halperin's top ten list of "maneuvers" was the use of "back channel messages." Halperin's key bureaucratic strategies: "1-report only what supports the stand you are taking 2- structure reporting of information so senior participants to see only what information you want them to see [...] 3-do not report facts which show danger 4- [...] present facts in what appears to be an authoritative manner 5-request a study from those who will give you the desired conclusion 6-keep away from senior participants who might report facts one wishes to have suppressed 7-expose participants [...] to those who hold correct views 8-get other governments to report facts which will be valuable 9-advise other participants on what to say 10-circumvent formal channels 11-distort the facts if necessary."[28]

Kissinger operated his "back channel" system with the help of the CIA. Ambassador William J. Porter was told it would provide "direct and private" communications between the White House and a few "key ambassadors," but exclude Secretary of State Rogers.

When Kissinger told him in 1969, Porter wrote in his diary, "Here's the Nixon–Kissinger secret diplomatic service shaping up, secret codes and all."²⁹

The back channel system grew so sophisticated that Rogers and State were not only denied information but fed disinformation. Middle East hand Nicholas Veliotes recalled how it operated: "I was a reasonably junior staffer, but I understood process, and to get a No-dist. cable [no distribution] to the Secretary of State one day, and then its equivalent in the backchannel to the National Security Advisor [...] which said, 'Disregard what I just said to the Secretary of State [...]' I saw a few things like that, but then how many do you need?"³⁰

The construction of a parallel system bypassing the State Department had profound implications. First, the Washington bureaucratic game was far more complex than most players ever suspected, and Rogers was repeatedly misled. Second, these conflicting messages caused tremendous confusion in foreign nations. Finally, from the historian's perspective, this undermines every effort to define what Nixon's foreign policy actually was at that time.

By October 1971 Soviet Ambassador Anatoly Dobrynin was told to inform Andrei Gromyko that Kissinger was "moving into the area [the Middle East] and quietly edging Rogers out." Thereafter Dobrynin observed that Moscow "preferred to use 'the Kissinger channel' [...] because the Kremlin knew from experience this channel was far more effective than the State Department." Dobrynin recalled NEA's Sisco telling Gromyko, in Rogers's presence, that Gromyko "did not quite understand Secretary Rogers." The image of an assistant secretary undermining the Secretary of State before a foreign official is shocking. Gromyko later met with Nixon who took yet another position. The affair left Gromyko "thoroughly unnerved."³¹

Kissinger moved within the NSC to organize or revive ad hoc entities like the Washington Special Actions Group, the 303 Committee and the Forty Committee that centered more control inside the White House. These groups were used to manage policy with groups of personnel who operated entirely outside bureaucratic channels and without Senate oversight. This rarely involved anyone from the State Department. Nixon allowed Kissinger to chair all these committees and to multiply the NSC's budget and staff exponentially. Middle East hand Edward Peck observed that even the name of the Forty Committee "was top secret." Nixon rarely appeared at these meetings, although they dealt with critical issues, and at one midnight session Kissinger ordered a nuclear alert without Nixon's presence. Before Nixon entered the White House, the 1968 NSC budget was $700,000, but three years later it had more than tripled to $2.2 million, and its staff had doubled, from 46 to 105.³²

Nixon's hostility toward diplomats was overt, telling Kissinger, "the little boys in the State Department [...] had better be careful because Rogers will brook no nonsense." Historian Walter Isaacson noted that in March 1969, Nixon "commiserated" with his NSC staff about "[h]ow hard it must be for them [...] to deal with all those 'impossible fags' in the State Department." Alexis Johnson chalked it up to "Nixon's longstanding paranoia that the Foreign Service consists solely of Democrats who despise Republicans, him in particular." Rogers never proved to be the taskmaster Nixon wanted, as he groused to Ehrlichman, "Rogers [is] always backing up his goddamned bureaucrats."³³

Kissinger recalled Nixon's view of the State Department: "The two institutions he most distrusted [were] the Foreign Service and the press." In his memoirs Kissinger warned the reader about US diplomats: "Woe to the uninitiated at the mercy of that extraordinary and dedicated band of experts." He later described them more impersonally: "A splendid instrument, staffed by knowledgeable, discreet and energetic individuals [... They do] require constant vigilance lest the convictions that led them into a penurious career tempt them to preempt decision-making." Other asides were more caustic. When journalist Richard Valeriani told him a former FSO was training his horse, Kissinger, who was flanked by two FSOs, responded: "At last, a Foreign Service officer is engaged in an activity up to his mental level."[34]

True to Halperin's strategy, Kissinger used careful leaks to Joseph Kraft and other columnists to build up his stature. Kissinger effectively managed his own press coverage to create an image of himself as the superstar of Middle East diplomacy. *Newsweek* ran a cartoon cover of Kissinger soaring through the air dressed as Superman with the caption "It's Super K!"[35]

In 1971 one of the most intense conflicts between Kissinger and the NEA began when a series of articles appeared in the American press, some authored by a journalist, Joseph Kraft, close to Kissinger. These articles were critical of the Middle East hands in general, and the initiative of senior diplomat in Cairo, Donald Bergus, in particular. The "Phantom Memo" controversy concerned a breakthrough offer from Cairo to enter talks with Israel over troop withdrawals in the Suez and Sinai regions. Bergus was building on Secretary of State Rogers' negotiations with Egypt. But details of the offer were revealed by Kraft in the Washington Post, which led to an Israeli rejection of a potential United Nations buffer zone and Arab–Israeli disengagement.[36] Within a few months a series of acidic features, most notably "Those Arabists at State," appeared in the *New York Times*, the *Washington Post* and *The New Yorker*.

The combination of Kissinger's bureaucratic skill and Nixon's hostility effectively shut out the State Department to such a degree that Senator Stuart Symington announced Rogers was "only the Secretary of State in name" and called hearings on "the lack of accountability." When Senators Stuart Symington and William J. Fulbright summoned Kissinger to answer to the Senate Foreign Relations Committee, Kissinger cited executive privilege. The senators demanded that Kissinger explain his "control of an NSC staff of 110 persons" and questioned why he functioned as "Secretary of State in everything but title." Symington's concern was the Senate's loss of "accountability" over foreign policy. Kissinger agreed to a meeting off the record. Nixon responded that Rogers was "chief adviser on foreign affairs and [...] people who think otherwise are misleading themselves and others." Symington backed down and Fulbright withdrew legislation barring executive privilege. Kissinger later sidestepped them when he used a secret side letter or memorandum of understanding to make additions to a treaty with Israel, which he claimed were not subject to Senate approval.[37]

When Secretary Rogers's top aide and ally, Alexis Johnson, suffered a heart attack he was replaced by Kissinger's back channel ally, William Porter. By September 1973 Kissinger had assumed the Secretary of State's post without relinquishing the NSC

Adviser's position, the only person ever to control both until President Gerald Ford pressed him to surrender it.

When the October War broke out, Middle East hand Edward Peck called Porter to tell him there was a war on, and Porter queried: "Has the Secretary sent for me or asked for me?" When Peck said no, Porter responded, "Well, when he does, call me." Peck observed, "And, Kissinger never did." With Rogers out, the secretaryship in hand and the powerful undersecretary's post under Porter, Kissinger had control over Middle East policy. Peck concluded, "That was sort of the end of it all."[38]

The White House asserted its view further down the chain of command. Nixon removed Assistant Secretary Parker Hart, a Middle East hand, in favor of Sisco. Hart only lasted one month into the Nixon administration after he criticized an Israel commando raid on Beirut December 28. He recalled his comments "hit the fan automatically with the American-Jewish community. They were all for getting that guy Hart out."[39]

His replacement at the NEA was Joseph Sisco. Kissinger was once heard shouting in the White House: "If I ever become Secretary of State, blood will run in the halls and the first one to go will be Sisco."[40] Kissinger grew to admire Sisco's ability to guard his own turf, and Sisco came to recognize his power. Kissinger's biographer claimed the switch came during the 1970 Jordanian crisis: "Until then Sisco had been a bureaucratic adversary [...] but from then on, he would be a backstage ally of Kissinger's." They also held similar views of the US–Israeli relationship. Sisco recalled: "I came in here with what all Arabists regard as a pro-Israel bias." Middle East hand Hermann Eilts was dismayed to find Sisco "who had for so long fought off Henry Kissinger's effort to intrude on the Middle East field [...] began to work, and had to work, very closely with Kissinger."[41]

The Sisco–Kissinger alliance signaled to the Middle East hands that their influence had been further reduced. Journalist Joseph Kraft asserted in 1971 that Sisco was assigned to clear out NEA: "Once in office, Sisco made a point of breaking up the Arabist concentration in the Bureau."[42] It was more a case of Middle East hands choosing to leave when they recognized Sisco would not be their advocate. Richard Parker accepted a post in Morocco in 1970: "I crossed swords with him on a number of occasions. I did not like working for him and very few of my colleagues did." Parker left when he found Sisco "working on a draft peace proposal involving Egypt without consulting me." Supportive of the effort, but dismayed at having no role in a key initiative in his area of expertise, Parker went to Morocco.[43]

During this era Middle East hands recognized how reduced the State Department role was. Andrew I. Killgore found that there was no longer any institutional strength to protect Arabists, who had once done their political reporting without fear of repercussions. During the Kissinger era, Killgore, a skilled Arabic linguist and Middle East hand, was assigned for three years to New Zealand. Despite efforts by Philip Habib and others in the State Department to get him back from exile, he remained in New Zealand until after Kissinger left office.[44]

Kissinger had particular problems with Middle East hands who served as the conduits for Sadat's peace offers. In 1971 Kissinger removed Donald Bergus from Cairo after the Egyptians sent a proposal that would have reopened the Suez Canal, known as "the Phantom Memo." In 1973 Kissinger ousted Bergus's successor, Joseph

N. Greene Jr, after Greene complained he had read evidence, in Arabic, of Kissinger's secret contacts with Egypt. It was a bizarre example of the usefulness of Arabic for information gathering. Kissinger reveled in Greene's reaction: "There is no fury like that of a Foreign Service officer bypassed, especially when he is head of a diplomatic mission, even a small, so-called Interests Section as in Cairo." Greene had read an Egyptian press report, in Arabic, of an interview in which Sadat revealed secret talks with Kissinger, then sent an unclassified cable describing the back channel contact. He was out of the Foreign Service within the year.[45] At that point Kissinger was not yet the Secretary.

Middle East hand William R. Crawford concluded that Kissinger had created "a duplicate Department of State in the White House." Kissinger summarized his Middle East experience in his memoirs: "If the reader finds the diplomacy outlined in this chapter an agonizing swamp of endless maneuvering and confusion, he knows how I felt." It seems the "agonizing swamp of endless maneuvering" was in part his own making. It was an arabesque, an intricate design. Most of those enmeshed in it only realized the complete pattern in hindsight, if at all. Kissinger's strategy may be a conscious or unconscious emulation of the diplomats he had studied. Of Metternich he wrote: "So dexterous were his combinations that during a decade they obscured the fact that what seemed the application of universal principles was in reality the *tour de force* of a solitary figure."[46] Much of the Nixon–Ford Middle East policy was precisely that, a tour de force by Dr. Henry Kissinger.

The Rogers Plan

Nixon made his first diplomatic initiative during the winter of 1968, in the interim between his election and inauguration. He sent William Scranton as his personal envoy to the Middle East. Scranton had worked at the State Department and was viewed as a practical, independent thinker. Joseph Sisco recalled Scranton had presidential approval: "Nixon indicated to Scranton he might really take a look at the situation."[47] Standing dramatically on the Allenby Bridge, literally the link between the Israeli-occupied West Bank and Jordan, Scranton told journalists: "America would do well to have a more evenhanded policy [...] We are interested, very interested, in Israel and its security, and we should be. But it is important to point out in the Middle East and to people around the word that we are interested in other countries in the area and have friends among them."[48] Scranton's comments set off a debate. Kissinger recalled its dramatic effect: "Shock waves of alarm spread to Israel and among Israel's supporters in the US."[49] What they feared and what alarmed Kissinger was the possibility of US leverage for what Israel termed an "imposed settlement." When Scranton elaborated on his "more evenhanded" comments, he said it was important for the United States to consider "the feelings of all persons and all countries in the Middle East and not necessarily espouse one nation over some other."[50] Kissinger related the event in his memoirs, but severed the last four words and altered Scranton's meaning: "and not necessarily espouse one."[51] A report appeared in *Newsweek*'s December 23, 1968 issue implying the Scranton mission was in trouble: "one of Nixon's chief foreign-policy advisers reportedly reassured the Israeli ambassador to Washington that Scranton was not in any sense authorized to speak for the new administration."[52]

The president-elect's press secretary, Ronald Ziegler, distanced Nixon from the statement: "His remarks are Scranton remarks, not Nixon remarks."[53] After a debriefing with Nixon, Scranton made a statement that reworded, but did not ultimately change, his original remarks: "We are very interested in Israel. But we are also interested in other nations there [...] We must mend our fences."[54] Mending fences is an accurate metaphor for the Scranton policy, as well as those of Rogers and NEA, in 1969. Fences are, of course, borders that both include and exclude. Resolving the refugee issue and settling the borders between Israel and her neighbors was inherent in that approach. Moreover, fence mending implies creating a better relationship. Nixon, however, had limitations on how far he would go to mend fences and had once commented: "I believe in building bridges but we should build only our end of the bridge."[55]

In the uproar of Scranton remarks and Ziegler's denials, another quotation was overlooked. When asked if a peace plan was in the works, Scranton responded, "Yes, certainly. We shall draw up a peace plan, but I can say nothing about it at the moment."[56] That became the Rogers Plan.

Secretary of State William Rogers had examined United Nations Resolution 242, ratified a year earlier, and his approach was legalistic, which reflected Scranton's "evenhanded" approach. The UN formula, known as "land for peace," involved Israeli withdrawal from occupied Arab territory in exchange for a firm commitment to peace and recognition of Israel. Rogers stressed: "We believe that this approach is *balanced* and fair."[57]

On the issue of final boundaries, Rogers accepted the UN position: "Those boundaries (1949 & 1967) were armistice lines, not final political borders. The Security Council resolution neither endorses nor precludes the armistice lines as the definitive political boundaries."[58]

Once in the White House Kissinger, Rogers, Sisco and the Middle East hands went to work executing Nixon's Middle East policy but often pursuing conflicting objectives. Nixon said he wanted to test Soviet intentions, Kissinger planned what he called a "stalemate" to force the Arabs to abandon the Soviets while making Israel secure, and Sisco wanted to checkmate the Soviets. Rogers and his Middle East hands wanted to negotiate a settlement to avoid war, defuse regional tensions, especially in the refugee camps, and thereby avert Soviet gains. Each reflected a side of Nixon's complex persona and thought they understood his objectives.

Joseph Sisco recalled that "President Nixon made very clear to me that what he wanted was a test of Soviet intentions in the Middle East." Kissinger's steadfast opposition to a broad solution won out: "I was always opposed to comprehensive solutions that would be rejected by both parties and that could only serve Soviet ends [...] My aim was to produce a stalemate."[59] And he did. Trying to deny the Soviets and to guarantee Israeli security he placed America as the roadblock. His stalemate destroyed the Rogers Plan as it damaged US credibility.

Secretary Rogers announced that his plan offered: "A just and lasting peace—a final settlement—not merely an interlude between wars. When contrasted with Kissinger's stalemate, Rogers' approach has a more compelling rationale: "We believe that a protracted period of no war, no peace, recurrent violence and spreading chaos would serve the interests of no nation, in or out of the Middle East."[60] The State Department approach was based upon moving forward in the belief that progress would benefit the United States as well.

Ultimately the Cold War view negated the regionalist approach, and the Middle East hands lost. So did Israel. The failed diplomatic resolution led to a low-level, but deadly, conflict with Egypt called the War of Attrition, and the Jordanian civil war exploded on its border, and, after a brief pause for Sadat's peace overtures, the October War. The United States suffered the continued closure of the Suez Canal, the OPEC oil embargo, a nuclear standoff with the Soviets during the October War and diminished regional influence. Ironically Moscow achieved heightened influence in Middle East, especially in Egypt, Syria and South Yemen, as they shipped arms and Soviet advisers into the region.

Assistant Secretary Joseph Sisco, who had drafted the language of UN Resolution 242, did much of the drafting for the Rogers Plan. He chose to do it without the Middle East hands and held to his earlier position that it should not specify the extent of Israeli withdrawal. Middle East hand Richard Curtiss recalled that when Nixon met with the heads of Defense, CIA and State to discuss the draft, they supported a return to pre-1967 lines, with only "insubstantial" border changes, as one participant concluded, "It is high time that the US stopped acting as Israel's attorney in the Middle East."[61] That was a view Israel feared might prevail.

Sisco began working with the Soviet Ambassador, Anatoly Dobrynin, to build a basis for negotiations, as summarized by NSC staffer William Quandt: "Final borders would be agreed upon by the parties. Minor adjustments in the 1967 lines were possible. There would be no imposed settlement. The four powers would work closely with and through [UN] Ambassador [Gunnar] Jarring. A final agreement would take the form of a contract signed by all parties. Peace would be achieved as part of a package settlement."[62] Talks continued between Sisco and Dobrynin throughout the year, and by December 1969 a more specific 10-point formula was ready. It dealt first with the UAR (Egyptian)–Israeli front and then the Jordanian–Israeli front. Discussion of the Syrian–Israeli front, the Golan Heights, was to follow. On the UAR–Israeli front there would be "a timetable for withdrawal of Israeli forces," an end to the state of war, "secure and recognized borders" with demilitarized zones and a guarantee for Israeli access to the Strait of Tiran and the Suez Canal, "a fair settlement of the refugee problem" and reciprocal recognition of "sovereignty, political independence and the right to live in peace." All of this was to be guaranteed in a contract and ratified by the UN.[63]

The problem was that neither the Israelis nor the Arabs trusted the other to move forward on such a momentous bargain, and the problem of how much territory was to be bargained remained central. Before the Six Day War such an exchange was viewed as complex, but after the occupation of the West Bank, the Sinai and the Golan Heights, it was immensely more difficult. Israel grew comfortable within its expanded boundaries. Arab demands for total withdrawal complicated matters. NSC Adviser Henry Kissinger's back channel communications signaled that the Rogers plan was dead. Hermann Eilts recalled being told by Rogers: "It's called the Rogers Plan, but it's really the Nixon plan, Nixon approved every bit of this, and then when I presented it, Kissinger pulled the rug out from under me.'"[64]

Rogers did not initially reveal the terms of his plan in public but conveyed it quietly. That was consonant with the quiet diplomacy tactics practiced by the Middle East hands. When asked about Israeli reports that future sales of Phantom jets would be kept secret, Rogers responded: "[I]n our system of government secrecy is not a very productive policy to follow!"[65]

Kissinger advised Nixon against the Rogers Plan, signaled to the Israelis that it had no White House support and afterward deflected the Middle East hands' effort to restart the process. This created the stalemate he had planned. Why prefer stalemate? Kissinger wrote: "My aim was to produce a stalemate until Moscow urged compromise or until, even better some moderate Arab regime decided that the route to progress was through Washington." As the Sisco–Dobrynin talks progressed, the entire military balance between Israel and the Arabs changed. The United States delivered Phantom jets to Israel in early September 1969. Israel felt a new sense of security, accompanied by a growing intransigence on negotiation or withdrawal while on the Arab side there was heightened, intense frustration. Prime Minister Golda Meir announced the Phantoms "helped bring peace to the Middle East." Middle East hand Richard Parker recalled that "ninety-six hours after the delivery" Israel launched a major raid into Egypt killing several hundred. He felt it was intended "to drive home the lesson" that Israel had the military edge and "to render Egypt defenseless against air attack." The raids progressed during the Rogers Plan negotiations, while Middle East hands warned the Soviets might step in. Journalist Seymour Hersh noted those warnings "were rejected out of hand by Kissinger." By late January Nasser had secured an air defense system and 14,000 Soviet advisers from Moscow.[66]

The continued US sale of arms, long opposed by the Middle East hands, escalated the Arab–Israeli conflict and gave Israel an unbeatable qualitative edge. But, as the United States gave Israel a sure sense of security, it heightened insecurity on the Arab side. The flaw in US policy was eerily predicted by Kissinger when he wrote about European politics circa 1812: "Could a power achieve all its wishes, it would strive for absolute security […] but […] absolute security for one power means absolute insecurity for all others." Kissinger concluded it would never lead to stability, since "were any one power *totally* satisfied, all of others would have to be *totally* dissatisfied and a revolutionary situation would ensue." After Egypt and Syria concluded diplomacy would never retrieve their territory they decided to attack in 1973. Kissinger wisely concluded in his study "The foundation of a stable order is *relative* security"—a situation in which no party had "a grievance of such magnitude" that conquest was the alternative. Kissinger ignored the advice of the Middle East hands and created an aura of "absolute security" for Israel. Ironically, that led to Israeli intransigence and Arab frustration.[67]

Arab reliance on Moscow also grew in part from their view that the White House was not being "evenhanded." Middle East hands recognized that the Arab perception of the United States had changed, as Richard Parker recalled: "[Sisco] was identified in the minds of Arab diplomats with what they considered false assurance of US intentions to make Israel withdraw [...] Sisco had difficulty convincing the Arabs of his sincerity as a result."[68] Michael Sterner concluded that Sisco viewed the region as part of the Cold War, epitomizing "the global as opposed to the regional viewpoint."[69]

For Sterner the NEA had been "a place where you could at least expect a dispassionate view of American foreign policy interests in the Middle East to prevail." But not under Sisco. Sterner found him too focused on short-term gains: "Joe was being too tactical and sacrificing too much of what should have been policy firmness for the sake of achieving short-lived tactical advances." William Quandt, then on the NSC staff, did not see Sisco as a regional specialist but someone whose "knowledge of the Middle East came from his years in Washington." Sisco conducted talks with the Soviets on the Rogers Plan, and Middle East hand Talcott Seelye traveled with him on a mission "to sell this plan in the area." While in Moscow, Seelye did not realize Kissinger was not supportive. Nixon stated in his memoirs the plan had no chance: "I knew the Rogers Plan could never be implemented, but I believed that it was important to let the Arab world know the US did not automatically dismiss its case."[70]

William Quandt, however, discerned a more subtle strategy, believing Nixon saw the State Department as "anxious to play a leading role," and he would let them: "If it should succeed there would be credit enough for everyone; if it were to fail, Nixon and Kissinger would be relatively free of blame."[71]

The Middle East hands had learned that quiet diplomacy could be effective. A decade earlier during the Joseph Johnson plan negotiations, both Johnson and William Crawford refused to release details of their proposal to the press, fearing that publicity would lead both sides to denounce it. Now Sisco argued that the Soviets were "misrepresenting" the Rogers plan in private to the Arabs and urged Rogers to go public. The ultimate undoing of the plan came when Rogers unwisely gave a hasty presentation on December 9, 1969, in hopes of saving it. Secretary Rogers stated American policy was "to encourage the Arabs to accept a permanent peace" and "to urge the Israelis to withdraw from occupied territory when their territorial integrity is assured."[72] In his speech Rogers emphasized Israel would not be pressed but remain secure so that renewed warfare would be forestalled. But as Seelye and others toiled, Kissinger's arabesque continued.

Israel at first raised concerns, but three weeks later issued a flat rejection. Rogers plowed onward, sending the Jordanian–Israel draft to King Hussein who quickly sent a positive response. Jordan's king had a million reasons in his kingdom to want an immediate settlement. The Palestinian refugees, known as the *fedayeen* in Jordan, outnumbered the king's subjects, and the nation was on the verge of a civil war, which nearly dragged in Israel.

David Korn, then a Middle East hand in Tel Aviv, argued it was the US proposal for the Jordanian front that had triggered Israel's refusal, noting that the initiative had "more serious domestic political implications in Israel than the one for Egypt."[73] The West Bank was arguably more important to the concept of *eretz Israel* (greater Israel) than Sinai. Prime Minister Golda Meir commented: "We didn't survive three wars in order to commit suicide." Israel's cabinet met on December 22, 1969, and firmly rejected Rogers: "Israel will not be sacrificed by any power or interpower policy and will reject any attempt to impose a forced solution on her [...] the proposal by the USA cannot but be interpreted by the Arab parties as an attempt to appease them at the expense of Israel." William Quandt observed Rogers had little time to worry about the rejection: "As Rogers was deploring the Israeli use of the word 'appease' the following day, the Soviets delivered an official note rejecting the Rogers proposals virtually in their entirety." AIPAC mobilized a campaign to oppose the Rogers Plan in Washington. Simha Flapan, an Israeli journalist, was at the American Jewish Committee (AJC) shortly after the Rogers Plan was announced. He was told the Israeli government had requested the AJC "arrange a demonstration protesting the Rogers Plan," which was held January 25–26, 1970. Historian Edward Tivnan records the level of pressure put on Congress to oppose the Rogers Plan: "fourteen hundred Jewish leaders from thirty-one states descended on Washington [...] AIPAC arranged appointments for them with 250 members of Congress."[74]

AIPAC made its point with overwhelming emphasis. Some of the opposition to the Rogers Plan was expressed directly to the NEA. Middle East hand Talcott Seelye noted the pressure put on Sisco and Rogers: "I recall [...] just about every other time I went in to see Sisco he was on the phone to [Israeli Ambassador Yitzhak] Rabin. And Rabin was always coming up to see the Secretary, etc. So one sensed the power of the Israel Embassy was quite considerable."[75]

Richard Parker called the Rogers Plan "a sincere effort to find a proposition the Arabs and Israel could both accept, but it was so watered down in the name of realism that there was not enough in it for either side." Parker felt it was the Israeli fear of a forced withdrawal from all of the Sinai as well as the provision to take in 100,000 refugees that were key to the rejection.

The failure of the Rogers Plan also led to new problems on the Egyptian front. In 1970 renewed hostilities broke out across the Suez Canal in what became known as the War of Attrition. Israel's Phantoms made raids deep into areas along the Nile that marked a new level of violence. Richard Parker has drawn a connection between the 1970 raids and an Israeli strategy promoted by Ambassador Rabin based on his reading of American intentions. In his memoirs Rabin said he realized in the months leading up to the Rogers Plan that "Nasser's standing could be undermined [...] Some sources have informed me that our military operations are the most encouraging breath of fresh air the American administration has enjoyed recently." Rabin argued the attacks would undermine Nasser: "A man would have to be blind, deaf and dumb not to sense how much the [US] administration favors our military operations."[76] Thus, the White House was Rabin's rationale for increasing military pressure on January 5, 1970, just after the Rogers Plan had been presented.

The collapse of the Rogers Plan and the Israeli raids had other ramifications. The Soviets delivered a note to Kissinger that he viewed as "a not very subtle hint that our innocent 1969 peace proposals had been a cover for Israeli deep penetration air raids." Dobrynin had warned Kissinger, who immediately advised Nixon to stick with "our policy of holding firm." The Egyptians were desperate and needed the Soviet surface-to-air missiles (SAMs), technicians, pilots and planes. Middle East hand Michael Sterner argued then that "ninety per cent of the Soviet presence in Egypt derives from Russia's role of providing military support to Egypt in its conflict with Israel."[77] A stalemate did not force Egypt to the US side, as Kissinger had originally theorized. Instead it forced them to turn to Moscow and tolerate a large contingent of Soviet advisers. For Israel, there were strategic consequences: they could no longer cross the Suez Canal without potentially engaging the Soviets. Egypt made tremendous sacrifices to obtain the SAMs, and in the October 1973 war they provided the air defense umbrella that allowed Egypt to inflict high casualties on the Israeli air force and recover half of the Sinai. Sadat told Rogers that Nasser was forced to Moscow in January 1970 by the Israeli raid and needed the Soviet SAMs "to defend our heartland and they only came after Israel began bombing our heartland." Sadat later stressed: "This was—and still is—quite a sacrifice for us, because we agreed that all the Soviet officers and men be paid in hard currency, not Egyptian money. We are paying through the nose for the maintenance of these Soviet SAM crews in Egypt."[78]

The failure of the Rogers Plan led Egypt to become a Soviet client and Israel felt secure enough to reject US mediation. Both continued bloody fighting across the canal and then Jordan exploded into civil war.

Crisis in Jordan, Black September 1970

As tensions rose between Israel and Egypt, Rogers worked to halt the War of Attrition. But America's ally in Jordan, King Hussein, was in deep trouble. The failure of the Rogers Plan was a terrible blow for the king who had a new generation of *fedayeen*, born in the refugee camps and raised in poverty, living in Jordan. The Palestinians, driven out of the West Bank in 1967, outnumbered the Hashemites and eventually took control of areas in Jordan, including parts of Amman. The collapse of the Rogers Plan in January 1970 also signaled to the Palestinians that diplomacy would not relieve their intolerable conditions. Middle East hand Robert Stookey estimated that by 1967, there were 2,350,000 Palestinians: 52 percent in Jordan, 13 percent in Syria and Lebanon, 17 percent in the Gaza Strip and 12 percent in Israel.[79]

In September 1970 Hussein was confronted by an increasingly powerful guerilla movement, led by Yasir Arafat, who was prepared to launch a takeover of Jordan. Talcott Seelye, country director for Jordanian affairs, realized the Palestine Liberation Organization (PLO) was becoming a state within a state by late 1970: "They were setting up roadblocks and interfering with the affairs of state and the government of Jordan. King Hussein [...] tried to persuade Arafat to cease and desist but was unsuccessful [...] So things were getting tenser and tenser [...] at one point there were attacks on the American embassy property." As ambassador to Jordan Harrison Symmes did not hold King Hussein in high esteem, had opposed aid to Jordan and had written a State Department paper entitled "Some Unthinkable Thoughts: A Jordan Without Hussein," which argued the United States should "cut its losses" since aid was "obstructing a possible solution to the problem of Palestine." The implication was Hussein was the obstruction to a Palestinian takeover in Jordan that would mean the refugees did not need to stay in the camps or return to Israel and the refugee problem would be solved. Rodger Davies informed Symmes in 1967 that he was chosen for the Jordan post because Nicholas Katzenbach felt "you have a balanced view toward Jordanian relations with the US."[80]

Washington took notice of Jordan in April 1970 when Assistant Secretary Joseph Sisco attempted to travel by land from Tel Aviv to Amman to evaluate the crisis. The *fedayeen* staged anti-Sisco demonstrations, a mob surrounded the embassy and Ambassador Symmes was told: "The fedayeen have requested you lower the American flag." Symmes refused and the mob removed it for him. Various means of delivering Sisco safely to the embassy were discussed, while King Hussein pressed for Sisco to make the visit to show support, informing Symmes: "I shall regard Sisco's not coming as a deliberate personal insult and I shall consider you responsible." Fearing this might lead to the assassination of NEA's senior officer, Symmes advised Sisco to skip Amman. King Hussein declared Symmes persona non grata and requested Washington recall him. Symmes was gone by May.[81]

The Nixon administration then left the post of ambassador to Jordan unfilled throughout the summer as the crisis deepened. In June an attempt had been made on King Hussein's life and the following day Embassy Amman cabled Kissinger, "The situation has fallen apart." Drawing on his philosophy of punishing those he viewed as in league with the Soviets, Kissinger moved to support the king. Kissinger viewed the king as a moderate: "Hussein had always advocated moderation, resisted the radical tide and avoided fashionable anti-Western slogans." It didn't hurt that the King's personal adviser, Zaid Rifai, had been Kissinger's student at Harvard. Kissinger saw the Jordanian crisis as "a test of our capacity to control events in the region."[82] But, the United States was not in control.

While Talcott Seelye recalled that the NEA was directly involved as advisers, Kissinger termed the State's response was "hardly electric." He regarded the State Department as "reluctant to add Jordan to a plate already overflowing" and convened the NSC's Washington Special Actions Group, to handle it. His rationalization for taking control was that "[t]he conventional wisdom of the Middle East experts [was] that Arabs were so excitable that any public warning was likely to drive them into a frenzy." Kissinger argued that Middle East experts held a negative stereotype of Arabs that "confuse[d] volubility with erratic behavior." He characterized his own view that Arab leaders were "circumspect and calculating."[83]

Nixon's new ambassador was a non-Arabist L. Dean Brown, sent off with this succinct advice from the president: "Keep me informed. Remember what I need. I don't want that State Department garbage." Brown grew to believe neither Nixon nor Kissinger understood the region and didn't want to listen to Middle East hands who did. Sisco informed him that Kissinger wanted Brown to go, but he protested, "I don't know anything about the Middle East." To which Sisco responded, "That's the idea." After making discreet inquiries, Brown summarized what he discovered: "The President and Henry Kissinger are fed up with the reporting from the Middle East. They don't understand a word of it. All these people are experts, Arabists, and it's all too long and too complicated." When the ambassador to Lebanon left his post due to illness, Kissinger sent L. Dean Brown as special envoy to Beirut, telling him to keep the embassy's political reports simple: "I can't understand a word they're saying. They send these long, lengthy telegrams about people I've never heard of and parties I've never heard of."[84] Kissinger, ever suspicious of Middle East hands, did not share their view of which regional forces motivated events.

He responded by sending envoys who did not know about the region, and he did not want to hear about the complexity of Lebanese politics.

When Brown arrived in Amman to present his credentials in September 1970, it was already in the midst of the crisis. To secure his safe arrival, an armored personal carrier was used; so, according to Seelye, rather than arrive at the embassy in a limousine, Brown "had to present his credentials in a tank." Events took a far more dangerous turn when a radical offshoot of the PLO, George Habash's Popular Front for the Liberation of Palestine (PFLP), hijacked four jetliners after Israel announced it was again pulling out of UN talks. The PFLP landed three of the planes and their passengers at Dawson's Field in Jordan.[85]

The NEA's Jordanian Task Force was headed by Talcott Seelye. They advised Secretary Rogers that Hussein had best act soon against the PLO, and Seelye argued: "If the Jordanian situation was calmed down then perhaps we could handle the hijacking situation. They were really two separate developments." The message was passed by Rogers to the Jordanian ambassador. Seelye concluded: "I don't know how much impact it had, probably marginal, but it happened to occur about the time that King Hussein, himself, presumably had decided it was time." Whether the NEA's advice was timely or just coincidental, Hussein moved at the right moment and unleashed his army on the *fedayeen*, in what Seelye recalled was "very, very bloody fighting."[86] Among the jetliner passengers were nearly a hundred Americans who had been evacuated from the planes and secreted around Amman as hostages. The NEA attempted to get the Red Cross in as neutral observers to assure their welfare while the State Department dealt with a deluge of telephone calls from relatives of the Americans. Seelye recalled one Palestinian charged with holding hostages "was shot trying to go out and get food to feed this American couple." Fortunately there were no American fatalities, and Seelye recalled everyone "emerged unscathed."[87]

The International Red Cross negotiated with the hijackers as the White House attempted to keep its European allies committed to a policy of no negotiation, since Israeli nationals and Israeli–Americans under dual passports were among the captives. The PFLP demanded the release of *fedayeen* in European and Israeli jails.

Kissinger reasoned, "We knew that Israel had a policy of never yielding to blackmail. It feared that if it ever yielded, no guerrillas could be held captive; terrorism would be encouraged. Our own view was roughly the same."[88] There was an incongruity between his policy and the fact that Israel freed 450 Palestinians in a phased exchange on September 29. Tragically, the White House stuck to this new no negotiations policy in 1973, which led to the deaths of two Middle East hands, Cleo Noel and George Moore, at the hands of Black September survivors of the Jordan fighting who expected the United States to negotiate.

Middle East hand David Korn, then in Tel Aviv, noted, "The Israelis loudly proclaimed a policy of refusing to pay ransom. They put up a tough front, but when they saw a possibility of freeing their people [...] they almost always sought a deal, albeit for the most part secretly."[89] Secretary Rogers publicly praised Brazil when it ransomed the US ambassador because they put his life "above all other considerations." When Nixon ordered the State Department to formulate its no negotiations policy in January 1973,

William Rogers, Alexis Johnson and William Macomber all refused to sign it. Two months later Cleo Noel and George Moore were murdered after Nixon announced the policy while Palestinian Black September guerrillas held the two Middle East hands hostage. They were shot to death when radio reports of the Nixon speech reached the Sudan.[90]

As if the situation was not already complex enough, Syria then mobilized armed forces and moved its tanks across the Jordanian border in support of the PLO in its confrontation with King Hussein's army. Kissinger convened an emergency meeting of the Washington Special Actions Group and his NSC deputy, Alexander Haig, requested Sisco come along. Sisco brought Seelye. Kissinger asked Seelye for a recommendation: "Do we respond with the US military or Israeli military?" Seelye said "The last thing we want is US military" He wanted to avoid sliding down the slippery slope: "I felt once you have the US military shedding Arab blood then you have ramifications to all of our embassies throughout the Middle East. While Israel is considered an instrumentality of the US, I didn't think the reactions against American institutions would be as bad." For the moment Kissinger decided against American forces. Seelye pointed out his experience of the event differs, following the discussion regarding the possibility of an Israeli air force action against the Syrian tanks. "The Israelis sent back word to us this operation could not be limited to an air operation, they would go in by land as well. We didn't like that idea in Washington. We figured that was the beginning of another occupation."[91] The matter was deferred for a few days.

According to Kissinger, Rabin called to inform him he "did not consider air strikes alone adequate; *ground* action might also be necessary" and requested an immediate response. Kissinger informed Nixon, and Nixon ordered Kissinger: "I have decided it. Don't ask anybody else. Tell him [Rabin] 'go.'" But Kissinger did not. He was concerned "an Israeli ground operation could produce a Mideast war," and polled Sisco (who agreed with Nixon). Secretary of Defense Melvin Laird could not decide. Kissinger, not yet even Secretary of State, had decided against acting on a direct presidential order. Nixon skimmed over events in his memoirs, saying only that he had "authorized Kissinger to call Ambassador Rabin and suggest [...] we would be fully in support of Israeli air strikes." The next morning the issue was discussed at an NSC meeting where Secretary Rogers opposed it.[92] Meanwhile Israel continued its mobilization.

By the next evening forces were in motion: the 82nd Airborne was on high alert, the Sixth Fleet was moved toward the Lebanese coast, the Israeli Defense Forces mobilized on Jordan's border. King Hussein waffled on Israeli assistance. Kissinger decided "to stop by a party at the Egyptian mission [...] to show that our policy was not anti-Arab." He found the Soviet ambassador deeply concerned but dismissed a comment that the Soviets were restraining Syria.[93]

But, according to historian Patrick Seale's interviews with Syria's Hafez al-Assad, the Syrians were very aware of American fleet movements and unwilling to oppose a combined Israeli–US operation: "Assad took the heavy hint and withdrew. He had no intention of committing himself to unequal combat with Israel, let alone with the US."[94] Meanwhile, Jordanian armed forces knocked out many Syrian tanks in heavy fighting, and Hafez Assad, commander of the air force, refused cover to the tank column and the remaining tanks were forced to retreat. What Nixon and Kissinger saw as a Soviet-inspired plot was a civil war. Middle East hands like Talcott Seelye realized it was rooted in the refugees' frustration, and the Syrian invasion was prompted by opportunism. Moreover, Asad feared the possibility of a joint US–Israeli operation. In 1973 he was willing to take on the Israel Defense Forces (IDF), but not the US armed forces in the bargain. Nixon's conclusion that Israel had become a major strategic ally was incorrect.

Middle East hands saw the explosion of long pent-up tensions rooted in decades of unresolved conflict. Cold Warriors saw Soviet plots. Kissinger drew a convoluted lesson from the events that, for him, magnified the victory: "The Soviets had backed off, raising by another notch the growing Arab disenchantment with Moscow."[95] But the crisis did not incline the leadership in Damascus or Cairo toward Washington, as Kissinger thought it would.

The Middle East hands, and especially Seelye, viewed it as a regional crisis: "Assad's action, together with the Jordanian air force action, caused the withdrawal of the column just at the point we were holding back authorizing the Israelis to move because they wanted to go in by land." Seelye felt that ultimate disposition might have had more consequences: "If we had authorized an [Israeli] ground attack, they would have gone in and probably would still be occupying the [Irbid] heights." Middle East hand Robert Stookey concluded that Nixon's analysis "ignored the long historical background of inter-Arab and Arab–Israeli animosities, which had little or nothing to do with Soviet ambitions." When questioned by journalists afterward, Seelye said: "Our intelligence indicated the Soviets were urging the Syrians to exercise restraint and not to get involved […] they had no hand in the PLO buildup in Jordan or the operation in Syria."[96]

Other events spun out of the Jordanian crisis: King Hussein's crackdown became known by the *fedayeen* as Black September for its deadly toll. It led to even more dangerous factionalism as the survivors formed a yet more radical commando unit, Black September, which targeted US diplomats and Israel. The *fedayeen* streamed into South Lebanon, and Israel's northern border became a new hot spot. Middle East hand Curtis Jones, posted to Beirut, found the Byzantine mire of Beirut factionalism further unbalanced by the arrival of more displaced refugees: "Lebanese politics became increasingly complicated."[97] Like falling dominos, the unresolved refugee issue first lit the fuse in Amman, destabilized Beirut and cost Israeli lives. The Palestinian presence led to the 1982–84 Israeli invasion of Lebanon, the creation of Israel's "security zone" in South Lebanon, and Operation Grapes of Wrath in 1996. America also suffered the consequences: in 1973 Black September murdered the ambassador at Khartoum and his aide. In 1976 the ambassador to Beirut and his aide were murdered, the Beirut Embassy was repeatedly bombed, as was the Marine barracks in 1983, with 241 American dead.

Kissinger's strategy had been to create a stalemate, reduce the Soviet role and draw "some moderate Arab regime" into Washington's orbit. Looking back in 1971, he concluded that it had all played out as he had planned: "the divisions within our government, the State Department's single-minded pursuit of unattainable goals—and the Soviet Union's lack of imagination—had produced the stalemate for which I had striven by design."[98] Upon the stalemate and its results Kissinger planned to build what he called "the peace process."

The Strange Case of Anwar Sadat 1971–74

Facing the continuing bloodshed of the War of Attrition, massive hard currency payments for Soviet air defense systems and the continued Israeli occupation of the Sinai Peninsula, Gamal Nasser was under great stress. After meeting with Arab diplomats to discuss the Jordanian conflict, Nasser collapsed and died in late September. The following spring his successor, Anwar Sadat, initiated his own peace offer. In February Sadat announced to the Egyptian National Assembly that 1971 was "The Year of Decision" and outlined his bold overture of peace to Israel: "If Israel withdrew her forces in Sinai to the Passes, I would be willing to reopen the Suez Canal; to have my forces cross to the East Bank [...] to make a solemn official declaration of a cease-fire; to restore diplomatic relations with the US; and to sign a peace agreement with Israel through [...] the UN."[99]

As William Quandt has pointed out, Sadat had every reason to expect a positive response, at least from the Americans. He was echoing what Secretary Rogers had said a month earlier, when he called 1971 the "year of decision in the Middle East." Sadat knew his offer included advantages to the United States—reopening the Suez canal would be a great economic boon. An oil tanker trip from Ras Tanura, Saudi Arabia, to Norfolk, Virginia, was 4,700 nautical miles, but traveling around Africa made the trip 11,810 nautical miles. Substantially more dangerous and expensive. For Israel a pact would signify recognition and peace. Sisco concluded that "the year of decision" did not resonate inside the Nixon White House: "We didn't really take it seriously. We should have, but we didn't."[100]

Neither did Israel. Ambassador Abba Eban urged his own government to respond, but the Israeli mood was intransigent. Worse yet, ultimately the Meir government would finish off Sadat's dramatic offer a year later when the Knesset declared: "the historic right of the Jewish people to the Land of Israel" and announced plans to settle Israelis in the occupied Arab territories. Up to this point, there had been no Israeli settlements. Later William Scranton, as President Ford's US UN representative termed the settlements "an obstacle to peace." His phrase became Washington shorthand for the US position. In March 1976 he criticized Israeli policies in the UN, terming "substantial resettlement of the Israeli civilian population in occupied territories [...] illegal [... and] is seen by my Government as an obstacle to the success of the negotiations for a just and final peace between Israel and its neighbors."[101]

The senior officer in Cairo, Middle East hand Donald Bergus, believed throughout 1971 that Sadat's offer held promise. Bergus and Michael Sterner were summoned to a personal meeting with Sadat in April, where Sadat displayed a map of proposed withdrawal lines. Sterner was elated: "We had certainly never heard anything like this from Nasser." Sadat soon added an additional incentive for the Americans by offering to send the Soviets packing. Here was something that should resonate in the White House. Bergus concluded, if this initiative drew an Israeli response, "you can write off war as a viable alternative in the Middle East."[102] He cabled Rogers who planned to fly to Cairo in May.

Anwar Sadat was an unknown quantity to many in Washington, but Middle East hands knew his long history. He had been with Nasser since the 1952 coup, and, unlike many other Middle East leaders, he had visited the United States. In February 1966 he had made an official tour of America, accompanied by Sterner, who first met him years earlier: "He was invited on a leadership grant to tour the US [...] I was made his escort officer because I was one of the few people in the government who knew him." Sadat visited Washington, Los Angeles, San Francisco, Sacramento and New York. Sterner brought him to sessions of Congress and state legislatures, recalling: "So he got the full flavor of American life. I think the big impression he went back with [...] was an impression of dynamism in the US [...] He associated openness, more open political systems, economic free enterprise and less state control over the economy as part of the American success story." Sterner recalled few Arab leaders had the experience of visiting the United States and their usual tours of Soviet and third-world locales were unimpressive. Sadat received a vision of a dynamic, democratic America from Sterner, and when he came to power he brought those ideas along with a desire for US cooperation. But Washington was unwilling, as Sterner found: "It was hard to get anybody to take Sadat seriously [...] I didn't know how strong Sadat would be and certainly didn't go around saying 'Listen, this is the man of the future' but I did send up memoranda to the Secretary of State saying, keep an open mind about this guy, I've spent some time with him and I think he thinks differently from Gamal Abdul Nasser."[103]

Sterner's instincts were correct, but he was not heeded. It would take another war to convince Kissinger that Sadat could negotiate and to convince the Israelis that they should.

Middle East tensions were reflected in the Kissinger versus Rogers antagonism. Kissinger was angered by renewed contacts with Egypt and the new offer by the Middle East hands and Rogers. Kissinger's arabesque continued after Rogers responded to Sadat. Kissinger threatened to resign over an action he deemed improper for a Secretary of State: "[Rogers] has written a letter to the Egyptian Foreign Minister." As Rogers's visit to Cairo neared, tensions escalated. Kissinger issued an ultimatum that demanded that all diplomatic action be approved by the NSC adviser: "All cables [...] especially the Middle East—must be cleared [...] all contact with [Soviet Ambassador] Dobrynin must be cleared." Even State Department talking points papers were to be cleared by Kissinger. He again threatened to resign because Rogers "has been holding policy meetings on the Middle East over at the State Department. That I cannot tolerate." Ehrlichman quipped his objections to public statements by Rogers made some sense: "Rogers was cut out of so many policy decisions by Henry that it *was* dangerous [...] he was often uninformed." Ehrlichman also observed the ultimatums were typed "without heading, address or signature" so as to be "unattributable."[104]

Kissinger also had a hand in shaping the official Israeli response to Sadat's offer. When Israel's counterproposal was drafted in mid-April, for a minor withdrawal but with no allowance for Egyptians to cross the canal in exchange for a ceasefire, Kissinger advised Ambassador Yitzhak Rabin. In his memoirs Kissinger recalled he told Rabin "to modify some elements that would have made the negotiation a total non-starter [...] the final Israeli version was certain to be unacceptable to Egypt."[105] In early May Rogers and Sisco took off for the Middle East, and Sadat promised them he would get rid of the Soviets. That alone should have drawn American interest. Kissinger warned Nixon: "It would be especially worrisome were his [Rogers's] presence to accelerate the diplomatic process."[106]

Rogers took the Sadat offer direct to the Israelis but got nowhere. Donald Bergus, however, retained hopes of working out the deal. Sterner felt the Middle East hands "really thought we had something promising here." Sadat's offer to open the canal and to sign a ceasefire would have meant official recognition of Israel, and should have been regarded as a major breakthrough. The problem, to Sterner, was Kissinger: "He tended to see things in terms of the US–Soviet chessboard on which Israel was our pawn and Egypt was the Soviet's pawn."[107]

With the negotiations losing momentum in late May Bergus was given a sheet of paper by the Egyptian Foreign Minister, Mahmoud Riad, which responded to the Israelis in a way that Bergus felt was "too stiff and negative." Bergus fiddled with the draft and returned a few days later with a text that meshed with what he knew Washington was looking for on Israel's behalf. It would make yet another offer to reopen the Suez Canal, one based upon US guidelines that should have been acceptable to Israel.[108] Bergus's handwritten notes were an effort to assist in producing an acceptable proposal. Sadat's acquiescence was communicated to Washington.

When no response came from Nixon to this proposal, which was supposed to match what Israel wanted, Sadat grew impatient. After waiting 70 days for a reply he complained of the snub, and journalist Joseph Kraft amplified the story into what was called "the Phantom Memo" in June. Kraft claimed he dubbed it the Phantom Memo because Bergus had been "very vague about the source." The title might have been an allusion to the ongoing dispute over the sale of Phantom jets to Israel which had been postponed in 1970. There was Israeli displeasure with the State Department's efforts to link concessions to Egypt with the jet sale. After the Bergus flap Meir was asked if the jets remained a problem and *Newsweek* reported "Mrs. Meir herself replied with a smile, 'Isn't that a phantom?'"[109]

According to Kraft, this appeared to be a move by Bergus. But, Rogers and Sadat had met a month earlier and were in regular communication. The initiative was deemed likely to succeed since it reflected what Israel wanted from an Egyptian offer.

But the biggest explosion came from Kissinger who called it "an extraordinary maneuver of which the White House was completely ignorant." He continued, "The incident not only revealed the State Department's bias toward an interim accord that was a stage toward an agreed (and unattainable) comprehensive settlement." Kissinger wrote that in April he had reframed Israel's response to make Rabin's offer "a total non-starter." From the view of Bergus and Sterner a comprehensive settlement was only unattainable if Sadat's peace offers were rejected. Kissinger argued the Bergus memo "magnified Cairo's disillusionment with American diplomacy; they thought us either incompetent or deceitful." Kissinger said: "The White House could no longer tell whether the parties were putting forward their own views or else interpretations of ours to force us into supporting publicly what we had told them privately."[110] Bergus evidently had used interpretations in helping the Egyptians draft the text, and that appears to have been, in Kissinger's view, his transgression.

Why had Bergus taken the risk? Both he and Sterner were convinced Egypt could be moved out of the Soviet orbit to American, as well as Israeli, advantage. Sterner commented, "We thought we were on the road to a major new opportunity." But that collapsed and Sterner concluded, "there was just no reciprocity [...] from the Israelis." There had been every reason to believe Sadat was a potential partner in peace, but Kissinger worked against it. Ambassador Rabin protested to Secretary Rogers on the grounds they had not been informed, even though the proposal was based on terms Rogers had discussed with them. In the words of NSC staffer Quandt: "Sadat soon realized it was not worth dealing with Rogers and Sisco any longer."[111]

Egypt then signed a friendship treaty with the Soviets. The end result was that Rogers was subjected to intense criticism, and Bergus was reassigned as "diplomat in residence" at the University of South Carolina. Later Sterner was moved from the Egyptian affairs desk in Washington to a post in the United Arab Emirates (UAE). Kissinger's stalemate remained intact.

A few months later, having made the Phantom Memo famous, journalist Joseph Kraft wrote an article on the Middle East hands. In "Letter from Cairo," he observed that Bergus and Sterner "like most of the other State Department Arab specialists, believe an Arab–Israeli settlement would lead to a diminution of the Soviet influence in Egypt." He pronounced that Sadat was "a mild public joke" and "a peacemonger"—perhaps an allusion to warmonger—and evidence of his skepticism. He dismissed Sadat's year of decision as "a tough-sounding way of saying [...] there has been an extension of the time when there is no war."[112]

Kraft continued his critique of the Middle East hands in a *New York Times Magazine* feature in November 1971, which included a composite photo of several Middle East hands, including Sterner and Bergus, with their faces superimposed over drawings of Lawrence of Arabia. Kraft argued Nixon, Rogers and Sisco "had cocked an ear" to listen to the Arabists and "the thrust of American policy is to put pressure on the Israelis." Later the Israeli daily *Ma'ariv* used the same illustration to lampoon the Arabists for their opposition to moving the US embassy from Tel Aviv to Jerusalem. Nixon ordered Kraft to be wiretapped in May 1969 to find out if Kissinger was leaking information to him. Kraft wrote a series of articles on Kissinger, one of which compared his accomplishments "in magnitude to the feats of Castlereagh and Bismarck"—a comment sure to delight the man who made both diplomats his dissertation topic.[113]

Two of Kissinger's regular dinner companions, journalists Rowland Evans and Robert Novak, chimed in with another attack on the Rogers's and Bergus's efforts, entitled "New Pressure on Israelis," which claimed the State Department was urging Nixon to push for a settlement rather than allow Israel to maintain a "semi-permanent occupation."[114] Despite the criticism, Sterner felt the verdict of history would be on the side of the Middle East hands: "I think Kissinger was wrong and we were right. The events of history demonstrated it. Had Israel responded in 1970 and 1971 they could have been spared the 1973 conflict."[115]

While Kissinger's entire approach was supposedly built upon a stalemate until Egypt abandoned the USSR, even after Sadat jailed communists and offered to get rid of his Soviet advisers, he did not draw a response. While the Middle East hands worked on peace offers that would have benefitted Israel as well as the United States, they were accused of being pro-Arab or worse.

Bergus, having been moved from a central position in Cairo to the periphery in South Carolina, busied himself producing a brief summary of his experiences in *The Middle East: Two Wars for the Price of One*. Bergus was returned to an overseas post only after Kissinger's departure in 1977. Other Middle East hands learned from Bergus's failed initiative, as George Lane recalled: "I am not aware of anybody else who tried that after Bergus got shot down doing it."[116]

Kissinger ordered the NSC staff to produce a paper in July that would destroy the Rogers proposal. One staffer was told, "It's got to be destroyed. Henry wants it cut down." The strategy was to appeal to Nixon's Cold War anxieties: "We played heavily on the Soviet angle. That was one thing you could always turn the President around with." As the NSC staff went to work there were some regrets, one said: "Rogers' proposal had some merit, and here we are destroying it because of bureaucratic rivalry." During 1972 nothing at all happened on the Middle East diplomatic front. According to NSC staffer William Quandt, the White House "explicitly told the State Department not to consider any new initiatives until after the elections." Nixon was absorbed with the reelection campaign. In Cairo Sadat took action in mid-1972, with no quid pro quo, and ousted the entire Soviet contingent. Other than a brief meeting and Kissinger's instructions to send what he called "a nothing message," there was no response. Quandt, an adviser at the Camp David talks, summarized the situation in 1972: "US Middle East policy consisted of little more than open support for Israel."[117]

Historian David Schoenbaum has argued the Israelis had three reasons not to negotiate by 1972: "the demonstrative absence of any Arab to talk to, the windfall of US arms and favor since 1970, and the apparent impregnability of Israel's strategic position each did its part to legitimize the status quo post bellum."[118]

Schoenbaum noted there was an economic advantage for Israel: in 1968 US military aid was $25 million per year, but by 1971 it had risen to $545 million, and Israel was spending 30 percent of GNP on defense. Incredibly, this defense spending did not harm the economy, since much was offset by the aid; thus Schoenbaum found, "while still enjoying guns and butter to an extent unknown before […] the surge of foreign capital in turn, fueled growth rates averaging nearly 12 per cent."[119]

There was genuine confidence within the Israeli Defense Forces (IDIF) in 1973. Diplomat Abba Eban found his position undercut by General Moshe Dayan's public statements on the occupied territories. Dayan visited Masada, a deeply symbolic spot—the site of an ancient Israeli defeat that led to a mass suicide—for a military ceremony in April 1973 and announced his vision of "a new State of Israel with broad frontiers, strong and solid, with the authority of the Israel Government extending from the Jordan to the Suez Canal." Conversely, Eban argued in 1973 there was "much talk of Israel's physical map, but little attention to the problem of her moral frontiers."[120] Yitzhak Rabin gave an interview in September 1973, less than three weeks before the October War, in which he stated that "Golda has better boundaries than King David or King Solomon."[121] Eban felt the warmth emanating from the White House, and the stalemate over boundaries was the major reason for Rabin's attitude: "The text was a warm celebration of the ceasefire lines, of the existing stability and of the Nixon administration."[122] Israel was confident in its position.

In the spring of 1973, a Libyan civilian airliner missed Cairo, its destination, when its French crew was deflected from their course by a sandstorm. Israeli forces in the Sinai picked up the jetliner as it strayed over the desert. Despite reversing course and returning westward, the plane was shot down by Israeli jets with 106 dead. Abba Eban noted in retrospect that there was a lack of care in which they dealt with the matter: "Some Israeli newspapers and broadcasts had been callous in discussing the dead passengers on a Libyan airliners mistakenly shot down by the Israeli air force on the unlikely assumption that the plane was on its way to attack the Dimona [nuclear] research reactor." The White House, in spite of the turmoil, received Ambassador Rabin a few days later. The Israeli delegation was present when the news arrived that Black September guerrillas had staged a hostage taking in Khartoum, the capital of Sudan, Egypt's southern neighbor. The targets of the hostage taking were two Middle East hands, Ambassador Cleo Noel and his deputy chief of mission George Moore. Middle East hand David Korn theorized in a study of the assassination that Moore was the target, and the event directly linked to the 1970 Jordanian crisis: the Black September survivors had confused the diplomat George Moore with a retired CIA officer whom they believed (incorrectly) had aided King Hussein in his crackdown.[123]

The captors demanded to exchange the diplomats for Sirhan Sirhan, the assassin of Robert F. Kennedy, and a group of Palestinian women held in Israeli jails.[124] The embassy, with both senior officers taken captive, contacted the State Department, which dispatched a negotiating team. Undersecretary of State William Macomber and the team flew to Khartoum, but arrived to find both Americans had just been murdered.

While the negotiating team was en route to Khartoum, Nixon had made statements about the crisis during a news conference. There were 10 topics discussed prior to that of the diplomats being taken hostage, and the penultimate topic, Martha Mitchell, had elicited Nixon's very firm and repeated refusal to comment because the matter was in the courts. Although that question elicited a "no comment," the subject of the hostages drew a response. Nixon made reference to his private discussion of the crisis with the wife of the Israeli ambassador in the White House. It was a controversial comment. Moreover, his response was not directed to the topic of reporter's question, confined to the ransom demand. Nixon instead responded on a broader manner, with two American lives at stake:

> "Q. Mr. President we have a crisis, of course, in the Sudan where the US Ambassador is being held hostage and one of the ransom demands is that Sirhan be released. I wonder if you have any comment on this, particularly on that demand.
>
> A. Last night I was sitting with the wife of Mr. Rabin and we were saying that the position of Ambassador, once so greatly sought after, now, in many places, becomes quite dangerous [...] As far as the US as a government giving in to blackmail demands, we cannot do so and we will not do so [...] Now, as to what can be done to get these people released, Mr. Macomber is on his way there for discussions; the Sudanese Government is working on the problem. We will do everything that we can to get them released, but we will not pay blackmail."[125]

In the minds of many at the State Department, the statement jeopardized the lives of Noel and Moore. Curtis Jones, a member of the negotiating team, recalled that "Nixon had committed a grievous error." When Macomber's team arrived in Khartoum they were told by the Sudanese that both men were dead, and Black September "had heard on the radio President Nixon's statement [...] (which) made further waiting pointless."[126]

The State Department immediately sent back a flash cable: "Request Embassy opinion whether there [is] any possibility that statement made by President at press conference three hours earlier could possibly have been conveyed to terrorists by time of shooting." Embassy Khartoum replied "BSO [Black September] heard at least paraphrase of President's statement " and relayed another Sudanese report "obvious that terrorists were carefully monitoring radio." There was link between Nixon's incautious words and the assassinations. His outspokenness went against the counsel of the NEA's Armin Meyer, who advised Nixon's aide to have him decline comment. Secretary Rogers had refused to comment. The State Department's top administrators had earlier refused to formalize a White House policy of no negotiations for diplomatic hostages. That was a policy that Secretary Rogers, Undersecretary Alexis Johnson and Deputy Secretary William Macomber had all refused to sign onto.[127]

The *New York Times* published an editorial that ran in the same issue as the transcript of the Nixon press conference and reports of the murders of Noel and Moore. It opened by referring to the two victims as "unwitting diplomats far from the scene of any grievance" and praised Nixon for being "appropriately blunt" and in "resist(ing) audacious blackmail demands." The *Times* described how the "Arab propaganda machinery was spinning forth outrage against Israel for the shooting-down of an unarmed Libyan airliner over the occupied Sinai peninsula last week." With such events less than a fortnight in the past, the editorial concluded: "the responsible partisans of the Arab and Palestinian cause" rather than complaining about the loss of 106 lives in the airliner shoot-down "have a far more urgent task in reining in their own insane, bloodstained fanatics."[128]

The assassinations sent a chill through the State Department. From retirement FSO Lee Dinsmore wrote an open letter to Secretary of State Kissinger, published in the *Foreign Service Journal*. Dinsmore stressed their professionalism and recalled how many Middle East hands had watched as their warnings were ignored: "If the State Department in March 1973 is not ready to face facts, to analyze them objectively, and professionally to present them to the President I fear we shall become enmeshed in the coils of the web we ourselves are spinning." Dinsmore pointed out that the threat of terrorism could be reduced: "It could be different and all Americans could relax. We could help Israel join the Near East and gain Arab good will and cooperation [...] May the US Government honor Cleo Noel and Curt Moore, and not merely praise them."[129]

By early 1973, the Rogers Plan was dead, two Middle East hands were victims of Palestinian reprisals and Kissinger's stalemate had dragged on for four years. In May Egypt made one last effort by secretly contacting Kissinger who asked for more concessions but felt there would be no "new negotiating process with an Israel that saw no need for it to begin with." The NSC sent a memo to Kissinger in May that Egypt would not attack, but the State Department sent what Kissinger later admitted was "the only farsighted estimate" advising "the resumption of hostilities by autumn will become a better than even bet."[130]

In fact, Asad and Sadat had begun to make plans to attack their own Israeli-occupied territories in October and win them back by force. The plan was originally scheduled for the holiest and most solemn day in the Israeli calendar, Yom Kippur, and fell within the Islamic holy month of Ramadan. The plan was for Egypt to make a bold attack across the Suez Canal and achieve a bridgehead in Sinai while Syria moved back onto the Golan Heights. Jordan's King Hussein was excluded from the planning.

As the attack neared Nixon shook up the State Department. Nixon was tired of Kissinger's maneuvers, but did not have the courage to fire him either. Throughout 1973 Kissinger campaigned to replace Rogers, until Nixon concluded Kissinger "wanted State, felt he deserved it, and let me know that he would resign if he didn't get it." As Morton Halperin had described in *Bureaucratic Politics*, a Secretary's threat to resign could "embarrass" a president into action. Nixon concluded, "With the Watergate problem, I didn't have any choices." Kissinger reveled in winning control of both NSC and the State Department. During his first press conference as Secretary, he was asked whether it should be "Mr. Secretary" or "Dr. Secretary." He responded, "If you just call me Excellency, it will be okay." He commented: "I've always acted alone [...] Americans admire that enormously" and then mixed his regional metaphors to conclude, "Americans admire the cowboy leading the caravan alone astride his horse."[131]

Kissinger was at the head of the State Department caravan in September 1973. The one person most opposed to the State Department approach was now the Middle East hands' senior officer. Kissinger had total control over foreign policy as NSC Adviser and Secretary of State. As the Watergate crisis loomed and possibly Nixon's resignation, Kissinger thought: "[M]y appointment was less an act of choice than a step taken against his will in the hope it would mitigate catastrophe." Kissinger had only a matter of days before the October War swept over Israel and tore apart his stalemate. Just before war broke out Kissinger still believed that his Middle East policy would "demonstrate that the road to peace led through Washington."[132] As the Middle East hands had warned, prolonged stalemate would lead to renewed conflict.

The Secretary of State had an enormous policy disaster on his hands, as America's closest regional ally was caught unawares. Only in the very last hours did Israel realize what was unfolding. Nicholas Veliotes, not an Arabist but a longtime Middle East veteran, arrived in Tel Aviv, and then visited the Bar–Lev line, the Israeli defenses, in August: "It seemed rather strange to stand there and wave to the Egyptian soldiers on the other side, and to see these enormous, what looked like sand ramparts, enormous things up in the sky"

When he discussed the threat with Israeli generals his concerns were brushed aside: "They were impatient with any questions" When he asked Dayan about the Egyptians, Dayan compared the Arab armies to "rusting freighters at anchor, slowly sinking into the water." American warnings were dismissed. Veliotes concluded, "Contrary to popular belief our guys saw something coming, but we were so mesmerized by the myth of Israeli intelligence invincibility."[133] On October 6, 1973, the Egyptians exploded across the Suez Canal and into the Sinai. Veliotes recalled the Israeli public was never really appraised of how near defeat the IDF was on the Syrian front: "[P]eople didn't really know how close it had come up in the north." By the ninth he received word the Israelis had "stopped them in the north" and received a copy of "their shopping list for resupply." Veliotes found he did not get the entire picture, mainly due to "Kissinger's operating style." For Veliotes in Tel Aviv, it was "utterly maddening to be at an overseas post in the middle of [...] that time [...] where you began to believe that he trusted the Israelis, but he didn't trust the Americans. We knew we weren't getting information."[134] He was incensed when US nuclear forces were put on alert, Israel was notified, but not the embassy.

Nixon and Kissinger got messages from Israel that the IDF was running out of all military supplies. Foot-dragging on sending the replacement equipment by Defense Secretary James Schlesinger, not the NEA, led President Nixon to order an airlift. When it moved slowly he allowed repainted El Al planes to lift-off directly from the United States. It was not a secret that could be kept and it had serious ramifications for America and US interests in the region. One of the few who spoke up to urge Secretary Kissinger not to undertake the resupply was Talcott Seelye, then US Ambassador to Tunisia.[135]

The cost to Israel in lives lost had been enormous and they had very nearly suffered a defeat. Historian Howard Sachar summed up "the bitter cost" to Israel: "2,552 dead and over 3,000 wounded in the eighteen days."[136] After the fighting ended, Nixon announced an additional resupply of $2.2 billion in arms to Israel, which further shocked the Arab world.

The Organization of Petroleum Exporting Countries (OPEC), unable to organize an embargo to force an Israeli withdrawal after the Six Day War, was able to organize one in 1973. They announced not only a cutoff of supply to the United States but a quadrupling of the price of oil to $14 per barrel. Within a matter of months the price escalated even further, through the insistence of the Shah of Iran, putatively an American ally, who eventually bumped the price into the $30 range. The embargo lasted well into March 1974, and it was not until much later that Libya and Syria relented.[137] The economic impact reverberated throughout the United States, causing a steep inflationary spiral and widespread unemployment as oil prices skyrocketed.

While the Middle East hand most closely connected with US energy policy, director of the White House Energy Office, James Akins, had raised the alarm about America's growing dependence on imported oil and predicted such difficulties as the oil embargo; his warnings went unheeded. Middle East hand Lee Dinsmore warned Congress a year before the October War in August 1972: "There are no aspects of our relations with the Arabs that are not affected by our position on the Arab–Israel issue." He stated "If, in a few years" the United States faced "the threat of an oil crisis," it would "almost certainly" be as a result of our position on Israel. He argued, "Rogers' proposal could bring the problem closer to a settlement" and warned if Arab oil producers abruptly halted production "a world crisis would develop overnight."[138]

In September 1972, Akins delivered a lecture on "World Energy Demands and the Middle East" at the Middle East Institute in Washington. He wrote "The Oil Crisis: This Time the Wolf is Here" for *Foreign Affairs* in April 1973, a half year before the embargo occurred. For his efforts he was cast in the role of scapegoat rather than as Paul Revere.

Forbes led with the headline "Don't Blame the Oil Companies: Blame the State Department." The articles opened by pointing out to the disgruntled businessman faced with an exponential increase in energy costs: "The next time you find yourself blaming the oil companies or the Israelis for the high price of gasoline and electricity consider for a moment another possibility: that the US Government itself is responsible [...] Forbes has concluded [...] OPEC gained its power over prices through the maneuverings of the State Department." Another story on Akins was titled "Serving Two Masters?" What most irked *Forbes* was that Akins "refuses to take seriously the talk these days of a drop in oil prices, much less any breakup of the OPEC oil cartel." In fact the price of oil increased the following year, 1977, and doubled by 1980. Akins's analysis remained correct.[139]

Forbes had taken Akins's repeated warnings of American vulnerability for advocacy of an embargo. What Akins had continually pointed out was that in the early 1970s America was becoming increasingly dependent upon OPEC exports. Akins argued in April 1973, six months before the October War, this could be avoided "by conserving energy and developing alternative sources of energy." Before the embargo his words were brushed aside, after the energy crisis no one wanted to hear it.[140]

OPEC's goal was to stop the resupply of Israel and save Egypt's Third Army, while the embargo did not leverage American cooperation, it did result in enormous economic damage to the United States with soaring transport costs, inflation and a half million unemployed. After the embargo, the United States could no longer assume secure access to Arab oil at a stable price, its longstanding goal.

As the crisis dragged on, Nixon sank under the pressures of Watergate. The remainder of his term was composed of a final Middle East tour in June of 1974, during which he reopened relations with Syria, promised Israel additional nuclear energy technology, and okayed billions in arms to the Shah of Iran. Another major problem arose in September when the PLO was declared the sole representative of the Palestinians by Egypt and Syria and then ratified by the Arab League in October 1974. Kissinger said the PLO was "treated as refugees in the UN, as terrorists in the US and Western Europe, as an opportunity by the Soviets, and as simultaneous inspiration and nuisance by the Arab world."[141]

The oil crisis continued to drag down the US economy, especially the automotive sector, and in January 1975 reached a critical stage. Kissinger threatened US military intervention. In an interview with *Business Week*, he said the United States would use military force in the Arab oil fields if there was "some actual strangulation of the industrialized world."[142] Congress produced a report, "Oil Fields as Military Objectives: A Feasibility Study," concluding the strategy was not feasible: "In short, success would largely depend on two prerequisites: 1–slight damage to key installations 2–Soviet abstinence from armed intervention."[143] The report concluded taking Arab oil by force could not be done. Price hikes and rationing must be accepted.

Gerald Ford: Kissinger's Second President

Ford arrived at the presidency with no experience in foreign affairs. While Ford was never a commanding presence in foreign policy, he made two decisive moves: he assured the American people he would retain Kissinger to provide continuity in foreign policy and he removed Kissinger as NSC Adviser. The first act reassured Americans that Ford would not be running foreign affairs, and the second assured Ford that Kissinger wouldn't be running it either. Ford said Kissinger "should only wear one hat." This nearly triggered Kissinger's resignation: "I resented the decision bitterly because I thought that it would undermine the perception of my position."[144]

Ford was proud of his strong Congressional record in favor of US aid to Israel and reiterated his position as president: "In all my public life, I have never wavered in my support for a free and secure Israel. There was never one vote or one speech that could be interpreted otherwise. All of my life, I have had great respect for the Jewish people."[145] By March 1975 Ford had become convinced Israel were "stalling" on disengagement and recalled his reaction: "Their tactics frustrated the Egyptians and made me mad as hell."[146] Ford made public his determination to achieve some success in Middle East negotiations, but his choice of leverage was made without the Middle East hands. Ford was willing to provide aid while moving forward on peace talks: "I wanted the Israelis to recognize that there had to be some *quid pro quo*. If we were going to build up their military capabilities, we in turn had to see some flexibility to achieve a fair, secure and permanent peace." When such flexibility did not materialize, Ford, aware of the political pressure that could be applied by AIPAC, cabled Premier Rabin and said, "I have given instructions for a reassessment of US policy in the region."[147]

What this meant was the reassessment would include US aid to Israel, which was temporarily frozen. Both Ford and Kissinger quickly found themselves in hot water. In May 1975, 76 Senators sent a letter to Ford, a "sense of the Senate," which apprised him they did not support such action and requested Ford "reiterate our nation's longstanding commitment to Israel's security by a policy of continued military supplies, and diplomatic and economic support." AIPAC had lobbied for the letter.[148]

Then some critics, particularly supporters of the Israeli right wing, quite unfairly attacked Kissinger, who had no direct connection to the Ford decision. The Middle East hands, even those serving as ambassadors in the region, were sidelined. Hermann Eilts was reduced to being a mailman, assigned to make more than 20 journeys between Washington and Cairo. Although Kissinger conferred with Israeli Ambassador Sacha Dinitz in Washington, he preferred to have the correspondence hand carried by Eilts to Cairo. When asked why this was done, Eilts responded simply, "That's the way Kissinger wanted to handle it."[149]

With Secretary Kissinger as arbiter, Egypt got a minor disengagement under the Sinai II Agreement but would have to wait for President Carter and to work through to the Camp David Accords. Jordan won neither a disengagement nor adjustment to the de facto borders although King Hussein implored Kissinger for even "a few kilometers." Syria had a minor movement but little of substance was achieved. Kissinger's strategy was directly at odds with the Middle East hands' Beirut Axioms, and his peace process created additional complications as it inched along.

Middle East hand Richard Murphy arrived as ambassador to Damascus to reopen US–Syrian relations in August 1974, then realized no effort would be made on that track: "I was out there in August of 1974, and there was a high expectation of further shuttles, further disengagements […] for a comprehensive peace agreement, but that never happened." When asked if a comprehensive settlement was the goal, he responded: "It was certainly my understanding that was what the goal was. What was not clear at that time—to me—was that the Israelis had only one early goal, to pay lip service to the comprehensive peace."[150]

During this era of shuttle diplomacy Kissinger became a one-man State Department. Middle East hands were rarely consulted. Kissinger steadfastly refused to have ambassadors present when he met with many heads of state, a policy totally contrary to normal diplomatic practice. The combination of shuttle diplomacy and back channels irked Hermann Eilts who found that "[i]t's awkward when an ambassador finds that the people to whom he is accredited know more about US policy, as a result of direct channels to the White House than they do. Very awkward." Kissinger made the press corps, rather than the diplomatic corps, his travel companions and confidantes. One journalist told NSC aide Roger Morris "We know more than most US ambassadors in the places we visit."[151]

The stalemate was finally broken when Sadat suggested Ford use a "buffer force" to ease the disengagement and break the deadlock with Israel. Ford then presented the idea to Prime Minister Yitzhak Rabin as a US initiative to speed Israeli acquiescence and better relations resumed.[152] Israeli did sign the Sinai II Agreement but held out for an American side letter banning all US–PLO meetings. After Israel signed, Ford reinstated the aid.

While this effort did succeed in moving the agreement forward it was costly for the American administration. The side letter made any future US role as an arbiter much more difficult. The Palestinian Memoranda, as it came to be known, excluded all American diplomats from all contacts with the PLO until the PLO recognized Israel and agreed to UN Resolution 242. This became, according to Hermann Eilts, "our greatest vulnerability" as mediators in the Arab–Israeli conflict. William Brewer recognized that it gave the Israelis a veto over American actions.[153] It totally excluded any Palestinians from negotiations, since the PLO had been chosen as "the sole legitimate representative of the Palestine people" at the Rabat Summit in October 1974. Thus, all possibilities of discussing a solution to the issue of the refugee issue was off the table as of September 1975, and Israel would not have to make any territorial concessions on the West Bank. US UN Ambassador Andrew Young was forced to resign over informal contacts with PLO representatives and Middle East hands were isolated from any contacts for more than a decade.

One aspect of Sinai II, the Multilateral Force, organized by Middle East hand Michael Sterner, successfully disengaged both parties and ultimately formed the model for the withdrawal process under the Camp David Accords. The Kissinger era ended with only a minor disengagement on the Syrian and Egyptian fronts. It did not mend fences, but instead built walls.

Anti-American hostility escalated in these years. Dr. Malcolm Kerr, one of their FSI Beirut professors warned in 1972 that America was increasingly viewed as a threatening presence. While the US had been "only casually affected" by events, he cautioned, "the impact on the peoples of the Near East has been traumatic." He feared those people might "gather together the means to react to their trauma in such a way as to cause us damage."[154] During the Kissinger years the Middle East hands were targeted for revenge.

In 1973 Middle East hands Cleo Noel and George Moore were murdered by Black September guerrillas seeking revenge for the US role in the Jordanian civil war. In 1974 NEA's Deputy Secretary, Rodger Davies and his assistant, were murdered in Cyprus, in revenge for what they suspected as American collusion in a coup. In 1976 US Ambassador to Lebanon Francis Meloy, his aide Robert Waring and their driver were murdered in Beirut on their way to meet with the president-elect of Lebanon.

Over the rest of Kissinger's tenure the US position did not improve. Seelye remained, under the watchful eye of 13 bodyguards. Hunt, his chargé, left to coordinate Kissinger's Sinai disengagement in Italy and was murdered while on duty.

Their successors in Beirut, Richard Parker and George Lane, completed Meloy's original mission in November 1976. Lane had extraordinary security to cross the Green Line, and recalled: "I had the best private army in Lebanon [...] I always traveled in a bulletproof car—an armored car with a lead car, and a follow car with four or five bodyguards in each car, carefully recruited from the elite of Lebanese security forces—one Druze, one Greek Orthodox, one Sunni, one Shia, all the religions were represented." His success in navigating across the city prompted an article in the *New York Times*.[155] It was a sad coda for the Middle East hands who only a decade earlier had lived, learned and prospered in Beirut.

It is the ultimate irony that after three decades of training the Department of State finally succeeded in establishing a corps of professional area experts just as President Nixon and Secretary of State Kissinger arrived. They made the White House the center of Middle East diplomacy and the Middle East hands irrelevant. Through bureaucratic reorganization Kissinger limited the State Department's role in the policy and used back channels to convey a contrary message to other governments. Secret diplomacy had replaced quiet diplomacy.

Kissinger addressed the American Foreign Service Association (AFSA), the Foreign Service officer's professional group, when they made him an honorary member at the end of his tenure: "I know the honor that has been bestowed on me by being given lifetime membership in an organization that its members believe I could never have joined except by Presidential appointment." He continued: "Thus it is appropriate that my last official public engagement should be a ceremony honoring those who have disagreed with me. And let me say, for the record now, that I forgive them. Not even the Foreign Service can be right 100 percent of the time."[156] From the start Kissinger believed the State Department would not support him, but he overlooked the fact that the careerists were loyal to the institution rather than to the man. They supported presidential policy even as it cost them their lives. Kissinger's manipulation of backchannel diplomacy isolated the Middle East experts and led to complications abroad. The Metternichean approach was unsuited to twentieth-century American foreign affairs.

The Middle East hands adhered to a set of values centered on the determination to resolve the Arab–Israeli conflict and to protect American national interests in the Middle East. They made the risky journey up the career ladder only to find a false summit, where few were willing to heed their advice and where they exerted little impact on policy.

EPILOGUE: BEIRUT AXIOMS; LESSONS LEARNED BY THE MIDDLE EAST HANDS

Area specialists trained in the Middle East Area Program (MEAP) became the core staff in the State Department's division of Near East and South Asian Affairs (NEA). Through language skill, academic training and hard work they built genuine area expertise. They based their policy recommendations upon what they had studied in their university training and the MEAP, the information they gathered using their language skills and their experience working as political reporting officers in posts across the region. Their worldview was shaped not just by education but also by their direct experience of tumultuous events and violence toward American diplomats and institutions in the region.

The Middle East hands were committed to promoting America's national interests and supporting US policy, but they did not have a homogenous point of view. They saw themselves as diplomatic professionals, with no commitment to any faction in the region or either side in the Arab–Israeli conflict. As political reporting officers they developed a discreet set of fundamental values rather than a dogmatic set of beliefs. Unlike the persistent Arabist stereotype, or the Orientalist reality, they were not apprenticed into a rigid policy system by senior officers.

From the foundation of their training, each Foreign Service officer (FSO) built their expertise without a rigid list of policy absolutes handed down from above. As regionalists, they recognized the Arab–Israeli conflict as the core problem facing US policy in the Middle East and one that endangered vital American interests. They saw the Soviets as opportunists and communism as a political philosophy that held little appeal for Arabs and Muslims. This clashed with the prevalent Cold War focus in Washington. Although Soviet subversion was a concern, it did not overrule everything else in their analysis.

The lessons learned by the Middle East hands can be summarized in six "Beirut Axioms."

1. A comprehensive peace, based upon defined borders and resolution of the refugee problem, should be negotiated between Arabs and Israelis. The refugee problem, if left unresolved, portended violence for the peoples of the region and difficulties for American interests there.
2. The United States should not be too closely allied with or identified as siding with any faction or regime, whether Arab or Israeli.
3. The Soviets were not the primary regional threat and could only win by default.

4. The United States should work with Arab moderates to undercut radicalism.
5. Arms transfers to all parties should be limited, and the United States should work to halt nuclear proliferation and promote Nuclear Non-Proliferation Treaty protocols.
6. Dispassionate analysis and a realistic determination of American national interests should be the guide to formulating and implementing Middle East foreign policy.

Conversely, globalists approached policy from a rigid formula of post–World War II policy absolutes based upon the Cold War conflict between the Soviet and American systems. From this perspective the Middle East was the arena for US–Soviet competition. They dismissed the Middle East hands' analysis as too complicated and failed to consider the regional factors that shaped events. Cold War globalists saw Israel as a Western ally threatened by Soviet-allied Arab states. This discounted Arab concerns over Israeli power and intransigence on relinquishing the occupied territories. In this period the globalist view led to widespread reversals of US policy: Egyptian and Syrian reliance on Soviet arms, major wars that cost thousands of lives (the Six Day War, War of Attrition and October War) and increasing complications in the disengagement process on a number of Arab-Israeli borders.

First Beirut Axiom

The foremost objective of the Middle East hands was a comprehensive settlement of the Arab–Israeli conflict. That must be based upon negotiation with all parties to the conflict, defined borders, and a resolution of the refugee problem, either by limited repatriation or compensation. They believed not only in Israel's right to exist and need for security but also that it was necessary for all parties, including Palestinians, to negotiate a solution. To that end they supported a number of initiatives, such as the Eric Johnston Plan, the Joseph Johnson Plan, the Rogers Peace Plan, and urged the United States to encourage an Israeli dialogue with Egypt and later Syria.

This was stalled when Henry Kissinger purposely created what he called a "bureaucratic stalemate" by which, he said, "We could block all diplomatic activity" and the result would be "an inconclusive course" that "only produced stagnation." Thus, he hoped to end Arab reliance on the Soviets and produce Arab concessions. In 1994 Kissinger summarized that approach to achieving peace as part of a larger globalist strategy against the Soviets: "It was not a starry-eyed quest for cooperation for its own sake but a method for conducting the geopolitical competition." Israeli scholars Boaz Vanetik and Zaki Shalom have drawn a connection between the stalemate policy and the onset of the October War.[1]

Middle East hands argued that prolonged stalemate would lead to renewed regional conflict and loss of life. They did not see the Cold War as the primary regional threat and reasoned that a comprehensive solution would materially improve the US position. Moreover, it would be in the best security interests of America's ally, Israel, to remove the rationale for any Arab group or state to launch a war.

What kind of peace did the Middle East hands envision? Ambassador James Akins summarized what he called "a just peace in the Middle East," which would resolve the longstanding problems of borders, the Palestinian refugees and Jerusalem. Akins described the way to a successful agreement: "If there is to be a final settlement [...] it will come as a result of American pressure on Israel to withdraw to its 1967 borders" This proposal included the reciprocity Israel had always wanted: "commercial and cultural exchanges" as well as the establishment of "diplomatic relations and security guarantees for all."[2]

Kissinger recalled that once in office in February 1969 he informed the head of the State Department's Near East division, "We did *not* want a quick success" in the Four Power peace negotiations at the United Nations. He admitted having "stonewalled" State Department's "various schemes for a comprehensive solution" between 1969 and 1971. At the start of Nixon's second term, Kissinger continued this approach: "I sought to delay any new State Department initiatives." Indeed, Kissinger's Middle East policy was not "a starry-eyed quest for cooperation." And it revealed his focus on the globalist perspective.[3]

Malcolm Kerr summarized the disappointment when these peace initiatives failed, noting they "start up amidst optimism but have eventually led to renewed frustration for the would-be promoters of peace." He also cited Israeli reluctance to negotiate or withdraw from the occupied territories. Kerr found this policy was based upon the Israeli *Galili Document*, which promulgated a policy of *ein breira*, or "no alternative," a determination to hold onto land and build settlements rather than negotiate. Kerr argued that "annexation with a good conscience" meant Israel was determined to live in a state of "permanent conflict with the Arabs." He reasoned that this policy grew out of "Israel's obsession with security, its preoccupation with territorial possession and military advantage by *faits accomplis*, its distrust of outside intermediaries and reluctance to take initiatives."[4]

Middle East hands continually supported American peace initiatives. William R. Crawford worked closely with both sides during the Eric Johnston and the Joseph Johnson peace initiatives. He had long argued, in the face of Israel and the resistance of the American Israel Public Affairs Committee (AIPAC), that efforts to negotiate a solution to the conflict would make Israel more secure rather than less secure. The Joseph Johnson Plan was designed to implement a blend of limited repatriation of Palestinian refugees from the 1948 war and to compensate and resettle others outside Israel. This would dissolve the United Nations refugee camps and reduce the potential for anti-Israeli violence. Despite his efforts the Joseph Johnson plan collapsed after he determined Israeli resistance to even such a limited effort.

The American effort assumed a comprehensive peace that would include all regional players in negotiations. This meant not only those states bordering Israel but required American negotiators to open channels to the Palestinian Liberation Organization (PLO). This effort was complicated in 1975 after the Sinai II Accords when Secretary of State Kissinger signed the "Palestinian Memoranda" with the Israeli government.[5] It was a side letter, or memorandum of understanding, between the United States and Israel that stated the United States would cease all contact until the PLO accepted UN Resolution 242 and recognized Israel. Due to its unique nature, this memorandum was never subject to Senate approval. Subsequently, American policy makers took what might be termed a strict constructionist interpretation of Kissinger's side letter and curtailed all PLO contacts.

Since the PLO was the only accepted representative, by agreement of the Arab states, the side letter eliminated any Palestinian representation in the negotiations and therefore kept discussion of refugee issues and the West Bank off the table for nearly two decades. Over the years many Middle East hands went on the record (in each case upon or after retiring from the State Department) in disagreement with this policy: Talcott Seelye in 1981; Michael Sterner in 1983 and in a 1985 *New York Times* editorial; Hermann Eilts's article "It's Time to Talk to the PLO," in 1985.[6] Seelye made the point succinctly upon his retirement in 1981: "To really find a solution to peace in the region we must start having relations with the PLO—a dialogue." His reasoning was based upon the following rationale: "It would strengthen moderates in the PLO and demonstrate to our Arab allies, such as Saudi Arabia, that we are serious." Seelye questioned whether Kissinger's pledge was binding, noting "that commitment is not a treaty and not a legal document." Seelye argued the lines of communication should be kept open: "We should be dealing with the PLO. Talking to them. Overtly, openly." When asked how such a dialogue should be opened, he answered, "You just have to pick up the phone."[7]

Over the decades American presidents took a strict constructionist view of the text. This complicated relations for diplomats abroad since PLO representatives were members of the diplomatic corps in many Middle East states. In 1979 President Carter forced the resignation of US UN representative Andrew Young for having informal contacts with the PLO. The Middle East hands went on the record in support of opening the dialogue many times, and subsequent events have shown their judgment to have been correct.

In December 1988 Arafat issued the required statement and Secretary of State George Shultz opened informal contacts, but the Israeli government objected and did not reciprocate. Upon his retirement as assistant secretary of State for NEA in 1989, Richard W. Murphy publicly urged the Israeli government to "pursue informal talks." He made the suggestion after a long series of efforts to bring both sides together, but despite his determination and the support of Secretary Shultz, those initiatives failed. Murphy observed changes in the Arab view of Israel, but felt these shifts in attitude were not reciprocated. He concluded that there had been: "A gradual, incremental change in Arab attitudes [...] not generally accepted by many people in this city."[8] Despite some movement by Arabs toward compromise with Israel, there was no consequent softening of Washington's pessimism.

Ironically, the diplomatic freeze was finally broken when Israel breached the stalemate in 1993, by initiating secret contacts with Arafat and the PLO in Oslo. This was not a result of American diplomacy. As a result, Israel and the PLO signed the 1993 Declaration of Principles. The Middle East hands were committed to using diplomacy as the route to a comprehensive peace settlement. Kissinger believed that a stalemate was viewed with skepticism. When Israel came to the same conclusion, they dealt with Arafat.

Middle East hands repeatedly argued that Washington should recognize the power of other parties to prevent a peace deal. They acknowledged the Syrian role in Lebanon and its relationship to the Israeli presence in its "security zone" since 1978. Hafez al-Assad's Syrian Ba'ath party had been ignored by Kissinger even after he reopened diplomatic relations in 1974. Middle East hand Richard Murphy was frustrated to find that the reopening of US relations did not lead to a similar opening on the Syrian–Israeli track. Murphy recommended the United States mediate disengagement in the Golan Heights using the model of the 1981 Multinational Force and Observers organized by Michael E. Sterner for the Sinai disengagement. Two decades later Yitzhak Rabin defended the idea that American involvement in a peacekeeping force could work in the Golan Heights, and the US Army colonel in charge of the Sinai operation agreed. Military disengagement was a key part of any comprehensive settlement. Middle East hand Michael Sterner organized the observer force through negotiations with both Egypt and Israel and used troops from Fiji, Columbia, the United States and other nations to successfully demilitarize the Sinai. Later both Prime Ministers Rabin and Shimon Peres stated it could be a model for any Israeli–Syrian disengagement in the Golan Heights.[9]

Murphy's suggestion to include Assad did not come from any great admiration for the Syrian leader but on the pragmatic political calculus that Assad could torpedo any deal that the United States brokered without him. And later he did.

Second Beirut Axiom

The Middle East hands argued that the United States should avoid becoming overly identified with any faction, whether Arab or Israeli. This meant support for unpopular Middle East regimes, for example, the Shah of Iran and the Maronite Christian minority in Lebanon, should be moderated as well as the Israeli "special relationship." They viewed the region dispassionately and argued that aggressive support of any faction, especially the use of CIA covert operations or the Sixth Fleet, could destabilize the entire region, as happened in Beirut. Historian Hugh Wilford has explored the negative impact of the CIA's "secret Arabists" who were "drawn from the Anglo-American elite" during the Truman and Eisenhower years.[10]

Middle East hand William Crawford pointed out that the United States should not be "tipped to one side or the other."[11] Raymond Hare, a founding father of the group, pointed out that America must recognize that there were limits upon our capability to control events. Since the 1950s American diplomats have found that the CIA's actions in Lebanon, Syria and Iran, as well as Kissinger's "back channel" or "dual track" diplomacy and Reagan-era activities in Iran–Contra, made conventional diplomatic contacts irrelevant.

While the Middle East hands acknowledged that the United States should support Israel's legitimate security concerns, they felt threat perception should be realistically evaluated. Often it appeared that the threat as perceived by an ally was unrealistic: as with Camille Chamoun's 1958 election crisis in Lebanon that led President Eisenhower to send in the Marine Corps.

Israel's border problems in the 1950s led to the Kibya and Gaza raids and played a central role in the 1967 Six Day War and the invasions of Lebanon in 1978 and 1982. In each case border issues were used as the pretext for military operations, overwhelming force was brought to bear and the result was war and more complex problems to disentangle. In the case of the Sinai and Golan Heights, prolonged Arab frustrations with unanswered peace feelers led to a joint Syrian and Egyptian attack in 1973 on the occupied territories held by Israel.

Decades earlier Kissinger wrote of European peace settlements in the Napoleonic era, arguing that "absolute security for one power means absolute insecurity for all others."[12] His comments are an almost prescient analysis of the Middle East situation he helped shape as Secretary of State. Up through 1973 Israel maintained all the territories occupied in 1967 and acquired new arms supplies from the United States to hold a significant military advantage over its neighbors, which helped to develop a sense of impregnable security and no need to negotiate. Yet Israeli forces in the Sinai and Golan Heights were attacked when the stalemate forced both Sadat and Assad to conclude they had nothing to lose. American promises to give Israel a qualitative edge in weaponry and not push for negotiations was supposed to create absolute security for Israel but instead made for the absolute insecurity of her neighbors, which led to renewed war. Middle East hands argued that undefined borders and large-scale arms transfers heightened the potential for conflict.

When Israeli Prime Minister Ehud Barak explained why he opened negotiations with Assad, he quoted Rabbi Yosef of the Shas party: "There were once those who said that Sharm el-Sheikh without peace was preferable [...] then we had 3,000 graves [a reference to the 1973 war] and the picture changed."[13]

The Middle East hands accepted that the security of Israel as fundamental to American policy, but what Israel did vis-à-vis its neighbors became a major complication for that policy in Egypt, Jordan, Lebanon and later Iraq. Meanwhile the policy recommendations of Middle East hands were often criticized as evidence of pro-Arab sympathies, ranging from hints of "localitis" to even anti-Semitism. Middle East hands knew that to understand Israel you must understand the tragic history of the Holocaust. They had joined the State Department at a time when support for Israeli security was already policy. Sterner recalled it was the earlier Orientalist generation who could not accept Israel: "The people who did go through [the bureaucratic battles over Israel] had a kind of scar, maybe a psychic scar [...] that was very hard to heal."[14] Most Middle East hands joined the State Department after the Orientalists, who took pride in fighting what they called "the battle of Palestine," retired.

American policy has always been presidential policy. Talcott Seelye pointed to the fact that the Middle East hands accepted the American commitment to Israel and its security: "Never, to my knowledge, did any of my colleagues ever question the basic US commitment to Israel's survivability." Donald Bergus recalled their focus was on the entire region, not just the Arab world: "I was proud of my knowledge of the countries in the area, including Israel." Bergus also pointed out that their goal was to be dispassionate: "Neither my American colleagues nor the Israelis with whom I worked saw me as 'tainted' by pro-Arab sentiments. To the contrary, I was sometimes accused of having a 'clinical' mind unlikely to be swayed by sentimental appeals of either side."[15]

There were limits to what became known as the American "special relationship" with Israel. In the 1980s Israeli strategic analysts pushed hard for an even more overt military alliance. They pointed out that prepositioning US arms in Israel and regular American military access to Israeli ports and air bases could be an advantage in the Cold War. This idea had wide support among the National Security Council (NSC) staffers in the Reagan and Bush administrations but far less support among Pentagon officials. Middle East hands strongly opposed it, fearing it might trigger even more anti-American reaction than the rumors of such an alliance in 1967. Sterner cited the centrality of the globalist view: "If you have that optic, then Israel naturally falls into place as an ally, being anti-Soviet, pro-democracy, etc."[16] Only the end of the Cold War could undercut that rationale.

During the Israeli invasion of Lebanon in 1982–84, the US goal was to get both Syrian and Israeli troops out of the civil war then raging in Lebanon. Secretary of State George Shultz went ahead without Syria in the negotiations and, while Assad was absent, set as the first condition a full Syrian withdrawal, followed by an Israeli withdrawal.

Middle East hand Robert Paganelli pointed out that Assad's cooperation was highly unlikely since the bargain had been struck without the presence of any Syrian representatives. Secretary Shultz refused to accept his advice and was determined to inform Assad of the withdrawal timetable, expecting his acquiescence. Shultz called Paganelli's advice "a virtual attack on everything that the US did in the Middle East." Middle East hand Richard Parker observed that Paganelli presented his case clearly and forcefully, with the support of all present except US ambassador to Israel Sam Lewis. Historian Patrick Seale later argued: "Paganelli knew the Syrian mind but Shultz gave him no credence." Journalist Robert Kaplan described Paganelli telling Secretary Shultz "The agreement is going to fall apart in your face."[17]

Shultz ignored Paganelli and notified Assad. The Americans watched as the agreement collapsed in a single day. Assad balked at being told to withdraw, and then Israel refused to budge. In the end there was a hard lesson: had Shultz followed Paganelli's advice the Americans might have averted some violence in Lebanon. Within months anti-US violence, including car bombings and kidnappings, took more than two hundred and fifty American lives. Paganelli's criticism was an attempt to rescue the initiative, but was made at the risk of his own career.

Third Beirut Axiom

The Soviet Union and communist subversion were not seen by Middle East hands as the primary regional problems. Communism was anathema to Arabs and in particular to Muslims. Communist movements had been persecuted by Nasser in Egypt and by other leaders in Syria and elsewhere. The only communist state in the region was South Yemen (formerly Aden), and the Marxist regime there was a symbol of Soviet ineptitude rather than a shining example of communist efficiency.

President Eisenhower wrote during the Suez Crisis: "The Soviets are the real enemy and all else must be viewed against the background of that truth."[18] Globalists ignored the power of Arab nationalism that impelled resistance to imperialism and superpower politics. Middle East hands felt the Soviets could only win if the United States allowed them to fish in troubled waters, as Laurence Pope noted: "The Soviet Union […] waits to pick up the pieces."[19]

In 1949 the first official appointed at the start of the Cold War to run NEA was George McGhee, an oilman and non-Arabist. He argued Truman's anti-Soviet policy was the reason why "a Soviet threat has not materialized" in the Middle East. Middle East hands had little faith in the Baghdad Pact, a regional anti-Soviet group organized by Secretary of State John Foster Dulles. Although Middle East hand Hermann Eilts was sent to the negotiations, most of his colleagues were deeply pessimistic. The pact attempted to secure the region against the Soviets but instead undercut domestic support for the leaders who joined. The agreement was rendered obsolete by anti-British and anti-Western revolts in July 1958. The Baghdad Pact collapsed along with the Iraq regime in 1958, and in a matter of hours, Washington nearly lost allies King Hussein in Jordan and Chamoun in Lebanon as well.

Middle East hands realized that the effectiveness of the Israeli military power was deeply feared in the Arab world, especially after the Suez War. Even NEA chief George McGhee was forced to later admit: "Perhaps [...] it was hopeless from the start for either the US or Britain to get the Arabs to see greater danger from Russia than from Israel."[20]

In those few lines McGhee touched upon the key difference between how Washington and the Middle East hands viewed the Soviet role in the region. Washington stressed the primacy of the threat of Soviet subversion. Middle East hands saw the Soviet threat as remote, but recognized the more immediate Arab fear of Israeli militarism. No amount of rhetoric made a Soviet invasion appear imminent in a region where border conflicts and four major Arab–Israeli wars had been fought.

Moreover, the Middle East hands did not see events moving at the instigation of a grand Soviet plot but rather were responses to political instability. To Middle East hands neither Moscow nor Washington was entirely in control of events or of their allies.

Michael Sterner, a Middle East hand with extensive experience in Yemeni and Egyptian affairs, observed that US policy needed to consider how to deal with Nasser and Arab nationalism. Egypt's Gamal Abdel Nasser had broad appeal across the Arab world and as leader of the nonaligned movement throughout the developing world. Nasser's influence even resonated, as Sterner recalled, "in a far off place like Aden." Sterner was less concerned about the potentially dangerous aspects of Nasser's brand of Arab nationalism, viewing it first as "something wholesome, a new phase of welcome self-determination in the world, providing they didn't start consorting with Moscow. That was a big proviso." Later arms deals and Arab reliance on Soviet military aid or economic barter deals became problematic: "We lacked confidence that these people had the ability to make deals with Moscow and not become the creatures of the Soviet Union."[21]

Middle East hands realized that if Washington was not more forthcoming then Arabs had only Moscow to resort to in the Cold War: Nasser bartered Egyptian cotton for Soviet wheat, bought arms in the Czech arms deal and got loans and expertise for the Aswan Dam project. When Egypt came under Israeli air attack during the War of Attrition, the Soviets quickly shipped planes, surface-to-air missile (SAM) air defense systems and military advisers. As desk officer for Egyptian Affairs, Sterner observed, "Ninety per cent of the Soviet presence in Egypt derives from Russia's role of providing military support to Egypt in its conflict with Israel."[22]

Otherwise, communism held little appeal. For decades the tiny Communist Party had been mainly organized among refugees living in Cairo. Once in power Nasser clamped down on them even while signing "friendship treaties" with Moscow. As his ambassador to the United States Salah Bassiouny pointed out: "Egypt's policy was anticommunist [...] [the Communists] were arrested." Nasser's action had an impact across the Arab world; as long as he suppressed Communism, then "all communist movements in the Arab world will be in a weak position."[23]

Middle East hands argued that Nasser was driven by anti-imperialism and his desire to lead the Arab nationalist movement with ambition for an even larger role in the non-aligned movement. Settling the Arab–Israeli conflict and US aid would greatly undercut any Soviet influence in Cairo. The Cold Warrior perspective viewed Nasser as an unreliable ally who would not toe the American anticommunist line and might deal with Moscow.

A similar stalemate was played out on the Syrian front. Richard Murphy, first a political reporting officer and later ambassador to Syria, was continually frustrated by the presence of "[t]he generous Soviet Union. The arms supplier at low prices." In a 1995 interview Murphy summarized what the Syrians wanted in 1974: "They were looking, as they are still looking, for [...] mutually respected relations, and normal relations, between themselves and the US."[24]

Arab nationalists did not want to be clients of either side. Murphy noted Damascus wanted "to play off one bloc against another and maintain your independence as a country." There was no sympathy for communism. Murphy noted that the Ba'ath had been "quick to persecute the local Communist parties." Syrians "saw themselves as not in one camp or another, just better understood by the Soviets."[25] In the Cold War Syria and Egypt alienated Washington by dealing with Moscow, which was anathema inside the Beltway.

What initiatives were proposed by the Middle East hands to undercut Soviet influence? In December 1958 Raymond Hare designed a program of food aid to reduce Egypt's dependence on Soviet wheat. Hare believed that a shipping surplus of American wheat to Egypt in exchange for minimal payments, which were then expended by the United States in Egypt as foreign aid, had a double effect in boosting the US image and Egypt's sense of independence. Middle East hand Rodger Davies concluded that food aid and working with Nasser could obtain Cold War objectives: "The best defense against Soviet influence is the health of Arab nationalism."[26]

There always was a disjunction between Washington's fears and the Middle East hands' perception of the Communist threat. Richard Parker compared Russian efforts to penetrate the region in the era of Catherine the Great and their Cold War methods: "Then, as now, the Russians exploited local discontents [and] military assistance was the primary instrument of penetration." Parker observed that Washington overemphasized the Cold War: "I think we overrated the Soviet menace."[27]

The prime example of what Communist could do for (or to) an Arab nation was in South Yemen. After the British withdrew from Aden the nation became independent and Marxist. After two decades of communist experimentation the regime collapsed. Later North and South Yemen merged, but the nation remained a vivid contrast to its richer neighbors on the Arabian Peninsula. Michael Sterner commented after a postunification visit to Yemen that Aden should be preserved "as a museum of Socialist incompetence."[28]

Fourth Beirut Axiom

Middle East hands argued that if the United States worked with Arab moderates this would prevent the rise of more radical elements. Although Arab nationalism had the potential to bring progress, it might also lead to instability. But change was inevitable, as President Kennedy pointed out in 1962: "Those who make peaceful revolution impossible will make violent revolution inevitable."[29]

From the Middle East hands' perspective, it was far better to accommodate Arab nationalism rather than to openly oppose Nasser and thus alienate his vast following across the Arab-speaking world and the developing world.

Middle East hand Andrew I. Killgore cabled a caution to Washington from Jerusalem in 1959: "Palestinians believe that US policy has been designed to bring about Nasser's downfall. As Nasser, in their minds, almost *is* Arab Nationalism, we are generally believed to oppose Arab Nationalism itself." Worse yet, Killgore's observation led to Arabs linking the Americans with the British: "The US therefore represents the hated 'imperialism.'" He projected his observations into the future, arguing that Nasserism could stem the advance of Communism: "If the rump of Palestine can be regarded as a kind of microcosm of the Arab world, our fight to keep Communism out of the Arab Middle East would be vastly strengthened by judicious support of Nasser."[30] Washington should not take policy positions that likened them to the British and French, both objects of hatred since their involvement with Israel in the 1956 Suez War against Egypt.

Richard Parker recalled that over time Nasser created problems elsewhere that undermined US support: "Our problems with Nasser all dealt with third countries. The Yemen, Israel, Jordan." While stationed in Jordan, Parker felt the Soviets were "not major players," but the Arab nationalists inside the Egyptian embassy were "engaged in a struggle for the soul of Jordan."[31]

The old diplomatic adage, where you stand depends upon where you sit, also applied to their varied views of Nasser over time.

Stationed in Aleppo in 1963 (then part of the UAR), Richard Murphy saw Nasser more negatively, as "a pretty imperious leader" who "was not a perfect thing for the Arab world or for American interests." Moreover, Nasser's mistakes in triggering an Israel attack in June 1967 reflected what Murphy termed "[t]he clumsiness of Egyptian diplomacy" and led to a fateful conflict, the Six Day War, "which maybe he hadn't ever intended."[32]

Many Middle East hands suffered the consequences when the Six Day War began in 1967. Murphy was left to literally hold the fort after most of the staff was evacuated: "[S]itting in the blacked-out embassy listening to Radio Cairo, as he [Nasser] announced that the Americans were involved [...] the Great Lie of June '67." Nasser's accusation that the American military had aided Israel led to a frightening backlash across the Middle East. Murphy recalled: "The burning of our consulate in Alexandria, the rough stuff that went on across North Africa, the mob scenes—which took their cue directly from Cairo—I think that pretty well confirmed my doubts about his leadership."[33]

Middle East hands were trapped inside embassies under Israeli air attack and besieged on the ground by anti-American mobs. These experiences left indelible impressions and were vivid indicators of the intense hatred that any hint of an American–Israeli alliance triggered. In the Mediterranean Sea off the Egyptian coast Israeli aircraft and torpedo boats attacked the US Navy's intelligence-gathering ship, the USS *Liberty*, leaving 34 American sailors dead and 171 wounded.[34]

In Syria the CIA had operated under diplomatic cover and been involved in a series of coups against the Ba'ath party that had only worsened the political situation. After repeatedly eliminating Syrian moderates, whom the CIA viewed as dangerous radicals, the agency left the field open to even more extreme elements. One splinter group overthrew another until Hafez al-Assad came to power in 1971.[35] Middle East hand Talcott Seelye found Syrian memories of the Eisenhower years still vivid when he was stationed in Damascus two decades later. He paid an official call on the Ba'ath Party chief and spent an icy half hour under the cold gaze of an officer who obviously knew well the CIA's role in Syria. Seelye recalled, "He showed exactly what he felt about me as the American representative."[36]

American support for the Shah of Iran in the 1970s seemed boundless, as President Nixon approved the shipment of millions in arms while the United States bought oil during the embargo and Carter toasted the Pahlavi regime. Total US arms sales to Iran since 1950 reached more than $11 billion. This ran against the advice of regional specialists. Nixon appointed former CIA director Richard Helms as US ambassador as a blunt message to those who feared the Shah's SAVAK security force. After the Iranian revolution of 1979 the Khomeini regime allowed the students to take over the US embassy that resulted in the 444-day hostage crisis and an incredible loss of American intelligence when the embassy files were captured.[37] Overt support for the Shah proved costly as Iran began exported fundamentalism. The anti-Western message resonated among Shi'ites working in gulf nations like Kuwait, Bahrain and Saudi Arabia.

Fifth Beirut Axiom

The United States should limit arms sales to all sides. Arms proliferation escalated conflicts, military aid consumed humanitarian aid dollars and balance of payments problems with oil-producing states could be dealt with by other means. In 1950 Raymond Hare negotiated the Tripartite Agreement, an effort to stem all arms sales to the Middle East by the United States, England and France. The deal was destroyed by the 1956 Suez War. Since then the United States has sold or transferred billions in arms and has assisted the establishment of a joint military research program with Israel to develop advanced missile systems, weapons systems and military aircraft.

Not only conventional weapons but also chemical and nuclear weapons have proliferated. Nuclear proliferation became a growing concern when a secret Israeli nuclear program, built with French help at Dimona, became public. This set off a cascade of proliferation as Iraq, Iran and Libya tried to rival the Israel program. In more recent decades the George H. W. Bush administration launched the Gulf War, and subsequently Washington has struggled to eliminate nuclear and chemical programs that were spurred by the presence of such weapons in the region.

When the Israeli government began construction of a nuclear reactor at Dimona, US intelligence informed President Eisenhower. Ike later advised John F. Kennedy, who refused to press Israel to halt the program. Later when the United States joined the Nuclear Non-Proliferation Treaty, it did not press Israel for its signature on the treaty, although Sterner and other Middle East hands suggested that the United States could have bargained for military assistance in exchange for an agreement to allow International Atomic Energy Agency inspections at Dimona.[38]

Instead, as word leaked out about the facility, and the Egyptians began their own small program; the threat of proliferation escalated as secret nuclear research programs began in Iraq, Iran and Libya. After the collapse of the Soviet Union, it is believed that Iran and Iraq sought engineers and materials from the remnants of the Soviet nuclear program. The advent of proliferation in the region also led to a preemptive Israeli attack on the Iraqi nuclear reactor at Osirak on June 7, 1981, which temporarily derailed Saddam Hussein's nuclear effort, but immensely complicated the George W. Bush administration's efforts to eliminate Iraq's weapons of mass destruction, as Saddam Hussein sought, literally, to bury the program deeper. During the first Gulf War American pilots took great risks to complete the destruction of Iraq's nuclear and chemical weapons. In the end it took the American military's occupation of Iraq to complete the search for weapons of mass destruction.

Sixth Beirut Axiom

Finally, the Middle East hands believed themselves to be professionals who were committed to protecting America's vital national interests. But what Michael Sterner called their "dispassionate view of American interests" was not always shared by Washington. Middle East hands thought they were protecting American interests yet their views, according to Sterner, "did not necessarily coincide with what presidents of either political party [...] decided was of national interest in this area." Lobbying by AIPAC, a highly effective organization with a multimillion dollar budget, also was a factor in Middle East foreign policy. Just as the China lobby shaped policy in the McCarthy era, AIPAC became a force that effectively shaped US Middle East policy in Congress and the White House.[39]

Middle East hands pushed comprehensive peace initiatives and limits on American arms transfers. Conversely, Israel's reluctance to relinquish occupied territory, its military involvement in Lebanon and elsewhere alienated neighboring states. This had serious ramifications for America in the Cold War. Richard Parker heard from his rivals, Soviet diplomats, about the consequences of US support for Israel: "The Soviets kept laughing at us and saying you're backing the wrong horse—and Israel is a millstone around your neck and so forth. And, that seemed pretty valid to some of us at some point."[40]

Elsewhere the Middle East hands still found their political reporting ran against Washington's Cold War worldview. After Edward Peck was sent to Iraq in 1977, he found

"There was no pro-Iraqi voice in the US government [...] nobody gave us any flack for it [criticism of Saddam]." Peck attempted to disabuse Washington of the conventional wisdom that Saddam Hussein could be a useful ally against Iran, and described Saddam as "[a] village thug who wore Pierre Cardin suits and had lovely bridgework and a nice mustache and all that." Peck then contrasted the Iraqi image with the PLO reality: "Arafat looks like a thug and really isn't and Saddam doesn't look it, but really is." Peck witnessed Hussein's brutal takeover in 1978, when Saddam "machine-gunned twenty-five of his closest associates" then "ruled Iraq with what can only be described as an iron hand [...] you step out of line and you are gone."[41]

Peck received a list of policy objectives and instructions from Washington headed by the order to "persuade the Iraqi government to abandon its hostility to Israel." He concluded, "I thought [that item] was a worthwhile objective, but somewhat unrealistic under the circumstances."[42] Peck realized that no amount of cabled reports would reshape the conventional wisdom.

Upon his return to Washington, Peck attempted to refuse the job of director of Egyptian Affairs because he anticipated difficulties with President Ronald Reagan's NSC staff. He understood the power of Cold War rhetoric on Middle East policy and that there would be even less of an audience for his perspective. Hoping to use his diverse language skills as his ticket out of Washington, Peck recalled how he pleaded with Deputy Assistant Secretary Morris Draper for a post elsewhere: "Morrie, what about Scandinavia? You are talking to the State Department's foremost Swedish and Arabic speaker. How many Swedish and Arabic speakers do you have?" Draper drily responded, "We don't really need very many," and assigned Peck to the Egyptian Affairs desk. Peck foresaw problems with Robert McFarlane, earlier Kissinger's military adviser on the NSC staff, then later President Reagan's special Middle East envoy and NSC adviser. At the start of the Iran–Iraq war, McFarlane bluntly informed Peck that Iraq's "best hope for salvation lies in lining up, arms linked, with Syria and Israel to stand against this hostile challenge." Peck told McFarlane that Iraq did not have good relations with either Syria or Israel but found that McFarlane was "literally unable to understand or accept the fact that the leaders of Iraq for one, and of Israel and Syria, for the other two, didn't see it that way at all."[43]

McFarlane later replaced State Department negotiator Philip Habib and in July 1983 undertook a mission for Reagan to Lebanon. Historian Theodore Draper detailed how McFarlane, as a special White House envoy, in September 1983 ordered US naval warships to open fire on military positions above Beirut in support of the Lebanese Armed Forces (LAF). The US Marines who were training the LAF were no longer viewed as neutral peacekeepers. Shortly afterward a massive truck bomb exploded under the US Marine Battalion Landing Team Headquarters in Beirut with 241 marines killed as the building collapsed.[44]

By the Reagan era Middle East hands, although regional experts with decades of experience in the region, were trumped in the policy making process by NSC staffers with no background in Middle East affairs, but whose strong ideological bent led them to ignore advice from area experts, which contradicted their conventional wisdom.

Washington's Conventional Wisdom

In 1973 Morton Halperin, an NSC staffer and aide to Henry Kissinger, codified Washington's Cold War axioms in what he called the "Shared Images" of national security interests in the Nixon White House. This summary provides a template for the Washington worldview and stands in stark contrast to the Beirut Axioms. In Washington the Cold War was foremost:

1. The preeminent feature of international politics is the conflict between communism and the Free World.
2. Every nation that falls to communism increases the power of the Soviet bloc.
3. The surest simple guide to US interests […] is opposition to communism.
4. Russian intentions […] are essentially expansionist [as are] Chinese intentions.
5. The main source of unrest, disorder, subversion and civil war in underdeveloped areas is communist influence and support.
6. The United States […] has the power, ability, responsibility and right to defend the Free World.
7. The United States has an obligation to aid any free people resisting communism.
8. Peace is indivisible. Therefore collective defense is necessary.
9. Concessions made under pressure constitute appeasement.
10. The Third World really matters […] it is the battleground.[45]

These axioms defined the Cold War conventional wisdom that repeatedly trumped the Middle East hands' worldview and the lessons they learned. During the Cold War, anti-communism became a holy writ that could not be challenged. Michael Sterner concluded that the US–Israel special relationship readily fit into this approach. Those who advocated working with Arabs to prevent their reliance on Moscow were ignored by those who emphasized an aggressive approach to fight the Soviets on the Cold War chessboard in the Middle East.

Halperin's Cold War axioms fit with his role in the Nixon White House as the person who designed the NSC takeover of the State Department's policy role. In 1970 policy analyst Graham Allison contrasted Washington's perspective with the "Axioms of Young Americans," which he argued opposed the Cold War view and intervention in Third World.[46]

Allison based his work on a 1969 *Time-Louis Harris* poll that found that only 9 percent of Americans favored US defense of Israel if it were attacked by the Arabs. He pointed out that the case of Israel particularly illustrated the contrast between the older generation of Cold Warriors and Young America. His conclusions align with the Middle East hands' opposition to an overtly Cold War analysis while Halperin deftly summarized Washington's conventional wisdom.

In the Eisenhower years Secretary John Foster Dulles continually favored regional anticommunist alliances, like the Baghdad Pact, driven by Cold War containment. The Eisenhower Doctrine decreed that the United States was prepared to halt communist aggression, but instead Ike was forced to use the CIA and later the US Marines to prop up the pro-American Camille Chamoun regime in Lebanon. Then Iraq and Jordan were all rattled by a political earthquake in July 1958. By the end of Ike's presidency Iraq had fallen, Syria was radicalized, Jordan's king nearly overthrown and Egypt further alienated from the United States.

In the Kennedy era the global view was put on hold for a rapprochement with Egypt, a program of food aid and economic development as well as the Joseph Johnson initiative of quiet diplomacy as Raymond Hare and Parker Hart had advocated. Joseph Johnson made a number of attempts to push his peace plan forward, but it failed. With the advent of Lyndon Baines Johnson to the presidency, the Israeli–American relationship warmed, and LBJ viewed Nasser as Moscow's ally. The Israeli success in attacking and defeating three Arab armies in the Six Day War redrew the map. As hawkish adviser Walter W. Rostow summarized for Lyndon Johnson, this was a powerful example of Israeli military skill: "Herewith the account, with a map, of the first day's turkey shoot." In a press conference a few months later, Undersecretary of State Eugene Rostow, argued Soviet influence in the Middle East had been "a fundamental fact of life" since 1955. In dramatic terms he concluded it was a Soviet "strategy for enveloping Europe and separating Europe from the United States, thus destroying NATO and altering the world balance of power against us." In 1976 Rostow testified before Congress against the sale of C-130 transports to Egypt's Anwar Sadat, arguing the United States had been "clinging to the myth of détente" and that the Carter administration had "systematically concealed the degree of Soviet involvement" in the region. Rather than abating, the Soviet threat in the Middle East "has increased in recent years," and he concluded, "The republic will be in peril" unless America understood the gravity of Soviet aims in the Middle East.[47]

In the Nixon–Ford era Henry Kissinger managed Middle East policy, and the stalemate he created led to conflict over the Sinai in the War of Attrition and the 1973 October War. Meanwhile the festering refugee problem ignited a civil war in Jordan and helped a civil war in Lebanon. By the end of Kissinger's tenure Lebanon was still embroiled in fighting and the "step-by-step" peace process had run its course. Nixon's massive arms shipments and CIA links to the Shah ultimately led to the loss of Iran and the hostage crisis that destroyed the Carter presidency.

Throughout these decades the Middle East hands argued their advice was a dispassionate analysis of America's best interests. Michael Sterner argued that Cold War chessboard was a faulty framework for analysis, and asked rhetorically: "[L]ook at things like Muammar Qaddafi throwing us out of Wheelus Air Force Base. What did he have to do with the Soviets? Yet, we lost a major Air Force training base, and the orientation of the country changed." He cited Iran as another example: "What about the Iranian revolution? We lost supposedly an enormous strategic asset—did that have anything to do with the Soviet Union? Of course not." Sterner concluded Washington's preoccupation with containing communism only created a Soviet opportunity: "The Soviets piled in later and tried to take advantage [...] But they were never, in my opinion, prime actors."[48]

Middle East hands saw the region's problems as exacerbated by the continuation of the Arab–Israeli conflict, but Washington viewed the problems as generated by the Cold War. Both agreed it was a strategically valuable area that had the potential to damage vital US interests. Middle East hands hoped Washington would follow the caution given by its first president to "avoid entangling alliances" and protect American interests in the Middle East.

Violence and the American Diplomats in the Middle East

In summing up three decades as a Middle East hand, Hermann Eilts reminisced about his role as an adviser to President Carter in the Israeli and Egyptian negotiations at Camp David and concluded, "It was worth a lifetime of experience." But he also lamented the fact that many of his fellow Middle East hands who had invested their careers in Arabic had paid a high price. They spent years in remote hardship posts, suffered violence and had little role in policy making: "If that is so, then you could just as well, and more comfortably, be in Paris."[49]

At the start that had been Eilts's own goal. He began his diplomatic career with an eye toward what he called the "European circuit." His combination of graduate school language training, fluency in German and US military service gave him a topnotch resume that promised a successful career with the State Department in European Affairs. But by chance, the one grant available to support his graduate studies required he learn Arabic to complete a project on Middle East issues. Although he initially refused, he later relented and became an Arabist by default. With Arabic training on his resume the State Department channeled him straight into a career in the Middle East. Eilts was first shipped to Tehran, then to the consulate general in Jerusalem.

Eilts arrived at ground zero in the Arab–Israeli conflict in May 1948 only days before the murder of the US Consul General Thomas Wasson. A chain of assassinations killed three other members of the consulate. Eilts knew the Middle East was a dangerous place, and, although he tried to reroute his career to European Affairs, the record of his Arabic training kept him in Middle East posts. He later became one of the youngest ambassadors in the Foreign Service, in large part because Arabic specialization was the path to advancement, but he remained ambivalent about being labeled as an Arabist.

Eilts was a key adviser to President Jimmy Carter in the most critical negotiations the United States mediated on the Arab–Israeli conflict between Israel's Menachim Begin and Egypt's Anwar Sadat. The drafting of the text of the framework for the Camp David Accords was completed in less than a fortnight in September 1978. Although Eilts was at the very center of a tremendously important peace initiative, he found his advice, based on a lifetime of area studies and diplomatic practice, had been ignored.

As a senior adviser to President Carter, Hermann Eilts, along with ambassador to Israel Samuel Lewis and William Quandt of the NSC, advised Carter. Although he was then a senior officer and former ambassador to Saudi Arabia, Eilts felt he was not heeded when he advised Carter on how to bring the two delegations together. He also felt the language of the Framework was: "[...] done in a hell of a big hurry, with the Israelis making all kinds of parenthetical and other insertions." The exchange of letters between Carter, Begin and Sadat reflects their differing interpretations of fundamental issues. After the negotiations the CIA intelligence officers who briefed Carter wrote a memoir of their experiences whose narrative proved that Orientalism was not dead within the CIA. Dr Jerrold Post, in a 1979 article for the CIA's in-house journal *Studies in Intelligence*, explained why their analysis of the negotiations focused on the personalities of Sadat and Begin. Post explained the CIA approach was based upon: "The strategic importance of the Middle East, *the relative imperviousness of the Near Eastern mind to Western perceptions*, and the highly personalized leadership styles of its rulers [...]" [emphasis in quotation mine]. This led the CIA, according to Post, to focus "a disproportionate share" of their intelligence efforts on analyzing the personalities of the leaders.[50] While the State Department focused on the political realities facing the president at Camp David, it was the CIA that approached the negotiations from a psychological perspective rooted in Orientalist perceptions of "the Near Eastern mind."[51]

Eilts watched as Carter pressured Sadat to make more concessions that he did not feel the Saudi Arabian government would support, particularly on the Palestinian issue. Carter had continually assured Sadat the Saudis would support the deal. Eilts remained deeply concerned when he found out there was to be no protracted settlement freeze in the occupied territories. He finally asked Carter how sure he was of Saudi support: "I said 'Mr. President I don't see all the traffic from Saudi Arabia, and you may have something from [Ambassador to Saudi Arabia] John West that I don't know about. Let me tell you Mr. President the Saudis aren't going to accept this. I know the Saudis, I know them better than most Americans. They are not going to accept this.'" Carter responded to Eilts, "Don't worry about the Saudis, I'll take care of them." But the Saudis did not "come along" despite Carter's efforts and a personal diplomatic mission by Secretary of State Cyrus Vance. The next day Begin sent Carter a letter that diverged from what Carter saw as the agreement and a flurry of letters between all the leaders continued. The Israeli interpretation was for a limited three-month halt to settlement activity in the occupied territories. Eilts summarized the result: "Camp David was a success but a very modest one. It turned out to be even more modest that we anticipated." Furthermore, "It also created ten years of turmoil in the area and if we had spent a little more time on it, we might have been better off."[52]

Arabic training brought great career rewards but their ability to shape policy, even through quiet diplomacy, was very limited. Eilts faced more of the violence other Middle East hands had encountered: in 1976 he narrowly escaped an assassination plot staged by Libya's Muammar Qadaffi.

His experience illustrates three common points in the career of almost every Middle East hand: first, anyone with significant linguistic talent was channeled into Arabic specialization and kept there by the State Department. Their experience of hostility and violence in the region left them with a realistic view of Arabs and Israelis, and they were not Orientalist romantics enamored of the Arabs. Second, those who became area specialists were evaluated and rated on the level of measurable skill they possessed rather than on any prior connections to the region or social status. The State Department needed people with significant language skill in Middle East posts and promoted them much more quickly than in any other regional bureau. Finally, those who did reach the ambassadorships and top post as assistant secretary of state for Near East Affairs found themselves with little influence on the formulation of policy. The price of advancement was a long string of hardship posts in an increasingly dangerous region where Middle East hands and their embassies were all too often the targets of terrorism and violence.

The top regional post in Washington, assistant secretary for Near East Affairs, was rarely filled by a Middle East hand. By the 1970s it was clear that reaching what Richard Parker once euphemistically called "the exalted ranks of the Foreign Service" was nearly impossible.

The erosion of the American position was in large part due to the perception that America was no longer an even Cold War handed arbiter. The Middle East hands were not naive or blind to the dangers but accepted the risks as their duty. Dr. Malcolm Kerr, one of their professors at the Beirut school, warned in his 1972 address to the Middle East Studies Association that America was increasingly seen by many in the region as a threatening presence. Kerr argued that while Americans had been "only casually affected" by the Arab-Israeli conflict and the Cold War, "the impact on the peoples of the Near East has been traumatic." He vividly illustrated the mix of positive and negatives that American policy had led to in the Middle East: "Have not all these quiet people brought their gifts and their illusions [...] sound finances and improved irrigation and the Suez assault in Egypt, the unification of Jerusalem and the demolition of Arab homes in Palestine and the USIS Libraries and PL-480 and Phantom aircraft."[53]

Despite America's good intentions, Kerr warned that the people of the Middle East might "gather together the means to react to their trauma in such a way as to cause us damage." He closed with a paraphrase of Arnold Toynbee's critique of the West: "This being the picture, should not we turn our head and move out of the light before our victims 'stagger to their feet and stab us in the back?'"[54]

Terrorism took the lives of a number of the Beirut school veterans. A year after Kerr's speech, Middle East hands Cleo Noel and George Moore were murdered in the Sudan; in 1974 NEA's deputy secretary, Rodger Davies, was murdered inside the US embassy in Cyprus. After the 1967 Six Day War very few new applicants volunteered for Arabic training in an area that had become a war zone. In 1975 the Beirut school was forced to close because it was too dangerous for Americans to travel in the city. In a report on the state of Arabic training a group of Middle East hands likened the region to the American West, concluding, "[T]he frontier has closed." They meant the era of career opportunity had ended, but in another way the pioneers found themselves alone in a dangerous area, which they had once freely roamed. Unlike the American West, over time instead of becoming safer, the pioneers of the Middle East area specialization remained trapped in an increasingly hostile environment.

In June 1976 the most high-ranking Middle East hands, all ambassadors, were summoned to Paris by Secretary of State Henry Kissinger. They met in the security tank of the embassy after the French police had whisked the Americans from the airport to the embassy.

This was an urgent meeting to deal with a diplomatic tragedy. The US ambassador to Lebanon, Francis Meloy and his aide FSO Robert Waring, as well as the embassy's chauffeur, had been captured while attempting to cross Beirut and murdered.

This was also the end of an era. The Beirut school had closed a year earlier as the war in Lebanon and inside Beirut escalated. In recent years a half dozen American diplomats were dead, and there was doubt the United States could even deliver a new ambassador into the embattled Beirut embassy. Kissinger and the Middle East hands discussed how to get Talcott Seelye into the embassy as special envoy to Lebanon. Seelye was shocked to find he had been selected for the hazardous assignment and faced the prospect with trepidation.[55]

Before Kissinger could even get the meeting underway Hermann Eilts recalled that he took the floor and asked the Secretary of State, when was the United States going to recognize the PLO? The United States was committed to not meeting with Palestinian representatives since a memorandum of understanding had been signed by Kissinger in September 1975. In this critical situation the Middle East hands present recognized the vital importance of PLO cooperation in getting Seelye safely into Beirut amid the fighting and the extent of his ability to move about the city. Seelye recalled that he restated his need for PLO contacts to secure his survival in Beirut, which Kissinger had earlier refused. Ambassadors Eilts, Seelye, Richard Murphy, Thomas Pickering and William Porter debated how to deal with the crisis.

The embassy was reopened with Special Envoy Talcott Seelye and his new chargé Leamon Ray Hunt, flown into Beirut wearing flak jackets, where they supervised the evacuation of American citizens by a naval task force. Kissinger had been exceedingly reluctant to change American policy, which denied contact with the PLO even to allow Seelye's request for indirect contacts to ensure his personal safety. Seelye made his own contacts once in Beirut.[56]

In the official transcript, the memorandum of conversation, Kissinger tells the group "I picked Meloy. As I said at the arrival ceremony for his body, I wanted him there. So he was my responsibility." They debated Talcott Seelye's potential to move about the city. Kissinger stated "Look, Talcott, your safety is overriding. But basically I want you to be less active than Brown [Meloy's predecessor] and more active than Meloy. I'm the one who cabled him to be more active. So I'm responsible." Later in the conversation, he stated, "Talking with the Palestinians won't end all our problems." He went on to discuss how that might impact the region: "I'm not so eager for Talcott to talk to them. It could be someone else." Seelye suggested having an American political officer with a radio working on the other side of the city for security reasons, although the person he had selected had backed away from the job, and concluded, "My life comes first." Kissinger responded, "We won't lose another Ambassador."[57]

Two years earlier a similar dilemma had faced William Crawford after Rodger Davies's murder in Cyprus. At that time Kissinger had also refused to allow any contact with the opposition under the Makarios regime. Crawford felt it was necessary to secure his own survival as he moved in to replace Davies in the embattled embassy.[58]

Following the Paris meeting the situation in Beirut did not improve. Seelye remained under the watchful eye of 13 bodyguards and finally left after a series of ominous events: a mortar shell landed in the embassy garden nearly killing his Marine guard, a 50-caliber round was fired into his bedroom, and he was forced to move into a secure area inside the embassy rather than the ambassadorial residence. Ray Hunt, Seelye's chargé, soon left for a post in Rome to coordinate the Sinai disengagement. Their successors, Richard Parker as ambassador and George Lane as chargé, became the new staff in Beirut.[59]

Lane managed to complete Meloy's original mission, crossing the Beirut Green Line with a team of eight bodyguards in November of 1976.[60] Ambassador Richard Parker left Beirut after little more than a year when the embassy discovered Meloy's murderers were gunning for him as well. Lane eventually left for an ambassadorship in North Yemen, having dodged sniper fire and narrowly missed yet another round shot through an embassy window.

Even Kissinger did not entirely escape the threats emanating from the region. In 1976 rumors circulated of a $150,000 contract put out on him by ultra-right-wing Israelis, which led President Ford to request a special extension of Secret Service protection for Kissinger's retirement.[61]

The others present at the Paris meeting had their own narrow escapes: Eilts was evacuated from Cairo after a Libyan assassination plot was uncovered. Murphy was shipped into Beirut in 1983, under tight security much like Seelye, to direct the investigation of yet another bombing of the embassy which killed 64 diplomatic staff.

A few years later Malcolm Kerr, who had warned them all of the risks of a backlash against American policy, was summoned from his teaching post at UCLA to become president of the American University of Beirut after president David Dodge was taken hostage. It was a request Kerr did not feel he could refuse, as the son of two American educators at the American University of Beirut (AUB). He was also a former AUB professor of history who had trained diplomats in the MEAP. But the AUB campus, the ultimate symbol of the benevolent side of the American presence, was literally surrounded by the armies of Syria, Israel, and various Lebanese warring factions.

In 1984 Kerr was shot in the back of the head by unknown assailants while walking into his office on the AUB campus. His murder was especially shocking since the AUB had always symbolized the most idealistic of American initiatives in the Middle East.

Leamon R. Hunt, working on the Sinai disengagement, died only a month after Kerr. He was murdered by Red Brigade terrorists in Italy while on duty as director of the Multi-National Force of Observers. He was coordinating peace observers for Kissinger's Sinai II Agreement between Egypt and Israel.

Richard Murphy gave his eulogy and vowed to renew the State Department's commitment to achieving peace: "Ray Hunt lost his life at the hands of terrorist assassins, as have too many others who have toiled for peace in the Middle East. His murder was as senseless as his life was meaningful. His death […] is a sad reminder of the long road ahead before a general peace and a broad reconciliation can prevail in that region […] [his] sacrifice in the cause of peace is one more reason to renew our faith and determination that this can and must be done."[62]

Years later, when eulogizing three more diplomats who had died on yet another peace mission, President Clinton summarized the Foreign Service's approach to its job and described the State Department's diplomats as "extraordinary Americans who made reason their weapon, freedom their cause, and peace their goal."[63]

The Middle East hands were the successors of the Orientalists and brought professionalism to American embassies in the Middle East. They tried to bring objectivity to the task of representing America in the region, protecting American interests and carrying out Washington's foreign policy. Although many were successful in their careers, this professional success came at enormous personal cost. While they accepted the risks, they hoped to promote what Hare and Hart termed quiet diplomacy, which would protect American interests and best the Soviets in the Cold War. They supported American initiatives like the Joseph Johnson Plan and the Rogers Peace Plan in the hopes they might achieve a comprehensive settlement of the Arab–Israeli conflict. They sought to avoid overt alliances with any Middle East leader or faction and to avoid anti-American violence. Instead, the erosion of the American position in the region, led to attacks on American consulates and embassies, as well as many Middle East hands, who endured the violence directed at American policy in the Middle East.

APPENDIX: BRIEF BIOGRAPHIES

James E. Akins, born in Ohio, 1926. Educated Akron University 1947, University Strasbourg, France, history 1951. US Navy 1945–46, relief worker, teacher Lebanon 1951–52. State Department 1953. Posts include: Damascus 1956–57, Beirut FSI school 1957, Kuwait, Baghdad, director Office of Fuels–Energy 1969, White House 1972–73, ambassador to Saudi Arabia 1973.

Arthur B. Allen, born West Virginia, 1920. Harvard 1941, USG physicist 1941–44, US Navy 1944–45. State 1947: Beirut, Algiers, Beirut FSI 1951, Johns Hopkins University. Posts Baghdad, Tripoli, Tunis, Washington Tunisian desk officer, NEA African affairs, Aleppo, Dhahran.

G. Norman Anderson, born Delaware, 1932. Columbia University 1954, MIA 1960, US Navy 1954–58, State 1960, Beirut FSI 1962, Russian language training 1966. Posts Moscow, ambassador to Sudan 1986.

Donald Bergus, born Indiana, 1920. University of Chicago 1942, State Department 1942, Baghdad, Athens, Beirut FSI 1946. Posts Jidda, University of Pennsylvania Arabic training 1949, Beirut, Washington Israeli–Jordanian affairs, NATO as Near East advisor 1959, Cairo, country director UAR 1966, US Interest Section Cairo 1967, academic affairs FSI 1973, ambassador to Sudan 1977.

Pierce K. Bullen, born Massachusetts, 1934. University of Florida 1955, master's 1958. State 1958, FSI Beirut 1959, Dhahran, Cairo, Voice of America Arabic.

Thomas J. Carolan, born Washington, DC, 1934. Georgetown University 1956, US Army 1957. State 1959, Beirut FSI 1962. Posts Dhahran, Beirut.

John R. Countryman, born New York, 1933. Fordham 1954, University of Miami master's 1961, State Department 1962, and Beirut FSI, 1966. Posts Dhahran, Tripoli, ambassador to Oman 1981.

William Rex Crawford, Jr., born Pennsylvania, 1928. Harvard 1948. US Navy 1948–49. University of Pennsylvania master's 1950, State Department 1951 Posts Jidda, Venice, Arabic 1955 and Beirut FSI 1956, Aden, Taiz, Washington Lebanon–Israeli affairs, Arab–Israeli affairs, Rabat, ambassador to YAR 1972, ambassador to Cyprus 1974.

Rodger Paul Davies, born California, 1921. University of California 1942, Hispanic languages. US Army Arabic linguist 1942–46. State 1946, Jidda, FSI Arabic 1948. Posts Damascus, Benghazi, Tripoli, Baghdad, deputy director NEA 1962, deputy assistant secretary NEA, acting assistant secretary, ambassador to Cyprus 1974. Assassinated Cyprus, 1974.

Francois M. Dickman, born Iowa, 1924. US Army 1943–46. University of Wyoming 1947, Fletcher School of Law & Diplomacy master's 1948, research Brookings Institution, State Department 1951, Arabic training FSI 1955, Beirut 1956. Posts Beirut, Khartoum, Washington UAR desk, Tunis, Jidda, Washington Gulf states affairs.

Lee F. Dinsmore, born Wisconsin, 1916. University of Wisconsin 1938, US Army 1945–46, private relief organization Gaza 1948–50. State 1952, Kirkuk, Baghdad, Kirkuk, international relations, assistant to assistant Secretary of State NEA1962, Iraq–Jordanian affairs 1965, Sanaa Chargé ad interim YAR 1967, Dhahran.

Edward P. Djerejian, born New York, 1939. Georgetown University 1960, US Army 1960–62. State 1962, Arabic 1964, FSI Beirut 1965. Beirut, Casablanca, ambassador to Syria 1988, NEA.

Morris Draper, born California, 1928. US Army 1946–47. University of Southern California 1952. State 1952: Baghdad, Beirut FSI 1959, Jidda, Washington international relations, Amman, special envoy.

William L. Eagleton, Jr., born Illinois, 1926. US Navy 1944–46. Yale 1948. State Department 1949, Damascus, Beirut FSI 1953, Baghdad, Washington international relations, Persian–Kurdish language training 1959, Tabriz, Chargé ad interim South Yemen 1967, USINT Algeria 1969, USINT Iraq 1980, ambassador to Syria 1984.

Hermann F. Eilts, born Germany, 1922. Ursinus College 1943, US Army 1942–45, SAIS master's 1947. State Department 1947, Tehran, Jidda, FSI Arabic 1950, University of Pennsylvania 1950. Posts Aden, Jidda & Sanaa, Baghdad, Washington, Baghdad pact–SEATO affairs, Arab Peninsular affairs, Tripoli, ambassador to Saudi Arabia 1965, USINT Cairo 1973, ambassador to Egypt 1974.

Fred Galanto, born Massachusetts, 1927. US Army 1944–46. Clark University 1949. UN Secretariat 1949. Institute d'Etudes Politiques, Paris 1951. State Department 1953 Beirut FSI 1959. Posts Basra, Washington, Algiers, Rome NATO, Luxembourg, Washington.

April Glaspie, born Canada, 1942. Mills College 1963, SAIS master's 1965. State Department 1966, Amman, Kuwait, Washington, Beirut FSI 1972, Amman, ambassador to Iraq, 1987, 1988.

Philip J. Griffin, born Washington, DC, 1932. Georgetown University 1954. US Army 1955–57. State Department 1957, Beirut FSI Arabic 1962. Posts Jerusalem, Dhahran, Washington, Dhahran, Chargé ad interim UAE 1972, Chargé ad interim Kuwait 1983.

Mark G. Hambley, born Idaho, 1948. American University 1969, Columbia University master's 1971. State Department 1971, FSI Arabic 1972, Beirut FSI 1973. Posts Sanaa, ambassador to Qatar 1989.

Hume A. Horan, born Washington, DC, 1934. Educated Harvard 1958, Harvard master's 1963. US Army 1954–56. State 1960, Baghdad, Beirut FSI 1963, country officer Libya, Amman, Jidda, ambassador to Sudan 1983, ambassador to Saudi Arabia 1987, ambassador to Ivory Coast 1992.

APPENDIX

Robert B. Houghton, born Massachusetts, 1921. Harvard 1942, State Department 1945, Jerusalem, FSI 1949, Damascus, London, Beirut FSI 1954, Jidda, Washington, Amman, country director Lebanon & Jordan, Beirut.

W. Nathaniel Howell, born Virginia, 1939. University of Virginia 1961, PhD 1965. State Department 1965, Beirut FSI 1970. Posts Abu Dhabi, Beirut, ambassador to Kuwait 1987.

Curtis F. Jones, born Maine, 1921. Bowdoin College 1942, US Army 1942–45, George Washington University master's 1968. State Department 1946, Beirut, Addis Ababa, FSI 1949, University of Pennsylvania Arabic 1949, Tripoli, Port Said, Damascus, officer UAR affairs, Aden, Beirut, NEA.

Andrew I. Killgore, born Alabama, 1919. Livingstone State College 1943, US Navy 1943–46, University of Alabama LLB 1949, State Department 1950, Frankfort, London, FSI 1955 and Beirut FSI 1956, Jerusalem, Amman, Washington international relations, Iraq–Jordan affairs, Baghdad, Tehran, Manama, Wellington, ambassador to Qatar 1977.

George M. Lane, born Maryland, 1928. Cornell 1951 French literature, Fletcher School of Law & Diplomacy master's 1957. State Department 1957, Washington international relations, Beirut FSI 1960. Posts Jidda, Aleppo, Rabat, Benghazi, Washington deputy director North African affairs, Beirut, ambassador to YAR (North Yemen) 1978.

Arthur Lowrie, born Pennsylvania, 1930. US Air Force 1951–54. Allegheny College 1955. State Department 1956, Beirut FSI 1961. Posts Khartoum, Tunis, Washington, USINT Iraq, 1972.

David L. Mack, born Oregon, 1940. Harvard 1962, master's 1964. State Department 1964, Baghdad, Aman, Jerusalem, Beirut FSI 1968. Posts Tripoli, Benghazi, Washington international relations, UNINT Iraq 1977, ambassador to UAE 1986.

Dayton S. Mak, born South Dakota, 1917. University Arizona 1939, US Army 1941–45, George Washington University master's 1964. State Department 1946, Arabic FSI 1948, Posts Dhahran, Jidda, Tripoli, London, Washington, Chargé Kuwait 1961, Beirut, research NEA.

Charles E. Marthinsen, born New Jersey, 1931. Gannon College 1953, US Army 1953–55. State Department 1953, Dacca, Beirut FSI 1960, Posts Jidda, Damascus, Cairo, Washington, Tripoli, ambassador to Qatar 1980.

James A. May, born California, 1921. US Army 1943–46. University California 1946. State Department 1947, Haifa, Rabat, Tunis, FSI 1954, Baghdad, Washington, Beirut FSI 1960. Posts Dhahran, Kuwait, Baida, Tripoli.

George C. Moore, born Ohio, 1925. US Army 1944–46. University of Southern California 1949, master's 1951. State Department 1950, Frankfort, Cairo, FSI 1956, Beirut FSI 1956. Posts Benghazi, Tripoli, Washington Arab Peninsula desk officer, acting country director, USINT Sudan 1969, Chargé ad interim Sudan 1972. Assassinated in Khartoum, 1973.

Richard W. Murphy, born Massachusetts, 1929. Harvard 1951, Cambridge University BA 1953. US Army 1953–55. State 1955, Beirut FSI 1959. Posts Aleppo, Jidda, Amman, Washington country director Arab Peninsula, ambassador to Syria 1974, ambassador to Saudi Arabia 1981, assistant Secretary of State for Near Eastern and South Asian Affairs 1983–89. Career ambassador 1985.

David G. Newton, born Massachusetts, 1935. Harvard 1957. State Department 1961, Zurich, Beirut FSI 1964, Sanaa, Washington, Near East studies University of Michigan 1969, Jidda, Sanaa, USINT Iraq 1984, Chargé ad interim 1984, ambassador to Iraq 1985.

Cleo A. Noel, Jr, born Oklahoma, 1918. University of Missouri 1939, Harvard master's 1940. US Navy 1941–45. State Department 1949 Dhahran, Marseille, Arabic FSI 1956, Beirut FSI 1956. Posts Khartoum, Washington officer in charge of Sudan affairs, USINT Sudan 1967, ambassador to Sudan 1972. Assassinated in Khartoum, 1973.

Robert P. Paganelli, born New York, 1931. US Air Force 1951–54. Hamilton College 1957, State Department 1958, Washington, FSI 1959, Beirut FSI 1960, Basra, Baghdad, Beirut, Damascus, Amman, Rome, ambassador to Qatar 1974, ambassador to Syria 1981.

Richard B. Parker, born in the Phillipines of American parents, 1923. US Army 1943–47. Kansas State 1947, master's 1948. State Department 1948, Jerusalem, Arabic FSI 1953, Beirut FSI 1953 and 1961. Posts Beirut, Amman, Washington international relations, Libyan desk officer, Beirut, Cairo, country director UAR, Rabat, Chargé ad interim Algeria 1974, ambassador to Algeria 1974, ambassador to Lebanon 1977, ambassador to Morocco 1978.

Edward L. Peck, born California, 1929. US Army 1946–49 and 1951–52. University of California 1956, George Washington University master's 1973. State Department 1957, Arabic Tangier 1962. Posts Tunis, Oran, Washington political affairs, Cairo.

Robert H. Pelletreau Jr, born New York, 1935. Yale 1957. US Navy 1957–58. Harvard LLB 1961. State 1962, Arabic Tangier 1962, Beirut, 1966. Posts Amman, Washington international relations, Algiers ambassador to Bahrain 1979, ambassador to Tunisia 1987.

James Placke, born Nebraska, 1935. University of Nebraska 1957, master's 1959. State Department 1958, Baghdad, Beirut FSI 1964. Posts Kuwait, Tripoli.

Laurence E. Pope, born New Haven, 1945. State Department 1969, Beirut FSI 1971, Rabat, Tripoli.

Christopher Ross, born Ecuador of American parents, 1943. Princeton 1965, SAIS 1967. State Department 1968, FSI 1968. Posts Rabat, Beirut, ambassador to Algeria 1988.

William A. Rugh, born New York, 1936. Oberlin College 1958, Johns Hopkins University master's 1961, Columbia University PhD 1967. State Department 1964, Beirut FSI 1964. Posts Jidda, ambassador to YAR 1984.

Thomas J. Scotes, born Maryland, 1932. University of Pennsylvania 1953. State Department 1955, Ishfahan, Tehran, Beirut FSI 1961. Posts Amman, Baghdad, Washington international relations, Tunis, Beirut, USINT Syria 1974, Chargé ad interim Syria 1974, ambassador to YAR 1974.

APPENDIX

Talcott W. Seelye, born in Lebanon of American parents 1922. US Army 1943–46. Amherst 1947. State Department 1949, Amman, Beirut FSI 1955. Posts Kuwait, Washington, Arab Peninsula affairs, Jidda DCM 1965, country director Lebanon, Jordan, ambassador to Tunisia 1972, ambassador to Syria 1978.

Edward Springer, born Oregon, 1931. University of Portland 1952, US Army 1952–54. State Department 1956, US UN, Beirut, Beirut FSI 1959, Cairo, Port Said, Tehran, Tripoli.

Michael E. Sterner, born New York, 1928. Harvard 1951. US Army 1954–56. State Department 1956, Aden, Sanaa, Beirut FSI 1958. Posts Cairo, Washington UAR desk officer, Arab–Israeli desk officer, director UAR, ambassador to UAE 1974.

William A. Stoltzfus, Jr, born in Lebanon of American parents, 1924. Princeton 1949. State Department 1949 Alexandria, Benghazi, FSI 1952, Beirut 1953. Posts Kuwait, Damascus, Jidda, Aden, Taiz, Washington, Jidda, ambassador to Kuwait, Bahrain & Qatar 1971, ambassador to Oman and UAE 1972.

Robert W. Stookey, born Iowa, 1917. University of Nebraska 1938, master's 1940. US Army 1941–46. State Department Arabic training 1946, Tangier, Ankara, FSI Beirut 1953. Posts Basra, Cairo, Jidda, Chargé YAR 1963.

Roscoe Suddarth, born Kentucky, 1935. Yale 1956, Oxford University master's 1958. State Department 1961, Beirut FSI 1963. Posts Taiz, Sanaa, Washington, ambassador to Jordan 1987.

Peter A. Sutherland, born New York, 1933. Harvard 1953. US Army 1953–56. Harvard LLB 1960, master's 1960. State Department 1961, Amman, Port Said, Jidda, Beirut FSI 1966. Posts Jerusalem, Washington, Tunis, ambassador to Bahrain 1980.

Harrison M. Symmes, born North Carolina, 1921. University of North Carolina 1942. US Army 1942–46. George Washington University master's 1948. State Department 1947, Alexandria, Damascus, FSI 1952. Posts Kuwait, Washington, Benghazi, Tripoli, deputy director NEA, country director Israel and Arab–Israel affairs, ambassador to Jordan 1967.

Terence A. Todman, born US Virgin Islands, 1926. US Army 1945–49, Polytech Institute 1951, Syracuse University master's 1952. State Department 1952, Beirut FSI 1960. Posts Tunis, Lome, ambassador to Chad 1969, assistant Secretary of State Inter–American Affairs 1977, Career ambassador 1989.

Winifred S. Weislogel, born Irvington, 1927. Union Junior College, Barnard College 1949, Otago University master's 1951. Fulbright Divison, Institute of International Education 1951–56. State Department 1956, Tripoli, Benghazi, FSI Tangier 1963, Rabat, Deputy Chief of Mission Lome.

Marshall W. Wiley, born Illinois, 1925. University of Chicago 1943. US Navy 1943–45, University Chicago JD 1948, MBA 1949. State 1958, Taiz, Beirut FSI 1961. Posts Amman, Washington, Cairo, director North African affairs, USINT Iraq 1975, ambassador to Oman 1978.

William D. Wolle, born Iowa, 1928. US Army 1946–47. Morningside College 1949, Columbia master's 1951. State 1951, Baghdad, Beirut FSI 1957. Posts Jidda, Washington, Arab–Israeli affairs, Kuwait, Amman, ambassador to Oman 1974, ambassador to UAE 1979.

David E. Zweifel, born Colorado, 1934. Oregon State 1957. US Navy 1957–62. State Department 1962, Portuguese language training 1962, Arabic Beirut FSI 1967. Posts Amman, ambassador to YAR 1981.

Note: The above career information is only partial. It was assembled from nonclassified sources including *Biographic Register of the Department of State*, between 1947 and its final edition 1974 (publication was suspended when it was suspected that terrorists had used the information to target FSOs.) Also, *Principal Officers of the Department of State and US Chiefs of Mission* and with the invaluable assistance of Ambassador George M. Lane.

NOTES

Introduction: America's Middle East Area Experts

1 Ambassador Richard W. Murphy, interview with the author, Washington, DC, June 9, 1993.
2 George Ball, "How to Save Israel In Spite of Herself," *Foreign Affairs*, April 1977, 453–71, quote 454.
3 Robert Kaplan wrote that Ambassador Richard B. Parker had decorated the study in his home with "ugly caricatures of Begin done by Arab artists." *The Arabists: The Romance of an American Elite*, first edition (New York: Free Press, 1993), 123. In fact the drawings were political cartoons of Richard Parker, not Menachim Begin. Letter to the author from Richard Parker, April 1994. When interviewing Parker I saw the images in his study, and they are of Parker.
4 Lewis was a research fellow at the Washington Institute for Near East Policy when he wrote the piece and later chief of "opposition research" compiling dossiers on Arabists for the American–Israeli Public Affairs Committee; see "Opposition Research at AIPAC," *Harpers*, October 1992; and "Mideast Institute's Experts and Ideas Ascendant," *Washington Post*, March 24, 1989. For quotation, see Michael Lewis, "Why Political Interference Is Good for the State Department," *Orbis*, spring 1988, 177–78 and 182.
5 Kaplan, *The Arabists*, 9.
6 Ambassador William R. Crawford, Jr., interview with the author, Washington, DC, June 10, 1993.
7 Quandt referred to Richard Murphy, *Views on Middle East Policy Formulation and Implementation and the State Department Role*, October 31, 1989, House 381-37.4, 49–80, quote 52–53.
8 The British *Oxford English Dictionary* (2nd ed., vol. 1, 1989) defines an Arabist as "[a] professed student of the language," while America's *Random House Dictionary* appends a second, uniquely American, variant: "A supporter of Arab interests" (2nd ed., 1987).
9 Bernard Lewis, "The Question of Orientalism," *New York Review of Books*, June 24, 1982.
10 William R. Lewis, *The British Empire in the Middle East 1945–51* (Oxford: Clarendon Press, 1984).
11 Said, *Orientalism*, 4 and 7
12 Said, *Orientalism*, 1978, 2–3, 7, 27; also *The Question of Palestine* (New York: Times Books, 1979), xiv.
13 Said, *Orientalism*, 322 and 324.
14 Sir Hamilton Gibb, *Area Studies Reconsidered* (London: School of Oriental and African Studies, 1963).
15 Said, *Orientalism*, 295. For a detailed discussion of Said and the taxonomy of the terms Orientalist, Near East and Middle East, see Osamah Khalil, "The Crossroads of the World: US and British Foreign Policy Doctrines and the Construct of the Middle East 1902–2007." On the development of Middle East studies in America, see Zachary Lockman, *Contending Visions of the Middle East: The History and Politics of Orientalism*. For a discussion of Said and the construction of the terms Near East and Middle East, see Osamah F. Khalil, "The Crossroads of the World: US and British Foreign Policy Doctrines and the Construct of the Middle East, 1902–2007," *Diplomatic History* 38, no. 2 (2014): 299–344. Also, chapter 6, "Said's *Orientalism*: A Book and Its Aftermath"; Zachary Lockman, *Contending Visions of the Middle East The History and Politics of Orientalism*, 2nd ed. (Cambridge University Press, New York, 2010); and Douglas Little, *American Orientalism: The United States and the Middle East since 1945* (Chapel Hill: University of North Carolina, 2002).

16 On Arabic language study in the ASTP, FSI and in academia, see R. Bayly Winder, "Four Decades of Middle Eastern Study," *The Middle East Journal* 41 (1987): 40–63; and Ernest N. McCarus, "The Study of Arabic in the US: A History of its Development," *Al-Arabiyya* 20 (1987): 13–27. On area studies, Richard D. Lambert et al., *Beyond Growth: The Next Stage in Language and Area Studies* (Washington: Association of American Universities, 1984).
17 On Orientalists of that era, see Philip Baram, *US State Department in the Middle East 1919–1945*, (Philadelphia: University of Pennsylvania Press, 1978).
18 Hare learned Arabic on his own after the State Department gave up on an experimental program in Paris where the French trained US Arabists during the 1930s. Hart learned his Arabic through tremendous personal effort, often at his own expense, at various regional posts.
19 Louis Menand, "The Trashing of Professionalism," *The New York Times Magazine*, March 5, 1995, 41–43.
20 Joseph Kraft, "Those Arabists in the State Department," *The New York Times Magazine*, November 7, 1971, 38–39, 82, 88–96; Robert Kaplan, "Tales From the Bazaar," *Atlantic Monthly*, August 1992, and *The Arabists: The Romance of an American Elite* (New York: Free Press, 1993); and Daniel Pipes, "Breaking All the Rules," *International Security* 9, no. 2](1984): 124–50; Amy Goott and Steven Rosen, *The Campaign to Discredit Israel*, AIPAC Papers on the US, 1983. A notable exception is John Solecki, "Arabists and the Myth," *Middle East Journal*, (1990): 446–57.
21 Donald C. Bergus, "Palestine: Focal Point of Tension," *Tensions in the Middle East*, Tenth Conference of the Middle East Institute, March 9–10, 1956, 33.
22 James Akins, "The Arabists" in "Arab Americans at the Crossroads," American-Arab Anti-Discrimination Committee conference, April 16, 1994, VHS.
23 Ambassador Michael Sterner, interview with the author, Washington, DC, June 10, 1993, and quoted by Kraft, "Those Arabists," 94.
24 Malcolm Kerr was dean of UCLA's Von Gruenbaum Middle East Studies Center and earlier a professor of area studies in the MEAP. *America's Middle East Policy: Kissinger, Carter and the Future* (Beirut: Institute for Palestine Studies, 1980), 10–11.
25 George Ball, *Diplomacy for a Crowded World* (Boston: Little, Brown, 1976), quote 121.
26 David Newsom, "The Terrorist Threat to Diplomacy," *Diplomacy and the American Democracy*, (Bloomington: Indiana University Press, 1988), 124–135. See also Lee Dinsmore, "Communication RE: The Near East to the Secretary," *Foreign Service Journal*, September 1973, 26, an open letter on the murders of Noel and Moore.
27 Richard B. Parker, "Middle East Studies and US Foreign Policy," in *The US and the Middle East*, ed. Hooshang Amirahamdi (Albany: State University of New York Press: 1992), 312.
28 Ambassador Hermann F. Eilts, "US Diplomacy in the Arab World Since Camp David," *The Challenge to US Interests in the Arab World*, address to the American-Arab Affairs Council at Milwaukee, Wisconsin, November 17–18, 1983.
29 See "Opposition Research at AIPAC," internal memo dated August 1990 by Michael Lewis, sent to Steven Rosen, AIPAC director of foreign policy issues, originally published in *The Village Voice*, then reprinted in *Harpers*, October 1992, 19–20.
30 AIPAC defines "anti-Israel" as the "[p]romotion of Arab interests becomes an anti-Israel activity when the main policies being advanced would reduce the security of Israel or weaken the bonds between the US and Israel." A. Goott and S. Rosen, *The Campaign to Discredit Israel*, AIPAC Papers on the United States (Washington, DC: American Israel Public Affairs Committee, 1983), 43.
31 David Ottaway, "Mideast Institute's Experts and Ideas Ascendant," *The Washington Post*, March 24, 1989; and Grace Halsell, "Clinton's Indyk Appointment One of Many from Pro-Israel Think Tank," *Washington Report on Middle East Affairs*, March 1993, 9–11. Indyk's change of citizenship from Australian to the United States was put through Congress before his ambassadorship began. On the development of AIPAC, see John J. Mearsheimer and Stephen M. Walt, *The Israel Lobby and US Foreign Policy* (New York: Farrar, Straus and Giroux, 2007).

32 Kraft, "Those Arabists."
33 Kraft, "Those Arabists."
34 James Akins, "This Time the Wolf is Here," *Foreign Affairs*, April 1973, and "Don't Blame the Oil Companies: Blame the State Department," *Forbes Magazine*, April 15, 1976.
35 The cover showed Ambassador Talcott Seelye striding past two turbaned Kevasses with raised swords, into what appears to be an Oriental palace. In fact Seelye was on his way to meet the president of Tunisia. Kaplan, *The Arabists: The Romance of an American Elite*, 1993.
36 Robert Kaplan, "Tales From the Bazaar," *Atlantic*, August 1992, and was the precursor of his book, *The Arabists*.
37 Neither Akins nor other Arabists accepted the Cold War argument made by AIPAC and Israel that it could serve as an anti-Soviet strategic asset. Ambassador James Akins, "The Arabists," American-Arab Anti-Discrimination Committee conference, April 16, 1994, VHS.
38 Teicher echoes the AIPAC position that Israel has strategic value as a site for "pre-positioning" personnel and equipment for rapid deployment in *Twin Pillars to Desert Storm: America's Flawed Vision in the Middle East from Nixon to Bush* (New York: William Morrow, 1993), 91–92, 96. See Steven J. Rosen, *The Strategic Value of Israel*, AIPAC Papers on US–Israel Relations, 1982. Rosen's paper dismissed the possible Arab or Islamic reaction briefly: "Arab publics already assume that the US is engaged in a strategic alliance with Israel." 12.
39 Teicher wrote, "These experts claimed to understand the Arab people and the Middle East because they had lived in Arab countries, and, therefore, knew 'firsthand' what the Arab world would tolerate," Teicher, *Twin Pillars to Desert Storm*, 92–93.
40 Rhodri Jeffreys-Jones, "The Socio-Educational Composition of the CIA Elite: A Statistical Note, *Journal of American Studies* 19 (1985): 421–24.
41 Teicher, *Twin Pillars to Desert Storm*, 93 and 256.
42 For Pelletreau's background, *The Biographic Register*, Department of State (Washington: US Government Printing Office, 1974), 267.
43 Winder, "Four Decades of Middle Eastern Study," 63; and Hume Horan, "A Plea For Arabists," *Foreign Service Journal* 50 (May 1973).
44 E. J. Kahn, *The China Hands: America's FSOs and What Befell Them* (New York: Viking Press, 1972), 7–8.
45 Richard Curtiss, *A Changing Image American Perceptions of the Arab-Israeli Dispute* (Washington: American Educational Trust, 1986), vii [emphasis in original].
46 Golda Meir, *My Life* (New York: Dell, 1975), 442.
47 Amin Maaloof, *The Crusades Through Arab Eyes* (New York, Shocken Books, 1984), 265. Maaloof observed the PLO named its fighting divisions after Arabs who defeated the Crusaders and "[t]he Arabs perceived the Suez expedition of 1956 as a Crusade by the French and the English, similar to that of 1191."
48 Hermann F. Eilts, "US Diplomacy in the Arab World since Camp David," *The Challenge to US Interests in the Arab World*, American-Arab Affairs Council conference, November 17–18, 1983.

1. The Orientalists Fade Away

1 Evan M. Wilson, "Decision on Palestine: The Setting and the Cast of Characters," *Foreign Service Journal* 56, no. 11 (1979): 13–17.
2 Thom Huebner, "Obituary Charles Albert Ferguson," *Language in Society* 28, no. 3 (1999): 431–37; "Review of Peter Abboud and Ernest McCarus, Elementary Modern Standard Arabic," *Modern Language Journal* 71, no. 4 (1987): 440–42.
3 Evan M. Wilson, *Decision on Palestine: How the U.S. Came to Recognize Israel* (Stanford, CA: Hoover Institution Press, 1979).
4 Evan Wilson, *A Calculated Risk: The U.S. Decision to Recognize Israel* (Covington, KY: Clerisy Press, 2008), 38.

5 Wilson, *Decision on Palestine*, 4–5.
6 John DeNovo, *American Interests in the Middle East 1900–1939* (Minneapolis: University of Minnesota Press, 1963), 208.
7 Philip Baram, *The Department of State in the Middle East* (Philadelphia: University of Pennsylvania Press, 1978), 86–88, 96.
8 Edward W. Said, *Orientalism* (New York: Vintage, 1979), 2–3; Janet Wallach, *Desert Queen: The Extraordinary of Life of Gertrude Bell* (New York: Nan A. Talese/Doubleday, 1996).
9 For the story of British Arabists, see Leslie McLoughlin, *In a Sea of Knowledge: British Arabists in the Twentieth Century* (London: Ithaca Press, 2002), on US rivalry 127–28 and Eban 116. For a collection of British Arabist memoirs, James Craig et al., *The Arabists of Shemlan, MECAS Memoirs 1944–1978*, volume I (London: MECAS Association, 2006).
10 Diane Sherlock, interview with John King Fairbank, *Harvard Magazine* (March–April 1979): 31–34.
11 Margaret Truman quoting a letter from Harry Truman, March 21, 1948, *Harry S. Truman* (New York: Morrow, 1973), 389.
12 William A. Eddy, *FDR Meets Ibn Saud*, Kohinur Series, number one (New York: American Friends of the Middle East, 1954); "King Ibn Saud: Our Faith and Your Iron," *Middle East Journal* 17, no. 3 (1963), 257–63. Baram, *The Department of State in the Middle East*, 76. On Eddy and the British Arabists, Loughlin, *In a Sea of Knowledge*, 123–24.
13 William A. Eddy, "How the Arabs See the West Today," *Address to the Middle East Institute* (lecture, Washington, December 19, 1950).
14 Eddy, "How the Arabs See the West Today," 2.
15 McLoughlin, *In a Sea of Knowledge*, 123.
16 For Truman-era diplomacy, which he terms as "presidential passivity," see Peter L. Hahn, *Caught in the Middle East US Policy toward the Arab-Israeli Conflict, 1945–1961* (Chapel Hill: University of North Carolina Press, 2004).
17 Eddy, *FDR Meets Ibn Saud*, 15.
18 Ibid., 34.
19 Loy Henderson, George Merriam and Secretary of State Byrnes's Memoranda on meeting in *Foreign Relations of the United States* [hereafter FRUS], Volume III (Washington: Government Printing Office, 1945).
20 Contrast "Conference of Chiefs of Mission in the Near East with President Truman, November 10, 1945," in *FRUS*, 11–18, with Eddy, *FDR Meets Ibn Saud*, 36–37.
21 For details on William Eddy and the CIA, see Hugh Wilford, *America's Great Game: The CIA's Secret Arabists and the Shaping of the Modern Middle East* (New York: Basic Books, 2013).
22 McGhee and Eddy correspondence, National Archives, State Department record group 59, 780.00/Box 4037.
23 Donald Davies quoted in E. J. Kahn, *The China Hands* (New York: Viking, 1975), 56.
24 William Yale Papers, Mugar Library Special Collections, Boston University, Boston, Massachusetts; also William Yale, *The Near East: A Modern History* (Ann Arbor: University of Michigan Press, 1958), 336–37. There are additional William Yale Papers in Houghton Library Archive, Harvard University, Cambridge, Massachusetts.
25 William Yale to his father, April 21, 1919, and May 21, 1919. His recommendations formed the "Yale Memorandum," separate from the King–Crane Report, in the William Yale Papers, Mugar Library Special Collections, Boston University, Boston, Massachusetts.
26 Baram, *The Department of State in the Middle East*, 84–86, 268.
27 Yale, *The Near East*, chapter 26 and quotation, 409.
28 William Yale Papers, Mugar Library Special Collections, Boston University, Boston, Massachusetts.
29 Edwin M. Wright, Harry Truman Presidential Library, oral history interview, 1974. For details on his CIA career, see Wilford, *America's Great Game*.

30 Edwin M. Wright, *The Great Zionist Coverup, A Study and Interpretation*, originally prepared for and by request of the Harry S. Truman Library, Independence, Missouri, 1975, v. This document was submitted to the Truman Library with Wright's oral history.
31 Loy Henderson was sent as ambassador to India and Nepal eight weeks after Truman recognized Israel. Wadsworth was sent to Turkey. "Memorandum of Conversation with His Royal Highness, Prince Faisal at Riyadh [Saudi, Arabia], August 24, 1956," 2, National Archives, Washington, RG 59, box 38, Projects Alpha, Mask and Omega, 1945–57.
32 Robert Schulzinger, *American Diplomacy in the Twentieth Century* (New York: Oxford University Press, 1984), 212.
33 Robert McClintock, "Suggestions for Improving the Foreign Service and Its Administration to Meet Its War and Post-War Responsibilities," *Foreign Service Journal* 22 (1945): 15 and 51–52.
34 William Lederer and E. Burdick, "A Factual Epilogue," *The Ugly American* (New York: Norton, 1958), 273; Dorothy McCardle, "Required Reading: State Dept Stays Up Late With Ugly American," *Washington Post*, January 11, 1959.
35 Ambassador William R. Crawford, interview with the author, Washington, June 10, 1993.
36 Ambassador Parker T. Hart ADST oral history interview, part two. in Frontline Diplomacy, The Foreign Affairs Oral History Collection of the Association for Diplomatic Studies and Training, Arlington, Virginia and Lauinger Library, Georgetown University, Washington, DC; also online www.adst.org [hereafter ADST interview].
37 Paul J. Hare, *Diplomatic Chronicles of the Middle East: A Biography of Raymond A. Hare*, (Washington, DC: Middle East Institute, 1993); and Raymond Hare, ADST oral history interview, Washington, DC.
38 Ambassador Parker T. Hart, ADST oral history interview, 37.
39 Ambassador Raymond Hare, interview with the author, Washington, DC, June 17, 1992.
40 Ambassador Parker T. Hart oral history interview, John F. Kennedy Library Oral History Program, recorded by Dennis J. O'Brien, April 15, 1969.
41 Ambassador Parker T. Hart, John F. Kennedy Presidential Library and Museum oral history interview, [hereafter JFKL] Boston, Massachusetts, June 10, 1970 [emphasis in original].
42 Ambassador Parker T. Hart, ADST oral history interview, first interview, January 27, 1989; and Ambassador Raymond Hare, interview with the author, Washington, DC, June 17, 1992.
43 Ambassador Parker T. Hart, ADST oral history interview, first interview, January 27, 1989.
44 "Shifting Diplomats," *Time Magazine* (July 30, 1956): 10.
45 Raymond Hare, "Capability and Foreign Policy," *US Department of State Bulletin* (July 1, 1957): 22–25.

2. The Middle East Hands Emerge

1 Louis E. Keefer, *Scholars in Foxholes: The Story of the Army Specialized Training Program in World War II* (Jefferson, NC: McFarland, 1988).
2 Curtis F. Jones, "The Army Specialized Training Program: Gateway to the Foreign Service," University of North Carolina, webpage accessed <www.unc.edu/depts/diplomat/AD_Issues/amdipl_6/jones_astp.html> "Our Founder: Charles Albert Ferguson, Ph.D.," Center for Applied Linguistics, <http://www.cal.org/who-we-are/our-founder> and "Obituary Charles Albert Ferguson," *Language in Society*, Cambridge University Press, vol. 28, 431–37.
3 Robert Kaplan, *The Arabists: The Romance of an American Elite* (New York: Free Press, 1993), first edition, 102, 7–8.
4 Kaplan classified Arabists into three types: the missionary types who were influenced by the missionary tradition and sympathetic to Arab nationalism, the birdwatchers who were dilettantes like the British and the Henderson types were supposed to have adopted Loy Henderson as their model and shared his anticommunism and supposed anti-Semitism, 99.
5 Hume Horan, "The Way to Language Success," *Foreign Service Journal* (December 1988): 35.

6 This material was compiled from *Biographic Register of the US Department of State* (Washington: Government Printing Office, various editions 1947 to its final edition 1974); author's interviews and the Association for Diplomatic Studies oral history interviews in Frontline Diplomacy, The Foreign Affairs Oral History Collection of the Association for Diplomatic Studies and Training, Arlington, Virginia and Lauinger Library, Georgetown University, Washington, DC; also online www.adst.org [hereafter ADST interview].
7 Kaplan, *The Arabists*, 114.
8 On Kreis program, see David Korn, *Assassination in Khartoum* (Bloomington: Indiana University Press, 1993), 65–66; Kaplan, *The Arabists*, 114. Talcott W. Seelye, interview with the author, Plainfield, Massachusetts, August 8, 1994; and Talcott Seelye ADST oral history interview, September 15, 1993.
9 Ambassador Paul J. Hare, interview with the author, Washington, DC, June 8, 1993.
10 Ambassador Andrew I. Killgore, interview with the author, June 16, 1992, Washington, DC; Albert Parry, *America Learns Russian* (Syracuse: Syracuse University Press, 1967), 151. In Cathal Nolan, *Notable US Ambassadors* (Westport, CT: Greenwood Press, 1997), those Southern diplomats from the postwar era are McGhee from Texas, Dodd from North Carolina and Dudley from Virginia. Although Raymond Hare was born in West Virginia his father was only briefly stationed there in government service, and he was raised in Maine. E. J. Kahn, "A Glossary of Old China Hands," in *China Hands* (New York: Viking Press, 1975).
11 For biographical information on Ambassador Terence Todman's career, see "Being Black in a Lily White State Department," www.adst.org; and his ADST oral history interview.
12 Nancy Light, "Subtle Sexism," *Foreign Service Journal* 65 (January 1988). For 1934 quotation, W. F. Ilchman, *Professional Diplomacy in the US* (Chicago: University of Chicago Press, 1961), 169, 234–235. Teresa Thomas, "American Women in the US Foreign Service: Area Specialization and Advancement in the post-1945 Era," paper presented at the Berkshire Conference of Women Historians, Rochester, New York, June 1999.
13 Teresa Thomas, "The Women's Action Organization and Advancement of Women Foreign Service Officers in the 1970's: 'It Is Not Militant, but It Is No Ladies Sewing Circle.'" Paper presented at the New England Historical Association conference, October 8, 2002. Those who formed the Women's Action Organization were mostly senior career women who had remained single and pursued careers in the Foreign Service. They realized their career goals might never be reached due to the solid resistance to women working as area specialists. These women knew posts in Russia, Asia, the Middle East and Africa required specialized language training, but women faced resistance in obtaining the few available seats in FSI's language and area specialization training programs. The few who did get into training found themselves repeatedly passed over by male administrators who had the power to select their own deputies in overseas posts. Despite the success of the Palmer suits, parity did not emerge. Once the last appeal was lost Secretary of State Cyrus Vance sought out the earlier generation, who were invited back with the promise of rapid promotion. Those who returned were not offered posts in regional bureaus like the NEA but in posts dealing with international treaties and protocols.
14 On rehiring women area specialists, see Teresa Thomas, "American Women in the US Foreign Service: Area Specialization and Advancement in the post-1945 Era," conference paper, Berkshire Conference of Women Historians, Rochester, New York, June 1999. For 1961 statistics, see William Barnes and J. H. Morgan, *The Foreign Service of the US: Origins, Development and Functions* (Washington: Historical Office Department of State, 1961), 306. For 1990 figures, see John Owens, "Crisis in the US Foreign Service," *Mediterranean Quarterly* 2, no. 3 (1991): 38.
15 Transcript of telephone conversation between President Lyndon B. Johnson and Dean Rusk, January 20, 1964, Lyndon Baines Johnson Presidential Library. Reference to transcript courtesy of Dr. David Paterson, State Department Historical Office, Washington, DC.
16 On Glaspie, see Richard Valeriani, *Travels with Henry* (New York: Berkeley Books, 1980), 241–42.
17 Cynthia Enloe, *Bananas, Beaches & Bases Making Feminist Sense of International Politics* (Berkeley: University of California Press, 1989), 116–17; and Jarine Bird, "Seeing Beyond the Veil,"

Foreign Service Journal (January 1985): 21; also Nancy Light, "Subtle Sexism," *Foreign Service Journal* 65 (1988): 33.
18 Richard F. Boyce, *The Diplomat's Wife* (New York: Harpers, 1956), 93.
19 In Carolyn G. Heilbrun, *Writing a Woman's Life* (New York: Norton, 1988), 36. Heilbrun quotes Flaubert discussing the "third sex" and using the term with a very different meaning. The origin of the phrase within the State Department goes back at least to the 1960s, and it has been used by a number of women, including references to the role of women in Muslim nations in Nancy Light's "Subtle Sexism," *Foreign Service Journal*, (January 1988). Jane Abell-Coon made a similar reference to the same term in her ADST oral history interview.
20 Richard B. Parker, ADST oral history interview, April 29, 1989. Stackhouse quoted in Kraft, "Those Arabists," *New York Times Magazine*, November 7, 1971, 88.
21 Ambassador William R. Crawford, interview with author, Washington, DC, June 10, 1993.
22 Ambassador George M. Lane, interview with the author, Worcester, Massachusetts, October 26, 1993. The first of the group to become ambassadors were Eilts 1965, Symmes 1967, Murphy 1971, Stoltzfus 1971, Crawford 1972, Seelye and Noel 1972, Akins 1973, Scotes, Wolle, Parker, Paganelli all in 1974 and Lane in 1975.
23 Ambassador Richard W. Murphy, interview with author, Washington, DC, June 9, 1993.
24 Kaplan, *The Arabists*, 119.
25 Ambassador Hermann F. Eilts, ADST oral history interview, Washington, DC, and Eilts, interview with the author, Boston, Massachusetts, March 11, 1993.
26 For a memoir describing diplomatic life in Jerusalem, Kai Bird, *Crossing Mandelbaum Gate Coming of Age Between the Arabs and Israelis, 1956–1978* (New York: Scribner, 2010), on the death of Thomas Wasson, 31.
27 "US Consul Dies of Wounds From a Sniper in Jerusalem: Thomas C. Wasson Shot Down While on Truce Commission Task," *New York Times*, May 23, 1948; "Second American Dies in Jerusalem: Machine-Gun Wounds are Fatal to Navy Aide—Burial of Consul Set for Today," *New York Times*, May 23, 1948; and "UN Palestine Truce Aide is Wounded in Jerusalem," *New York Times*, May 27, 1948; "British Legionnaires Sentenced," *New York Times*, May 23, 1948.
28 Ambassador Hermann F. Eilts, ADST oral history interview; and interview with the author, Boston, Massachusetts, March 11, 1993.

3. Landfall: Language Training in Beirut, 1946

1 On ASTP training, see Louis E. Keefer, *Scholars in Foxholes: A Study of the Army Specialized Training Program* (Jefferson, NC: McFarland, 1988).
2 Roy F. Nichols, *Advance Agents of American Destiny* (Philadelphia: University of Pennsylvania Press, 1956), 137.
3 "The Spoken Word: Dr. Henry Lee Smith Uses Language, All Kinds, to Teach Linguistics on TV," *New York Times*, May 11 1958, II, 11; *Who Was Who in America* (New Providence, NJ: Marquis Publishing,) Dr. Smith's papers are at the University of Buffalo, SUNY. NB: Dr. Henry Lee Smith, Jr. is *not* to be confused with Dr. Harlie L. Smith Jr., an FSI linguist in the 1970s.
4 Jester and Smith, "Language Training for the Foreign Service and the Department of State," *American Foreign Service Journal* 23, no. 9 (1946): 35.
5 Smith became a celebrity thanks to US Army publicity: "Let's Learn Language," *Time*, January 25, 1943, 41–43; and *National Geographic* 84 (1943): 698. "Language Training for the Foreign Service," *American Foreign Service Journal* 23, no. 9 (1946).
6 Leslie McLoughlin, *In a Sea of Knowledge: British Arabists in the Twentieth Century* (Reading, UK: Ithaca Press, 2002), 36, 122.
7 For an artistic approach to Arabic writing Gabriel Mandel Khan, *Arabic Script: Styles, Variants and Calligraphic Adaptations* (New York: Abbeville Press, 2001). Maksoud Feghali's *Spoken Lebanese*

(Boone, NC: Parkway Press, 1999) explains how a phonetic system can be used to learn the Lebanese dialect. Today the State Department's updated short program is Karin Ryding and Abdelnour Zaiback, *Formal Spoken Arabic FAST Course* (Washington: Georgetown University Press, 1993).

8 Ambassador Richard W. Murphy, interview with the author, Washington, DC, June 9, 1993.
9 Ambassador George M. Lane, interview with the author, Worcester, Massachusetts, October 26, 1993; and Ernest McCarus, "A Lust for Language," *Paths to the Middle East*, 188; also Ambassador Dayton Mak, interview with the author, Washington, DC, June 15, 1992.
10 Davies, letter to Hume Horan and Charles Cecil, May 20, 1974, copy in possession of the author.
11 Charles A. Ferguson, "Diglossia," in *Word, Journal of the International Linguistic Association* (1959): 325–340; Charles A. Ferguson, Haim Blanc et al. *Contributions to Arabic Linguistics, Harvard Middle Eastern Monographs* (Cambridge, MA: Center for Middle East Studies of Harvard University, 1964), 151.
12 "Recruitment & Training for the Foreign Service of the United States," United States Congress, Committee on Foreign Relations, Senate Staff Study (Washington: Government Printing Office, 1958), February 28, 1958.
13 Monteagle Stearns, "Report on Hard Language Proficiency in the Foreign Service: Arabic, Chinese, Japanese, Russian," Department of State, May 21, 1986. Leon and Leila Poullada, "Our Tongue–Tied Foreign Service," *American Foreign Service Journal*, June 1957, 24. For Richard W. Murphy quote, author's interview, June 9, 1993.
14 On Soviet program, see Jacob Ornstein, "Foreign Language: Chink in America's Armor," *Foreign Service Journal* (February 1959): 44–48; and "To Win the 'Languages Race' with Russia," *New York Times*, September 15, 1957, 45–46, 54–57; and Monteagle Stearns, "Report on Hard Language Proficiency," 5–6.
15 Charles A. Ferguson, "Introduction," and R. S. Harrell, "A Linguistic Analysis of Egyptian Radio Arabic," *Contributions to Arabic Linguistics* (Cambridge, MA: CMES, 1960).
16 Stearns, "Report on Hard Language Proficiency in the Foreign Service," Appendix C, 2.
17 Ambassadors: Eilts 1965, Symmes 1967, Todman 1969, Brewer 1970, Murphy 1971, Stoltzfus 1971, Crawford, 1972, Noel 1972, Seelye 1972, Akins 1973, Davies 1974, Paganelli 1974, Parker 1974, Scotes 1974, Sterner 1974, Wolle 1974, Dickman 1976, Bergus, 1977, Killgore 1977, Lane 1978, Wiley 1978, Pelletreau 1979, Horan 1980, Marthinsen 1980, Sutherland 1980, Countryman 1981, Zweifel 1981, Eagleton 1984, Rugh 1984, Newton 1985, Mack 1986, Howell 1987, Suddarth 1987, Djerejian 1988, Glaspie 1988, Ross 1988, Hambley 1989.
18 Frank Snowden Hopkins, "Should the Foreign Service Officer Specialize?" *American Foreign Service Journal* 24, no. 7 (July 1947): 11–13, 48–50.
19 Dayton Mak, Association for Diplomatic History oral history interview, August 9, 1989, in Frontline Diplomacy, The Foreign Affairs Oral History Collection of the Association for Diplomatic Studies and Training, Arlington, Virginia and Lauinger Library, Georgetown University, Washington, DC; also online www.adst.org [hereafter ADST interview]. Also, Dayton Mak, interview with the author, Washington, DC, June 15, 1992.
20 Joseph Kraft, "Those Arabists at State," *New York Times Magazine*, November 7, 1971, 88.
21 Hopkins, "Should the Foreign Service Officer Specialize?" *American Foreign Service Journal* 24, no. 7 (July 1947): 11–13, 48–50.
22 Curtis F. Jones, "The Education of an Arabist," *Foreign Service Journal*, December 6, 1982; and Jones, ADST oral history interview, March 29, 1994.
23 Dayton Mak heard the Arabist proverb from George Wadsworth, Ambassador Dayton Mak, interview with the author, Washington, DC, June 15, 1992. Robert Kaplan quotes Alfred Atherton as being similar anecdote from James Moose; *The Arabists*, 126.
24 Ambassador Parker T. Hart, ADST oral history interview, part one, 31–32.
25 Talcott W. Seelye, ADST oral history interview, September 15, 1993.

26 Ambassador Hermann Eilts, interview with the author, March 11, 1993, Boston, Massachusetts.
27 Ambassador William R. Crawford, interview with the author, Washington, DC, June 10, 1993.
28 George Makdisi, "The Unconventional Education of a Syro-Lebanese Intellectual," in Aleya Rouchdy, ed., *The Arabic Language in America* (Detroit, MI: Wayne State University Press, 1992), 210.
29 Donald Bergus, letter to the author, February 23, 1994.
30 For academic view, see Paul Lunde and J. Wintle, *A Dictionary of Arabic and Islamic Proverbs* (London: Routlege and Keegan, 1984), vii. For quotation on Arab view, Abdel Aziz Hussein, Minister of State for Kuwait, *As the Arabs Say: Arabic Quotations Recalled and Interpreted*, volume II, (Washington, DC: Sabbagh Management Corp, 1985), viii.
31 Dayton Mak, "Some Syrian Arabic Proverbs," *Journal of the American Oriental Society* 69, no. 4 (1949). Mak, interview with the author, June 15, 1992. Rodger Davies, *Southwestern Journal of Anthropology* 5 (1949): 244–52; Arthur Allen, *Journal of the American Oriental Society* 75, no. 2 (1955): 122–125. Hermann Eilts, "Along the Storied Incense Roads of Aden," *National Geographic* 111, no. 2](1957), 233–54; and review "Cairo to Riyadh Diary," *Middle East Journal* 5, no. 3 (summer 1951).
32 The hefty series of volumes began as an FSI typescript in 1955 and was later published as Peter F. Abboud and Ernest N. McCarus, *Elementary Modern Standard Arabic Part One and Part Two* (Ann Arbor: Department of Near Eastern Studies, University of Michigan, 1968). Roger Allen, "Teaching Arabic in the US," in Rouchdy, *The Arabic Language in America*, 222–50. Gibb taught Oriental studies at Oxford and Harvard, *Area Studies Reconsidered* (London: School of Oriental and African Studies, University of London, 1963), 14; and *Reflections on the Past, Visions for the Future*, ed. Don Babai (Cambridge, MA: Harvard University Press, 2004), 7.
33 Ambassador Dayton Mak, ADST oral history interview, Washington, DC, August 9, 1989. Ryding and Zaiback, *Formal Spoken Arabic FAST Course*, vii.
34 Ambassador Harrison M. Symmes, ADST oral history interview, February 25, 1989.
35 Ambassador Dayton Mak, interview with the author, Washington, DC, June 15, 1992.
36 Ambassador Hermann Eilts, ADST oral history interview, August 12 and 13, 1988; and interview with the author, Boston, Massachusetts, March 11, 1993.
37 *Toward a Stronger Foreign Service*, Report of the Secretary of State's Public Committee on Personnel, [hereafter *The Wriston Report*], June 1954, 45; also "Loyalty and Security in the Department of State," US State Department publication #3841, October 1950.
38 *The Wriston Report*, 13–14.
39 "Proficiency and in Recruiting for the Foreign Service," Committee on Foreign Relations, US Senate, 86th Congress, First Session, April 16, 1959, 77; and "The Formulation & Administration of United States Foreign Policy," Brookings Institution, January 1960, Study #9, in *US Foreign Policy, Compilation of Studies*, 87th Congress, First Session, Document #24, March 15, 1964, 935.
40 *The Wriston Report*, 48; and "US Aide Takes Oath, Hoskins Director of Foreign Service Institute," *New York Times*, March 9, 1955. Also Henry Pringle, "School for Modern Diplomats," *Saturday Evening Post*, January 3, 1959: 90. On Hoskins, "New Director of Textron to Guide Merchandising," *New York Times*, March 20, 1947, 41.
41 Harold B. Hoskins, "The Need for More Effective American Representation in the Middle East—Private & Government," 10th Annual Conference on Middle Eastern Affairs, *Middle East Institute Proceedings*, 1956, 37–38.
42 Henry Lee Smith, Jr, "Language Training for the Foreign Service and the Department of State," *American Foreign Service Journal* 23, no. 10 (1946): 13; and Smith, "Training in Languages," *New York Times*, April 5, 1952. Also, Hoskins, "The New FSI Training Program," *Foreign Service Journal* 32, no. 11 (1955): 51.

43 Hoskins, "The Department of State and the Quest for Quality," Address to the College English Association Institute, April 5, 1955 in *US Department of State Bulletin* (May 16, 1955): 816–19.
44 Hoskins, "The Need for More Effective American Representation in the Middle East," *Middle East Institute Proceedings* (1956), 34–38.
45 Harold Hoskins, "The Need for More Effective Representation," Middle East Institute Proceedings, 1956, 37–38.
46 For Chinese 28 months, Russian 20 months, Japanese 36 months. See Appendix VIII, "Current Foreign Service Institute Courses 1958: Department of State, Foreign Service Institute" in "Recruitment & Training for the Foreign Service of the United States," Senate Staff Study, February 28, 1958, 194.
47 Ambassador Andrew I. Killgore, interview with the author, Washington, DC, June 6, 1992.
48 Ibid; Ambassador Richard B. Parker, ADST oral history interview, April 21, 1989.
49 Ambassador Richard B. Parker, ADST oral history interview, April 21, 1989. Parker achieved an S-4/R-4 rating [meaning a top rating in speaking/reading], after completing two programs at Beirut. *Biographic Register*, Department of State publication, Washington: Government Printing Office, title page.
50 Ambassador Richard B. Parker, ADST oral history interview, April 21, 1989; interview with the author, Washington, DC, June 11, 1993. For an overview of his career, see Richard B. Parker, *Memoirs of a Foreign Service Arabist* (Washington: ADST-DACOR Diplomats and Diplomacy Books, 2013).
51 Ambassador William R. Crawford, interview with the author, Washington, DC, June 10, 1993. Decades later FSI would settle on what they termed Formal Spoken Arabic or FSA, describing it as "[a] form of Arabic lingua franca [...] the most efficient, flexible and useful brand of Arabic for Foreign Service personnel," Ryding and Zaiback, *Formal Spoken Arabic*, vii.
52 Ambassador Talcott W. Seelye, interview with the author, Plainfield, Massachusetts, August 8, 1994; and Ambassador Michael E. Sterner, interview with the author, Washington DC, June 10, 1993.
53 Remarks by Talcott Seelye, panel "The Arabists," "Arab Americans at the Crossroads Conference," American-Arab Anti-Discrimination conference, April 16, 1994, VHS.
54 Ambassador Richard B. Parker, interview with the author, Washington, DC, June 11, 1993.
55 Ambassador William R. Crawford, Jr, interview with the author, Washington, DC, June 10, 1993.
56 Ambassador Richard B. Parker, interview with the author, Washington, DC, June 11, 1993.
57 "The Foreign Service: A Manchester Guardian Inquiry" reprinted in *Foreign Service Journal* 30, no. 4 (April 1956): 19.
58 Leslie McLoughlin, *In a Sea of Knowledge: British Arabists in the Twentieth Century* (Reading, UK: Ithaca Press, 2002), 120–22. For personal reflections by British Arabists, see James Craig et al., *The Arabists of Shemlan, MECAS Memoirs 1944–1978* (London: Stacey International, 2006).
59 For cost, see Francis J. Carmody, "ASTP Gives No Help to French Teachers," *Modern Language Journal* 30 (1946): 518. "Recruitment & Training for the Foreign Service of the United States," Senate Staff Study, February 28, 1958.
60 James Reston, "Foreign Service Woes: A Comment on Inability of US Envoys to Talk Language of Nations They're in," *New York Times*, March 19, 1958, 14. "CIA Chief Sees 'Pressing Need' for Language Studies," *New York Times*, February 8, 1958, 8; and James Reston, "Diplomacy and Congress: Dulles Has to Argue for His Budget In the Midst of Urgent Deliberations," *New York Times*, May 22, 1958, 12.
61 James Reston, "Diplomacy and Congress: Dulles Has to Argue for His Budget In the Midst of Urgent Deliberations," and "Is French at Nice The Best for US? Dulles Hears Differently," *New York Times*, May 22, 1958, 1; also Reston, "Many US Envoys Held Inadequate," *New York Times*, June 24, 1958, 29.
62 Ernest N. McCarus, "History of Arabic Study in the United States," in Rouchdy, *The Arabic Language in America*, 209–213; Menahim Mansoor "Education News: Arabic," *New York Times*, November 2, 1958, IV, 9.

63 Jacob Ornstein, "To Win the 'Languages Race' with Russia," *New York Times*, September 15, 1957, 45 & 52; "Proficiency and in Recruiting for the Foreign Service," Hearing before a Subcommittee of the Committee on Foreign Relations, US Senate, 86th Congress, 1st Session, April 16, 1959.
64 Earle Russell, quoted by Beatrice Russell, *Living in State* (New York: D. McKay, 1959), 181–82.
65 Leon and Leila Poullada, "Our Tongue–Tied Foreign Service," *Foreign Service Journal* 34, no. 6 (June 1957): 25; Menahem Mansour, "Education News: Arabic," *New York Times*, November 2, 1958, 9.

4. Filling the Cold War Linguist Gap: The Middle East Area Program in Beirut

1 Beatrice Russell, *Living in State* (New York: D. McKay, 1959), 182.
2 Quoting Beatrice Russell, *Living in State* (New York: D. McKay, 1959), 182.
3 Dr. Snow, held a doctorate in linguistics from the University of Michigan, codified the grammar of Modern Standard Arabic and was director of the FSI Arabic school. Dr. James Snow, interview with the author, June 10, 1993.
4 For how the area changed, see Samir Khalaf "Ras–Beirut Adrift," in *Quest for Understanding Arabic and Islamic Studies in Memory of Malcolm H. Kerr*, eds. Samir Seikaly, Ramzi Baalbaki, and Peter Dodd (Beirut: American University of Beirut Press, 1991), 71–96.
5 Ambassador George M. Lane, interview with the author, Worcester, Massachusetts, October 26, 1993.
6 Posts: Aden (Eagleton) 1967; Bahrain, 1972 (Stoltzfus); Sudan (Noel) 1972, Yemen (Crawford) 1972 and Syria (Murphy) 1974; United Arab Emirates (Sterner) 1974; Kuwait (Stoltzfus); Oman (Wolle) 1974; Qatar (Paganelli) 1974. Quotation, Ambassador George M. Lane, interview with the author, October 26, 1993.
7 Of the 10, Naff studied Ernest McCarus, director of the Foreign Service Institute Arabic program; George Makdisi, who worked briefly at the FSI Washington; and others who taught at the AUB, including Charles Issawi and Farhat Ziadeh. See Thomas Naff, *Paths to the Middle East: Ten Scholars Look Back* (Albany: State University of New York Press, 1993), x–xiii.
8 Henry Lee Smith Jr., "Language Training for the Foreign Service & the Department of State," *American Foreign Service Journal* 23, no. 9 (1946): 68.
9 Ernest McCarus, "A Lust for Language," in *Paths to the Middle East*, 188; and introduction, Ernest McCarus and Peter Abboud, *Elementary Modern Standard Arabic I, Pronunciation and Writing* (New York: Cambridge University Press, 1983). James Craig, "MEACAS: An Overview," in *The Arabists of Shemlan, MECAS Memoirs 1944–78*, (London: Stacey International, 2006), 9.
10 Ambassador Michael E. Sterner, Foreign Affairs Oral History Collection, Association for Diplomatic Studies and Training, Arlington, VA, www.adst.org. [hereafter ADST] Association for Diplomatic Studies interview, March 2, 1990; and interview with the author, Washington, DC, June 10, 1993.
11 David Cowan, *An Introduction to Modern Literary Arabic* (Cambridge: Cambridge University Press, 1958 [1968]). Regarding "Thatcher's Club," in Leslie McLoughlin, *In a Sea of Knowledge: British Arabists* (Reading, UK: Ithaca Press, 2002), 122.
12 Richard S. Harrell, "A Linguistic Analysis of Egyptian Radio Arabic," in *Contribution to Arabic Linguistics, Harvard Middle Eastern Monographs III*, ed. Charles A. Ferguson (Cambridge, MA: Center for Middle East Studies of Harvard University, 1964), for analysis of Nasser's Arabic.
13 Ernest N. McCarus, "A Lust for Language" and Roger Allen, "Teaching Arabic in the United States: Past, Present, and Future," in *Paths to the Middle East*, 181–98. For Snow's role, see "Introduction," in *Modern Written Arabic*, vol. 1, ed. Harlie L. Smith, Jr. (Washington: Foreign Service Institute, Department of State, 1969), iii; and James A. Snow, *A Grammar of Modern Written Arabic Clauses*, PhD dissertation, University of Michigan, 1965); and James A. Snow, interview with the author, June 15 and 23, 1992; and June 10, 1993.

14 For the changing political situation on the AUB campus, see Betty S. Anderson, *The American University of Beirut Arab Nationalism and Liberal Education* (Austin: University of Texas Press, 2011).
15 Ambassador George M. Lane, interview with the author, Worcester, Massachusetts, October 26, 1993. On Arab proverbs, Isa Sabbagh, *As the Arabs Say Arabic Quotations Recalled and Interpreted*, vols. I and II (Washington: Sabbagh Management Corp, 1983–1985).
16 Ambassador Talcott W. Seelye, interview with the author, Plainfield, Massachusetts, August 8, 1994. Henry Kissinger later recalled, "I had asked Meloy to show the flag by calling on the newly elected Sarkis," Henry Kissinger, *Years of Renewal the Concluding Volume of His Classic Memoirs* (New York: Touchstone, 1999), 1047–48.
17 Ambassador Talcott W. Seelye, interview with the author, Plainfield, Massachusetts, August 8, 1994.
18 Ambassador William D. Brewer, Association for Diplomatic Studies interview, August 2, 1988.
19 Ambassador William D. Brewer, Association for Diplomatic Studies interview, August 2, 1988.
20 Ambassador Michael E. Sterner, Association for Diplomatic Studies interview, March 2, 1990.
21 Ibid.
22 Cecil visited Israel with two other FSI students in 1971 for eight days and traveled through Jerusalem and the Golan heights with the Jerusalem Deputy Chief of Mission's driver, a Yemeni Jew. Charles Cecil, letter to the author, Abidjan, Ivory Coast, January 22, 1995.
23 Ambassador Richard W. Murphy, interview with the author, June 9, 1993.
24 Beatrice Russell, *Living in State*, 247–51.
25 Beatrice Russell, "We Like the Foreign-Service Life," *Saturday Evening Post*, June 18, 1955; and Beatrice Russell, "Ahlan Wasahlan and All That," *Living in State*, 179–83.
26 Russell, *Living in State*, 182.
27 "Earle Russell Dies Trying to Cross Sahara," June 30, 1971, *Washington Post*, and "H. Earl[e] Russell Jr, Diplomat Dies Driving In the Sahara," *New York Times*, June 30, 1971.
28 Parker, *Memoirs of a Foreign Service Arabist*, 186.
29 Parker, *Memoirs of a Foreign Service Arabist*, 186. Edward Peck, "Reflections: An Unusual Expression of Gratitude," *Foreign Service Journal* 91, no. 11 (2014): www.afsa.org.
30 Ambassador Richard B. Parker, interview with the author, June 11, 1993.
31 Ambassador Andrew I. Killgore, interview with the author, June 16, 1992.
32 Ambassador Michael E. Sterner, interview with the author, Washington, DC, June 10, 1993.
33 William Rugh, *Arab Perceptions of American Foreign Policy during the October War*, Special Study #2 (Washington: The Middle East Institute, 1976); and William Rugh, *The Arab Press: News Media and Political Process in the Arab World* (Syracuse, NY: Syracuse University Press, 1979).
34 Rugh, *The Arab Press*, xvii and 159, 167.
35 Rugh, *The Arab Press*, xvii–xviii.
36 William Rugh, *American Encounters with Arabs: The 'Soft Power' of US Public Diplomacy in the Middle East* (Westport, CT: Praeger Security International, 2006).
37 Rugh, *The Arab Press*, xvii–xviii.
38 Ambassador Talcott W. Seelye, Association for Diplomatic Studies interview, September 15, 1993.
39 Memo from Arabic-trained Foreign Service officers to the Department of State, September–October 1967, by Richard Dawson, Hume Horan, William Crawford, George Lane et al. Drafts from Lane and Dawson. Monteagle Stearns, "Report on Hard Language Proficiency in the Foreign Service: Arabic, Chinese, Japanese, Russian," Department of State, May 21, 1986.
40 For statistics, "American University of Beirut Begins its 102nd Year 1967–68," *Middle East Studies Bulletin* 1, no. 2 (1967).
41 Hisham Shirabi, "Looking Back at AUB," *The Jerusalem Quarterly* 30 (1984): 43–49.
42 Ambassador Richard W. Murphy, interview with the author, Washington, DC, June 9, 1993.

43 Ambassador George M. Lane, interview with the author, Worcester, Massachusetts, October 26, 1993.
44 Hand notes taken at FSI Special Area Course, American University of Beirut, October 17, 1960 to December 12, 1960, Ambassador George M. Lane.
45 Robert Kaplan, *The Arabists* (New York: Free Press, 1993), 185.
46 On the problems after the Six Day War, see chapter 6, "'Guerilla U' The Contested Nature of Authority," in Anderson, *The American University of Beirut.*
47 For information on the AUB, see "Programs in Middle East Studies, American University of Beirut," *MESA Bulletin*, February 1, 1973.
48 Preface to the third edition, Zeine N. Zeine, *The Emergence of Arab Nationalism with a Background Study of Arab-Turkish Relations in the Near East* (Delmar, NY: Caravan Book, 1973 [1958]), vii.
49 Zeine, *The Emergence of Arab Nationalism*, 1973, 9–11 and 125–126.
50 Zeine, *The Emergence of Arab Nationalism*, 129–134 and 138–139.
51 FSO Charles Cecil, Abidjan, letter to the author, January 22, 1995.
52 See biographical sketch accompanying Nabih Amin Faris, "A View of Arab Unity," in *Political and Social Thought in the Contemporary Middle East*, ed. Kemal H. Karpat (New York: Praeger, 1968), 259.
53 Nabih Faris, "Arab Unity and Ideology," *Political and Social Thought in the Contemporary Middle East*, 262; and Malcolm H. Kerr, *The Arab Cold War* (London: Oxford University Press, 1965).
54 Constantine K. Zurayk, *More Than Conquers: Selected Addresses Delivered at the AUB 1953–66*, (Beirut: American University of Beirut, 1968), 9–11.
55 See "Having Nothing, and Yet Possessing All Things," Baccalaureate Address, June 1955, in Zurayk, *More Than Conquers*, 28–33.
56 Tareq K. Ismael, *The Arab Left* (Syracuse, NY: Syracuse University Press, 1976), 102.
57 George M. Lane, personal correspondence.
58 Ambassador Michael E. Sterner, interview with the author, Washington, June 10, 1993.
59 Constantine K. Zurayk, *The Meaning of the Disaster, [Ma'na al-Nakbah]*, translated from the Arabic by R. Bayly Winder, English edition (Beirut: Khayat's College Book Cooperative, 1956), 29–30 and 40.
60 Zurayk, *The Meaning of Disaster*, 39–40.
61 Ibid.
62 Harold B. Hoskins, "The Need for More Effective American Representation in the Middle East—Private and Government," Address to the Middle East Institute (Washington: Middle East Institute, 1956), March 9, 1956.
63 The attack occurred in the fall of 1977 shortly after Kerr returned from a sabbatical and taught at the American University of Cairo. Ann Z. Kerr, *Come With Me From Lebanon* (Syracuse, NY: Syracuse University Press, 1994), 167.
64 Malcolm Kerr and Antun Aqiqi, *Lebanon in the Last Years of Feudalism, 1840–1868, A Contemporary Account by Antun Dahir Al-Aqiqi and Other Documents* (Beirut: Catholic Press, 1959), xii.
65 Kaplan, *The Arabists*, 210.
66 Ambassador William R. Crawford, interview with the author, Washington, DC, June 10, 1993. Also, Richard N. Curtiss, *A Changing Image: American Perceptions of the Arab–Israeli Dispute*, (Washington: American Educational Trust, 1982), vii.
67 Ambassador L. Dean Brown, Association for Diplomatic Studies interview, Washington, DC.
68 Malcolm H. Kerr, "The 1960 Lebanese Parliamentary Elections," *Middle Eastern Affairs*, October 1960, 267. Malcolm Kerr, review of Menahim Mansoor, *English-Arabic Political, Diplomatic and Conference Terms*, in *The Muslim World* 51, no. 3 (1961): 239–40. For Kerr's biting analysis of the players in the conflict, see "Lebanese Views on the 1958 Crisis," *Middle East Journal* 15, no. 2 (1961): 211–17.
69 Malcolm Kerr, "The Middle East: Present Problems and Future," Address by Malcolm Kerr, American Foreign Service Association Opening Banquet, April 30, 1968, copy in Vertical File, G. K. Keiser Library, Middle East Institute, Washington, DC, accessed 1994.

70 Ibid. When Kerr gave this address: African-American unrest on the UCLA campus was high, President Lyndon Johnson had ended his election bid a month earlier, Rev. Martin Luther King's assassination had touched off riots in April and Columbia University was paralyzed by student protests in the same month.
71 Malcolm Kerr, *Regional Arab Politics and the Conflict with Israel*, RN 5966–FF October 1969, Research Program on Economic and Political Problems and Prospects (Santa Maria, CA: RAND Corporation, 1969), v and 50.
72 Malcolm Kerr, "The West and the Middle East: The Light and the Shadow," 1972 Presidential Address, Middle East Studies Association, *MESA Bulletin*, February 1, 1973.
73 Malcolm H. Kerr, "Nixon's Second Term: Policy Prospects in the Middle East," *Journal of Palestine Studies* 2, no. 3] (1973): 14–29. James Akins, "This Time the Wolf Is Here," *Foreign Affairs* 51, no. 3 (1973). Teresa Thomas, "The Diplomat Who Cried Wolf: James Akins and the OPEC Oil Embargo," conference paper, New York Political Science Association conference, Albany, New York, May 1998.
74 Malcolm Kerr, *America's Middle East Policy: Kissinger, Carter and the Future* (Beirut: Institute for Palestine Studies, 1980), 8–11.
75 Ibid., 18–19.
76 Kerr placed Kissinger alongside Rostow, Bundy, Haig, Scowcroft and Brzezinski in that category; see Ibid., 18. Elsewhere John Connally, Henry Jackson and Ronald Reagan, 30.
77 Kerr, *America's Middle East Policy*, 30–31.
78 Ibid., 10.
79 David D. Newsom, "Miracle or Mirage; Reflections on US Diplomacy and the Arabs," *Middle East Journal* 35, no. 3 (1981): 299–313.
80 Hume Horan, "Plea for Arabists," *Foreign Service Journal* 50, no. 5 (1973). Horan's three factors: the 1967 war made the Arabic language "unwise and untimely," the government's need for Southeast Asian specialists in the context of the Vietnam War and the "loss of career acceleration" caused by the amount of time required by the Arabic program. Also, James A. Snow interviews with the author, June 15 and 23, 1992; and June 10, 1993.
81 Collective letter from Arabic-trained officers to the Department of State, copy of text from Ambassador George Lane. Also Richard Dawson, letters to the author November 24, 1994 and December 17, 1994; and Hume Horan correspondence with the author November 2, 1994.
82 For brief outline of Israeli military actions and Lebanese political situation, see Congressional Quarterly, *The Middle East* (Washington: Congressional Quarterly, 1994), 45, 291–301. For more details, Robert Fisk, *Pity the Nation: The Abduction of Lebanon* (New York: Athenaeum, 1990); and Zeev Schiff and Ehud Yaari, *Israel's Lebanon War* (New York: Simon and Schuster, 1984).
83 For an account of his life, Ann Zwicker Kerr, *Come with Me from Lebanon: An American Family Odyssey* (New York: Syracuse University Press, 1994).
84 Richard B. Parker, "Middle East Studies and US Foreign Policy," *The United States & the Middle East*, ed. Hooshang Amirahmadi (Albany: State University of New York Press, 1991), 312.
85 Parker, "Middle East Studies and US Foreign Policy," 312–13.

5. "The Departure of Kings, Old Men, and Christians": The Eisenhower Years

1 Letter from William D. Brewer to the author, February 17, 1996.
2 Salim Yacub, *Containing Arab Nationalism: The Eisenhower Doctrine and the Middle East* (Chapel Hill: University of North Carolina Press, 2004), 238.
3 Ambassador Joseph C. Green, John Foster Dulles oral history collection, Public Policy Papers, Department of Rare Books and Special Collection, Princeton University Library, October 16, 1965, 17. [hereafter John Foster Dulles Oral History collection, Princeton University];

US Department of State, *Principal Officers of the Department of State and US Chiefs of Mission* (Washington: Department of State, Office of the Historian, 1991), 107.
4 Ambassador Joseph C. Green, John Foster Dulles Oral History collection, Princeton University, October 16, 1965, 28–29.
5 Leonard Mosley, *Dulles: A Biography of Eleanor, Allen and John Foster Dulles and their Family Network* (New York: Dial Press, 1978), 509 and 85–87. Memorandum of Conversation, Dulles, Hakim, Chamoun et al., American Embassy Beirut, Lebanon, May 16, 1953, 2, in Secretary's Trip to the Near East and South Asia, May 9–29, 1953, National Archives, Washington, DC, [record group] RG 59, 780 1–250, Box 4037.
6 Ambassador Hermann F. Eilts, ADST oral history interview, in Frontline Diplomacy, The Foreign Affairs Oral History Collection of the Association for Diplomatic Studies and Training, Arlington, Virginia and Lauinger Library, Georgetown University, Washington, DC; also online www.adst.org [hereafter ADST interview]. Also, Hermann F. Eilts, interview with the author, Boston, Massachusetts, March 11, 1993. Ambassador Talcott W. Seelye, interview with the author, Plainfield, Massachusetts, August 8, 1994.
7 Ambassador Richard B. Parker, ADST oral history interview, April 21, 1989; interview with the author, Washington, June 11, 1993.
8 Ambassador Harrison Symmes, ADST oral history interview, February 5, 1989.
9 Anatoly Dobrynin, *In Confidence Moscow's Ambassador to America's Six Cold War Presidents* (New York: Times Books, 1995), 25–29 [emphasis in original].
10 Memorandum of Conversation with Near East Hands, American Embassy Beirut, Lebanon, May 17, 1953, 4, Secretary's Trip to Near East and South Asia, May 9–29, 1953, National Archives, Washington, RG 59, 780 1–250, Box 4037.
11 Ambassador Joseph C. Green, The John Foster Dulles oral history collection, Princeton University, 41–42.
12 Memorandum of Conversation with Near East Hands, May 17, 1953, 1–4, in Secretary's Trip to the Near East and South Asia, May 9–29, 1953, National Archives, Washington, DC, RG 59, 780 1–250, Box 4037.
13 Meeting with President (of Lebanon) Camille Chamoun, May 18, 1953, in Secretary's Trip to the Near East and South Asia, May 9–29, 1953, National Archives, Washington, DC, RG 59, 780 1–250, Box 4037.
14 Meeting with President Camille Chamoun, May 18, 1953, in Secretary's Trip to the Near East and South Asia, May 9–29, 1953, National Archives, Washington, DC, RG 59, 780 1–250, Box 4037.
15 Entry for January 27, 1959, Dwight Eisenhower, *The Eisenhower Diaries*, ed. Robert Ferrell (New York: Norton, 1981).
16 After the 1948 Arab–Israeli War, the United Nations Relief Works Agency (UNRWA) was set up to help them. UNRWA registered 750,000 refugees in 1948. Following the 1967 Six Day War, the total of Palestinian refugees in the region was estimated at one million three hundred thousand, and by 1998 the number was estimated at three millions six hundred thousand with 20 percent living in Gaza, 15 percent in the West Bank, 38 percent in Jordan, 9.5 percent in Lebanon, 9.5 percent in Syria, 3 percent in Saudi Arabia and 5 percent scattered elsewhere. Source, UNRWA figures in *National Geographic*, February 2000. As of March 2000, the total Palestinian refugee populations living in exile and in UNRWA camps: 579,987 in the West Bank; 818,771 in Gaza; 1,554,375 in Jordan; 381,163 in Syria and 375,218 in Lebanon, *Boston Globe*, July 18, 2000.
17 Joseph C. Green to Secretary of State, September 27, 1952, Embtel 238, Secret Security Information, National Archives, Washington, DC, RG 59, 780.00/–250. Response: Acheson (signed by John D. Jernegan), to Embassy Amman, October 1, 1952, National Archives, Washington, DC, RG 59, 780.00/–250.
18 Yacub, *Containing Arab Nationalism*, 39, 74.
19 Isaac Alteras, *Eisenhower and Israel: US–Israeli Relations 1953–60* (Gainesville: University of Florida Press, 1993), 118; and *Foreign Relations of the United States* [hereafter *FRUS*], *1952–54, Near and Middle East*, volume IX, part one, xxii.

20. "The Secretary of State to the Chairman of the Advisory Board for International Development (Johnston)," October 13, 1953, *FRUS 1952–54 Near and Middle East*, volume IX, 1349.
21. For the plan's antecedents, see David M. Wishart, "The Breakdown of the Johnston Negotiations over the Jordan Waters," *Middle Eastern Studies* 26, no. 4 (1990): 536–46, especially 537–38. For details on the geographical complications from the perspective of a Jordanian negotiator, see Munther J. Haddadin, "Water in the Middle East Peace Process," *The Geographical Journal* 168, no. 4): 324–40.
22. Talcott Seelye to Department, October 13, 1953, Amman cable #29, at National Archives, Washington, DC, RG 59, 780.00/–250; and "To Byroade from Johnston," signed Dillon, Embassy Paris, October 15, 1953, cable #15, at National Archives, Washington, DC, RG 59, 780.00/–250.
23. "The Chargé in Jordan (Seelye) to the Department of State," October 15, 1953, *FRUS 1952–54 Near and Middle East*, volume IX, 1358–59. Ariel Sharon, *Warrior: The Autobiography of Ariel Sharon* (New York: Simon and Schuster, 1989), 86, 92. Alteras, *Eisenhower and Israel*, 83, 93.
24. Sharon, *Warrior*, 166; and Howard Sachar, *A History of Israel* (New York: Knopf, 1976), 520, 618.
25. "The Chargé in Jordan (Lynch) to the Department of State," October 22, 1953, *FRUS 1952–54, Near and Middle East*, volume IX, 1381–82.
26. Alteras, *Eisenhower and Israel*, 121. Lavon quote, State Department cable Tel Aviv, 569; and November 3, 1953 quote in NEA report, "Trends in Israel," *FRUS*, volume IX, part one, 1408.
27. Hugh Wilford, *America's Great Game: The CIA's Secret Arabists and the Shaping of the Modern Middle East* (New York: Basic Books, 2013), 197. Wilford also noted this led to a blowup between Byroade and Nasser after which Roosevelt and Johnston together cabled Washington "urging his recall," 198, on crypto-diplomacy, 200–01.
28. Text undated, cover letter, November 10, 1953, *FRUS Near and Middle East Volume IX part one*, 1407–08.
29. "Suggested Main Points of Approach Toward Israel–Arab Settlement," January 14, 1955, "Memo Prepared in the Bureau of NEA [...] discussions with and [...] concurrences of Mr. Hare, Mr. Jernegan," *FRUS*, volume XIV, *Arab-Israeli Dispute 1955–57*, 9–15.
30. Ambassador Talcott W. Seelye, interview with the author, August 8, 1994; and ADST oral history interview, September 15, 1993. On later events, "Israel, Jordan and Palestinians Reach Historic Water Agreement," *Chicago Tribune*, February 14, 1996, 10.
31. Alteras, *Eisenhower and Israel*, 90–91. Ambassador William D. Brewer, Association for Diplomatic Studies oral history interview, August 2, 1988.
32. Ambassador William D. Brewer, ADST oral history interview, August 2, 1988. Ambassador Richard B. Parker, ADST oral history interview, April 21, 1989.
33. Sachar, *A History of Israel*, 458.
34. Secretary of State J.F. Dulles to American Embassies, "United States–United Kingdom Policy in the Middle East," sent to: Amman, Baghdad, Beirut, Cairo, Damascus, Jidda, Khartoum, Tel Aviv, London, May 18, 1956, National Archives, RG 59, Box 3699, 780.00/5–1856.
35. Bureau of NEA memo, March 28, 1956, "US Policy in the Near East," *FRUS, Arab-Israeli Dispute 1955–57*, 413–14. This was approved by Eisenhower the same day, "Memorandum from the Secretary of State to the President," March 28, 1956, *FRUS, Arab–Israeli Dispute 1955–57*, volume XV, 419.
36. Evelyn Shuckburgh and John Chamley, *Descent to Suez: Diaries 1951–56* (New York: Norton, 1987), 362–364 [emphasis in original].
37. Eisenhower, *Waging Peace, 1956–61: The White House Years* (Garden City, NY: Doubleday, 1965), 183, 684–85.
38. Memcon, February 15, 1957, "Israeli Withdrawal," with Abba Eban, Reuven Shiloah, Dulles, drafted by Rountree, *FRUS*, volume XVII, 189–94. Ambassador Richard B. Parker, ADST oral history interview, April 21, 1989.
39. Address by President Dwight Eisenhower, "Developments in Eastern Europe and the Middle East," US Department of State *Bulletin*, (November 12, 1956): 744–45. "Informal Record of

a Meeting December 3 in the Secretary's Office," Executive Secretariat, December 3, 1956, 780.00/12–356, National Archives, RG 59, Box 3699.
40 Ambassador Talcott W. Seelye, ADST oral history interview, September 15, 1993.
41 "Consul William D. Brewer, Kuwait City to David D. Newsom, officer-in-charge Arabian Peninsula and Iraq Affairs," November 27, 1956, in National Archives, Washington, DC, RG 59, 780.00/11–2756, Box 3669.
42 Quoted in editorial note #183, President's January 5, 1957 proposal, in *FRUS, Near East Region 1955–57*, volume XII, 437–438.
43 "Memorandum of a meeting, White House, January 1, 1957," in *FRUS, Near East Region 1955–57*, volume XII, 432.
44 Salim Yacub, *Containing Arab Nationalism*, 179–80.
45 "Secretary of State to President's Special Assistant (Richards)," March 9, 1957, in *FRUS, Near East Region*, volume XII, 454–55.
46 *FRUS, Near East Region volume XII*, 486, 525–30. On Knesset vote: 59 to 5 [Communist Party members] and 39 abstentions, see Alteras, *Eisenhower and Israel*, 305–06.
47 Ambassador George Wadsworth, "Telegram to the Department," October 31, 1955, in *FRUS 1955–57, Near East*, volume XIII, 748–49.
48 "Soviet Bloc and Egyptian Activities in Yemen, Memo from Wilkins to Rountree," in *FRUS 1955–57, Near East*, volume XIII, 752–54.
49 "Telegram from Embassy in Ethiopia to the Department," April 15, 1957, in *FRUS 1955–57, Near East*, volume XIII, 755–61; and *FRUS, Near East Region*, volume XII, 536.
50 Richard Parker, Lakeland's colleague, recorded the incident in *The Politics of Miscalculation in the Middle East* (Bloomington: Indiana University Press, 1993), 102, 253. William D. Brewer's letter to the author, February 17, 1996. William Lakeland, letter to the author October 9, 1995.
51 Mohammed Heikal, *The Cairo Documents* (Garden City, NY: Doubleday, 1973), 126, 138–39. On Soviet purge of Arabists, Garay Menicucci, see "Glasnost, the Coup and Soviet Arabist Historians," *International Journal of Middle East Studies* 24, no. 4 (1992): 559–77.
52 Heikal, *The Cairo Documents*, 140.
53 Drafted by Donald Bergus, *FRUS, Near East Region 1958–60*, volume XII, 4–5.
54 "Memo of Discussion, 352nd Meeting of the National Security Council," January 22, 1958, *FRUS Near East Region 1958–60*, volume XII, 614, quotes 618.
55 Shuckburgh, *Descent to Suez*, February 12, 1956 entry, 333.
56 *Foreign Relations of the United States 1958–60, Near East Region*, volume XII, NSC 5801/01, document 5, 21–22
57 Ambassador Richard B. Parker, ADST oral history interview, April 21, 1989.
58 "Meeting in President's Office," Monday, July 14, 1958, 10:55 am, *FRUS Lebanon-Jordan 1958–60*, microfiche edition, 5, document 160.
59 "Memorandum for the Record President's meeting," Monday July 14, 1958, 2:35 pm, *FRUS Lebanon-Jordan 1958–60*, microfiche edition, 5, document 161.
60 "Staff notes," July 15, 1958, 9:00 am, *FRUS Lebanon-Jordan 1958–60*, microfiche edition, 6, document 181. Ambassador Richard B. Parker, ADST oral history interview, April 21, 1989.
61 Richard B. Parker, "Middle East Studies and US Foreign Policy," in *The US and the Middle East: A Search for New Perspectives*, ed. Hooshang Amirahamadi (Albany: State University of New York Press, 1993), 320–21.
62 Wilford quotes on CIA Arabists' exit in *America's Great Game*, 284–85; "Telephone Call from the Vice President," to Secretary Dulles, July 15, 1958, 6:49 pm, in *FRUS Lebanon-Jordan 1958–60*, microfiche edition, 6, document 187.
63 "Ambassador Robert McClintock to Secretary Dulles," January 20, 1959, *in FRUS Lebanon-Jordan 1958–60*, microfiche edition, doc 850/6.
64 Dulles quoted in "Memorandum of Conference with President Eisenhower," Washington, July 23, 1958, *FRUS, Near East, 1958–60*, volume XII, 98.

65 Ambassador William D. Brewer, ADST oral history interview, August 2, 1988. Ambassador Talcott W. Seelye, interview with the author, Plainfield, MA, August 8, 1994.
66 Curiously the two-page chart and cover letter dated August 20, 1957, are stamped "filed September 12, 1958," meaning they were on Murphy's desk from mid-1957 until the fall of 1958, within which time the Lebanon landings occurred. "Admiral Arleigh Burke, Chief of Naval Operations, to Deputy Under Secretary Murphy," August 20, 1957 in National Archives, RG 59 box 3700, General Records of the Department of State 1955–59, 780.00/8–2057.
67 *Biographic Register* (Washington: Government Printing Office, 1970), 269. For quotes, "Ambassador Robert McClintock (Beirut) to Secretary of State," January 20, 1959, *FRUS Lebanon-Jordan 1958–60*, microfiche, document 850/6.
68 "Ambassador Raymond Hare (Cairo) to Secretary of State," January 24, 1959, *FRUS Lebanon-Jordan 1958–60*, microfiche, document 543.
69 "Ambassador Raymond Hare (Cairo) to Secretary of State," section two of two, July 18, 1958, *FRUS Lebanon-Jordan 1958–60*, microfiche, doc 268. Robert Murphy to Secretary of State, from Addis Ababa, August 8, 1958, section four of five, *FRUS Lebanon-Jordan 1958–60*, microfiche, doc 387.
70 "Ambassador Raymond Hare (Cairo) to Secretary of State," section two of two, July 18, 1958, *FRUS Lebanon-Jordan 1958–60*, microfiche, doc 268. Ambassador Richard B. Parker, ADST oral history interview, April 21, 1989.
71 "Ambassador Henry Byroade (Capetown) to Secretary of State (Dulles)," Eyes only for Secretary, No Distribution, Top Secret, Cable #2, July 15, 1958 National Archives, Washington, RG 59, 1955–59, 780.00/7–1558. "John Foster Dulles to Capetown," top secret, Eyes only for Ambassador from Secretary, July 16, 1958, National Archives, Washington, RG 59, 1955–59, 780.00/7–1558.
72 Ambassador Raymond Hare, interview with the author, Washington, DC, June 17, 1992.
73 Richard Parker, *The Politics of Miscalculation*, 102.
74 Ambassador Parker T. Hart, Association for Diplomatic Studies interview, January 27, 1989.
75 For an account of how CIA covert aid backfired when used by Nasser to establish a radio station for propaganda, Voice of the Arabs, see Hugh Wilford, *America's Great Game: The CIA's Secret Arabists and the Shaping of the Modern Middle East* (New York: Basic Books: 2013), 157.
76 Mohammed Heikal, *The Cairo Documents*, 190–92.
77 "Telegram from the Embassy in the UAR [Hare] to the Department," December 1, 1958, *FRUS Arab-Israeli Dispute, UAR*, volume XIII, 502–05.
78 Ambassador Raymond Hare, ADST oral history interview, summer 1987.
79 Ambassador Raymond Hare, ADST oral history interview, summer 1987.
80 Paul J. Hare, *Diplomatic Chronicles of the Middle East: A Biography of Ambassador Raymond A. Hare*, (Lanham, MD: Middle East Institute, 1993), 122.
81 Heikal, *The Cairo Documents*, 188–89. Eisenhower, *Waging Peace*, 584–85. William J. Burns, *Economic Aid & American Policy toward Egypt 1955–1981* (Albany: State University of New York Press, 1985), 1985, Hare 118; *Foreign Relations of the United States 1961–63, Near East, volume XVII*, document 195, Bowles to Washington, February 21, 1962, 482
82 Ambassador Armin H. Meyer, ADST oral history interview, February 8, 1989.

6. Quiet Diplomacy in Action: The Kennedy and Johnson Years

1 Ambassador Armin H. Meyer, Association for Diplomatic Studies oral history interview, part one, 1989, in Frontline Diplomacy, The Foreign Affairs Oral History Collection of the Association for Diplomatic Studies and Training, Arlington, Virginia and Lauinger Library, Georgetown University, Washington, DC; also online www.adst.org [hereafter ADST interview]."John F. Kennedy to Dean Rusk," May 13, 1963, President's Office Files, Box 88 A, folder "Departs and Agencies—State Department 4/63–5/63 in John F. Kennedy Presidential Library.

2 *Public Papers of the Presidents of the United States, John F. Kennedy*, 1961, 27.
3 *Foreign Service Journal*, volume 38, no. 4 (April 1961): 24–25.
4 John F. Kennedy, "The Great Period of the Foreign Service," *Foreign Service Journal* (July 1962): page 29.
5 The phrase is an often repeated cautionary adage used by American diplomats. Quoted in Frank Kessler, *The Dilemmas of Presidential Leadership* (Englewood Cliffs, NJ: Prentice Hall, 1982), 101.
6 *Foreign Service Journal*, April 1961 and Arthur Schlesinger, *A Thousand Days: John F. Kennedy in the White House* (Boston: Houghton, Mifflin, 1965), 411. Kennedy, "The Great Period of the Foreign Service," *Foreign Service Journal* 39, no. 7 (July 1962): 28–29.
7 For the history, see John Dumbrell, "The Action Intellectuals," chapter seven, in *A Companion to John F. Kennedy*, ed. Marc J. Selverstone (Hoboken, NJ: Wiley Blackwell, 2014). Original Theodore H. White article, "The Action Intellectuals," three part series in *Life Magazine*, relevant article in June 9, 1967, issue. For quotes on Bundy, see Kai Bird, *The Color of Truth McGeorge Bundy and William Bundy: Brothers in Arms* (New York: Touchstone Books, 1998), 210, 189 and 188.
8 Dean Rusk, *As I Saw It* (New York: W. W. Norton, 1990), 509, 33–57; and Schlesinger, *A Thousand Days*, 432. Abba Eban, *Personal Witness: Israel through My Eyes* (New York: G. P. Putnam's, 1992), 383.
9 Ambassador Armin H. Meyer, Foreign Affairs Oral History Collection, Association for Diplomatic Studies and Training, Arlington, VA, www.adst.org. Hereafter ADST oral history interview, Washington, DC, April 1990.
10 Schlesinger, *A Thousand Days*, 509.
11 Schlesinger, *A Thousand Days*, 554. John F. Kennedy, *Public Papers of the Presidents of the United States: John F. Kennedy* (Washington: Government Printing Office, 1962–64), 223.
12 Isaiah L. Kenen quoted by Avi Shlaim, "Sleepless Afternoons," *London Review of Books*, February 25, 1993. Myron Kaufmann, "The State Department," in *The Coming Destruction of Israel* (New York: New American Library, 1970).
13 Ambassador William R. Crawford, ADST oral history interview, October 24, 1988.
14 Mordechai Gazit, *President Kennedy's Policy toward the Arab States and Israel: Analysis and Documents* (Tel Aviv: Shiloah Center for Middle Eastern and African Studies, 1983), 46–48. George Lenczowski, *American Presidents and the Middle East* (Durham, NC: Duke University Press, 1990), 71. Lewis J. Paper, *The Promise and the Performance: The Leadership of John F. Kennedy*, (New York: Crown Publishers, 1975), 334.
15 Avner Cohen, "Most Favored Nation: The US carries a big stick on proliferation, but talks softly regarding Israel," *Bulletin of the Atomic Scientists* (January–February, 1995): 44–53, 51–53.
16 JFK quote, *Foreign Relations of the United States*, (hereafter *FRUS*), *FRUS Near East, 1962–63*, volume XVIII (Washington: Government Printing Office), 276–283. Jordan and Hart, "JFK's Support of Jewish Causes Recalled," *Boston Globe*, October 24, 1994. Herbert S. Parmet, *JFK: The Presidency of John F. Kennedy* (New York: Dial Press, 1983), 227–28. Speeches to Zionist Organization of America and B'nai B'rith, Gazit, *President Kennedy's Policy*, 31–61.
17 Robert Komer had nearly as many page citations as Kennedy in *FRUS Near East 1962–63* and fell a few short of Dean Rusk, see index 870–71, 876–77.
18 Warren I. Cohen, "Lyndon Johnson versus Gamal Abdul Nasser," in *Lyndon Johnson Confronts the World 1963–68*, ed. Cohen and Nancy Bernkopf Tucker (New York: Cambridge University Press), 283–84.
19 "Memorandum from Robert W. Komer, National Security Council Staff to President Kennedy," December 22, 1962, in *FRUS, Near East 1961–63*, volume XVIII, 272. Ambassador Michael E. Sterner, interview with the author, Washington, DC, June 10, 1993.
20 "Notes on Presidential-Bipartisan Congressional Leadership Meeting," Memcon, August 12, 1956, *FRUS, Suez Crisis 1955–57*, volume XVII, 190, 195. Armin Meyer ADST oral history interview. On oil, see Steven Spiegel, *The Other Arab-Israeli Conflict: Making America's Middle East Policy from Truman to Reagan* (Chicago: University of Chicago Press, 1985), 120.

21 Ambassador Armin H. Meyer, ADST oral history interview, Washington, DC, 1989. Peter Braestrup, "Johnson Gets Out and Meets the Folks in Lebanon," "US Official's Visit Stirs Israel Anew" and "US Call Trip Personal," *New York Times*, August 24, 1962.
22 Schlesinger, *A Thousand Days*, 567.
23 Quoting comment of Deputy Assistant Secretary of State of NEA, Mr. James P. Grant, in *Foreign Relations of the US, 1961–63, Near East 1962–63*, volume XVIII, April 27, 1963, document 222, 483–84.
24 Quoting comment of Deputy Assistant Secretary of State of NEA, Mr. James P. Grant, in *Foreign Relations of the US, 1961–63, Near East 1962–63*, volume XVIII, April 27, 1963, document 222, 483–84.
25 Herbert Parmet, *JFK: The Presidency of John F. Kennedy*, 228.
26 "Memorandum from Acting Secretary of State Bowles to President Kennedy," May 6, 1961, [Meyer] in *FRUS Near East 1961–62*, 100–101; and UAR letter, "Telegram from the Department of State to the Embassy in the United Arab Republic," May 11, 1961, [Meyer and Palmer], 113.
27 "Draft Deptel re: Ben-Gurion visit to NY, 5/10/61" sent to Cairo, Beirut, Amman, Baghdad, Jidda, Tel Aviv and Taiz NIACT [Night Action] in *JFK National Security Files* microfilm, National Archives NLKL-77–179, NSF country file Israel 3-61-5-61, box 118.
28 Note in *FRUS Near East 1961–62*, 113.
29 "Text of Kennedy Letter to Arab Leaders," *New York Times*, June 26, 1961; and Dana Adams Schmidt, "US Said to Study a Visit by Nasser Official," May 11, 1961, text to Lebanon, Jordan, Iraq, Saudi Arabia and the Yemen, *FRUS Near East 1961–62*, 110–13.
30 "Israelis Weigh Messages," *New York Times*, June 26, 1961.
31 "Memorandum from President Kennedy to his Special Assistant for National Security Affairs, Bundy," July 10, 1961, *FRUS Near East 1961–62*, document 83, 183.
32 Rusk to Kennedy, in *FRUS, Near East 1961–63*, volume XVII, document 86, 191 and 193.
33 Ambassador Armin H. Meyer, Association for Diplomatic Studies oral history interview, part one, 1989. "Israelis Weigh Messages," *New York Times*, June 25, 1961. "Memorandum from President Kennedy to his Special Assistant for National Security Affairs, Bundy," July 10, 1961, *FRUS Near East 1961–62*, document 83, 183. "Memorandum from Secretary of State Rusk to President Kennedy," July 13, 1961, and "The Letters to Arab Leaders."
34 Gazit, *President Kennedy's Policy*, 16.
35 Kennedy quote "Memcon Ambassador Hart's Call on the President," June 29, 1961, in *FRUS Near East 1962–62*, 169–70. Hart request in Ambassador Parker Hart, oral history #3, John F. Kennedy Presidential Library, interview with Dennis J. O'Brien, June 10, 1970.
36 Ambassador Parker Hart, oral history #3, John F. Kennedy Presidential Library, interview with Dennis J. O'Brien, June 10, 1970.
37 Ambassador Parker Hart, oral history #3, John F. Kennedy Presidential Library, interview with Dennis J. O'Brien, June 10, 1970.
38 "Memcon Ambassador Hart's Call on the President," June 29, 1961, in *FRUS Near East 1961–62*, 169–70. Ambassador Parker T. Hart, John F. Kennedy Presidential Library, Boston, Massachusetts, second oral history interview, Virginia, May 27, 1969 [hereafter JFK Presidential Library]. Ambassador Richard W. Murphy, interview with the author, June 9, 1993.
39 Ambassador Armin Meyer, ADST oral history interview, 1989.
40 Ambassador William Brewer, ADST oral history interview, August 2, 1988.
41 Ambassador William Brewer, ADST oral history interview, August 2, 1988; and Ambassador Armin Meyer, ADST oral history interview, 1989.
42 Ambassador Armin Meyer, ADST oral history interview, part one, 1989.
43 Assistant Secretary Phillips Talbot, JFK Library oral history, quoted in Parmet, *JFK*, 226. Ambassador Armin Meyer, ADST interview, part one, 1989.
44 "Memorandum from the President's Deputy Special Counsel (Feldman) to President Kennedy," May 26, 1961, *FRUS Near East 1961–63*, 130. Ambassador Hermann F. Eilts, interview with the author, Boston, Mass., March 11, 1993.

NOTES 217

45 "Memorandum from Acting Secretary of States Bowles to President Kennedy," [drafted by Meyer], April 28, 1961, *FRUS Near East 1961–63*, 91–92 and note.
46 Parmet, *JFK*, 226. Ambassador Armin H. Meyer, ADST oral history interview, 1989.
47 Ambassador William R. Crawford, ADST oral history interview, October 24, 1988. Rusk, *As I Saw It*, 125.
48 Ambassador William R. Crawford, letter to the author, March 1, 1996; and interview with the author, June 10, 1993.
49 Ambassador William R. Crawford, interview with the author, June 10, 1993.
50 United National Resolution 194, quoted by Joseph Johnson, in "Arab vs. Israeli: A Persistent Challenge to Americans," *Middle East Journal* 18, no. 1 (1964,): 1–13.
51 "Memorandum for the President, Dean Rusk, Dr. Joseph Johnson's Proposals on the Palestine Refugee Problem," August 7, 1962, drafted by W. R. Crawford, John F. Kennedy Presidential Library, (hereafter JFK Library) Boston, Massachusetts, declassified February 13, 1996, from National Security Files; Countries: Israel, General 9/6/62–9/5/62, Box 118.
52 "The Johnson Plan: Considerations for the United States," drafted by W. R. Crawford, 1. JFK Library, Boston, Massachusetts, declassified February 13, 1996, National Security Files; Countries: Israel, General 9/6/62–9/5/62, Box 118.
53 "The Johnson Plan: Considerations for the United States," drafted by William Crawford, 5–7, John F. Kennedy Presidential Library, Boston, Massachusetts, National Security Files; Countries: Israel, General 9/6/62–9/5/62, Box 118.
54 "The Johnson Plan: Considerations for the United States," drafted by William Crawford, 5–7, John F. Kennedy Presidential Library, Boston, Massachusetts, National Security Files; Countries: Israel, General 9/6/62–9/5/62, Box 118.
55 "The Johnson Plan: Considerations for the United States," drafted by W. R. Crawford, 5–7, JFK Library, Boston, Massachusetts, National Security Files; Countries: Israel, General 9/6/62–9/5/62, Box 118.
56 Rusk, *As I Saw It*, 383.
57 Ambassador William R. Crawford, ADST interview, October 24, 1988.
58 The original plan was still classified in 1978: Parmet, *JFK*, 234. A 1994 request by the author to the JFK library yielded multiple copies, some classified and some declassified, but not the original. A complete copy was declassified for the author in 1996. Mary M. Kennefick, archivist, JFK Library located "The Johnson Plan" [copy] in the National Security Files: Countries: Israel, General."
59 Ambassador William R. Crawford, interview with the author, Washington, DC, June 10, 1993. Inquiries to the JFK Library resulted in the location of four copies, none bearing the note: Suzanne K. Forbes, Archivist JFK Library to the author December 29, 1994.
60 Spiegel, *The Other Arab–Israeli Conflict*, 110–117, quote 447.
61 "Memorandum from Robert W. Komer of the NSC Staff to the President's Special Assistant for National Security Affairs, [McGeorge] Bundy," September 14, 1962, 96–97.
62 Parmet, *JFK*, 233.
63 Parmet, *JFK*, 252–53.
64 Parmet, *JFK*, 233, 252–53. Gazit, *President Kennedy's Policy*, 40, 42.
65 Parmet, *JFK*, on Johnson plan 226–235, quotes 233–35. Rusk, *As I Saw It*, 382–83.
66 Ambassador Armin H. Meyer, ADST oral history interview, Washington, DC, 1989. Joseph E. Johnson, "Arab vs. Israeli: A Persistent Challenge to Americans," *The Middle East Journal* 18, no. 1 (winter 1964): 1–13.
67 Ambassador Armin Meyer, ADST oral history interview, Washington, DC, April 1990.
68 Ambassador Armin Meyer, ADST oral history interview, Washington, DC, April 1990.
69 Ambassador William R. Crawford Jr, interview with the author, Washington, DC, June 10, 1993. Ambassador Armin H. Meyer, ADST oral history interview, Washington, DC, April 1990.
70 "Memorandum from Robert W. Komer of the National Security Council Staff to President Kennedy," Foreign Relations of the United States, Near East 1962–63, December 22, 1962, 272.

71 Avner Cohen, "Most Favored Nation," *Bulletin of the Atomic Scientists* 51, no. 1 (January/February 1995): 52. "Memo of Conversation with Israel Foreign Minister Meir," December 27, 1962, *FRUS Near East 1962–63*, 276–83.
72 Ambassador Curtis F. Jones, ADST oral history interview, March 29, 1994.
73 Ambassador William R. Crawford, interview with the author, Washington, DC, June 10, 1993. Joseph Kraft, "Those Arabists in the State Department," *New York Times Magazine*, November 7, 1971, 82.
74 Ambassador Lucius Battle, ADST oral history interview, July 10, 1991.
75 Ambassador Lucius D. Battle, ADST oral history interview, July 10, 1991.
76 Ambassador Lucius D. Battle, ADST oral history interview, July 10, 1991.
77 Heikal, *The Cairo Documents*, 229.
78 Heikal, *The Cairo Documents*, 229. For Parker's analysis, see *The Politics of Miscalculation*, 104–106.
79 "US Embassy Cairo telegram #5030 to Department of State March 4, 1967, Lucius Battle," text in Parker, *Political Miscalculations*, Document 13, 242–244. Ambassador Lucius Battle, ADST oral history interview, Washington, DC, July 10, 1991.
80 Dayton Mak, "Some Syrian Arabic Proverbs," *Journal of the American Oriental Society* 69, no. 4 (1949): 223–38. Ambassador Richard B. Parker, ADST oral history interview, April 21, 1989.
81 For Kerr quote, see Parker, *Political Miscalculations*, 100. Ambassador William D. Brewer, ADST oral history, Washington, DC, August 2, 1988.
82 Ambassador Lucius Battle, ADST oral history interview, July 10, 1991.
83 "Richard Parker Am Embassy Cairo, to Sec State Washington," May 25, 1967, reprinted Robert H. Miller, *Inside an Embassy: The Political Role of Diplomats Abroad* (Washington: Congressional Quarterly, 1992), 121–122.
84 "Richard Nolte, AmEmbassy Cairo, to Sec State Washington," May 27, 1967, text in Miller, *Inside an Embassy*, 123–24.
85 Parker, *The Politics of Miscalculation*, 107.
86 Ambassador Richard B. Parker, ADST oral history interview, April 21, 1989.
87 Eban, *Abba Eban: An Autobiography* (New York: Random House, 1977), 111. Fortas quote in Quandt, *Peace Process*, 47.
88 Ship's position 31–35.5 north and 33–29 East; James Ennes, *Assault on the Liberty: The True Story of the Israeli Attack on an American Intelligence Ship* (New York: Random House, 1979), Appendix F, 310. Ambassador Harrison Symmes, ADST oral history interview, February 25, 1989. "Ambassador Walworth Barbour, AmEmbassy Tel Aviv, to Sec State Washington," June 7, 1967, LBJ National Security Microfilm, #00082.
89 Johnson quoted in George Lenczowski, *American Presidents and the Middle East*, 110–12. Ennes, *Attack on the Liberty*, 346–50, 3. For the debate over Israeli intentions, see A. Jay Cristol, *The Liberty Incident: The 1967 Israeli Attack on the US Navy Spy Ship* (Washington: Brassey's, 2002).
90 Rusk, *As I Saw It*, 388.
91 Rusk, *As I Saw It*, 388. For Rusk and Israeli government notes, see Ennes, *Assault on the Liberty*, 356–59.
92 Parker, *Politics of Miscalculation in the Middle East*.
93 "Memcon John F. Kennedy and Golda Meir," December 27, 1962, Gazit, *President Kennedy's Policy Toward the Arab States and Israel*, 112–13. Merle Miller, *Lyndon: An Oral Biography* (New York: Putnam, 1980), 476.
94 "Memorandum Hal Saunders to WWR [Walt Whitman Rostow]," July 24, 1968 with appended, "62% in Poll Expect an Arab-Israel War in 5 Years," *New York Times*, July 24, 1968, Lyndon B. Johnson National Security Files, The Middle East National Security Files, 1963–69, ed. G. C. Herring, [hereafter LBJ Files], reel 7, #00364–5. Harris Poll in Graham T. Allison, "Cool It: The Foreign Policy of Young America," *Foreign Policy* 1 (1970–71): 144–60, 144.
95 Quandt, *Peace Process*, 38. George Ball, "How to Save Israel in Spite of Herself," *Foreign Affairs* 55, no. 3 (1977): 453–71; and "How to Avert a Middle East War," *Atlantic Monthly*, January 1975, 6–11.

96 "Memorandum Hall Saunders to WWR [Walt Whitman Rostow], July 24, 1968 with appended, "62% in Poll Expect an Arab-Israel War in 5 Years," *New York Times*, July 24, 1968.
97 "Dixon Donnelley to the Secretary," [copy bears typed address "Mr. Walt W. Rostow"] June 8, 1967, "Public Mail on the Arab-Israeli Crisis, Information Memorandum," LBJ Microfilm, Reel #1, 00433.
98 "Dixon Donnelley to the Secretary," [address "Mr. Walt W. Rostow"] June 8, 1967; "Public Mail on the Arab-Israeli Crisis, Information Memorandum," LBJ Microfilm, Reel #1, 00431; Benjamin H. Read, Executive Secretary, "Memorandum for Mr. Walt W. Rostow: Public Mail on the Arab–Israeli Crisis addressed to Secretary of State," June 8, 1967, LBJ Microfilm, reel #1, 00430.
99 Lenczowski, *American Presidents*, 114.
100 Ambassador Walworth Barbour, AmEmbassy Tel Aviv to Sec State Washington, June 7, 1967, LBJ Presidential Library, LBJ National Security Microfilm, reel 1, #00091–00092.
101 The identity of the Israeli informant was sanitized. "Ambassador Walworth Barbour, AmEmbassy Tel Aviv, to Sec State Washington," June 7, 1967, LBJ National Security Microfilm, #00091–00092.
102 "Ambassador Walworth Barbour, AmEmbassy Tel Aviv, to Sec State Washington," June 6, 1967, #3971 LBJ National Security Microfilm, #00091–00092 and #00097.
103 "Secretary of State Dean Rusk to Walworth Barbour, AmEmbassy Tel Aviv," June 7, 1967, LBJ Microfilm, #00102. To Tel Aviv, Ref Amman #4095, "sent DX to Ben Read, receipted for June 6 8:30 a.m. AJO," LBJ Microfilm, #00128. Ambassador Richard W. Murphy, interview with the author, New York, February 23, 1995.
104 Ambassador Hermann Eilts, Jidda to Secretary of State," June 6, 1967, LBJ microfilm, #00184–00185; and Secretary State Rusk, June 7, 1967, "Circular all Posts," State #209202, LBJ NS Microfilm.
105 Hal Saunders, "Memorandum for McGB [McGeorge Bundy] Subject: The Agenda and Status of Work," June 7, 1967, LBJ microfilm, #00531.
106 John P. Roche, "Eyes only memorandum for the President," copy to Walt Rostow, June 6, 1967, LBJ microfilm, #00571 (emphasis in original).
107 Congressional Quarterly, *The Middle East*, seventh edition, 1990, 22.
108 Eban, *Abba Eban*, 443.
109 Quote in Eban, *Abba Eban: An Autobiography*, 443. LBJ's comment also quoted by Eugene Rostow in *The Middle Eastern Crisis and Beyond*, USIS *Byliner*, #F068–7, January 1968, vertical files, Middle East Institute, Washington, DC, accessed 1994. It was first made by Goldberg on June 4, repeated by LBJ on June 19; text in Lenczowski, *US Interests in the Middle East* (Washington: American Enterprise Institute for Public Policy Research, October 1968), 119–20.
110 Eban, *Abba Eban*, 443–44.
111 Eban, in Caradon, Goldberg, El-Zayyat, Eban, *UN Security Council Resolution 242: A Case Study in Diplomatic Ambiguity* (Institute for the Study of Diplomacy, 1981), 43.
112 Eban, *Abba Eban*, 450–52.
113 Richard N. Curtiss, *A Changing Image American Perceptions of the Arab–Israeli Dispute* (Washington: American Educational Trust, 1986), 105; Eban, *Abba Eban*, 452.
114 Edward M. Stack, *Reading French in the Arts and Sciences* (Boston: Houghton, Mifflin, 1987), 16.
115 Arthur Goldberg in *UN Security Council Resolution 242: A Case Study in Diplomatic Ambiguity*, 13, 22–23, 32. Text of Resolution 242 [UN Security Council doc S/RES/242 (1967) (S/8247) November 22, 1967, in Congressional Quarterly, *The Middle East*, seventh edition, 1990, 301. Curtiss, *A Changing Image*, 105.
116 Eban, *Abba Eban*, 453.
117 Parker, *Political Miscalculations*, 128.
118 Eban, *Abba Eban*, 360.
119 Rusk, *As I Saw It*, 380–81; Parker, *Political Miscalculations*, 128–30. In retirement Parker organized a twenty-fifth anniversary meeting of participants to set the record straight. Richard B. Parker, ed., *The Six Day War, A Retrospective* (Gainesville: University Press of Florida, 1996).

7. Kissinger's Arabesque: The Nixon and Ford Years

1. Robert Kaplan, *The Arabists: Romance of an American Elite*, first edition (New York: Free Press, 1993,), 9.
2. On the Nixon–Kissinger control of foreign policy, see Joan Hoff, "A Revisionist's View of Nixon's Foreign Policy," *Presidential Studies Quarterly* 26, no. 1 (1996): 107–29. For the Kissinger stalemate policy and its impact, see Vanetik Boaz and Zaki Shalom, "The White House Middle East Policy in 1973 as a Catalyst for the Outbreak of the Yom Kippur War," *Israel Studies* 16, no. 1 (2011): 53–78; and their book length study *The Nixon Administration and the Middle East Peace Process, 1969–1973: From the Rogers Plan to the Outbreak of the Yom Kippur War* (London: Sussex Academic Press, 2013), 228–31, 259.
3. "Memorandum of Discussion at the 352nd Meeting of the NSC," January 22, 1958, *Foreign Relations of the US, 1958–60* (hereafter *FRUS*), volume XIII, 10–11.
4. "Memorandum of a Conversation, Vice President Nixon's Residence, Washington," March 13, 1960, *FRUS 1958–60*, volume XIII, 295.
5. Warren Weaver, Jr., "Nixon Reserved on Middle East," *New York Times*, June 1, 1967, 17.
6. Ambassador George M. Lane, interview with the author, fall 1995.
7. *New York Times*, June 7, 1967, 21; and June 22, 1967, 3.
8. The Time–Louis Harris Poll of May 2, 1969, asked if Thailand, Italy, West Berlin or Israel were attacked, would the respondent favor sending US troops? Thailand 25 percent, Italy 27 percent, West Berlin 26 percent and Israel 9 percent in Graham Allison, "Cool It: The Foreign Policy of Young America," *Foreign Policy*, no.1 (1970–71): 144–160.
9. Richard Nixon, *RN: The Memoirs of Richard Nixon* (New York: Grossett and Dunlop, 1978), 477.
10. Seymour M. Hersh, *The Price of Power: Kissinger in the Nixon White House* (New York: Summit Books, 1983), 234.
11. Stephen Ambrose, *Nixon* (New York: Simon and Schuster, 1987), voting figures 617. Hersh, *The Price of Power*, 214; Henry Kissinger, *White House Years* (Boston: Little Brown, 1979), 370. For examples of Nixon comments from the tapes, see <millercenter.org/presidentialrecordings/rmn–524–027 and George Lardner Jr and Michael Dobbs, "New Tapes Reveal Depth of Nixon's Anti-Semitism," *Washington Post*, October 6, 1999, A31.
12. Hersh, *The Price of Power*, 13, 27. Joseph Kraft, "In Search of Kissinger," *Harper's*, January 1971, 54–61 and 57–58.
13. Kissinger, *Diplomacy* (New York: Simon and Schuster, 1994), 740; Kissinger, *White House Years*, 370.
14. Congressional Quarterly, *The Middle East*, 7th ed. (Washington: Congressional Quarterly, 1990), 54–55. On Congress, see American Israeli Public Affairs Committee (AIPAC) *Near East Report*, October 27, 1976; John L. Moore et al., "The Israel Lobby," *The Washington Lobby* (Washington: Congressional Quarterly, 1979), 141–143.
15. D. Ottaway, "Mideast Institute's Experts and Ideas Ascendant," *Washington Post*, March 23, 1989; "Clinton's Indyk Appointment One of Many from Pro-Israel Think Tank," *Washington Report on Middle East Affairs*, March 1993, 10. John J. Mearsheimer and Stephen M. Walt, *The Israel Lobby and US Foreign Policy* (New York: Farrar, Straus and Giroux, 2007).
16. Undersecretary of State Joseph Sisco, ADST oral history interview, March 19, 1990 in Frontline Diplomacy, The Foreign Affairs Oral History Collection of the Association for Diplomatic Studies and Training, Arlington, Virginia and Lauinger Library, Georgetown University, Washington, DC; also online www.adst.org [hereafter ADST interview].
17. Cook, "A New Administration Takes Shape," *Time*, December 20, 1968. Hersh, *The Price of Power*, 32–33.
18. John Ehrlichman, *Witness to Power: The Nixon Years* (New York: Simon and Schuster, 1982), 271; Hersh, *The Price of Power*, 409; Kissinger, *White House Years*, 31.
19. Nixon, *RN*, 433.

20 Undersecretary Joseph J. Sisco, ADST oral history interview, March 19, 1990. *The Biographic Register of the US Department of State* (Washington: Government Printing Office, 1974), 318.
21 Undersecretary of State Joseph Sisco, ADST oral history interview, March 19, 1990.
22 Kissinger, *White House Years*, 341; Undersecretary of State Joseph Sisco, ADST oral history interview, March 19, 1990.
23 Joseph J. Sisco, *Middle East Negotiations: A Conversation with Joseph Sisco, with Basic Documents* (Washington: American Enterprise Institute for Public Policy Research, 1980), 31–32.
24 Nixon, *RN*, 340; *American Heritage Dictionary of the English Language* (New York: Dell, 1970), 66.
25 Walter Isaacson, *Kissinger: A Biography* (New York: Simon and Schuster, 1992), 763.
26 Robert Schulzinger, *Henry Kissinger: Doctor of Diplomacy* (New York: Columbia University Press, 1989), 207–10; Roger Morris, *Uncertain Greatness: Henry Kissinger and American Foreign Policy* (New York: Harper and Row, 1977), 277–78, 293.
27 U. Alexis Johnson, "Caught in the Nutcracker," *Foreign Service Journal*, September 1984. William Rogers refused to write a memoir and did not respond to the author's request for an interview. Halperin and Morris quote in Hersh, *The Price of Power*, 29–36.
28 Morton Halperin, *Bureaucratic Politics* (Washington: Brookings Institution, 1974), 158–166, 179, 225–27.
29 Porter quoted in Hersh, *The Price of Power*, 42–44.
30 Ambassador Nicholas A. Veliotes, ADST oral history interview, Washington, DC, January 29 and May 1, 1990.
31 Anatoly Dobrynin, *In Confidence Moscow's Ambassador to America's Six Cold War Presidents* (New York: Times Books, 1995), 235–36, 204–05.
32 Kissinger, *White House Years*, 183, 660; Isaacson, *Kissinger*, 205. Edward Peck, ADST oral history interview, June 29, 1989. Gerald and Deborah Strober, *Nixon: An Oral History of His Presidency* (New York: Harper Collins, 1994), 82.
33 Kissinger, *White House Years*, 26; Isaacson, *Kissinger*, 197; Johnson, "Caught in the Nutcracker," 29; John Ehrlichman, *Witness to Power*, 291.
34 Kissinger, *White House Years*, 28; *Years of Upheaval*, 442–43; Richard Valeriani, *Travels with Henry* (Boston: Houghton Mifflin, 1979), 352.
35 "Super K's Mideast Triumph," in same issue as "We Are Going to Survive" on Nixon and impeachment, *Newsweek*, June 10, 1974.
36 For details of the negotiations, see Richard Parker, *The Politics of Miscalculation in the Middle East*, Bloomington: Indiana University Press, 1993, 130–45; and Steven Spiegel, *The Other Arab–Israeli Conflict* (Chicago: University of Chicago Press, 1985), 206–8.
37 "Symington Hits Kissinger Role as the 'Real' Secretary of State," *Washington Post*, March 3, 1971; "Symington Cools Dispute on Rogers, Kissinger Roles," *Washington Post*, March 6, 1971; "It's Rogers, Not Kissinger in Top Spot, Nixon Asserts," *Milwaukee Journal*, March 3, 1971.
38 Ambassador Edward Peck, ADST oral history interview, Washington, DC, interview one, June 29, 1989.
39 Ambassador Parker T. Hart, ADST oral history interview, January 27, 1989.
40 Comment was made in summer 1970 while Rogers and Sisco worked on a cease-fire in the War of Attrition, quoted in Hersh, *Price of Power*, 228.
41 Joseph Kraft, "Those Arabists in the State Department," *New York Times Magazine*, November 7, 1971, 89; Ambassador Hermann Eilts, interview with the author, Boston, Massachusetts, March 11, 1993; Isaacson, *Kissinger*, 304; Hersh, *The Price of Power*, 412.
42 Kraft, "Those Arabists," *New York Times Magazine*.
43 Ambassador Richard B. Parker, ADST oral history interview, April 21, 1989, and letter to the author April 28, 1994; Kaplan, *The Arabists*, 152–156.
44 Ambassador Andrew I. Killgore, interview with the author, Washington, DC, June 6, 1992.
45 Isaacson, *Kissinger*, 512; and Kissinger, *Years of Upheaval*, 224–25. Joseph Nathaniel Greene Jr. (born 1920) *is not to be confused with* Joseph Coy Green who served Dulles in Jordan. Michael Michaud, "Confessions of a GLOPee," *Foreign Service Journal* 54 (1977): 5–7.

46 Kissinger, *White House Years*, 340; and *A World Restored*, 322.
47 Undersecretary of State Joseph Sisco, ADST oral history interview, March 19, 1990.
48 Lenczowski, *American Presidents and the Middle East*, 120. Andrew Carveley, *US–UAR Diplomatic Relations and Zionist Pressures* (St. Louis, MO: DH-TE International, 1969), 6.
49 Kissinger, *White House Years*, 50–51.
50 Mission Impossible Scranton's Fact Finding tour of the Middle East, *Newsweek*, December 23, 1968, 36.
51 Kissinger, *White House Years*, 51.
52 Kissinger, *White House Years*, 50–51; *Newsweek*, December 23, 1968. Rogers, *A Lasting Peace in the Middle East*. Ambassador Hermann F. Eilts, interview with the author, Boston, Massachusetts, March 11, 1993.
53 "His Own Man Politically: William Warren Scranton," *New York Times*, December 14, 1968; and "Scranton Urges Policy in Mideast by 'Evenhanded,'" *New York Times*, December 10, 1968 and December 11, 1968.
54 "Scranton Urges Policy in Mideast be 'Evenhanded,'" *New York Times*, December 10, 1968.
55 "Lakeside Speech at the Bohemian Grove," in Nixon, *RN*, 284.
56 "Scranton Speaks in Rome," *New York Times*, December 12, 1968.
57 "William Rogers Nominated," *New York Times*, December 11, 1968; Rogers, *A Lasting Peace in the Middle East*.
58 Rogers's address, quoted Abba Eban, *Abba Eban: An Autobiography* (New York: Random House, 1977), 452.
59 Kissinger, *White House Years*, 1279.
60 George Lenczowski, *American Presidents and the Middle East* (Durham, NC: Duke University Press, 1990), 120. William P. Rogers, *A Lasting Peace in the Middle East: An American View*, Department of State publication #8507, 1970. Emphasis in Rogers's quotation.
61 Richard H. Curtiss, *A Changing Image American Perceptions of the Arab–Israeli Dispute* (Washington: American Educational Trust, 1986), 107.
62 William Quandt, *Decade of Decision: American Policy toward the Arab–Israeli Conflict 1967–76*, (Berkeley, CA: University of California Press, 1977), 84.
63 Quandt, *Decade of Decision*, 89–91. Quandt summarizes the text from a retranslation of the Arabic, noting "the exact English text of the Oct. 29 document has not been publicly released."
64 Ambassador Hermann F. Eilts, interview with the author, Boston, Massachusetts, March 11, 1993.
65 "Secretary Rogers' News Conference of March 23, 1970," Department of State press release #100, 11.
66 Richard Parker, *Politics of Miscalculation in the Middle East* (Bloomington: Indiana University Press, 1993), 137–146; Hersh, *The Price of Power*, 225.
67 Kissinger, *A World Restored*, 144–45 [emphasis in original].
68 Parker, *The Politics of Miscalculation*, 133.
69 Ambassador Richard B. Parker, interview with the author, Washington, DC, June 11, 1993. Ambassador Michael Sterner, ADST oral history interview, Washington, DC, March 2, 1990.
70 Ambassador Michael Sterner, ADST oral history interview, March 2, 1990; Quandt, *Decade of Decisions*, 26, 74–75; Ambassador Talcott Seelye, ADST oral history interview, September 15, 1993; Nixon, *RN*, 479.
71 Quandt, *Decades of Decision*, 77.
72 Undersecretary Sisco, ADST oral history interview, March 9, 1990; David Korn, "US–Soviet Negotiations of 1969 and the Rogers Plan," *Middle East Journal* 44, no. 1 (1990): 47; William P. Rogers, "A Lasting Peace in the Middle East: An American View," address to the Galaxy Conference, Dec 9, 1969, Department of State publication #8507, January 1970.
73 Korn, "Rogers Plan," 48.
74 Edward Tivnan, *The Lobby Jewish Political Power and American Foreign Policy* (New York: Simon and Schuster, 1987), 71–72; Quandt, *Decade of Decision*, 91–92.

75 Ambassador Talcott Seelye, ADST oral history interview, September 15, 1993.
76 Parker, *The Politics of Miscalculation*, 138–39.
77 Kissinger, *White House Years*, 561. Michael Sterner, quoted in Joseph Kraft, "Letter From Cairo," *The New Yorker*, September 18, 1971, 100.
78 "Sadat: 'We Are Now Back to Square One,'" interview with Arnaud de Borchgrave, *Newsweek*, (December 13, 1971): 43–47.
79 Robert Stookey, *America and the Arab States: An Uneasy Encounter* (New York: Wiley, 1975), 227.
80 Ambassador Harrison M. Symmes, ADST oral history interview, February 25, 1989. Ambassador Seelye, ADST oral history interview, September 15, 1993.
81 Ambassador Harrison M. Symmes, ADST oral history interview, February 25, 1989.
82 Kissinger, *White House Years*, 596.
83 Kissinger, *White House Years*, 596–98.
84 Ambassador L. Dean Brown, ADST oral history interview, Washington, DC.
85 Kai Bird, son of an American diplomat and friend of one hostage, has written a personal memoir of the Jordan crisis in chapter seven, *Crossing Mandelbaum Gate: Coming of Age between the Arabs and Israelis, 1956–1978*, (New York: Scribners, 2010).
86 Ambassador Talcott Seelye, ADST oral history interview, September 15, 1993.
87 Ambassador Talcott Seelye, ADST oral history interview, September 15, 1993.
88 Kissinger, *White House Years*, 601.
89 David Korn, *Assassination in Khartoum* (Bloomington: Indiana University Press, 1993), 110.
90 Kissinger, *White House Years*, 601; Hersh, *The Price of Power*, 237; David Korn, *Assassination in Khartoum* (Bloomington: Indiana University Press, 1993), 110–11, 121.
91 Ambassador Talcott Seelye, ADST oral history interview, September 15, 1993.
92 Ambassador Talcott Seelye, ADST oral history interview, September 15, 1993; Kissinger, *White House Years*, 622–26; Nixon, *RN*, 484–85.
93 Kissinger, *White House Years*, 629.
94 Patrick Seale, *Asad of Syria: The Struggle for the Middle East* (Berkeley: University of California Press, 1989), 160.
95 Kissinger, *White House Years*, 629, 631.
96 Ambassador Talcott Seelye, ADST oral history interview, September 15, 1993. Stookey, *America and the Arab States*, 232.
97 Foreign Service officer Curtis F. Jones, ADST oral history interview, March 29, 1994.
98 Kissinger, *White House Years*, 1279, 1289.
99 Quandt, *Decade of Decisions*, 143; Sadat quoted in Tivnan, *The Lobby*, 75–76.
100 Congressional Research Service, "Oil Fields as Military Objectives: A Feasibility Study: proposed for the Special Subcommittee on investigations of the Committee on International Relations," (Washington: Government Printing Office, 1975), 23; Undersecretary Sisco, ADST oral history interview, March 19, 1990.
101 *Department of State Bulletin*, April 19, 1976, 528; quote in Stephen L. Spiegel, *The Other Arab–Israeli Conflict: Making America's Middle East Policy from Truman to Reagan* (Chicago: University of Chicago Press, 1985), 306–7; Tivnan, *The Lobby*, 75–76.
102 Hersh, *The Price of Power*, 404.
103 Ambassador Michael Sterner, ADST oral history interview, March 2, 1990.
104 John Ehrlichman, *Witness to Power* (New York: Simon and Schuster, 1975), 269, 270–72 (emphasis in original).
105 John Ehrlichmann, *Witness to Power* (New York: Simon & Schuster, 1975), 270.
106 Kissinger, *White House Years*, 1282; Hersh, *The Price of Power*, 408–9.
107 Ambassador Michael Sterner, ADST oral history interview, March 2, 1990.
108 For a full account of the Bergus "Phantom Memorandum," see Hersh, 409–11; and Sterner's ADST interview. Kissinger, *White House Years*, 1283–84; Spiegel, *The Other Arab Israeli Conflict*, 207–8. Note there were two Riads in the Egyptian foreign ministry: Mahmoud and Mohammad.

109 Joseph Kraft, "The Phantom Memorandum," Washington *Post*, June 27, 1971; "The Phantom Smile," *Newsweek*, December 17, 1971.
110 Kissinger, *White House Years*, 1283.
111 Ambassador Michael Sterner, ADST oral history interview, March 2, 1990. Kraft, "The Phantom Memorandum," *Washington Post*, June 27, 1971; "Letter from Cairo," *The New Yorker*, September 18, 1971; Quandt, *Peace Process*, 130.
112 Kraft, "Letter from Cairo," *The New Yorker*, Sept 18, 1971; and "In Search of Kissinger," *Harper's*, (January 1971): 54; Ambassador Michael Sterner, ADST oral history interview, March 2, 1990.61; Richard Valeriani, *Travels with Henry*.
113 Isaacson, *Kissinger*, 228, 358, 500–01. Kraft, "Letter from Cairo," *The New Yorker*, September 18, 1971, 76, 81–100; and "Those Arabists," *New York Times Magazine*, November 7, 1971.
114 Rowland Evans and Robert Novak, "New Pressure on Israelis," *Washington Post*, March 3, 1971; Isaacson, *Kissinger*, 228, 358, 500–01. NSC aide Roger Morris observed Kissinger was "the best single source" for journalists in the Nixon years, quote in Roger Morris, *Uncertain Greatness: Henry Kissinger and American Foreign Policy* (New York: Harper and Row, 1977), 195.
115 Ambassador Michael Sterner, ADST oral history interview, March 2, 1990.
116 Ambassador George M. Lane, interview with the author, Worcester, Massachusetts, October 26, 1993.
117 On NSC staff comments, see Hersh, *The Price of Power*, 412. Quandt, *Peace Process*, 132.
118 David Schoenbaum, *The United States and the State of Israel* (New York: Oxford University Press, 1993), 186.
119 Schoenbaum, *The US and the State of Israel*, 187–88.
120 Eban, *Autobiography*, 487.
121 Eban, *Autobiography*, 487–88.
122 Eban, *Abba Eban*, 487–89, 495.
123 Korn, *Assassination in Khartoum*, 248–49; and Eban, *Abba Eban*, 491.
124 Korn, *Assassination in Khartoum*, 166.
125 "Transcript of President's News Conference on Foreign and Domestic Matters," *New York Times*, March 3, 1973, 12, (dateline March 2).
126 Ambassador Talcott Seelye interview with the author, Plainfield, Massachusetts, August 8, 1994. Korn, *Assassination in Khartoum*, 151, 177.
127 The White House demanded the State Department draft a "no negotiations, no-concessions" policy, which the State Department personnel realized was in contravention of other US policies (the FBI puts negotiation at a premium in domestic cases). Korn realized it "declared forfeit the lives of American diplomats," Korn, *Assassination in Khartoum*, 111, 121, 178.
128 Unsigned *New York Times* editorial, March 3, 1973, 30.
129 FSO Lee F. Dinsmore, "Communication RE: The Near East to the Secretary," *Foreign Service Journal*, September 1973, 26.
130 Kissinger, *Years of Upheaval*, 227, 462.
131 Isaacson, *Kissinger*, 502–3, Kissinger quotation, 504. Morris, *Uncertain Greatness*, 2.
132 Kissinger, *Years of Upheaval*, chapter ten, and quotation, 471.
133 Ambassador Nicholas Veliotes, ADST oral history interview, September 17, 1991.
134 Ambassador Nicholas Veliotes, ADST oral history interviews, June 25, November 20, 1990, September 17, 1991.
135 Undersecretary George Ball commented: "He [Seelye] had the wisdom and temerity to send a cable to our then Secretary of State, Henry Kissinger, imploring him not to send arms," Ball, ADC Arabists Panel, (video), April 16, 1994.
136 Howard Sachar, *A History of Israel* (New York: Knopf, 1976), 786–87.
137 See *Oil Fields as US Objectives: A Feasibility Study*, August 21, 1975; and Stookey, *America and the Arab States*, 253.
138 Dinsmore testimony in *US Interests in and Policy Toward the Persian Gulf*, House Committee on Foreign Affairs, Subcommittee on the Near East, 92nd Congress (Washington: Government Printing Office, 1972), August 15, 1972.

139 "Don't Blame the Oil Companies: Blame the State Department," *Forbes Magazine*, April 15, 1976; Congressional Quarterly, *The Middle East*, seventh edition, 108.
140 James Akins, "The Oil Crisis: This Time the Wolf is Here," *Foreign Affairs* 51, no. 3 (April 1973): 462–90, quotation 490.
141 Kissinger, *Years of Upheaval*, 623–25.
142 Kissinger quotation, *Business Week*, December 23, 1974; and the *US Department of State Bulletin*, January 27, 1975.
143 "Oil Fields as Military Objectives: A Feasibility Study," prepared for the Special Subcommittee on Investigations, August 21, 1975, 76.
144 Gerald R. Ford, *A Time to Heal: The Autobiography of Gerald R. Ford* (New York: Harper and Row, 1979), 325–26. Kissinger, *Years of Upheaval*, 435–36.
145 Ford, *A Time to Heal*, 286.
146 Ford, *A Time to Heal*, 246–47.
147 Ford, *A Time to Heal*, 245–48.
148 Lenczowski, *American Presidents*, 149–51.
149 Ford, *A Time to Heal*, 247, 286–7, and Ambassador Hermann F. Eilts, ADST oral history interview, August 1 and 13, 1988.
150 Ambassador Richard W. Murphy, interview with the author, New York, NY, February 23, 1995.
151 Ambassador Hermann F. Eilts, interview with the author, Boston, Massachusetts, March 11, 1993. Morris, *Uncertain Greatness*, 263.
152 Ford, *A Time to Heal*, 287–92.
153 Ambassador Hermann F. Eilts, ADST oral history interview, August, 1988. When State published the documents in *The Quest for Peace*, 1983, they omitted the Memoranda of Agreement, see *Journal of Palestine Studies* 13, no. 3(1984): 139. Quandt describes the text leaked to the *New York Times* September 17, 1975: "A special memo dealing with Geneva [...] with respect to the Palestinians: no recognition of and no negotiation with the PLO until the PLO recognizes Israel's right to exist and accepts UN Resolutions 242 and 338." Quandt, *Decade of Decisions*, 274–75.
154 In the quotation Malcolm Kerr combined a reference to the impact of Graham Greene's *The Quiet American* with Arnold Toynbee's *The Western Question*, 1972 Presidential Address, Middle East Studies Association, *MESA Bulletin*, February 1, 1973.
155 "US Envoy Crosses Beirut Line," *New York Times*, November 6, 1976, 3. Quotation in Ambassador George M. Lane, ADST oral history interview, August 27, 1990.
156 "Excerpts from Secretary Kissinger's Address," *Foreign Service Journal*, March 1977, 4–5.

Epilogue: Beirut Axioms; Lessons Learned by the Middle East Hands

1 For a detailed discussion of the Kissinger stalemate policy and its impact, see Vanetik Boaz and Zaki Shalom, "The White House Middle East Policy in 1973 as a Catalyst for the Outbreak of the Yom Kippur War," *Israel Studies* 16, no. 1 (2011): 53–78; and their book-length study *The Nixon Administration and the Middle East Peace Process, 1969–1973: From the Rogers Plan to the Outbreak of the Yom Kippur War* (London: Sussex Academic Press, 2013), especially 228–31, 259. Quotations from Henry Kissinger, *White House Years* (Boston: Little Brown, 1979), 379; and Kissinger, *Diplomacy* (New York: Simon & Schuster, 1994), 737.
2 James Akins, "Saudi Arabia, Soviet Activities and Gulf Security" and "The Impact of the Iranian Events upon Persian Gulf and United States Security," in *American Foreign Policy Institute Studies*, ed. Z. M. Szaz (Washington, DC: American Foreign Policy Institute, 1979), 10; and "The Arabists," panel discussion James Akins, Andrew Killgore, Talcott Seelye, Arab-American Anti-Discrimination Committee convention, April 16, 1994 [VHS].

3 Emphasis in original. For Kissinger on Four Power talks, see Kissinger, *White House Years*, 354. For "stonewalled" quotation, see Henry Kissinger, *Years of Upheaval* (Boston: Little Brown, 1982), 207. Kissinger, *Diplomacy*, 740.
4 Malcolm Kerr, *The Elusive Peace in the Middle East* (Albany: State University of New York Press, 1975), 5–8.
5 Congressional Quarterly, *The Middle East*, 7th ed. (Washington: Congressional Quarterly, 1990), 65.
6 Michael Sterner, "Managing US–Israeli Relations," *American-Arab Affairs* 6 (1983): 16–17 and "For US–Palestinian Talks: Even if Israel is Dissatisfied," *New York Times*, July 31, 1985; Hermann Eilts, "It's Time to Talk to the PLO," in *Facing the PLO Question*, ed. Meir Merhav, Philip Klutznick and Hermann Eilts (Washington: Foundation for Middle East Peace, 1985); Richard Murphy, "A Departing Envoy's Grim Afghan View," *New York Times*, January 30, 1989.
7 "Retiring US Envoy Urges Links to PLO," *Washington Post*, September 1, 1981. The *Post* interviewed Seelye and contained direct quotes that Seelye regards as accurate. Subsequent wire reports, in particular, "A US Envoy Assails Begin as 'Blind,'" paraphrased the *Post*, and Seelye regarded those quotations as less accurate, *New York Times*, September 1, 1981.
8 Richard Murphy, "A Departing Envoy's Grim Afghan View," *New York Times*, January 30, 1989. For an account of how the PLO logjam was broken by an April 1988 visit by American Jewish leaders, working through Swedish diplomats, see William Quandt, *Peace Process American Diplomacy and the Arab–Israeli Conflict since 1967* (Washington: Brookings Institution Press, 1993), 368–72.
9 Richard Murphy, "Gives Mideast Talks a Boost," *New York Times*, February 21, 1992. "Rabin Raps Foes of US Golan Force," *Boston Globe*, June 28, 1994. Col. Thomas Pianka, "US Troops on the Golan? It Worked in Sinai," *New York Times*, July 8, 1994. See Michael E. Sterner, ADST oral history interview, March 2, 1990, in Frontline Diplomacy, The Foreign Affairs Oral History Collection of the Association for Diplomatic Studies and Training, Arlington, Virginia and Lauinger Library, Georgetown University, Washington, DC; also online www.adst.org [hereafter ADST interview]. Also, "For Sinai Military Observers, Boredom," *New York Times*, January 22, 1995.
10 For the CIA's own "secret Arabists" and the results of their covert activities, see Hugh Wilford, *America's Great Game The CIA's Secret Arabists and the Shaping of the Modern Middle East* (New York: Basic Books, 2013), quotation, xx; and memoirs by Wilbur Eveland, *Ropes of Sand* (New York: Norton, 1980); and Miles Copeland, *The Game of Nations: the Amorality of Power Politics* (New York: Simon and Schuster, 1970).
11 Ambassador William R. Crawford, interview with the author, Washington, DC, June 10, 1993.
12 Henry Kissinger, *A World Restored Metternich, Castlereagh and the Problems of Peace 1812–1822* (Boston: Houghton Mifflin, 1957), 145.
13 "Looking for Camp David," *New York Times*, January 9, 2000.
14 Ambassador Michael E. Sterner, interview with the author, Washington, DC, June 10, 1993.
15 Ambassador Donald Bergus, letter to the author, February 23, 1994.
16 For a critique of US–Israeli Rapid Deployment Force, see Camille Mansour, "Israel as a Strategic Asset," *Beyond Alliance the US–Israeli Special Relationship*, 33–34. For proposal, see Steven J. Rosen, *The Strategic Value of Israel*, AIPAC Papers on US–Israel Relations, #1, 1982, and Howard Teicher, *Twin Pillars to Desert Storm* (New York: William Morris, 1993). Ambassador Michael E. Sterner, interview with author, Washington, DC, June 10, 1993.
17 George Shultz, *Turmoil and Triumph: My Years as Secretary of State* (New York: Scribner's, 1993), 201; Patrick Seale, *Assad, the Struggle for the Middle East* (Berkeley: University of California Press, 1989), 407. Robert Kaplan, *The Arabists: The Romance of an American Elite* (New York: Free Press, 1993), 188. Richard Parker, *Politics of Miscalculation in the Middle East*, (Bloomington: Indiana University Press, 1993), 201–4.

18 Dwight Eisenhower to Winston Churchill, November 27, 1956, *Waging Peace 1956–61: The White House Years* (Garden City, NY: Doubleday, 1965), 681.
19 Laurence Pope, "The Arabist Myth," *Foreign Service Journal*, January 1985, 33.
20 George McGhee, *The US-Turkish-NATO Middle East Connection: How the Truman Doctrine Contained the Soviets in the Middle East* (New York: St Martin's Press, 1990), xiii, xv, 158.
21 Ambassador Michael E. Sterner, Association for Diplomatic Studies interview, March 2, 1990.
22 Sterner quoted in Joseph Kraft, "Letter from Cairo," *The New Yorker*, September 18, 1971, 99–100.
23 Selma Botman, *Egypt from Independence to Revolution* (Syracuse: Syracuse University Press, 1991),135. Bassiouny, quote in Richard Parker, *The Six Day War: A Retrospective* (Gainesville, FL: University Press of Florida, 1996), 66.
24 Ambassador Richard W. Murphy, interview with the author, New York, February 23, 1995.
25 Ibid.
26 Rodger Davies quoted in Joseph Kraft, "Those Arabists in the State Department," *New York Times Magazine*, November 7, 1971, 81. For Akins on Soviet interests, "Saudi Arabia, Soviet Activities and Gulf Security," in Z. M. Szaz, *The Impact of the Iranian Events upon the Persian Gulf and United States Security* (Washington: American Foreign Policy Institute Studies on Middle East Policy, 1979).
27 Ambassador Richard B. Parker, interview with the author, Washington, DC, June 11, 1993; and Richard Parker, "Catherine the Great's Oriental Project," *Foreign Service Journal* (December 1970): 42.
28 Ambassador Michael E. Sterner, interview with the author, Washington, DC, June 10, 1993.
29 Quote from President John F. Kennedy's 1962 speech, in Walter LaFeber, *Inevitable Revolutions* (New York: Norton, 1984), 154.
30 "Politics and the Drouth," [secret] dispatch #74, signed by Albert B. Franklin, Consul General, reporting officer Andrew I. Killgore, January 13, 1959 [emphasis in original], 3 in National Archives 784.00/1-359.
31 Ambassador Richard B. Parker, Association for Diplomatic Studies interview; and interview with the author, Washington, DC, June 11, 1993.
32 Ambassador Richard W. Murphy, interview with the author, New York, February 23, 1995.
33 Ibid. See also Stephen Green, *Taking Sides America's Secret Relations with a Militant Israel* (Brattleboro, VT: Amana Books, 1988), 180–243.
34 George Lenczowski, *American Presidents and the Middle East* (Durham, NC: Duke University Press, 1992), 110–11. James Ennes, *Assault on the Liberty: The True Story of the Israeli Attack on an American Intelligence Ship* (New York: Random House, 1979).
35 For the CIA role in Syria, Douglas Little, "Cold War and Covert Action: The US & Syria, 1945–58," *Middle East Journal* 44, no. 1 (1990): 51–75.
36 Ambassador Talcott W. Seelye, Association for Diplomatic Studies interview, September 15, 1993.
37 Total US arms sales to Iran since 1950 totaled $11,176,039,000. Defense Intelligence Agency, cited in Congressional Quarterly, *The Middle East* 7th ed. (Washington: Congressional Quarterly, 1990),, 73. For the story of one US diplomat/hostage, see Moorhead Kennedy, *The Ayatollah in the Cathedral Reflections of a Hostage* (New York: Hill and Wang, 1986). The Iranian students salvaged shredded US secret documents, reassembled and published them in *Documents from the Nest of Spies* (Teheran, Iran: Islamic Revolution Guard Corps, undated) full set in National Security Archive, George Washington University, Washington, DC.
38 Avner Cohen, "Most Favored Nation: The US Carries a Big Stick on Proliferation, but Talks Softly regarding Israel," *The Bulletin of Atomic Scientists* (January/February 1995): 44–53. Also, Ambassador Michael E. Sterner, ADST oral history interview, March 2, 1990; and Ambassador William R. Crawford, ADST oral history interview, October 24, 1988.
39 AIPAC's political impact detailed in Congressional Quarterly, *The Middle East*, 7th edition, 1990, 54–55.

40 Ambassador Richard B. Parker, interview with the author, Washington, DC, June 11, 1993.
41 Ambassador Edward Peck, ADST oral history interview, June 29, 1989.
42 Ambassador Edward Peck, ADST oral history interview, June 29, 1989.
43 Ambassador Edward Peck, Association for Diplomatic Studies interview, June 29, 1989.
44 For an account of McFarlane's rise as Reagan's special Middle East envoy and NSC adviser, see Theodore Draper, *A Very Thin Line: The Iran–Contra Affairs* (New York: Hill and Wang, 1991), 28–29. For an account of the McFarlane orders from State Department negotiator Philip Habib's perspective, see John Boykin, *Cursed Is the Peacemaker* (Belmont, CA: Applegate Press, 2002), 310–11.
45 Morton Halperin, *Bureaucratic Politics and Foreign Policy* (Washington: Brookings Institution Study, 1969–1973 [1974]), 11–12.
46 Graham Allison, "Cool It: The Foreign Policy of Young America," *Foreign Policy* (1970–71): 144–60.
47 Eugene V. Rostow, "Opening Statement before Subcommittee on Foreign Assistance," US Senate, March 31, 1976, in *Middle East Review* (spring 1976). Undersecretary of State January 19, 1968, Voice of America statement; and USIS *Byliner*, January 1968. Walter W. Rostow to LBJ, National Security File, NSC, June 5, 1967, LBJ Library, quoted in Green, *Taking Sides*, 350.
48 Ambassador Michael E. Sterner, interview with the author, Washington, DC, June 10, 1993.
49 Ambassador Hermann F. Eilts, interview with the author, Boston, Massachusetts, March 11, 1993.
50 Text of the correspondence "Annex to the Framework Agreements, Exchanges of Letters," President Jimmy Carter Presidential Library, webpage accessed at www.jimmycarterlibrary.org/documents/CampDavid. For CIA quotation and documents released under the Freedom of Information Act and a timeline, see www.foia.cia.gov/carter-camp-david/docs/carterPublication.pdfc
51 Jerrold Post, MD, "Personality Profiles in Support of the Camp David Summit," *Studies in Intelligence* 23, (1979); "President Carter and the Role of Intelligence in the Camp David Accords," www.foia.cia.gov/carter-camp-david/docs/carterPublication.pdfc
52 Ambassador Hermann F. Eilts, ADST oral history interview; and interview with the author, Boston, Massachusetts, March 11, 1993.
53 Malcolm Kerr, 1972 Presidential Address to the Middle East Studies Association, reprinted in *MESA Bulletin*, February 1, 1973.
54 In the quote Kerr combined a reference to the impact of Graham Greene's *The Quiet American* and Arnold Toynbee's *The Western Question*, in 1972 Presidential Address to the Middle East Studies Association, reprinted in *MESA Bulletin*, February 1, 1973.
55 Talcott Seelye, ADST oral history interview, September 15, 1993, in Frontline Diplomacy, The Foreign Affairs Oral History Collection of the Association for Diplomatic Studies and Training, Arlington, Virginia and Lauinger Library, Georgetown University, Washington, DC; also ADST interview.
56 Ambassador Talcott Seelye, ADST oral history interview, September 15, 1993; and interview with the author, August 8, 1994.
57 *Foreign Relations of the United States*, 1969–1976, volume XXVI, Arab-Israeli Dispute, 1974–1976, document 290, Paris, June 22, 1976, 5–7:35 pm, Memorandum of Conversation, 1035–52.
58 Crawford had concluded, in the wake of Makarios's suspicions that the United States was behind his own near assassination, that it would be safer to rebuild contacts: "[F]rom my point of view, not to mention my safety, it really had to be done [...] We had just had an ambassador who got killed." Ambassador William R. Crawford, ADST oral history interview, October 24, 1988.
59 Parker explained his own reluctance at that point in his career to becoming the next ambassador: "I didn't want to go to Beirut and get shot at. I had had enough danger in my life." Richard B. Parker, ADST oral history interview, April 21, 1989.

60 "US Envoy Crosses Beirut Line," *New York Times*, November 6, 1976, 3. Ambassador George M. Lane, ADST oral history interview, August 27, 1990.
61 "Kissinger Protection Likely; Death Plot Reported" and "Likud Leader Derides Report," both in *New York Times*, January 14, 1977.
62 For quotation, "Assistant Secretary Murphy's Eulogy" and "Leamon R. Hunt is buried at Arlington Cemetery," both in *State Magazine*, The Department of State, Washington, DC (1984): 2–5.
63 President William J. Clinton, address at memorial service for FSO Robert Frasure, Joseph Kruzel and S. Nelson Drew, Fort Myer, Virginia, quoted in *Boston Globe*, August 24, 1995.

BIBLIOGRAPHY

Archives and Manuscript Collections

American University of Beirut, University Archive, Beirut, Lebanon. Middle East Area Program papers.
Amherst College, Archives and Special Collections, Frost Library. Amherst, Massachusetts.
George Camp Keiser Library, Middle East Institute. Washington, DC Raymond Hare papers in Library's Vertical Files.
Harry S. Truman Library, Independence, Missouri. Edwin M. Wright papers.
Harvard University, Government Documents Division, Widener Library, Cambridge, Massachusetts. Declassified Documents, Carrolton Press, microfiche edition:
Department of State Special Files. Documents on American Foreign Relations.
Dwight D. Eisenhower Diaries, microfilm edition.
Foreign Relations of the United States, microfiche supplements.
United States. Department of State: Central Files for Middle East.
United States. House of Representatives records.
United States. Senate Foreign Relations Committee records.
Houghton Library, Harvard University. Cambridge, Massachusetts. William Yale papers.
Lauinger Library Special Collections, Georgetown University. Washington, DC. Frontline Diplomacy, The Foreign Affairs Oral History Collection of the Association for Diplomatic Studies and Training.
Library of Congress, Washington, DC. Averell Harriman papers. Loy Henderson papers.
John Fitzgerald Kennedy Presidential Library and Museum. Boston, Massachusetts. Country files: Israel, general. Joseph Johnson Refugee Plan. John F. Kennedy National Security Files, microfilm.
Lyndon Baines Johnson Presidential Library. Austin, Texas. Lyndon Baines Johnson National Security Files,
Middle East National Security Files, 1963–69, microfilm edition.
Mugar Library Special Collections, Boston University. Boston, Massachusetts. William Yale Papers.
National Archives, Washington, DC and College Park, Maryland. Record Group 59. General Records of the Department of State.
National Archives, Washington National Records Center, Suitland, Maryland. Foreign Service Post files. Record Group 84. Records of Embassies, consulates, 120.00 files.
Princeton University Special Collections, Seeley G. Mudd Manuscript Library, Princeton, New Jersey. John Foster Dulles Papers.

Oral History Interviews

Harry S. Truman Presidential Library, Independence, Missouri.
Oral history interviews: Edwin M. Wright.
John Fitzgerald Kennedy Presidential Library and Museum, Boston, Massachusetts.

Oral history interviews: Raymond A. Hare, Parker T. Hart, Dean Rusk.
Association for Diplomatic Studies & Training. Arlington, Virginia and Lauinger Library, Georgetown University, Washington, DC ADST Foreign Affairs Oral History program interviews: Lucius Battle, Donald Bergus, William D. Brewer, L. Dean Brown, William R. Crawford Jr, Arthur Day, Hermann F. Eilts, Raymond A. Hare, Parker T. Hart, Andrew I. Killgore, David A. Korn, George M. Lane, Arthur Lowrie, Armin H. Meyer, Richard B. Parker, Edward L. Peck, Talcott W. Seelye, Joseph J. Sisco, Michael E. Sterner, Harrison Symmes, Nicholas A. Veliotes, Winifred Weislogel, Marshall Wiley.
Author's oral history interviews and personal correspondence: Donald Bergus, William D. Brewer, Charles Cecil, William R. Crawford Jr, Richard Dawson, Hermann F. Eilts, Paul J. Hare, Raymond A. Hare, Hume Horan, Fred J. Galanto, Andrew I. Killgore, William Lakeland, George M. Lane, Dayton Mak, Richard W. Murphy, Richard B. Parker, Talcott W. Seelye, James A. Snow, Michael E. Sterner, Winifred Weislogel.

Published Materials

Abed, Shukri. "Israeli Arabism: The Latest Incarnation of Orientalism," Occasional Paper #6, Washington: International Center for Research and Public Policy, 1986.
Akins, James. "Saudi Arabia, Soviet Activities and Gulf Security." In *The Impact of Iranian Events upon Persian Gulf and United States Security*. Edited by Z. M. Szaz. Washington: American Foreign Policy Institute Studies, 1979.
———. "This Time the Wolf is Here," *Foreign Affairs*, April 1973.
Allen, Arthur. "Some Iraqi Proverbs and Proverbial Phrases," *Journal of the American Oriental Society* 75, no. 2 (April–June 1955): 122–25.
Allison, Graham, "Cool It: The Foreign Policy of Young America," *Foreign Policy* (Winter 1970–1971): 144–60.
Alteras, Isaac. *Eisenhower and Israel: US–Israeli Relations 1953–60*. Gainsville: University Press of Florida, 1993.
Amirahmadi, Hooshang, ed. *The US and the Middle East: A Search for New Perspectives*. New York: SUNY Press, 1993.
Anderson, Betty S. *The American University of Beirut: Arab Nationalism and Liberal Education*. Austin: University of Texas Press, 2011.
Andrew, Christopher and V. Mitrokhin. *The Sword and the Shield: The Mitrokhin Archive and the Secret History of the KGB*. New York: Basic Books, 1999.
Arabists Discussion Panel: George Ball, Talcott Seelye, Andrew Killgore, and James Akins. Convention of the American-Arab Anti-Discrimination Committee, VHS, April 16, 1994.
Badeau, John B. *The Middle East Remembered*. Washington: Middle East Institute, 1983.
Ball, George. *Diplomacy for a Crowded World*. Boston: Little Brown, 1976.
———. "How to Avert a Middle East War," *Atlantic Monthly*, no. 235, January 1975.
———. "How to Save Israel in Spite of Herself," *Foreign Affairs* 55 (April 1977).
Baram, Philip. *The Department of State in the Middle East 1919–45*. Philadelphia: University of Pennsylvania Press, 1978.
Barnes, William and J. H. Morgan, *The Foreign Service of the US: Origins, Development & Functions*. Washington: Historical Office Department of State, 1961.
Bergus, Donald. *The Middle East: Two Wars for the Price of One*. Columbia: University of South Carolina, 1973.
———. "Palestine: Focal Point of Tension," Tenth Middle East Institute Conference, March 9–10, 1956.
Bird, Eugene. "The Israelization of American Policy," *Washington Report on Middle East Affairs*, March 1994.
Bird, Kai. *Crossing Mandelbaum Gate: Coming of Age Between the Arabs and Israelis, 1956–78*. New York: Scribner, 2010.

———. *The Good Spy: The Life and Death of Robert Ames*. New York: Crown Publishers, 2014.

Blechman, Barry M. and S. Kaplan. *Force Without War: US Armed Forces as a Political Instrument*. Washington: Brookings Institution, 1978.

Botman, Selma. *Egypt from Independence to Revolution*. New York: Syracuse University Press, 1991.

Brown, L. Carl. *Diplomacy in the Middle East*. London: I. B. Tauris, 2004.

Burns, William J. *Economic Aid and American Policy toward Egypt, 1955–81*. New York: SUNY Press, 1985.

Buheiry, Marwan. *US Threats of Intervention against Arab Oil: 1973–79*. Beirut: Institute for Palestine Studies, 1980.

Burns, E. L. M. *Between Arab and Israeli*. Beirut: Institute for Palestine Studies, 1969.

Burns, William J. *Economic Aid and American Policy toward Egypt*. Albany: SUNY Press, 1985.

Caradon, A. Goldberg, N. El-Zayyat, Abba Eban. *UN Security Council Resolution 242: A Case Study in Diplomatic Ambiguity*. Georgetown University Institute for the Study of Diplomacy, 1981.

Chomsky, Noam. *The Fateful Triangle: The US, Israel and the Palestinians*. Boston: South End Press, 1983.

Cohen, Avner. "Most Favored Nation: The US Carries a Big Stick on Proliferation, But Talks Softly Regarding Israel," *Bulletin of Atomic Scientists* 51, no. 1 (January/February 1995).

Cohen, Bernard C. *The Public's Impact on Foreign Policy*. Boston: Little, Brown, 1973.

Cohen, Warren I. and Nancy Bernkopf Tucker. *Lyndon Johnson Confronts the World: American Foreign Policy, 1963–68*. New York: Cambridge University Press, 1994.

Coll, Steve. *Ghost Wars: The Secret History of the CIA, Afghanistan and Bin Laden*. New York: Penguin, 2004.

Cook, Blanche Wiesen. *The Declassified Eisenhower*. New York: Penguin Books, 1984.

Copeland, Miles. *The Game of Nations*, New York: Simon & Schuster, 1969.

Curtiss, Richard. *A Changing Image: American Perceptions of the Arab–Israeli Dispute*, Washington, DC: American Educational Trust, 1986.

Daniel, Robert L. *American Philanthropy in the Near East 1820–1960*. Athens: Ohio University Press, 1970.

Davies, Rodger. "Syrian Arabic Kinship Terms." *Southwestern Journal of Anthropology* 5 (1949): 244–52.

Dawn, C. Ernest. *From Ottomanism to Arabism: Essays on the Origins of Arab Nationalism*. Chicago: University of Illinois Press, 1973.

DeNovo, John A. *American Interest and Policies in the Middle East, 1900–1939*. Minneapolis: University of Minnesota Press, 1963.

DeSantis, Hugh. *The Diplomacy of Silence: The American Foreign Service, the Soviet Union and the Cold War 1933–1947*. Chicago: University of Chicago Press, 1980.

Dester, I. M., Leslie Gelb and Anthony Lake. *Our Own Worst Enemy: The Unmaking of American Foreign Policy*. New York: Simon and Schuster, 1984.

Dinsmore, Lee. "Communication RE: The Near East to the Secretary," *Foreign Service Journal* 50, no. 9 (September 1973): 26.

Dobrynin, Anatoly. *In Confidence Moscow's Ambassador to America's Six Cold War Presidents*. New York: Times Books, 1995.

Eban, Abba. *An Autobiography*. New York: Random House, 1977.

———. *Personal Witness: Israel through My Eyes*. New York: Putnam, 1992.

Eddy, William. *FDR Meets Ibn Saud*. Kohinur Series, #1, American Friends of the Middle East, 1954.

———. "How the Arabs See the West Today," Middle East Institute Conference, Washington, DC, December 19, 1950.

Ehrlichman, John. *Witness to Power: The Nixon Years*. New York: Pocket Books, 1982.

Eilts, Hermann F. "It's Time to Talk to the PLO in Facing the PLO Question." In *Facing the PLO Question*. Edited by Meir Merhav. Washington: Foundation for Middle East Peace, 1985.

———. *US Diplomacy in the Arab World Since Camp David, The Challenge to US Interests in the Arab World*. American–Arab Affairs Council, Milwaukee, Wisconsin, November 17–18, 1983.

Eisenhower, Dwight. *The White House Years: Waging Peace*. New York: Doubleday, 1965.
———. "Developments in Eastern Europe and the Middle East," US Department of State Bulletin, November 12, 1956.
———. *The Eisenhower Diaries*. Edited by Robert Ferrell. New York: Norton, 1981.
Etheredge, Lloyd S. *A World of Men: The Private Sources of American Foreign Policy*. London: MIT Press, 1978.
Eveland, Wilbur. *Ropes of Sand: America's Failure in the Middle East*. London: W. W. Norton, 1980.
Faris, Nabih A. "A View of Arab Unity." In *Political and Social Thought in the Contemporary Middle East*. Edited by K. Karpat. New York: Praeger, 1968, 259–62.
Ferguson, Charles. "Diglossia," *Word*, 1959. Reprinted in Haim Blanc, *Contributions to Arabic Linguistics*, Harvard Middle Eastern Monographs III, Center for Middle East Studies, 1964.
Fink, Carole. *Cold War: An International History*. Boulder, CO: Westview Press, 2014.
Ford, Gerald. *A Time to Heal*. New York: Harper & Row, 1979.
Fuller, C. Dale. *Training of Specialists in International Relations*. Washington: American Council on Education, 1957.
Gazit, Mordechai. *President Kennedy's Policy toward the Arab States and Israel*. Tel Aviv: Shiloah Center, 1983.
Gibb, Sir Hamilton. *Area Studies Reconsidered*. London: University of London School of Oriental & African Studies, 1963.
Goehlert, Robert and E. Hoffmeister. *The Department of State and American Diplomacy*. New York: Garland, 1986.
Golan, Matti. *The Secret Conversations of Henry Kissinger: Step-by-Step Diplomacy in the Middle East*. New York: Quadrangle, 1976.
Goot, Amy and S. Rosen. *The Campaign to Discredit Israel*, AIPAC Papers on the US, 1983.
Grabill, Joseph L. *Protestant Diplomacy and the Near East: Missionary Influence on American Policy 1810–1927*. Minneapolis: University of Minnesota Press, 1971.
Hahn, Peter L. *Caught in the Middle East: US Policy Toward the Arab–Israeli Conflict, 1945–1961*. Chapel Hill: University of North Carolina Press, 2004.
Halperin, Morton H. *Bureaucratic Politics and Foreign Policy*. Washington: Brookings Institution, 1974.
Hare, Paul J. *Diplomatic Chronicles of the Middle East: A Biography of Ambassador Raymond A. Hare*, Washington, DC: Middle East Institute, 1993.
Hare, Raymond A. "Capability and Foreign Policy," *US Department of State Bulletin*, July 1, 1957.
Harr, John Ensor. *The Professional Diplomat*. Princeton, NJ: Princeton University Press, 1969.
Hart, Parker. *Saudi Arabia and the United States: Birth of a Security Partnership*. Bloomington: Indiana University Press, 1998.
Hart, Parker T. "Reflections of an FSO Wife," *Foreign Service Journal* (January 1954).
Heikal, Mohammed H. *The Cairo Documents*. New York: Doubleday, 1973.
Hersh, Seymour. *The Price of Power: Kissinger in the White House*. New York: Summit Books, 1983.
Hopkins, Frank S. "Career Classroom: The Foreign Service Institute Trains Young and Older Diplomats in the New Diplomacy," *New York Times Magazine*, December 5, 1948.
———. "Should the FSO Specialize?" *American Foreign Service Journal* 24, no. 7 (July 1947).
Horan, Hume. "A Plea for Arabists," *Foreign Service Journal* 50, no. 5 (May 1973).
———. "The Way to Language Success," *Foreign Service Journal* vol. 65, no. 12 (December 1988).
Hoskins, Harold. "The Need for More Effective American Representation in the Middle East—Private and Government," *Middle East Institute Tenth Conference*, 1956.
———. "The Department of State and the Quest for Quality." Address April 5, 1955, *US Department of State Bulletin*, May 16, 1955.
Huntington, Samuel. "The Clash of Civilizations?" *Foreign Affairs* 72, no. 3 (Summer 1993): 22–49.
Ilchmann, Warren F. *Professional Diplomacy in the US*. Chicago: University of Chicago Press, 1961.

Institute for the Study of Diplomacy, Diplomats and Terrorists, volumes I and II, monographs, published by Edmund A. Walsh School of Foreign Service, Georgetown University, Washington, 1982.

Isaacson, Walter. *Kissinger: A Biography*. New York: Simon & Schuster, 1992.

Jacobs, Matthew F. *Imagining the Middle East: The Building of an American Foreign Policy, 1918–1967*. Chapel Hill: University of North Carolina Press, 2011.

Jeffreys-Jones, Rhodri. "The Socio-Educational Composition of other CIA Elite: A Statistical Note." *Journal of American Studies*, vol. 19, 1985, 421–44.

Johnson, Joseph. "Arab vs. Israeli: A Persistent Challenge to Americans," *Middle East Journal* xvii (Winter 1964).

Johnson, Ural Alexis. "Caught in the Nutcracker." *Foreign Service Journal* 61, no. 9 (September 1984).

———. *The Right Hand of Power*. New Jersey: Prentice-Hall, 1984.

Jones, Curtis F. "The Education of an Arabist," *Foreign Service Journal* 49, no. 12 (December 1972).

Kahn, E. J. *The China Hands: America's Foreign Service Officers and What Befell Them*. New York: Viking Press, 1975.

Kaplan, Robert D. *The Arabists: The Romance of an American Elite*. New York: Free Press, 1993.

———. "Tales from the Bazaar." *Atlantic Monthly*, August 1992.

Katz, Samuel. *Battleground: Fact and Fantasy in Palestine*. New York: Bantam Books, 1973.

Kaufman, Myron S. *The Coming Destruction of Israel*. New York: Signet, 1970.

Kedourie, Elie. *Arab Political Memoirs and Other Studies*. London: Frank Cass, 1974.

Kerr, Ann Zwicker. *Come With Me From Lebanon An American Family Odyssey*. New York: Syracuse University Press, 1994.

Kennedy, John F. "The Great Period of the Foreign Service." *Address to the American Foreign Service Association*, Washington, DC, May 31, 1962.

Kerr, Malcolm H. "American Policy toward Egypt 1955–1971." *Ford Foundation Arms Control and Foreign Policy Seminar Paper*, 1973.

———. *America's Middle East Policy: Kissinger, Carter, and the Future*, Beirut: Institute for Palestine Studies, 1980.

———. *The Arab Cold War: Nasir and His Rivals, 1958–1970*. 3rd edition. London and New York: Oxford University Press, 1971.

———. *The Elusive Peace in the Middle East*. Albany: SUNY Press, 1975.

———. "The Emergence of a Socialist Ideology in Egypt," *Middle East Journal* xvi (Spring 1962): 127–44.

———. "Lebanese Views on the 1958 Crisis," *Middle East Journal* xv (Spring 1961): 211–17.

———. *Lebanon in the Last Years of Feudalism, 1840–1868, A Contemporary Account by Antun Dahir Al-Aqiqi and other documents*. Beirut: AUB, 1959.

———. "The Middle East: Present Problems and Future." *Address to the American Foreign Service Association Opening Banquet*, April 30, 1968.

———. "The 1960 Lebanese Parliamentary Elections," *Middle Eastern Affairs* (October 1960): 266–75.

———. "Nixon's Second Term: Policy Prospects in the Middle East." *Journal of Palestine Studies* 2, no. 3 (spring 1973): 14–29.

———. "The Quest for International and Regional Stability: The Middle East Role." *Address to the American Academy of Political Science Conference*. Columbia University, December 13–14, 1968.

———. *Regional Arab Politics and the Conflict with Israel*. Rand Corporation Study # RN 5966–FF, October 1969.

———. "Review of Said's Orientalism." *International Journal of Middle East Studies* 12 (1980): 544–47.

———. "Toward Peace in the Middle East: The Conditions of a General Settlement," [undated typescript, circa summer 1976], Raymond Hare Papers in Vertical Files, Middle East Institute, George Camp Keiser Library, Washington, DC.

———. "The West and the Middle East: The Light and the Shadow." 1972 Presidential Address, Middle East Studies Association, *MESA Bulletin*, February 1, 1973.

Kerr, Malcolm, A. Becker and B. Hansen. *Economics and Politics of the Middle East*. New York: American Elsevier, 1975.

Khalil, Osamah. *At the Crossroads of Empire: The United States, the Middle East, and the Politics of Knowledge, 1902–2002*. PhD dissertation, University of California, Berkeley, 2011.

Kissinger, Henry A. *A World Restored: Metternich, Castlereagh and the Problems of Peace 1812–1822*. Boston: Little Brown, 1957.

———. *White House Years*. Boston: Little Brown, 1979.

———. *Years of Upheaval*. Boston: Little Brown, 1982.

Korn, David A. *Assassination in Khartoum*. Bloomington: University of Indiana Press, 1993.

———. "US–Soviet Negotiations of 1969 and the Rogers Plan." *Middle East Journal* 44, no. 1 (winter 1990).

Kraft, Joseph. "In Search of Kissinger," *Harper's*, January 1971, 57–58.

———. "Letter From Cairo." *New Yorker*, September 18, 1971, 99–100.

———. "Phantom Memo." *Washington Post*, June 27, 1971.

———. "Those Arabists in the State Department," *New York Times Magazine*, November 7, 1971.

Kramer, Martin. *Ivory Towers on Sand: The Failure of Middle Eastern Studies in America*. Washington: Washington Institute for Near East Policy, 2001.

Lambert, Richard D., et al. *Beyond Growth: The Next Stage in Language and Area Studies*, Washington: Association of American Universities, April 1984.

Lane, George M. "Who and What Are the Arabists?" *Georgetown Compass: A Journal of International Affairs* (spring 1994): 106–8.

Leacacos, John P. *Fires in the In-Basket: The ABC's of the State Department*. Cleveland: World Books, 1968.

Lederer, William and E. Burdick. *The Ugly American*. New York: Norton, 1958.

Lenczowski, George. *American Presidents and the Middle East*. Durham, NC: Duke University Press, 1992.

Lewis, Bernard. "The Question of Orientalism." *New York Review of Books*, June 24, 1982.

Lewis, Michael. "Why Political Interference Is Good for the State Department." *Orbis*, Spring 1988.

Light, Nancy. "Subtle Sexism." *Foreign Service Journal* 65, no. 1 (January 1988).Little, Douglas J. *American Orientalism: The United States and the Middle East since 1945*. Chapel Hill: University of North Carolina Press, 2002.

———. "Cold War and Covert Action: The US and Syria 1945–58." *Middle East Journal* 44, no. 1 (winter 1990).

———. "From Even-Handed to Empty-Handed." In *Kennedy's Quest for Victory: American Foreign Policy 1961 to 1963*. Edited by Thomas Paterson New York: Oxford University Press, 156–77.

———. "New Frontier on the Nile: JFK, Nasser and Arabism," *Journal of American History* 75, no. 2 (September 1988): 501–27.

———. "Pipeline Politics: America, TAPLINE, and the Arabs." *Harvard Business History Review* (Summer 1990): 255–85.

Lockman, Zachary. *Contending Visions of the Middle East: The History and Politics of Orientalism*. 2nd edition. New York: Cambridge University Press, 2010.

Mak, Dayton. "Some Syrian Arabic Proverbs." *Journal of the American Oriental Society* 69, no. 4, December 1949.

Mansour, Camille. *Beyond Alliance: Israel in US Foreign Policy*. New York: Columbia University Press, 1994.

McCarus, Ernest N. "History of Arabic Study in the US." In *The Arabic Language in America*, 209–13. Edited by Aleya Rouchdy. Detroit: Wayne State University, 1992, 209–13.

———. "Lust for Language." In *Paths to the Middle East: Ten Scholars Look Back*. Edited by Thomas Naff. Albany: State University of New York Press, 1993.

———. "The Study of Arabic in the US: A History of its Development." *Journal of the American Association of Teachers of Arabic* 20 (1987): 13–27.

McClintock, Robert M. "Suggestions for Improving the Foreign Service to Meet Its War and Post–War Responsibilities." *American Foreign Service Journal* 22, no. 9 (September 1945).

McLoughlin, Leslie. *In a Sea of Knowledge British Arabists in the Twentieth Century*. Cornell, NY: Ithaca Press, 2002.

Mearsheimer, John J. and Stephen M. Walt. *The Israel Lobby and US Foreign Policy*. New York: Farrar, Straus and Giroux, 2007.

Menand, Louis. "The Trashing of Professionalism." *New York Times Magazine*, March 5, 1995, 41–43.

Meir, Golda. *My Life*. New York: Dell Books, 1975.

Menicucci, Garay. "Glasnost, the Coup and Soviet Arabist Historians." *International Journal of Middle East Studies* 24 (November 1992).

Miller, R. H. *Inside an Embassy*. Washington: Institute for the Study of Diplomacy, 1992.

Morris, Roger. *Uncertain Greatness: Henry Kissinger and American Foreign Policy*. New York: Harper & Row, 1977.

Moseley, Leonard. *Dulles: A Biography of Eleanor, Allen and John Foster Dulles and their Family Network*. New York: Dial Press, 1978.

Naff, Thomas, ed. *Paths to the Middle East: Ten Scholars Look Back*. New York: Berkeley, 1979.

Newsom, David. "Miracle or Mirage: Reflections on US Diplomacy." *Middle East Journal* (Summer 1981): 299–313.

———. "The Terrorist Threat to Diplomacy." In *Diplomacy and the American Democracy*. Bloomington: Indiana University Press, 1988, 124–35.

Nixon, Richard M. *RN: The Memoirs of Richard Nixon*. New York: Grossett, 1978.

———. "Transcript of President's News Conference on Foreign and Domestic Matters," *New York Times*, March 3, 1973.

Nolan, Cathal. *Notable US Ambassadors since 1775: A Biographical Dictionary*, Westport, CT: Greenwood Press, 1997.

"Opposition Research at AIPAC." *Harper's*. October 1992.

Ornstein, Jacob. "To Win the 'Languages Race' with Russia, *New York Times*, September 15, 1957.

Ottaway, David. "Mideast Institute's Experts and Ideas Ascendant," *Washington Post*, March 24, 1989.

Owens, John. "Crisis in the US Foreign Service," *Mediterranean Quarterly* 2, no. 3 (Summer 1991).

Painter, David. *Oil and the American Century*. Baltimore, MD: Johns Hopkins University Press, 1986.

Parker, Richard B. "Middle East Studies and US Foreign Policy." In *The US and the Middle East: A Search for New Perspectives*. Edited by Hooshang Amirahmadi. Albany: SUNY Press, 1993.

———. *Memoirs of a Foreign Service Arabist*. Washington: ADST-DACOR Books, 2013.

———. *The Politics of Miscalculation in the Middle East*. Bloomington: Indiana University Press, 1993.

Parmet, Herbert. *JFK: The Presidency of John F. Kennedy*. New York: Penguin, 1983.

Peck, Edward. "Reflections: An Unusual Expression of Gratitude." *Foreign Service Journal* (November 2014).

Penrose, Stephen Jr. *That They May Have Life: The Story of the American University of Beirut 1866–1941*. New York: AUB, 1941.

Parry, Albert. *America Learns Russian*. Syracuse: Syracuse University Press, 1967.

Pipes, Daniel. "Breaking All the Rules: American Debate Over the Middle East," *International Security* 9, no. 2 (Fall 1984): 124–50.

Pope, Laurence. "The Arabist Myth." *Foreign Service Journal* 62, no. 1 (January 1985).

Poullada, Leon and Leila. "Our Tongue-Tied Foreign Service." *Foreign Service Journal* 34, no. 6 (June 1957).

Prados, John. *Presidents' Secret Wars: CIA and Pentagon Covert Operations since World War II*. New York: William Morrow, 1986.

Pringle, Henry and K. "School for Modern Diplomats," *Saturday Evening Post*, January 3, 1959.
Propas, Frederic L. "Creating a Hard Line toward Russia: The Training of State Department Soviet Experts, 1927–1937." *Diplomatic History* 8, no. 3 (spring 1984): 209–26.
Quandt, William. *Camp David Peacemaking and Politics*. Washington: Brookings Institution, 1986.
———. *Decade of Decisions: American Policy toward the Arab–Israeli Conflict, 1967–76*. Berkeley: University of California Press, 1977.
———. *The Middle East Ten Years after Camp David*. Washington: Brookings Institution, 1988.
———. *Peace Process: American Diplomacy and the Arab–Israeli Conflict since 1967*. Washington: Brookings Institution, 1993.
Rafael, Gideon. *Destination Peace: Three Decades of Israeli Foreign Policy: A Personal Memoir*. New York: Stein and Day, 1981.
Rogers, William Pierce. *A Lasting Peace in the Middle East: An American View*. Department of State publication #8507, Address to the Galaxy Conference, December 9, 1969.
———. "Secretary Rogers' News Conference," transcript dated March 23, 1970, Department of State press release #100, 11.
Rosen, Steven J. *The Strategic Value of Israel*, AIPAC Papers on US–Israel Relations, 1982.
Rosenburg, Cheryl. *Israel and the American National Interest: A Critical Examination*. Urbana: University of Illinois Press, 1986.
Rouchdy, A. ed. *The Arabic Language in America*. Detroit, MI: Wayne State University Press, 1992.
Rubenberg, Cheryl. *Israel and the American National Interest*. Chicago: University of Illinois Press, 1986.
Rugh, William. *American Encounters with Arabs: The "Soft Power" of US Public Diplomacy in the Middle East*. Westport, CT: Praeger Security International, 2006.
———. *The Arab Press: News Media and Political Process in the Arab World*. Syracuse, NY: Syracuse University Press, 1979.
Rusk, Dean. *As I Saw It*. New York: W. W. Norton, 1990.
Russell, Beatrice. *Living in State*. New York: D. McKay, 1959.
———. "We Like the Foreign Service Life." *Saturday Evening Post*, June 18, 1955.
Sachar, Howard M. *A History of Israel: From the Rise of Zionism to Our Time*. New York: Knopf, 1976.
Sabbagh, Isa K. *As the Arabs Say*. vols. I and II. Washington: Sabbagh Management, 1983, 1985.
Sadat, Anwar. "Interview with Arnaud de Borchgrave." *Newsweek*, December 13, 1971.
Said, Edward W. *The Palestine Question and the American Context*. Beirut: Institute for Palestine Studies, 1979.
———. *Covering Islam: Arabs and the American Media*. New York: Pantheon, 1981.
———. *Orientalism*. New York: Vintage Books, 1979.
Saunders, Harold H. *Conversations with Harold H. Saunders: US Policy for the Middle East in the 1980s*. Washington: American Enterprise Institute for Public Policy Research, 1982.
———. *The Other Walls: The Politics of the Arab–Israeli Peace Process*. Washington: AEI Public Policy Research, 1985.
Schlesinger, Arthur. *A Thousand Days*. Boston: Houghton-Mifflin, 1965.
Schuckburgh, Evelyn. *Descent to Suez 1951–56*. New York: W. W. Norton, 1986.
Schulzinger, Robert. *Henry Kissinger: The Doctor of Diplomacy*. New York: Columbia University Press, 1989.
———. *The Making of the Diplomatic Mind: The Training, Outlook and Style of US Foreign Service Officers 1908–31*, Middletown: Wesleyan University Press, 1975.
Schoenbaum, David. *The United States and the State of Israel*. New York: Oxford University Press, 1993.
Sisco, Joseph J. *Middle East Negotiations: A Conversation with Joseph Sisco*. American Enterprise Institute Studies in Foreign Policy, 1980.
Smith, Henry Lee Jr. and Perry Jester. "Language Training for the Foreign Service and the Department of State." *American Foreign Service Journal* 23, no. 9 (September 1946).

Snow, James A. *A Grammar of Modern Written Arabic Clauses*. PhD diss, University of Michigan, Ann Arbor, 1965.
Solecki, John. "Arabists and the Myth," *Middle East Journal* 44, no. 3 (summer 1990): 446–57.
Spiegel, Stephen. *The Other Arab-Israeli Conflict*. Chicago: University of Chicago, 1985.
Sterner, Michael E. "Managing US–Israeli Relations." *American-Arab Affairs*. Fall 1983, 16–17.
Stookey, Robert. *America and the Arab World: An Uneasy Encounter*. New York: Wiley & Sons, 1975.
Strober, Gerald. *Nixon: An Oral History of His Presidency*. New York: HarperCollins, 1994.
Suddarth, Roscoe. "Diplomacy in a Yemeni Jail." *Foreign Service Journal* (October 1971).
Teicher, Howard and G. R. Teicher. *Twin Pillars to Desert Storm*. New York: Morrow, 1993.
Tempest, Paul, ed. *The Arabists of Shemlan*: MECAS Memoirs, 1944–78, vol. I. London: Stacey International, 2006.
Thomas, Baylis. *How Israel Was Won: A Concise History of the Arab–Israeli Conflict*. Lanham, MD: Lexington Books, 1999.
Thomas, Evan. *The Very Best Men: The Daring Early Years of the CIA*. New York: Simon & Schuster, 2006.
Thomas, Teresa A. "Review of Kaplan's The Arabists," *Middle East Journal* 49, no. 1 (winter 1995): 157–59.
Tivnan, Edward. *The Lobby: Jewish Political Power and American Foreign Policy*. New York: Summit Books, 1987.
Tobin, Gary A. *Jewish Perceptions of Antisemitism*. New York: Plenum Press, 1988.
Trice, Robert H. Jr. *Domestic Political Interest and American Policy in the Middle East: Pro-Israel, Pro-Arab and Corporate Non-Governmental Actors and the Making of American Foreign Policy*, PhD diss. University of Wisconsin, Madison, 1974.
Tucker, Nancy Bernkopf, ed. *China Confidential American Diplomats and Sino-American Relations, 1945–1996*. New York: Columbia University Press, 2001.
United States. Congress. House of Representatives. *Oil Fields as Military Objectives: A Feasibility Study*, August 21, 1975.
———. *Views on Middle East Policy Formulation and Implementation and the State Department Role*, October 31, 1989, House 381–37.4.
United States. Congress. Senate. *Improvement in Standards of Language Proficiency and in Recruiting for the Foreign Service*, April 16, 1959.
———. *Recruitment and Training for the Foreign Service of the US*, Staff Study for the Committee on Foreign Relations, February 28, 1958.
———. *Proficiency and Recruiting for the Foreign Service: to Establish Standards of Foreign Language Proficiency*. Hearings, April 16, 1959.
United States. Department of State. *Foreign Relations of the United States*. Various volumes and microfilm editions, 1952–1963.
———. *The Biographic Register of the United States Department of State*. Washington: US Government Printing Office, various editions through 1974.
———. *Principal Officers of the Department of State and United States Chiefs of Mission 1778–1990*. Washington: Government Printing Office, January 1991.
———. *Report on Hard Language Proficiency in the Foreign Service, A Study by Monteagle Stearns*.
———. *Toward a Stronger Foreign Service: The Wriston Report*. Washington: US Government Printing Office, June 1954.
"US College in the Near East: Its Methods and Courses are Western," *Life*, 1957.
Valeriani, Richard. *Travels with Henry*. New York: Berkeley Books, 1980.
Vent, Myron. "AID and AUB: Partners in Middle East Development." *Higher Education*, April 1963.
Weil, Martin. *A Pretty Good Club: The Founding Fathers of the US Foreign Service*. New York: W. W. Norton, 1978.
Weiner, Tim. *Legacy of Ashes: The History of the CIA*. New York: Anchor Books, 2008.

Wilford, Hugh. *America's Great Game: The CIA's Secret Arabists and the Shaping of the Modern Middle East.* New York: Basic Books, 2013.
Wilson, Evan. *Decision on Palestine.* Stanford: Hoover Institution Press at Stanford University, 1979.
Wynder, R. Bayly. "Four Decades of Middle Eastern Study," *Middle East Journal* 41 (1987): 40–63.
Yacub, Salim. *Containing Arab Nationalism: The Eisenhower Doctrine and the Middle East.* Chapel Hill: University of North Carolina Press, 2004.
Zeine, Zeine N. *The Emergence of Arab Nationalism with a Background Study of Arab-Turkish Relations in the Near East.* New York: Caravan Books, 1958.
Zurayk, Constantine K. *More Than Conquerors: Selected Addresses Delivered at the American University of Beirut 1956–66.* Beirut: AUB, 1968.
———. *The Meaning of Disaster* [Ma'na al–Nakbah]. Beirut: AUB, 1956.

INDEX

A

Abell-Coon, Jane 42
Acheson, Dean, on role of White House aides 110
action intellectuals 109–10, 113
air bases: US in Libya 111, 183; US in Saudi Arabia 111
Akins, James E.: brief biography of 191; on goals of Middle East hands 10, 14; on oil crisis 13–14, 164–65; technical personality type of 38; on US vulnerability 81; *see also* Middle East Area Program (MEAP); Middle East hand(s)
Allen, Arthur B.: brief biography of 191; publications of 56; *see also* Middle East Area Program (MEAP); Middle East hand(s)
Allen, George 85
Allison, Graham 136–37, 182
Alteras, Isaac 92, 94, 99
American Encounters with Arabs (Rugh) 72
American Foreign Service Association (AFSA) 168
American Israel Public Affairs Committee (AIPAC): affect on US policy 2, 180; and Crawford 171; and Ford administration 166; on Israeli risk-taking 3; and Johnson administration 138; opposition to Rogers Peace Plan by 150; overview of 12–13, 111–12; and US aid to Israel 138
American University of Beirut (AUB): on Arab nationalism 75–76; closure/relocation to Cairo 83, 186; course content at 74; faculty of 74–79; founding of 73; kidnappings of staff of 83; on Ottoman empire 75; overview of 73–79; physical attacks on 83–84; radicalization of student body at 74, 76, 78; on role of Islam 76; on role of US in Middle East 75; *see also* McCarus, Ernest
Anderson, G. Norman: brief biography of 191; skilled linguist personality type of 37; *see also* Middle East Area Program (MEAP); Middle East hand(s)

anti-Semitism: Middle East hands charged with 3–4, 13, 174; Orientalists charged with 20
Antonius, George 6
Arab Awakening, The (Antonius) 6
Arab League: PLO recognized by 165; and three noes of Khartoum 130
Arab nationalism: Beirut Axioms on 86, 176, 178; and Islam 75–78; J. F. Dulles on 88, 103; Middle East hands on 176, 178; and Nasser 176, 178–79; Zurayk on 77–78
Arab Press: News Media and Political Processes in the Arab World, The (Rugh) 71–72
Arabian American Oil Company (ARAMCO) 13, 25, 95
Arabic language: changes after advent of mass media 50–51; number of speakers of 63; *see also* language training, British program; language training, US program
Arab-Israeli conflict, Beirut Axioms on 86
Arab-Israeli war (1948), and right of return of refugees 3
Arabist: as pejorative term 5, 14–15; *see also* Middle East hand(s)
Arabists: The Romance of an American Elite, The (Kaplan) 4, 14, 44
Arafat, Yasir: becomes leader of PLO 140; and Palestinian Memoranda 172; and plan to takeover Jordan 151
area studies 61
Army Specialized Training Program (ASTP) 7, 33–34, 39, 48–49
Assad, Hafez al: assumes power 179; and attacks on Jordan 154; and negotiations with Barak 174; and peace negotiations 82, 172–73; plans to win back occupied territories 163; retreats from Jordan 154–55; *see also* Syria
Aswan Dam 96, 176
audiolingual language learning 49, 62
Axioms of Young America 136–37, 182

B

Ba'ath party (Syria) 172–73, 179
Badeau, John 122
Baghdad, revolution in 1958 102
Baghdad Pact 88, 101, 114, 176, 182
Ball, George 3–4, 10–11, 82, 125, 127
Barak, Ehud 82, 174
Baram, Philip 20–21, 23, 26, 34, 38–40, 67
Barbour, Walworth 129
Battle, Lucius 121–24
Begin, Menachim 44–45, 184–85
Beirut: attack on US Marine barracks in 12, 155; attacks on American embassy in 12, 83, 155, 188; closure of training program in 16; as dangerous location 74
Beirut Axioms: and Arab nationalism 86, 176, 178; Axiom 1-comprehensive peace and refugee problem 170; Axiom 2-US should not side with any faction/regime 173–75; Axiom 3-Soviets not primary threat and win by default 175–78; Axiom 4-work with Arab moderates to undercut radicalism 178–79; Axiom 5-arms transfers and nuclear proliferation 179–80; Axiom 6-national interests as guide for Middle East foreign policy 180–81; and Baghdad Pact 176; Globalist view on 170; key areas of 86; and Kissinger 166, 170–71; Middle East hands view on 170–71, 176–78; overview of 114, 169–81; and PLO 171–72; and settlement of Arab-Israeli conflict 86, 170; and Six Day War 178–79; and Suez Crisis 175; summary of 9, 110, 114, 169–70; and Syria 179; and US support for Shah of Iran 179
Bell, Gertrude 6, 21
Ben-Gurion, David: and Hawk missile sale 119–20; meeting with J. F. Kennedy 114–16; meeting with Nixon on refugee problem 136; and Richards Mission 99
Bergus, Donald 1, 36; brief biography of 191; career path of 86; and Kissinger 144; on Middle East hands as pro-Arab 174; and Phantom Memo controversy 143–44, 158; reassignment after Egypt-Soviet friendship treaty 159–60; on solution to Arab-Israeli conflict 9–10, 45; and "Year of Decision, The" 156, 158–59; *see also* Middle East Area Program (MEAP); Middle East hand(s)
Bernadotte, Folke 44
Bird, Kai 110
Black September 153–55, 161–62
Bowles, Chester 107

Brazil, and ransom of US ambassador 153
Brewer, William: on consequences of failure of Eric Johnston Plan 94; on dealing with Nasser 124; on experience of NEA desk officers 85; on goal of Middle East hands 69; on Marine landings in Lebanon 103; on taking advantage of pro-American sentiment after Suez War 97; and normalization of relations with Egypt 110, 116; and Palestinian Memoranda 167; on risks involved in being Middle East hand 69; on US-UAR relationship 100
Brown, L. Dean 79, 152–53
Brzezinski, Zbigniew 82
Buchanan, Patrick 136
Bullen, Pierce K.: brief biography of 191; *see also* Middle East Area Program (MEAP); Middle East hand(s)
Bundy, McGeorge: appointed Special Assistant for National Security 110; and Ben-Gurion's visit to Kennedy 115; influence over foreign policy 110; and refugees 129–30; and Yemen 113
Bunger, Miles 92
Burdick, Eugene 29, 47
Burgess, Donald 101
Burns, Findley 129
Burns, William 107
Burton, Richard 6
Byroade, Henry 85, 93, 105–06

C

Camp David Accords 45, 184–85
Campbell, Joseph 27
Caradon (Lord) 131–32, 139
Carleton, Alford 88–89
Carolan, Thomas J.: brief biography of 191; *see also* Middle East Area Program (MEAP); Middle East hand(s)
Carter, Jimmy: and Camp David talks 45, 184–85; Eilts as advisor to 184–85; Kerr as advisor to 78; and resignation of Andrew Young 172; support for Pahlavi regime 179
Carter administration: hostage crisis under 183; and Soviet threat 183
Cecil, Charles 70, 75
Central Intelligence Agency (CIA): and Camp David talks 184–85; and Chamoun regime in Lebanon 182–83; covert actions during Eric Johnston Plan 93–95; educational level of personnel dealing with foreign policy 15; Middle East hands on 173; and Orientalism

184–85; provision of technical training to Egypt 106–07; relationship with State Department under Eisenhower 87; role in Syria 179; and secret Arabists during Truman/Eisenhower years 173; and Shah of Iran 183
Chamoun, Camille 89–90, 102, 173, 182–83
chemical weapons 179–80
China hands: Fairbank on 22; lack of opportunities for 52; and McCarthyism 2–3, 16, 20, 86; origins in missionary community 40
Churchill, Winston 24
Clifford, Clark 27
Clinton, Bill, praise for Middle East hands 188
Coghill, Patrick 89
Cohen, Warren I. 113
Cold War axioms 76, 182–84
Communism: and Baghdad Pact 88, 101, 114, 176, 182; in Egypt 100–01, 159, 177; Eisenhower administration view on 86, 182–83; Middle East hands on 177; in South Yemen 177–78; and Syria 177; in Yemen 178; *see also* Soviet Union
Conference of Presidents of Jewish Organizations 12
Congress, support of early language program by 47, 58
Copeland, Miles 86, 93
Countryman, John R.: brief biography of 191; *see also* Middle East Area Program (MEAP); Middle East hand(s)
Crabb, Cecil 111
Crawford, William Rex: brief biography of 191; career path of 42–43; and Eric Johnston Plan 171; on expertise gained from area experience 79; on Hart and Hare 29; intelligence gathering in Yemen by 99–100; on Israeli lobbyists 112; and Joseph Johnson Plan 110–11, 117–21, 149, 171; on Kissinger 145; on living conditions in Saudi Arabia 54; on need for Middle East specialization 5; on NSC under Johnson administration 122; on regional dialects 60; and risks of being Middle East hand 69, 187; on skill rating metric 61; skilled linguist personality type of 37; on US not being overidentified with Arabs/Israelis 173; *see also* Middle East Area Program (MEAP); Middle East hand(s)
crypto-diplomacy 93
Curtiss, Richard 16, 131–32, 147

D

Davies, Rodger P.: on appointment of Symmes to Jordan 151; brief biography of 191; on language learning 50; murder of 69, 167–68, 186–87; publications of 56; skilled linguist personality type of 37; on UN Resolution 242 132; on undercutting Soviet influence with food aid 177; *see also* Middle East Area Program (MEAP); Middle East hand(s)
Dawson, Richard 83
Dayan, Moshe 160, 163
Declaration of Principles (1993) 4, 10, 172
Defense Department, on Israeli-Arab policy, 1958 101
DeNovo, John 20
DeSantis, Hugh 67
Dickman, Francois M.: brief biography of 192; political science personality type of 36–37; *see also* Middle East Area Program (MEAP); Middle East hand(s)
Dimona nuclear facility (Israel) 112, 121, 133, 179–80
Dinitz, Sacha 166
Dinsmore, Lee F.: on assassinations of diplomats 162; brief biography of 192; on oil crisis 164; *see also* Middle East Area Program (MEAP); Middle East hand(s)
Djerejian, Edward P.: brief biography of 192; and Orientalist stereotype 15; *see also* Orientalist(s)
Dobrynin, Anatoly 88, 142, 147, 157
Dodge, David 83
Donnelley, Dixon 127–28
Draper, Morris: brief biography of 192; career path of 181; on McFarlane 181; *see also* Middle East Area Program (MEAP); Middle East hand(s)
Drumbell, John 110
Dulles, Allen 27, 62, 87, 102
Dulles, Eleanor 87
Dulles, John Foster: and Arab nationalism 88, 103; death of 106; and Eddy 25, 88–89; and Eisenhower Doctrine 98; family background of 87; on Foreign Service 86; Globalist view of 81, 103; inflexibility toward new leadership in Middle East 105–06; and Israeli occupation of Gaza 97; on Israeli-Arab policy, 1958 101; on Khrushchev 101; language training program, support of 58; Middle East hands on 88; and Nasser 10, 87–88, 93; and Operation Alpha 91;

and Orientalists 88–89; refugee camp visit by 89; and Richards Mission 98; on Soviet arms to Yemen 99; on Soviet threat 76, 89–90; Soviets on 88; and State Department shakeup, 1956 31; and Suez Canal 95–96; and US-British policy linkage 89–91, 95; and water plan for Egypt 100; and wheat aid to Egypt 106

E
Eagleton, William L., Jr.: brief biography of 192; *see also* Middle East Area Program (MEAP); Middle East hand(s)
Eban, Abba: on boundaries of Israel 160; on Dean Rusk 110; and importance of US presidential policy 128; and Richards Mission 99; on UN Resolution 242 130–32
Eddy, William 22–25, 39, 88–89
Egypt: Communists in 100–01, 159, 177; and crisis, 1967 122; downing of Mecom Oil Company plane by 122–23; and Eisenhower administration 183; and Johnson administration 122–25; and Kennedy administration 110, 113–14, 183; and Kissinger 144–45, 162; occupied territories, attack on 173–74; and October War (1973) 163–64; reaction to US arms delivery to Israel 148; and Rogers Peace Plan failure 150–51; signs friendship treaty with Soviets 159; and Sinai II Agreement 166; Soviet military aid to 147, 150–51, 176, 183; US wheat aid to 107, 121–24; and War of Attrition 147–48, 150, 183; water plan for 100; *see also* Nasser, Gamal; Palestinian Liberation Organization (PLO); Rogers Peace Plan; Six Day War; United Arab Republic (UAR)
Ehrlichman, John 139, 142, 157
Eilts, Hermann F.: as advisor to Carter 184–85; on area experience as Arabic program requirement 54; assassination plot against 185, 188; and Baghdad Pact 176; brief biography of 192; career path of 37, 44–45, 86, 184–85; on complexity of Middle Eastern issues 17; and Ford administration 166–67; J. F. Dulles relationship with 88; on lack of influence of Middle East hands 12; on Palestinian Memoranda 172; political science personality type of 36; and refugee problem 117; and risks of being Middle East hand 187; on Rogers Peace Plan 147–48; shirt-sleeve diplomacy by 111; on Sisco-Kissinger alliance 144; on Six Day War, US role in 129; on specialized language training 56–57; *see also* Middle East Area Program (MEAP); Middle East hand(s)
Eisenhower, Dwight D.: appointments to Near East Affairs by 85–86; on influence of Soviets in Middle East 76; response to election of Chamoun 173; and Suez War 96–97, 175; and William Rogers 138
Eisenhower administration: and aid program to Egypt 107; and Communism 86, 182–83; and Eric Johnston plan 91–95; and Globalist view 81; language program support by 47, 58, 62; linkage of US-British Middle East policy under 89–91, 95; Middle East Area Program under 1; policy initiatives under 90–108; quiet diplomacy during 106–08; and Suez War 95–97; US-Israeli relationship under 86–87; *see also* Dulles, John Foster; Eisenhower Doctrine
Eisenhower Doctrine 98–104, 182–83; and decline of US position in Middle East 105–06; and "Long-Range US Policy Toward the Near East" 101–02; and Marine landings in Lebanon 102–05; overview of 98; and Richards Mission 98–100, 108
England: *see* Great Britain
Eric Johnston Plan: covert CIA actions during 93–95; disposition of ambassadors after failure of 94; failure of 93–95, 108; Middle East hands support of 2; overview of 91–95; reception of 92–93; Seelye on 91–92
Evans, Rowland 159
Eveland, Wilbur 93

F
fadayeen 149, 151, 153, 155
Fairbank, John K. 16, 22
Faisal (Saudi Arabia) 28, 30–31, 61, 115
Faris, Nabih 74–76
Farouk (Egypt) 24
Feldman, Meyer "Mike" 112, 116–17, 119
Ferguson, Charles 7; as ASTP director 55; brings Modern Standard Arabic to US universities 19; establishes language school at Beirut 1, 47; on expansion of Middle Eastern studies in academia 55; joins State Department 34; language training materials developed by 56; resigns from Beirut language school 60; success of language program of 56; teaching method of 33–34, 55–56; use of native informants by 55

Flapan, Simha 150
Food for Peace program 31, 107, 110–11, 114
Ford, Gerald, and administration: Israel-US relationship during 138, 166; Kissinger removed as NSC advisor 165–66; and Middle East hands 166–67; and Palestinian Memoranda 167; and shuttle diplomacy 166–67; and Sinai II Agreement 166–67
Foreign policy as presidential policy in US 2–3, 128, 140, 174
Foreign Service Institute (FSI): *see* language training, US program; Middle East Area Program (MEAP); Middle East hand(s)
Foreign Service Officer (FSO): *see* Middle East Area Program (MEAP); Middle East hand(s)
Foreign Service Reform Act (1946) 28, 48
Fortas, Abe 125
Forty Committee 140, 142
France: and building of Dimona facility 179; and Suez War 90–91, 96–97
Fulbright, William J. 10, 143

G

Galanto, Fred: brief biography of 192; *see also* Middle East Area Program (MEAP); Middle East hand(s)
Galili Document 171
Gaza Strip: Israeli attacks on Arabs in 93–95, 173; Israeli occupation of 97; numbers of Palestinian refugees in 151; wheat aid to Palestinian refugees in 117
Gazit, Mordechai 112, 115, 119–20, 127
GI Bill 7, 33, 35, 37, 39
Gibb, H.A.R. 7
Glaspie, April: brief biography of 192; as early woman Arabist 41–42; *see also* Middle East Area Program (MEAP); Middle East hand(s)
Globalist view: on Arab nationalists 10; of Dulles 81, 103; on Israel 174–75; and Kissinger 81, 170; Middle East hands on 81–82; and Nixon 81; overview of 170; *vs.* Regionalist view 10–11, 81–83
Golan Heights 173–74
Goldberg, Arthur 128, 130–32, 139
Great Britain: linkage of Middle East policy with US 89–91, 95; and Suez War 87, 91, 95–97; and Yemen 99–100; *see also* language training, British program
Green, Joseph C. 86–87, 89–90, 94
Greene, Joseph N., Jr., Kissinger removes from Cairo 144–45

Griffin, Philip J.: brief biography of 192; *see also* Middle East Area Program (MEAP); Middle East hand(s)
Gromyko, Andrei 131, 142
Gulf War, and weapons proliferation 179–80

H

Haass, Richard 13
Habash, George 78, 153
Habib, Philip 144
Haig, Alexander 154
Halperin, Morton 141, 163, 182
Hambley, Mark G.: brief biography of 192; *see also* Middle East Area Program (MEAP); Middle East hand(s)
Hare, Paul J. 39, 107
Hare, Raymond: appointed Inspector General of the Foreign Service 85; background of 8, 29; on French language school 30; lack of military service 39; on Marine landings in Lebanon 104–05; as model for Middle East hands 31–32; and quiet diplomacy 31, 106–07, 183; on refugees 93; retires from NEA 121; and Tripartite Agreement 179; on undercutting Soviet influence with food aid 177; on US capability to control events 173; and US-Egypt relationship 106–07, 123; *see also* Middle East hand(s); Orientalist(s)
Harman, Avraham 114, 125
Harriman, Averill 44
Hart, Parker: background of 8, 29–31; and Ben-Gurion's visit to Kennedy 115; on Israeli occupation 132–33; lack of military service 39; on living conditions in Middle East 54; as model for Middle East hands 31–32; Nixon removes in favor of Sisco 144; obtains seat for Killgore at Beirut language program 59; on quiet diplomacy 183; on wheat aid to Egypt 106; *see also* Middle East hand(s); Orientalist(s)
Hawk missiles 119–20, 133
Heikal, Mohammed 100, 107, 122–23
Helms, Richard 179
Henderson, Loy 27, 62
Hersh, Seymour 137, 148
Herter, Christian 62, 106
hijackings 153
Hitti, Philip 7
Holocaust 24, 174
Hopkins, Frank 53

Horan, Hume A.: brief biography of 192; on lack of interest in Arabic training 83; skilled linguist personality type of 37; *see also* Middle East Area Program (MEAP); Middle East hand(s)
Hoskins, Harold B. 57–58, 60, 62, 78
Houghton, Robert B.: brief biography of 193; *see also* Middle East Area Program (MEAP); Middle East hand(s)
Howell, W. Nathaniel: brief biography of 193; *see also* Middle East Area Program (MEAP); Middle East hand(s)
Hunt, Leamon Ray 12, 187; murder of 168, 188
Hussein (Jordan): assassination attempt on 152; and *fedayeen* 153, 155; Kissinger's support of 152; and L. B. Johnson 122; and October War (1973) 163; requests US to recall Symmes 152; and Rogers Peace Plan 149; Symmes on 151; *see also* Jordan
Hussein, Saddam 180–81

I

Idris, Mohammad 98
Indyk, Martin 13, 138
International Atomic Energy Agency (IAEA) 112, 121, 180
International Bank for Redevelopment 116
International Red Cross, and PLFP hijackings 153
Iran: and embassy hostage crisis 179; and nuclear weapons 180; revolution in 183; and Richards Mission 98–99; US support for 179, 183
Iran-Contra, Middle East hands on 173
Iraq: and chemical weapons 180; and nuclear weapons 180; revolution in 105, 108, 183; and Richards Mission 98–99
Isaacson, Walter 142
Islam: and Arab nationalism 75–78; and political decline of Arabs 75–76
Israel: and absolute security 148, 174; and boundaries/occupied territories 156, 160, 173–74; and Declaration of Principles 4, 10, 172; Dimona nuclear facility in 112, 121, 133, 179–80; and Eric Johnston Plan 92–95; evenhanded policy, response to 145–46; and Ford administration 138, 166; and Hawk missile sales 119–20; and invasion of Lebanon, 1982–84 155; and Johnson administration 126–30, 133, 183; and Jordan 154; Joseph Johnson Plan rejected by 119; Libyan airliner shot down by 161; military aid/defense spending 160; and nuclear energy technology aid 165; numbers of Palestinian refugees in 151; and October War (1973) 163–64; Osirak nuclear reactor, attack by 180; and Phantom jet sales 148, 158; and prisoner exchanges/ransom 153; and Richards Mission 99; Rogers Peace Plan rejected by 149–50; and settlements in occupied territories 156; Six Day War victory, reaction to 128–29; stalemate strategy, consequences of 150–51; and Suez War 90–91, 96–97; US arms sales to 148; US joint military research program with 179; US military aid to 127–29, 138, 160; US "special relationship" with 1–2, 129, 133, 174–75; USS *Liberty* attack by 11, 125–26, 179; and War of Attrition 147, 150–51, 183; "Year of Decision, The" peace plan, response to 156–59; *see also* American Israel Public Affairs Committee (AIPAC); Joseph Johnson Plan; Rogers Peace Plan
Israeli Defense Forces (IDF) 11, 154, 160, 164
Israeli-Jordanian-Palestinian Authority water agreement 94
Issawi, Charles 79

J

Jacobson, Eddie 22
Japanese hands 52
Jarring, Gunner 132, 147
Jeffrey-Jones, Rhodri 15
Johnson, Alexis 141–43, 153–54, 162
Johnson, Joseph 117–20, 149; *see also* Joseph Johnson Plan
Johnson, Lyndon B. (as president): appoints Battle as NEA Assistant Secretary 123–24; and area specialists 121–22; and Israel 126–27, 130, 133; promotion of women as ambassadors 41; and UN Resolution 242 130–32; *see also* Johnson administration
Johnson, Lyndon B. (as vice president): attitude toward Middle East 113; and Yemen 113
Johnson, Park 88–89
Johnson administration: Egypt-American relationship under 122–25; and events leading to Six Day War 124–27; and Israeli attack on USS *Liberty* 11, 125–26, 179; Israeli-American relationship under 183; and military aid to Israel 129; and public opinion on military aid to Israel

127–28; and Six Day War 124–29; and UN Resolution 242 130–32, 171
Johnston, Eric 86; and reception of Eric Johnston plan 92; *see also* Eric Johnston Plan
Jones, Curtis F.: brief biography of 193; career after J. F. Kennedy assassination 121; on diplomats taken hostage 161–62; joins Moroccan Arabic language program 33–34; moves to State Department 34; on new breed of diplomat 53; on refugees in Lebanon 155; *see also* Middle East Area Program (MEAP); Middle East hand(s)
Jones, Elizabeth 41–42
Jones, G. Lewis 43, 85
Jordan: attacks on US embassy property in 151; civil war in 147; and crisis, 1970 151–55; and decline of US position in Middle East 105; and Eric Johnston Plan 92; and Ford administration 166; Israeli raid on Qibya 92; and jetliner hijackings by PFLP 153; L. D. Brown appointed ambassador to 152; near-collapse of monarchy in 108; PLO plan to takeover 151; PLO/Syrian invasion of 154–55; refugees in 151, 155; revolution in 183; and Rogers Peace Plan 149; and Six Day War ceasefire 129; US opposition to arms sales to 138; *see also* Hussein (Jordan); Six Day War
Jordan River diversion: *see* Eric Johnston Plan
Jordanian Task Force (NEA) 153
Joseph Johnson Plan 2, 110–11; and aftermath of Six Day War 129–30; avoidance of publicizing 149; drafting of initiative 110–11, 117–19, 171; failure of 120–21, 133, 183; and Hawk missile sales 119–20; overview of 117–21, 171

K

Kamel, Mustafa 13
Kaplan, Robert: Arabic language training of 44; on ease of picking up language skills 79; on Middle East hands 4, 14–15, 34, 38; on Paganelli 175; on radicalization of student body at AUB 74
Katzenbach, Nicholas 151
Keefer, Louis 33
Kenen, Isaiah L. 111
Kennedy, John F. 63; action intellectuals of 109–10, 113; approach toward Middle East 111; area specialists, views on 121–22; assassination of 121; correspondence on Ben-Gurion meeting 114–16; and Faisal 115; Food for Peace program of 31, 107, 110–11, 114; Jewish concerns supported by 112, 127, 133; Meir meets with 112, 121; quiet diplomacy under 110; on revolution 178; support of area specialists by 109; *see also* Kennedy administration
Kennedy, Robert F. 161
Kennedy administration: and "Anticipated Israel Objections" list 118–19; and financial costs of UN refugee camps 116–18; normalization of relations with Nasser under 110; and quiet diplomacy 110, 113–21; and refugees 110–11, 116–21; and Yemen 113
Kerr, Malcolm: and anti-American hostility 167; on Arab-Israeli conflict 80; background of 7–8, 78–79; on dangers of being Middle East hand 186; on effect of Western influence on Middle East 80–81; on failure of peace initiatives 171; on Globalist *vs.* Regionalist view 10, 81–82; on inherent volatility of Lebanon 80–82; at MEAP 74–75; murder of 12, 83–84, 188; on Nasser 76, 124; on volatility of refugee camps 80
Khalil, Osamah 197
Khartoum, murder of Middle East hands at 155, 161–62
Khomeini regime, and hostage crisis 179
Khrushchev, Nikita 100–01
Kibya raids, causes of 173
Killgore, Andrew I.: on Arab nationalism 178; brief biography of 193; on lack of institutional strength to protect Arabists 144; on obtaining seat in Beirut language program 59; on pressures of training 71; technical personality type of 37; on US regional underrepresentation of Middle East hands 40; *see also* Middle East Area Program (MEAP); Middle East hand(s)
King-Crane Commission 25
Kissinger, Henry: alliance with Sisco 144; on Arab League recognition of PLO 165; backchannel diplomacy of 135, 141–42, 147, 168; background of 137; contract put out on life of 188; convenes emergency meeting on Jordan 154; disobeys direct presidential order 154; dual track diplomacy of 173; on flaw in US policy 148; and gendered assignments 41–42; and Globalist view 81; Hersh on

137, 148; and Israel 137–38, 150–51, 157–59; and Jordan 152–53; Kraft on 159; and Lebanon 152–53; and Meloy 68–69, 186–87; on Middle East hands 79, 141, 143–45, 152–53, 159, 168; National Security Council expansion by 137, 140–45; on Nixon's personal views on Jews 137; and no negotiations policy 153; and October War (1973) 163–64, 170, 183; on oil crisis 165; and Palestinian Memoranda 171; peace strategy of 11, 174, 183; and Phantom Memo 158–59; and risks of being Middle East hand 186–87; on Rogers 139, 157; and Rogers Peace Plan 147–48, 150; and Sadat/Egypt 157–59; and Scranton 145; as Secretary of State 143–44, 163–64; self-image making by 143; sends non-Arabist as Special Envoy to Beirut 152–53; and Sinai II Agreement 166; and Soviet threat 76, 137, 158; stalemate strategy of 146, 148, 150–51, 155, 159, 170–71; and "Year of Decision, The" 157–59

Komer, Robert 82, 111–13, 119, 121
Korn, David 149, 153, 161
Kraft, Joseph 13–15, 122, 143–44, 158–59
Kreis Resident Officer 38
Kuwait 12, 97

L

Lacharriere, Guy 132
Laird, Melvin 154
Lakeland, William 100
land for peace: *see* UN Resolution 242
Lane, George M.: brief biography of 193; on British *vs.* US language learning methods 49–50; on career advancement 66; career path of 37, 43; on failure of Bergus initiative 160; on learning through proverbs 68; and murder of US ambassador to Lebanon 2, 168; on Nixon during Six Day War 136; on Palestinian failings 77; and risks of being Middle East hand 69, 187–88; *see also* Middle East Area Program (MEAP); Middle East hand(s)
language training, British program: and dialect learning 67; establishment of 21–22; focus of 62; grammar-translation method of 49–50; location of 68; rejection of area specialists 61–62; training materials for 56; US training *vs.* 68; *see also* language training, US program

language training, Soviet program 50–51, 67, 73
language training, US program: age of candidates 54–55; and audiolingual method 49, 62; British training *vs.* 68; competition for seats in 52; and dialect learning 59–60; early program at Beirut 1, 47–48, 58, 62; first attempts to train Arabists in Algiers 48; first director of 48; funding issues 62; key objective of 60; and linguist gap 58; methodology of 68; Moroccan school 50; and native informants 55; need for 48, 61–63, 68–69; origins of 5, 33–34, 49; recruitment for 51, 58–59; senior diplomat views on 48, 53–54; and skill maintenance 61; and skills rating metric 61; and social distinctions in spoken Arabic 50; specialized programs 56–57; success of FSI six-month program of 56; successful students in 59–60; teaching methods of 6–7; *see also* language training, British program; Middle East Area Program (MEAP)
Language-Designated Post (LDP) 43, 57
Lavon, Pinhas 93
Lawrence, T. E. 21
Lawrence of Arabia 6, 14
Lebanon: CIA and Chamoun regime in 182–83; civil war in 105, 108; and Eric Johnston Plan 92; Israeli invasions of 12, 155, 173, 175; Kerr on 79–80; Marine landings in 102–05; refugees in 151, 155; revolution in, 1958 102; *see also* language training, US program
L'Ecole des Langues Orientales Vivantes 30
Lederer, William 29, 47
Lenczowski, George 126
Lewis, Bernard 5
Lewis, Michael 4
Lewis, Samuel 45, 184
Libya: airliner shot down by Israel 161; and nuclear weapons 180; and oil embargo 164; and Qaddafi 183, 185, 188; and Richards Mission 98–99; US air base in 111, 183
linguist gap 58
linguist personality type 37
Lockman, Zachary 197
Lodge, Henry Cabot 26
"Long-Range US Policy Toward the Near East" (NSC #5801) 101–02
Lowrie, Arthur: brief biography of 193; *see also* Middle East Area Program (MEAP); Middle East hand(s)

INDEX   249

M
Maaloof, Amin 16
Mack, David L.: brief biography of 193;
   see also Middle East Area Program (MEAP);
   Middle East hand(s)
Macomber, William 153–54, 161–62
majlis (parliament) 60
Mak, Dayton S. 53, 55–56; brief biography
   of 193; see also Middle East Area Program
   (MEAP); Middle East hand(s)
Makarios regime 187
Makdisi, George 55 brief biography of 193;
   see also Middle East Area Program (MEAP);
   Middle East hand(s)
Mansoor, Menahim 63
Marine Battalion Landing Team, attack on 2
Marshall, George C. 86
Marthinsen, Charles E.: brief biography of
   193; see also Middle East Area Program
   (MEAP); Middle East hand(s)
May, James A.: brief biography of 193;
   see also Middle East Area Program (MEAP);
   Middle East hand(s)
McCarthy, Joseph 57, 86
McCarthyism, and China hands 2–3, 16,
   20, 86
McCarus, Ernest: at AUB 65, 67–68;
   background of 66–67; takes over FSI
   program 63; teaching methods of 67; use
   of Arabic proverbs to teach culture and
   language 68; see also American University of
   Beirut (AUB)
McClintock, Robert 28, 103–05, 115
McFarlane, Robert 15, 82, 181
McGhee, George 25, 176
McLoughlin, Leslie 23
McNamara, Robert: appointed Secretary
   of Defense 110; on Israeli attack on USS
   Liberty 126
Mearshimer, John 13, 138
Mecom, John 122–23
Mecom Oil Company 122–23
media: Arabic language, changes after advent
   of mass media 50–51; attacks on Middle
   East hands 3; Nasser's use of 67–68
Meir, Golda: on Israel 121; and Joseph
   Johnson Plan 119; meeting with J. F.
   Kennedy 112, 121; on Nixon 137; on
   Rogers Peace Plan 149; on US Phantom
   deliveries 148; on Zionism 16
Meloy, Francis 68–69, 83, 167–68, 186–87
Menand, Louis 9

Meyer, Armin: appointment to Israel 109; and
   Ben-Gurion's visit to J. F. Kennedy 115;
   and Joseph Johnson Plan 117, 120; and
   normalization of relations with Egypt 116;
   on policy of J. F. Kennedy toward Nasser
   110; and refugee problem 116–17; and
   US-Egyptian relations 105; visits refugee
   camps 108, 113
Middle East Area Program (MEAP): Arabic
   proverbs as teaching method of 68; area
   studies, 1957 to 1975 73–83; critique
   of 72–73; development of 7–8, 35–36;
   establishment of 33, 65; field experience
   as component of 69–71; first director of
   66–67; goals of 65, 73–74; history/overview
   of 1–4; instruction methods of 71; J. F.
   Kennedy's support of 109; location of
   65–66, 68, 73–79; Nixon's hostility toward
   142; professionalization of 8–9; rationale for
   65; and Regional perspective 76; and team/
   individual area training 67; see also language
   training, US program; Middle East hand(s)
Middle East Centre for Arab Studies (MECAS):
   see language training, British program
Middle East hand(s) 146; accusations of
   pro-Arab sympathies 174; and aftermath
   of Six Day War 125, 129; anti-Semitism
   charges against 3–4, 13, 174; and anti-US
   hostility 77; on Arab nationalism 176, 178;
   on area experience as Arabic program
   requirement 54; and Ben-Gurion's visit to
   Kennedy 115; brief biographies of 191–96;
   Bureau of Near East Affairs diplomats
   vs. 1; career opportunities for 51–53, 66,
   186; career path, typical 42–45; common
   points in careers of 185; on Communism
   177; criticism of 3–4, 9, 12–16, 79, 159;
   defining 4–6; description of typical 34–36,
   38–39; diplomatic initiatives supported by
   2; educational level of 15–16; and Egypt
   110, 114, 116, 144–45, 156, 158–59;
   and Eisenhower administration 106–08;
   first black 40; first woman 41; and Ford
   administration 166–67; gender diversity
   of 40–42; geographic origins of 39–40;
   and GI Bill 7, 33, 35, 37, 39; on Iran-
   Contra 173; on J. F. Dulles 88; and Johnson
   administration 133, 178–79; and Jordan
   152, 155; and Joseph Johnson Plan 117,
   120–21; journalistic attacks on 3, 13–15;
   Kissinger on 79, 141, 143–45, 152–53,
   159, 168; lack of influence of 3, 12, 82;

length of posting under Eisenhower 86; and living conditions in Middle East 54; on Marine landings in Lebanon 103–05; military background of 36, 39; on military support of Egypt by Soviets 150; on Nasser 178–79; and Nixon administration 135–37, 149; and no negotiations policy 153–54; on oil crisis 13–14, 164–65; Orientalists *vs.* 34, 36, 38–39; overview of 169; on Palestinian Memoranda 172; and personal risk 66; personality types of 36–38; policy outlook of 2–3, 9, 86; precursors of 28–32; professionalization of 51; as Public Affairs officers 71–72; and quiet diplomacy 106–08, 113–14, 148–49; racial diversity of 40; recruitment of 35, 52–53; and refugee problem 114; Regionalist view of 10–11; risks involved in being 69–71; on Rogers Peace Plan failure 149–50; on roots of contemporary events 16–17; on Sadat 156–57; shirt-sleeve diplomacy by 111; and Six Day War 133, 178–79; on Soviet threat 176–78, 183–84; stereotype of 4, 14–15, 34; and US Phantom deliveries to Israel 148; on US relationship with Israel 174; value of 52; violence toward 2–3, 68–69, 81, 161–62, 167–68, 184–89; and "Year of Decision, The" 156, 158–59; *see also* Beirut Axioms; language training, US program; Middle East Area Program (MEAP); *individual hand*
Middle East Institute, establishment of 19
Middle East Studies Association, establishment of 19
Mitchell, Martha 161
Modern Standard Arabic (MSA) 60; and dialect learning 67; emergence of 51, 67; first university-level courses in 19; textbooks for 66, 68
Moore, George C.: brief biography of 193; murder of 81, 121, 153–54, 161–62, 167–68, 186; personality type of 38; *see also* Middle East Area Program (MEAP); Middle East hand(s)
Moose, James 30, 53–54
Morgenthau, Hans 10
Morocco, FSI school in 50
Morris, Roger 141, 167
Murphy, Richard W.: and American Embassy attacks, 1983 70; on Arab-Israeli talks 172; on Assad 173; as assistant to Hart 115; on AUB faculty 74; brief biography of 194; on British language learning method 49; career path of 37, 43–44; on Communism 177; field experience of 70; and Ford administration 166–67; on lack of influence of Middle East hands 3; on Nasser 178–79; and Orientalist stereotype 15; political science personality type of 36; and risks of being Middle East hand 187–88; on Soviet language learning program 50–51; on Syrian-Israeli talks 173; *see also* Middle East Area Program (MEAP); Middle East hand(s); Orientalist(s)
Murphy, Robert 104–05

N

Naff, Ernest 66
Nasser, Gamal: on aid *vs.* independence 123; as Arab Nationalism itself 178–79; attempt to unify Arab nations 76; Cold Warrior perspective on 177; and Communists 100–01; death of 156; demands removal of UN peacekeepers 126; and Free Officer's movement 106; Globalist *vs.* Regionalist view on 10; and J. F. Dulles 10, 87–88, 93; and L. B. Johnson 113, 123; and Marine landings at Beirut 104; media use by 67–68; Middle East hands on 178–79; Murphy's meeting with 105; and nationalism 176, 178; Parker on 124, 132; and Radio Cairo 106–07; and social distinctions in spoken Arabic 50; and Soviet military aid 148, 151; and Soviet wheat aid 106; and Suez Canal 95–96; and US wheat aid 123
National Association of Arab Americans (AAAA) 138
National Security Council (NSC): and Johnson administration 122; and Joseph Johnson Plan in aftermath of Six Day War 129–30; and Kissinger 141, 160, 162; and "Long-Range US Policy Toward the Near East" 101–02; and Nixon administration 137, 140–45; and Rogers Peace Plan 160; and Yemen War 112–13
nationalism: *see* Arab nationalism
Near East and South Asian Affairs (NEA) 19, 66; Battle appointed as Assistant Secretary of 123–24; on failure of Eric Johnston Plan 93–95; foreign policy "three stage rocket" of, 1958 110–11; hiring/promotions reforms 28; and jetliner hijackings by PFLP 153; Jordanian Task Force of 153; Middle East hands *vs.* diplomats of 1; on refugees 93; Sisco becomes director of 139; and Soviet military aid to Yemen 99; State Department

employees *vs.* diplomats of 20; and Suez Canal 96; Talbot resigns as chief of 121; and technical aid to Yemen 100; typical desk officer 20–21; and US-Egypt relations 106; *see also* Orientalist(s); State Department
Nes, David 125
neutralism 102
Newson, David 11–12, 82
Newton, David G.: brief biography of 194; *see also* Middle East Area Program (MEAP); Middle East hand(s)
Niles, David 27
Nixon, Pat 90
Nixon, Richard M. (as president): appoints Kissinger Secretary of State 163; appoints L. Dean Brown ambassador of Jordan 152; conflicting objectives of Middle East policy of 137, 146; criticism of Middle East Hands 79; on diplomats taken hostage 161–62; and Globalist view 81; Kissinger disobeys direct order of 154; Kraft on 159; on Marine landings in Beirut 103; Middle East hands, view of 142; personal views on Jews 137; policy of as vice president/president 135–36; and rearming of Israel after October War (1973) 164; and Rogers Peace Plan 145–46, 149; on Soviet influence in Middle East 76; and Soviet threat 136–37, 146; State Department, view on 143; support for Shah of Iran 179, 183; and Watergate 163, 165; willingness to support Israel 136; *see also* Kissinger, Henry; Nixon administration
Nixon, Richard M. (as vice president): on Foreign Service 90; Middle East policy of 135–36; on Six Day War 136
Nixon administration: evenhanded policy under 145–46; and Jordan crisis, 1970 151–55; Jordanian ambassador post left unfilled under 152; and Middle East hands 135; National Security Council budget under 142; and no negotiations policy 153–54, 162; and Palestinian refugees 140; public opinion on military aid to Israel and Soviet threat during 136–37; quiet diplomacy during 148–49; and secret diplomacy 135; and UN Resolution 242 139–40; and "Year of Decision, The" 156; *see also* Kissinger, Henry
no negotiations policy 153–54, 162
Noel, Cleo A.: brief biography of 194; and Kreis Program 38; murder of 81, 153–54, 161–62, 167–68, 186; political science personality type of 36–37; *see also* Middle East Area Program (MEAP); Middle East hand(s)
Nolte, Richard 122, 124–25
Novak, Robert 159
NSC #5801, "Long-Range US Policy Toward the Near East" 101–02
nuclear power: Dimona facility 112, 121, 133, 179–80; Osirak nuclear reactor 180
nuclear weapons 111; proliferation of 179–80

O

October War (1973): consequences for US 147; and Kissinger 163–64, 170, 183; Rugh on 72, 194; Soviet aid to Egypt during 151; US aid to Israeli Defense Forces during 11, 164
oil, role in US Middle East policy 1
oil crisis/embargo: consequences to US 147, 164–65; Dinsmore on 164; *Forbes Magazine* on 14, 164–65; *Foreign Affairs* on 13–14, 164; Kissinger on 165; and Libya 164; Middle East hands on 13–14, 164–65; and Shah of Iran 164; and Syria 164
Olayan, Sulyman 30
Operation Alpha 91
Operation Grapes of Wrath 155
Operation Omega 96
Operation Peace for Galilee 12, 175
Organization of Petroleum Exporting Countries (OPEC) 13–14, 147, 164–65; *see also* oil crisis/embargo
Orientalism (Said) 6–7, 21
Orientalism, meaning of term 21
Orientalist(s): anti-Semitism charges against 20; area experience as requirement of 19–20; British 21–23; and CIA 184–85; commonalities among 27–28; defining 8; differences/similarities between US and British 22–23; educational endeavors of 21; entrenched power of 21; first generation proselytizers 21; and John Foster Dulles 88–89; key problem of 22; Middle East hands, difference from 34, 36, 38–39; missionary connection of 25–29; modern usage of term 6; original usage of term 6; overview of 19; stereotype of 14; Truman's relationship with 13, 19–20, 22, 24–28; and Zionism 8, 28; *see also* Near East and South Asian Affairs (NEA); *individual Orientalist*
Ornstein, Jacob 63

Osirak nuclear reactor 180
Ottoman Empire 75

P

Paganelli, Robert P.: brief biography of 175, 194; and Israel-Syria relations 175; *see also* Middle East Area Program (MEAP); Middle East hand(s)
Pahlavi, Reza 98
Pakistan, women Arabists in 42
Palestinian Conciliation Commission (PCC) 114; *see also* Joseph Johnson Plan
Palestinian failings, blame for 77–78
Palestinian Liberation Organization (PLO): Arab League recognition of 11, 165; Arafat becomes leader of 140; Beirut Axioms on 171–72; and Declaration of Principles 4, 10, 172; Jordan invasion by 154–55; Jordan takeover planned by 151, 154; and Palestinian Memoranda 167, 171–72; Seelye on 151
Palestinian Memoranda 167, 171–72
Palmer, Alison 41
Paper, Louis 112
Parker, Richard B.: on aftermath of US arms delivery to Israel 148; on Arab nationalism 178; on area studies 61; on attack on US by Nasser 123; and Baghdad revolution, 1958 102; on Beirut experiences 12; brief biography of 194; career path of 42; on changes in Arab perception of US 148–49; on Communist threat 177; on death of Russell 71; on demands of being Middle East hand 71; on Eric Johnston Plan failure 94; and events leading to Six Day War 124–25, 127; on J. F. Dulles 88, 97; and Lebanon revolution, 1958 102; on Marine landings in Lebanon 102–03, 105; on Nasser 124, 132; on Paganelli 175; and risks of being Middle East hand 69, 168, 187–88; on Rogers Peace Plan 150; on Sisco 144; on Soviet reaction to US support for Israel 180; success at Beirut language training program 59–60; technical personality type of 38; on UN Resolution 242 132; on US policy lack of success 84; *see also* Middle East Area Program (MEAP); Middle East hand(s)
Parmet, Herbert 114, 120
Peck, Edward L.: brief biography of 194; on control of Middle East policy by Kissinger 144; field experience of 71; on Forty Committee 142; in Iraq 180–81; *see also* Middle East Area Program (MEAP); Middle East hand(s)
Pelletreau, Robert H., Jr.: brief biography of 194; educational level of 16; and Orientalist stereotype 15; technical personality type of 37; *see also* Orientalist(s)
Peres, Shimon, on military disengagement 173
Peretz, Don 120
"Phantom Memo" controversy 143–44, 158
Pickering, Thomas 187
Pike Committee 140
PL-480 (wheat aid to Egypt) 121–23
Placke, James: brief biography of 194; *see also* Middle East Area Program (MEAP); Middle East hand(s)
political science personality type 36–37
Pope, Laurence E.: brief biography of 194; on Soviet Union 175; *see also* Middle East Area Program (MEAP); Middle East hand(s)
Popular Front for the Liberation of Palestine (PFLP), jetliner hijackings by 153
Porter, William 143–44, 187
Post, Jerrold 184–85
professionalism, defining 8–9

Q

Qaddafi, Muammar 183, 185, 188
Quandt, William: as advisor to Carter at Camp David talks 45, 184; on Arabists 5; on Middle East policy and election of 1972 160; on Rogers Peace Plan 147, 149–50; on "Year of Decision, The" 156
quiet diplomacy 2; Hare on 31, 106–07, 183; Hart on 183; and Kennedy administration 110, 113–21; and Nixon administration 148

R

Rabat Summit 167
Rabin, Yitzhak (as ambassador) 4; and Israeli borders 160; and military disengagement 173; on need for ground action 154; and peace negotiations 82; and Rogers Peace Plan 150; and "Year of Decision, The" 159
Rabin, Yitzhak (as Premier), relationship with Ford 166
racial diversity of Middle East hands 40
radio Arabic 60, 67
Radio Cairo "Voice of the Arabs" 106–07
Rayburn, Sam 102
Reagan, Ronald, sends peacekeeping forces to Beirut 83

refugees: and Bundy 129–30; camps as breeding grounds for radicals 78, 121, 183; *fadayeen* in Jordan 149, 151, 153, 155; J. F. Dulles visits camps 89; Jones on refugees in Lebanon 155; and Joseph Johnson Plan 110–11; and Kennedy administration 110–11, 116–21; Kerr on volatility of 80; L. B. Johnson visits Shatila camp 113; Meyer visits camps 108; Nixon on 135–36; numbers in 1967 151; numbers in Gaza Strip 151; numbers in UN camps 90; right of return of 3; Sabra and Shatila camps 77, 113; wheat aid to 117; *see also* Eric Johnston Plan; Joseph Johnson Plan; Rogers Peace Plan

Regionalist view: on Arab nationalists 10; *vs.* Globalist view 10–11, 81–83; Middle East hands on 81–82

Reston, James 62

Revolutionary Command (Free Officers; Egypt) 95–96

Riad, Mohammad 132–33, 158

Rice, Frank 59

Richards, James 86; background of 98; on Soviets in Yemen 99; *see also* Richards mission

Richards Mission: failure of 108; size of aid package as unacceptable 98–99

Rifai, Zaid 152

Roche, John P. 130

Rockefeller, Nelson 137

Rockwell, Stuart 102–03

Rogers, William P. 10, 137, 140–41; background of 138–39; on diplomats taken hostage 162; and Egypt-Soviet friendship treaty 159; and Kissinger 139, 141–44, 157; Kraft on 159; on Middle East policy of Nixon 146; Nixon on 142; and peace plan of Sadat 157; publicizing of Rogers Peace Plan through speech by 149; on ransom 153; refusal to sign no negotiations policy 153–54, 162; replaced by Kissinger 135, 163; and UN Resolution 242 139–40; and "Year of Decision, The" 158–59; *see also* Rogers Peace Plan

Rogers Peace Plan 136, 145–51; consequences of failure of 147; drafting of 147; effect of stalemate strategy of Kissinger on 146; events leading up to 145–46; Kissinger orders NSC to produce paper to destroy 160; Middle East hands support of 2–3; and Nixon 136; Parker on 150; publicizing through speech by Rogers 149; rationale of 146–47; on UAR-Israeli front 147–48

Rooney, John 62

Roosevelt, Archie 103

Roosevelt, Franklin D. 23–24

Roosevelt, Kim 93, 103

Ross, Christopher: brief biography of 194; *see also* Middle East Area Program (MEAP); Middle East hand(s)

Ross, Dennis 13

Rostow, Eugene 82

Rostow, Walter W. 110, 127, 183

Rountree, William 85

Rugh, William A.: brief biography of 194; on October War (1973) 72, 194; political analysis of Arab journalism by 71–72; *see also* Middle East Area Program (MEAP); Middle East hand(s)

Rusk, Dean 10, 41; and aftermath of Six Day War 129; and Ben-Gurion's visit to Kennedy 115; and Bundy 110; and events leading to Six Day War 125; and Israeli territorial expansion 126; on Israeli withdrawal 132; and Joseph Johnson Plan 117, 119, 133; personality of 110; and public opinion on Arab-Israeli crisis 127–28; on US-Israel relationship 132; and Yemen 113

Russell, Beatrice 70–71

Russell, Earl: career path of 37, 70–71; death of 70–71; field experience of 70; on need for Arabic speakers 63; political science personality type of 36; on rationale for Middle East Area Program 65; shirt-sleeve diplomacy by 111

Russia hands 40, 52

S

Sachar, Howard 92, 95, 164

Sadat, Anwar: background of 156–57; and Camp David talks 45, 184–85; Israeli response to peace plan of 156–59; Kissinger's response to peace plan of 157–59; Kraft on peace plan of 159; Middle East hands reaction to peace plan of 156; Nixon administration reaction to peace plan 156; offer to reopen Suez Canal by 156, 158; ousts Soviet contingent 160; and peace plan, "Year of Decision, The" 156; plans to win back Israeli-occupied territories 163; Sterner's relationship with 60; on War of Attrition 151

Said, Edward 6–7, 21

Said, Nuri al- 98
Salibi, Kamal 74
Saltonstall, Leverett 63
Sands, William 1
Saud, Abdul Aziz al- 23–24, 106
Saudi Arabia: accusations of US aid to Israel during Six Day War 129; ARAMCO in 13, 25, 95; and Ben-Gurion's visit to J. F. Kennedy 115; US air base in 111; view of L. B. Johnson toward 113; women Arabists in 42
Saunders, Harold 127, 129–30
Schlesinger, Arthur: on area specialists under Eisenhower 109; on Dean Rusk 110; on J. F. Kennedy and Nasser 113; on J. F. Kennedy as knowledgeable on Middle East 111; on US military aid to Israel 164
Schlesinger, James 140
Schoenbaum, David 160
Schulzinger, Robert 28
Scotes, Thomas J.: brief biography of 194; *see also* Middle East Area Program (MEAP); Middle East hand(s)
Scranton, William 145–46, 156
Seale, Patrick 154, 175
Seelye, Talcott W.: on Arabic language skill importance 61, 72; on area experience as Arabic program requirement 54; brief biography of 195; on death of Meloy 69; dialect learning program of 60; and emergency WSAG meeting 154; on Eric Johnston Plan 91–92; and Ford administration 168; on Israeli raid on Qibya 92; and jetliner hijackings by PFLP 153; on John Foster Dulles 88; on Jordanian crisis, 1970 155; and Kreis Program 38; on Marine landings in Lebanon 104; on meeting with Ba'ath Party 179; on Palestinian Memoranda 172; on PLO 151; on pro-American sentiment after Suez War 97; on resupplying Israel during October War (1973) 164; retained after failure of Eric Johnston Plan 94; and risks of being Middle East hand 69, 186–87; on Rogers Peace Plan 149–50; on US commitment to Israel and security 174; *see also* Middle East Area Program (MEAP); Middle East hand(s)
Selassie, Haile 24
Senior Interdepartmental Group (SIG) 141
Shah of Iran 164–65
Shaler, William 48
Shalom, Zaki 170
Sharon, Ariel, on water issue 92

Shirabi, Hisham 73
shirt-sleeve diplomacy 47, 70, 111
Shuckburgh, Evelyn 96
Shultz, George 172, 175
Sinai 126, 173–74
Sinai II Agreement 166–67
Sirhan, Sirhan 161
Sisco, Joseph: background of 139; demonstrations against, in Jordan 152; on drafting of Rogers Peace Plan 147; and emergency WSAG meeting 154; Global perspective of 82; and Israel 138; Kissinger's alliance with 144; Kraft on 159; Parker on 144; on Rogers 142; and Rogers Peace Plan 148–50; on Scranton 145; and Soviet threat 146; and UN Resolution 242, drafting of 139; on "Year of Decision, The" 156
Six Day War 3, 11; aftermath of 125, 127–28, 183; events leading to 124–27, 173; and Middle East hands 125, 129, 178–79; and public opinion on military aid to Israel 127–28; reaction to victory by Israel 128–29; Sisco on 139; and Soviet Union 126–27; Vice President Nixon on 136; Zurayk on Arab loss 77
skilled linguist personality type 37
Smith, Henry Lee, Jr.: and ASTP 48–49; on expertise of director of Middle East Area Program 67; language learning method of 49, 56
Snow, James A. 65–66, 83
South Yemen: Communists in 177–78; Soviet arms/advisor shipments to 147; *see also* Yemen
Soviet Union: on Baghdad Pact 101; Beirut Axioms on 175–78; Carter administration and threat of 183; and Cold War linguist gap 47; containment of, as US policy objective 1–2, 10; Egypt, military aid to 147, 150–51, 176, 183; and Eric Johnston Plan failure 94; influence in Middle East 76; J. F. Dulles on threat of 76, 89–90; Kissinger on threat of 76, 137, 158; language training program of 50–51, 67, 73; Middle East, military aid to 147; Middle East hands on threat of 176–78, 183–84; Nixon on threat of 136–37, 146; public opinion on threat of 136–37; reaction to US support for Israel 180; Rogers Peace Plan rejected by 150; Sisco on threat of 146; and Six Day War 126–27; South Yemen, military aid to 147;

Sterner on threat of 10, 182–83; and Yemen 99–100; *see also* Communism
Speigel, Steven 113
Springer, Edward: brief biography of 195; *see also* Middle East Area Program (MEAP); Middle East hand(s)
Stackhouse, Heywood 37–38, 42
Stark, Freya 6
State Department: and Arabic program at Paris 30; and Arabic program of FSI 7; and CIA under Eisenhower 87; and closure of training program in Beirut 16; and first language program divorced from Orientalism 7; on Israeli-Arab policy, 1958 101; and Kissinger 141–44, 162; Language-Designated Post of 43, 57; on Marine landings in Lebanon 104–05; Nixon's view of 143; violence against personnel of 11–12; *see also* language training, US program; Middle East Area Program (MEAP); Middle East hand(s); Near East and South Asian Affairs (NEA)
Sterner, Michael E.: on Arab nationalism 176; brief biography of 195; on Communism in Yemen 178; on Globalist view 175; on importance of Middle East hands 69; on Israel/Israelis 69–70; on Kissinger 158; on media use by Nasser 67–68; on Middle East hand *vs.* presidential view 180; on military disengagement 173; organizes Multilateral Force 167; on Palestinian failings 77; on Palestinian Memoranda 172; and Phantom Memo 158–59; reassignment after Egypt-Soviet friendship treaty 159; Sadat's relationship with 60, 157; on Sisco and global view 149; on Soviet threat 10, 182–83; and "Year of Decision, The" 156, 158–59; *see also* Middle East Area Program (MEAP); Middle East hand(s)
Stimson, Henry 33
Stino (Doctor) 123
Stolzfus, William A., Jr.: brief biography of 195; and J. F. Dulles 88–89; on language training program 56; *see also* Middle East Area Program (MEAP); Middle East hand(s)
Stookey, Robert W.: brief biography of 195; on Nixon 155; on numbers of Palestinian refugees 151; *see also* Middle East Area Program (MEAP); Middle East hand(s)
Suddarth, Roscoe: brief biography of 195; *see also* Middle East Area Program (MEAP); Middle East hand(s)

Suez Canal: closure of 125, 147; need for clearing/deepening of 116; and "Phantom Memo" controversy 143–44; and "Year of Decision, The" 156, 158
Suez War 90, 95–97, 179
Sutherland, Peter A.: brief biography of 195; *see also* Middle East Area Program (MEAP); Middle East hand(s)
Symington, Stuart 143
Symmes, Harrison M.: as ambassador in Amman 122, 151–52; brief biography of 195; on J. F. Dulles 88; on success of Arabic language training program 56; *see also* Middle East Area Program (MEAP); Middle East hand(s)
Syria: attack on occupied territories by 173–74; and Communism 177; and Eric Johnston Plan 92, 94; and Ford administration 166; Israel's relationship with 94, 172–73; and Jordan 154–55; Nixon reopens relations with 165; numbers of refugees in 151; and October War (1973) 163–64; and oil embargo 164; radicalization of 183; role of CIA in 179; Soviet arms/advisor shipments 147; *see also* Assad, Hafez al; Palestinian Liberation Organization (PLO); Six Day War; United Arab Republic (UAR)

T

Talbot, Phillips: and assassination of J. F. Kennedy 121; assignment to Greece 121; joins State Department 110; and Joseph Johnson Plan 119; and refugee problem 114, 116; resigns as NEA chief 121
TAPline 23, 25, 88
Tasca, Henry 136
technical personality type 37–38
Teicher, Howard 15–16
Tennes; *see* Valley Authority (TVA) 91, 93
"Those Arabists at State" (Kraft) 13–15
303 Committee 142
Tilden, Bill 107
Tivnan, Edward 150
Todman, Terence A.: brief biography of 195; as first black Middle East hand 40; *see also* Middle East Area Program (MEAP); Middle East hand(s)
Toynbee, Arnold 80
Tripartite Agreement 179
Tripartite Declaration 31

Truman, Harry/administration: on foreign policy as presidential policy 2–3; and Orientalists 13, 19–20, 22, 24–28
Twin Pillars to Desert Storm: America's Flawed Vision in the Middle East from Nixon to Bush (Teicher) 15
Ugly American, The (Lederer & Burdick) 29, 47, 50

U

UN Resolution 194 118
UN Resolution 242 130–32; Arabs on 130–31; Curtiss on 131–32; drafting of 139; Eban on 130–32; English and French text, differences between 131–32; final text of 132; Goldberg on 128, 130–32; and L. B. Johnson 130–32; and Palestinian Memoranda 171; Rogers on 146
United Arab Republic (UAR): creation of 114; US relationship with 100; *see also* Egypt; Syria
United Arab States, attempts to form 76
United Nations Works and Relief Agency (UNWRA) 110–11
United States Information Agency (USIA), attacks on libraries of 83, 122
USS *Liberty* 11, 125–26, 179

V

Valeriani, Richard 143
Vance, Cyrus 10, 185
Vanetik, Boaz 170
Veliotes, Nicholas 142, 163–64

W

Wadsworth, George 24, 28, 99
Wallach, Janet 21
Walt, Stephen 13, 138
Walworth, Israel 125–26, 128–29
War of Attrition 147, 150–51, 183
Waring, Robert 83, 167–68, 186
Washington Institute for Near East Policy (WINEP) 13, 138
Washington Special Actions Group (WSAG) 142, 152, 154
Wasson, Thomas 11, 44, 184
water allocation: *see* Eric Johnston Plan
Watergate 163, 165
Weislogel, Winifred S.: brief biography of 195; as first woman Arabist 41; *see also* Middle East Area Program (MEAP); Middle East hand(s)
Weizmann, Chaim 22
"West and the Middle East: The Light and the Shadow, The" (Kerr) 80–81

Wheeler (General) 116
Wheelus Air Force Base 183
White, Theodore H. 109–10
Wiley, Marshall W.: brief biography of 195; technical personality type of 37; *see also* Middle East Area Program (MEAP); Middle East hand(s)
Wilford, Hugh 25, 93, 103, 173
Wilson, Evan 19–20
Wilsonian ideals 21, 73
Winder, R. Bayly 16
Wolle, William D.: brief biography of 196; *see also* Middle East Area Program (MEAP); Middle East hand(s)
women Arabists: gendered duties of 41–42; marriage policy for 40–42; reluctance of State Department to hire 40; serving in Muslim countries 42; Weislogel as first 41
Wright, Edwin M. 27
Wriston, Henry 62
Wriston Committee 57
Wriston Report, The 57, 85

Y

Yacub, Salim 86, 98
Yale, William 25–27
Yarmuk Dam project 91–92, 94
Yemen: and Bundy 113; Communism in 178; failure of Richards Mission in 99–100; and Kennedy administration 113; Soviet military aid to 99; US technical aid to 100; *see also* South Yemen
Yergin, Daniel 67
Young, Andrew 167, 172
Young America, Axioms of 136–37, 182

Z

Zayyat, N. el- 132
Zayidi, Nicola 74
Zeine, Zeine N. 74–75
Ziadeh, Nicola 74
Ziegler, Ronald 146
Zionists/Zionism: Green on 90; Kraft on 14, 16; Meir on 16; as obstacle to establishment of United Arab States 78; and Orientalists 8, 28; and Truman 25, 27; and Wright 27; Yale on 26
Zurayk, Constantine 74, 76–78
Zweifel, David E.: brief biography of 196; *see also* Middle East Area Program (MEAP); Middle East hand(s)

www.ingramcontent.com/pod-product-compliance
Lightning Source LLC
Chambersburg PA
CBHW021823300426
44114CB00009BA/290